Passions, Politics and the Limits of Society

Helsinki Yearbook of Intellectual History

Edited by Heikki Haara and Koen Stapelbroek

Volume 1

Passions, Politics and the Limits of Society

Edited by
Heikki Haara, Mikko Immanen, and Koen Stapelbroek

DE GRUYTER
OLDENBOURG

ISBN 978-3-11-067979-3
e-ISBN (PDF) 978-3-11-067986-1
e-ISBN (EPUB) 978-3-11-067996-0
ISSN 2698-6205

Library of Congress Control Number: 2020936595

Bibliographic information published by the Deutsche Nationalbibliothek
The Deutsche Nationalbibliothek lists this publication in the Deutsche Nationalbibliografie; detailed bibliographic data are available on the Internet at http://dnb.dnb.de.

Cover image: Bernard Picart, Frontispiece to a 1732 edition of Samuel Pufendorf's *Introduction à l'histoire générale et politique de l'univers*
Printing and binding: CPI books GmbH, Leck

www.degruyter.com

Table of Contents

Part II Natural Law, Political Economy and History: Essays in Honour of Kari Saastamoinen

Heikki Haara & Koen Stapelbroek

Intellectual History and Helsinki: Editorial Introduction

It is our great pleasure to present this first issue of the Yearbook of the Helsinki Centre for Intellectual History. Entitled *Passions, Politics and the Limits of Society*, this book brings together in a single volume a range of essays that engage with the changing shape of moral and political inquiry in the early modern period. It also acquaints the reader with the activities of the Centre. By now, it is nearly three and a half years since the Helsinki Centre for Intellectual History was established.[1] In the meantime, the Centre has become something of an international reference point; this publication may therefore be seen as a sign confirming that both intellectual history in general and scholarly life in Helsinki are doing well.

Other than providing an internationally recognisable point of reference, the Centre – including its website, seminar series and communicative functions – was set up as a local platform for discussion and an exchange of ideas across different historical sub-disciplines and adjacent fields in the social sciences, thereby transcending institutional as well as disciplinary boundaries. The aim of this publication format, an annual volume to highlight initiatives organised in Helsinki or by members of the Centre, is to provide further international visibility to the community of scholars at the University of Helsinki who are involved in fields of intellectual history. Indeed, as agreed by the initiators from the outset and by the membership of the Centre, intellectual history, on our understanding, can take many different forms, be applied in different academic disciplines and to a wide range of historical periods and sources.

The study of ideas in history has a rich and distinguished history in Helsinki and in Finnish academic life. It is our hope that the existence of our Centre may contribute to its further development and also preserve and promote a deeper understanding of the history of intellectual history in Helsinki and Finland.

The Yearbook of the Helsinki Centre for Intellectual History, likewise, is intended to serve as a forum for frontline research of intellectual history broadly construed. It refuses to confine itself to any one discipline or historical period but understands the diversity of the field and promotes the study of intellectual

1 For the partner institutions of the Centre within the University of Helsinki, the events hosted by the Centre and its partners and other activities, see: www.helsinki.fi/centre-for-intellectual-history.

https://doi.org/10.1515/9783110679861-001

history from a range of methodological and cross-disciplinary perspectives. The first volume of the Yearbook reflects the aims of the Centre. We wish to thank Rabea Rittgerodt at de Gruyter for her support and confidence in this new book series and this volume. We also owe thanks to our external readers for their perceptive comments and suggestions.

The opening chapter of the present volume, "The State of Intellectual History: Local and Global" by Richard Whatmore, is a fully revised version and further development of his inaugural lecture at the Centre. Originally presented in Helsinki as a "pep talk", it engages with the relevance and potential future of the field of intellectual history in a changing world in which understanding the nature and history of political and social challenges is often as hard and essential as coming to grips with their actual appearance and the development of policy or other responses. Citing István Hont, Whatmore suggests that we will not likely see the emergence of "a world where intellectual history came to prominence as a discipline in any general public sphere". Nevertheless, one might increasingly be able to agree that "eighteenth and nineteenth-century authors are better guides for those who determine our future than the pontifications of economists, journalists and civil servants who have not been schooled in intellectual history".

The first part of the yearbook, following the chapter by Whatmore, is entitled *Inclusion and Exclusion in the History of Ideas* and provides seven chapters that were originally presented as papers in the first thematic conference organised under the auspices of the Centre in December 2017 in Helsinki. We are proud that our keynote speakers László Kontler and Eva Piirimäe have allowed us to publish their revised and extended texts as, respectively, "Inventing 'Humanity': Early-Modern Perspectives" and "Human Rights and their Realisation in the World: Herder's Debate with Kant." Kontler shows how the historicisation of nature as a process contributed to the invention and development of the ordering concept of "humanity", while Piirimäe traces the actual principles of what later became the idea of human rights back to the moral philosophical debates between Herder and others in the eighteenth century. The theme of "Inclusion and Exclusion" is further developed in papers by Justin Begley, Ben Dew, Tatiana Artemyeva, Çağlar Çömez and Fabio Mengali, who from different perspectives approach the theme of inclusion and exclusion in the history of ideas, including those of the recognition of social, cultural, religious or ethnic difference, and the conceptualisation of tolerance, citizenship and human rights.

The second part of the volume, entitled *Natural Law, Political Economy and History* is a collection of essays in honour of Kari Saastamoinen. Besides his reputation as an internationally well-known scholar, who has published influential work on Pufendorf, Locke and the history of liberalism and equality, Kari has been a mentor to all but an entire generation of intellectual historians in Helsinki. The first contribution to this part is Markku Peltonen's aptly entitled "Kari Saastamoinen – An Appreciation", which is followed by chapters by Heikki Haara and Tim Stuart-Buttle, Mikko Tolonen, Aino Lahdenranta, Adriana Luna-Fabritius, Ere Nokkala, Laura Tarkka-Robinson and by Jani Marjanen and Jussi Kurunmäki. The chapters in this part discuss debates on natural law, human nature and political economy in early-modern Europe. Its contributions explore the sorts of political and moral visions that were relevant in post-Hobbesian moral philosophy and the development of political and economic thought in the Enlightenment.

The connection of Kari to Pufendorf and Kari's role as a mentor to young scholars has also inspired the selection of the cover illustration of this Yearbook, Bernard Picart's depiction of Clio revealing the theatre of history to a young student. The drawing was used as the frontispiece of the 1732 edition of Samuel Pufendorf's *Introduction à l'histoire générale et politique de l'univers* which was originally published in 1682. Pufendorf's book was a widely-printed and translated European best-seller that appealed to both politicians and general readers who attempted to understand the links between politics and history. This same linkage remains central for intellectual historians wishing to explore and remap the terrain of their field to come to grips with the globalised present.

Richard Whatmore

1 The State of Intellectual History: Local and Global

Introduction: The point of Intellectual History

The novelist Iris Murdoch, in a letter to the polymath Raymond Queneau written in 1947, noted that she was about to take a class discussing "whether Socrates was a utilitarian?" Had it been possible to communicate with Murdoch at the time, an intellectual historian might would have informed her that the question was a foolish one, if her aim was to understand either Socrates or utilitarianism. The point of intellectual history is to illuminate the past by taking seriously the utterances and arguments of historical actors. Taking seriously the thoughts of previous generations does not, as is so often claimed, lead to scepticism and relativism, developing a perspective somehow above and distanced from the present, and necessarily disdainful of political commitment or particular decision today. Rather, the very point of intellectual history has always been to deepen engagement with issues in question. It might be the case that contemporaries recognised limits upon argument that are now in shadow for us. There are lost traditions of intellectual endeavour, the recovery of which, sometimes entailing an understanding of why they failed, can only enrich those that have survived or which are of recent vintage. The result is always a better sense of human action, of why someone advocated a programme or practice, of why a stand was taken, and of the range of options open to our ancestors.

One of the major criticisms of intellectual historians has been that we make the study of history a purely antiquarian enterprise, by severing any relationship between past and present. In a global world, where we look to history to help illuminate the problems of the present, this can be a devastating critique. In being overly 'local' and in ignoring the present, the intellectual historian becomes irrelevant to the world, a relatively pointless addition to any faculty. The argument of this article, which builds on points made in *What is Intellectual History?*, is that this attack is misconceived.[1] Intellectual historians underscore how difficult many of the choices faced by historical actors are. We are the inheritors of the tradition of searching for unintended consequences in the history of ideas that so marked the brilliant scholarship of David Hume, Edward Gibbon,

1 Richard Whatmore, *What is Intellectual History?* (Cambridge: Polity Press, 2015).

https://doi.org/10.1515/9783110679861-002

Adam Smith, William Robertson, Adam Ferguson and so many fellow luminaries of the enlightenment era. An example of an unintended consequence of great relevance to the present is the association of radical agrarian critiques of commercial society with dictatorship, genocide and extremist forms of nationalism. When François Fénelon in his *Telemachus*, composed in the 1690s and never intended for publication, defended the strategy of transferring populations from the towns to the countryside, it was an element of a careful strategy to protect modern populations from the worst effects of luxury and selfishness. That such a strategy became a blueprint for the brutal crushing of 'counter-revolutionaries' and intellectuals that later defined the regimes of Mao Zedong or Pol Pot, is a story worthy of recollection.

Another example is the unintended association of the French Declaration of the Rights of Man and the Citizen with terror and civil war in the 1790s. This linkage was obvious to contemporaries on the grounds that the assertion of universal rights, purportedly derived from nature, were accompanied by the abandonment of every existing law. In other words, the association between devotion to the rights of man and the citizen and the practice of terror was not surprising. A further fact of profound historical importance is the admiration of so many republicans and democrats for generals or strongmen, who clothe themselves in the garb of a patriotic monarch expressing the interests of all of humanity. Intellectual historians, in making connections between traditions and ideologies that today are presumed antithetical, or in puncturing the commonplace assumption of the superiority of the contemporary West, have a significant role to play in the formation of successful civic identities. By reconstructing historic ideologies in their richness and diversity, we can better understand the choices we face in the present.

In many respects intellectual history is the form of historical enquiry most suited to our global world. Intellectual historians are used to dealing with long spans of time, the translation of ideas across cultures and their necessary adaptation to new circumstances, and the inevitability of the revision of ideas and of their misunderstanding.

Challenges to Intellectual History

Should we therefore be celebrating the success of intellectual history as a modern academic subject? Darrin McMahon and Samuel Moyn have written that, "[i]t is difficult to remember a time when intellectual history figured so centrally in the larger historical enterprise as well as in the humanities as a whole."[2] David Armitage has gone further, arguing that intellectual history is best placed to deal with the kinds of questions about long-term historical change across continents raised by the way we live today. Armitage has called this "a history *in* ideas".[3] Increasingly we seem to have accepted John Burrow's definition of intellectual history as the process of recovering "what people in the past meant by the things they said and what these things 'meant' to them", employing the metaphors of the intellectual historian as an eavesdropper upon the conversations of the past, as a translator between the cultures identifiable today and those of the past, and of an explorer studying worlds full of assumptions and beliefs alien to our own.[4] Donald Winch used to say that as intellectual historians we are always playing away-matches, because we can never presume home support wherever we happen to be, whether among historians, literature scholars, philosophers or social scientists. I think we can now say that we have a home team, because we have support in certain institutions, where cross-disciplinary engagement is encouraged; but we still have a lot of work to do to be certain that what we are doing today will continue into the future, especially as the founding generation passes on.

Another reason for avoiding excessive optimism is because the history of ideas or intellectual history tends to flourish in times of uncertainty about the future, and when people are seeking alternatives to scepticism, cynicism and utopian schemes for the end of history or the construction of near-perfect societies. As such, both the history of ideas and its new variant, intellectual history, especially marked late twentieth-century thought. Both subject areas can be seen to be products of twentieth-century speculation about the relationship between ideas and historical processes, which became ever more prominent within humanistic scholarship. Part of the reason was a growing scepticism about the claims of the positive sciences of the nineteenth century, themselves founded upon definitions of rational human activity, and of human health and wellbeing that could be universalised. If the confidence of nineteenth-century philoso-

---

2 Darrin M. McMahon and Samuel Moyn, "Introduction: Interim Intellectual History," in *Rethinking Modern European Intellectual History*, ed. Darrin M. McMahon and Samuel Moyn (Oxford: Oxford University Press, 2014), 3.

3 David Armitage, "What's the Big Idea? Intellectual History and the Longue Durée," *History of European Ideas* 38 (2012): 493–507; "Globalizing Jeremy Bentham," *History of Political Thought* 32 (2011): 63–82.

4 John W. Burrow, "Intellectual History in English Academic Life: Reflections on a Revolution," in *Advances in Intellectual History*, ed. Richard Whatmore and Brian Young (London: Palgrave Macmillan, 2006), 8–24.

phers, or the nihilism of those who rejected their philosophies, could be shown to have a relationship with the outbreak of world wars, or the unparalleled institutionalised violence of the first half of the twentieth century, then something was amiss with the human sciences, and they needed to be rethought. Another significant issue was the relationship between the disciplines that were organised within universities, and more especially the nature of social science and its relationship to arts and humanities disciplines. A further factor was uncertainty about the veracity of Marxism, in its various forms, and more particularly about the capacity of Marxist states to maintain themselves both economically and militarily against the capitalist West. More philosophers began to argue, with the sceptic Ludwig Wittgenstein, that language determined every aspect of human behaviour. Wittgenstein, in *Philosophical Investigations* and *On Certainty*, described language as a phenomenon so intimately connected with human action that the kinds of language available to actors could be said to constrain or facilitate change; words really should be conceived to be deeds. With no human science on the horizon that will restore the kinds of certainty that generated the Whig historiographies of the past, intellectual history may well flourish, but only because of trouble we are in.

Laslett and the Foundation Story

It tends to be sensible to know your enemies. As such, we need to recall the kinds of criticism levelled against the founding generation of intellectual historians, John Pocock, Quentin Skinner and John Dunn. Identifying such a generation is contentious of course. Many believe, with good reason, that their work as intellectual historians is rather inspired by *Begriffsgeschichte* or "conceptual history", founded on the scholarly monument of the multivolume lexicon of the *Geschichtliche Grundbegriffe* that appeared between 1972 and 1997. Reinhart Koselleck's brilliant *Begriffsgeschichte*, if it failed to make the study of language in different historical contexts scientific, nevertheless established a framework for understanding the transition from early-modern to modern thought during the *Sattelzeit* between 1750 and 1850, that has yet to be bettered. The aspiration of combatting extreme ideologies employing false historical teleologies was shared by Anglophone intellectual history and there is a great deal of overlap.[5] Alternatively, you might be following a method associated with Michel Foucault, seeking

5 Kari Palonen, "An Application of Conceptual History to Itself: From Method to Theory in Reinhart Koselleck's 'Begriffsgeschichte,'" *Finnish Yearbook of Political Thought* 1 (1997): 39–69.

out the 'epistemes' or discursive formations operating beneath the consciousness of historical actors, constructing an archaeology of linked historic concepts, and a genealogy showing the often irrational employment of such concepts in human social relations. There is much in common with so-called Anglophone approaches.

What is the Anglophone method? It is associated everywhere with the 'Cambridge School', so named because the founding authors were associated with the University of Cambridge when writing some of the works that transformed the field of intellectual history.[6] The label has been widely criticised, not least by John Pocock, for the good reason that his own connection with Cambridge had been relatively short-lived and not especially significant. Nevertheless, the label has stuck. What were the leading members of the Cambridge School advocating that was different? Pocock, John Dunn, and Quentin Skinner proposed that texts be treated as products of specific historical contexts, by which they meant ideological contexts formed through linguistic practice. In working out the meaning of the texts, Dunn and Skinner identified the intentions of an author as the principal guide to the nature of the text, although neither unproblematic as an intellectual objective, nor sufficient in terms of understanding an author's work. Skinner memorably said that the goal of the historian was to reveal what the author of a particular text 'was doing', encompassing what the author had intended to do and had succeeded in doing as interpreted by the responses of other authors. One of the anticipated consequences of the method was indicated by the original title of Skinner's essay: 'The Unimportance of the Great Texts in the History of Political Thought.'[7]

Among the most significant claims asserted by Pocock, Dunn and Skinner, but emphasised especially by Pocock in all of his methodological writings, was that the language or discourse in which an author was working, meaning the set of assumptions that he or she was adopting and employing in the articulation of their arguments, set limits to the argument itself. Language or discourse comprised a grammar and a rhetoric; it also comprised sets of assumptions about the use and implications of ideas, which amounted to a complex structure. Authors living within communities of language users could innovate and alter existing languages, but the point was to search for exactly this because existing languages were employed in articulating what was happening in the ideological and material present. The three authors opposed approaches found-

6 Mark Bevir, "The Contextual Approach," in *The Oxford Handbook of the History of Political Philosophy*, ed. George Klosko (Oxford: Oxford University Press, 2011), 11–23.

7 Petri Koikkalainen and Sami Syrjämäki, "Quentin Skinner *On Encountering the Past,*" *Finnish Yearbook of Political Thought* 6 (2002): 34–63.

ed on the presumption of fixed concepts of historical analysis, of meta-theoretical assumptions about human nature, and of opaque or a-historical theoretical vocabularies.

Pocock went on to say that in communicating through speech acts, individuals drew upon the existing traditions or languages that were available to them in formulating arguments. In so doing, language in Pocock's view acquired a structure, often called discourse, where discourses were series of speech acts performed by individuals in particular social and historical contexts. The speech acts confirmed or modified the discourses or paradigms that they operated in, and did so sometimes consciously and explicitly and sometimes unconsciously and implicitly.[8] Working historians needed to search for paradigms or discourses that operated historically, such as the kind of republicanism that fuelled argument across the Atlantic world in early-modern times, the equally prominent advocacy of ancient constitutionalism or of Enlightenment historiography in the eighteenth century in its Arminian, Anglican, and Voltairean variants. The key fact was that such paradigms became prominent through use, imposed particular ways of thinking upon historical actors, could be seen to have evolved and to have been transformed in different circumstances and sometimes to have collapsed and disappeared; Pocock's work has entailed the study of the ascent and near disappearance of a series of paradigms. The student who follows this method in Pocock's view discovers numerous rationales for advocating particular political strategies and learns that a number of rationales at any one point, often contradicting one another, can be seen to have made sense to historical actors and to have been justified accordingly. The historian learns prudence in consequence. History becomes the study of the making of decisions in circumstances where there is no black and white. Necessity cannot be found. Rather, history becomes a series of contingent choices, several of which make sense. Prudence requires the historian to distinguish between the background ideological traditions or languages that authors drew upon in formulating their ideas, and the specific utterances that made up a claim or argument. Pocock distinguishes between 'langue' and 'parole', the language and the utterance, and has continued to refer to this distinction in all of his work.[9]

8 J. G. A. Pocock, "Languages and their Implications: The Transformation of the Study of Political Thought" and "On the Non-Revolutionary Character of Paradigms: A Self-Criticism and Afterpiece," in J. G. A. Pocock, *Politics, Language & Time: Essays on Political Thought and History* (Chicago: University of Chicago Press, 1989), 3–41, 273–291.

9 J. G. A. Pocock, "The State of the Art," in J. G. A. Pocock, *Virtue, Commerce, and History: Essays on Political Thought and History, Chiefly in the Eighteenth Century* (Cambridge: Cambridge University Press, 1985), 1–33; Id. "The Concept of a Language and the Métier d'Historien: Some Con-

The assumption, of course, that Pocock, Skinner and Dunn were doing identical things in researching historical ideas is a mistake. John Pocock associated himself with Michael Oakeshott's view that research questions formulated within the humanities are best described as an on-going conversation. He also prioritised paradigms over intentions.[10] Quentin Skinner had been trained in Oxford language philosophy and had a clearer sense of the need to address problems posed by Wittgenstein for the human sciences. John Dunn, having written a brilliant account of the relationship between John Locke's politics and Calvinism, quickly moved towards the study of present politics rather than the history of ideas. In so doing he was following Peter Laslett, the person John Pocock has called the founder of the study of historical ideas in Cambridge and elsewhere, having 'revealed the mystery of contextualisation'.[11] Pocock introduced himself to Laslett in the late 1940s, being aware that Laslett was working on his edition of Robert Filmer, published in 1949, and the diverse idiomatic responses to Filmer by Locke, Algernon Sidney, William Petyt, Henry Neville and others. In 1956 Pocock met Laslett again at Cambridge, and realised that while his forthcoming edition of Locke, which appeared in 1960, was brilliant, Laslett was no longer an intellectual historian. Laslett II had become interested in the capacity of logical positivism to address contemporary problems, which Pocock in turn traced to Karl Popper's *The Open Society and its Enemies*. Within a few years Laslett III had emerged, studying the extent to which patriarchal social structures in the family and in the state mirrored the sixteenth- and seventeenth-century reality. The investigation of social structures through the techniques of historical demography, Laslett decided, was more important than the study of the works of individual thinkers using contextual analysis. Laslett's point was that it was better to rely on the techniques of the contemporary social sciences if you wanted to understand the past, and at the same time make a link between historical research and contemporary social issues. It remains significant that the first modern intellectual historian of the Cambridge School rejected the discipline he had done so much to create.

---

siderations on Practice," in J. G. A. Pocock, *The Languages of Political Theory in Early-Modern Europe*, ed. Anthony Pagden (Cambridge: Cambridge University Press), 19–38.

10 J. G. A. Pocock, *Politics, Language & Time: Essays on Political Thought and History* (Chicago: University of Chicago Press, 1971), 25.

11 J. G. A. Pocock, Private correspondence with the author, November 18, 2015.

Attacking Cambridge

With such definitional problems in mind, how did critics respond to the Cambridge historians? With vitriol is the answer. Skinner in particular was attacked for being too much of a philosopher, for not being able to pin down an author's intentions, for pursuing research questions of purely antiquarian interest, and for leading the humanities down a cul-de-sac characterised by narrowness and irrelevance.[12] The claim that intellectual history was not connected to present politics in particular was reiterated time and time again. This was seen to be pure madness, because the study of ideas historically had always been connected to the issues of the present. In making the study of ideas a matter of history meant that intellectual historians were retreating into an ivory tower.[13] A presumed contrast between such writers as Isaiah Berlin and the Cambridge historians was particularly marked here, or indeed with Foucault. The Cambridge historians just got it wrong. Lewis Namier, the advocate of prosopography in historical analysis, seemed to have it right in stating that the study of ideas was 'flapdoodle', in his *England in the Age of the American Revolution* (1930), because what really motivated human beings was self-interest. Ideas were misleading because they masked the true source of social action.

The different accusation Antonio Gramsci levelled at Benedetto Croce is also worth recalling, of practising 'despicable Pontius Pilatism', for not taking a stand on issues of concern to the mass of the people, for not wanting to take responsibility in public argument, and for not engaging directly in contemporary poli-

---

12 See for example *Margaret Leslie*, "*In Defence of Anachronism*," *Political Studies* 18 (1970): 433–470; *Charles D. Tarlton*, "*Historicity*, Meaning, and Revisionism in the Study of Political Thought," *History and Theory* 12 (1973): 307–328; Bhikhu Parekh and R. N. Berki, "The History of Political Ideas: A Critique of Q. Skinner's Methodology," *Journal of the History of Ideas* 34 (1973): 163–184; John Keane, "On the 'New' History: Quentin Skinner's Proposal for a New History of Political Ideology," *Telos* 47 (1981): 174–183. For an overview see Conal Condren, *The Status and Appraisal of Classic Texts* (Princeton, NJ: Princeton University Press, 1985) and Mark Bevir, *The Logic of the History of Ideas* (Cambridge: Cambridge University Press, 1999), 48–52.

13 *Tarlton*, "*Historicity*, Meaning, and Revisionism," 307–328; John G. Gunnell, "Interpretation and the History of Political Theory: Apology and Epistemology," *American Political Science Review* 76 (1982): 317–327; Kenneth Minogue, "Method in Intellectual History: Quentin Skinner's *Foundations*," in *Meaning and Context: Quentin Skinner and his Critics*, ed. James Tully (Princeton, NJ: Princeton University Press, 1988), 176–193; Robert Wokler, "The Professoriate of Political Thought in England since 1914: A Tale of Three Chairs," in *The History of Political Thought in National Context*, ed. Dario Castiglione and Iain Hampsher-Monk (Cambridge: Cambridge University Press, 2001), 134–158.

tics.[14] E. P. Thompson took the position of Gramsci with regard to Cambridge school historians. In his *Customs in Common* (1991) Thompson reconstructed the views of ordinary people in the eighteenth century supportive of the 'moral economy', which Adam Smith and the advocates of capitalist social relations were stated to have sought to refute and undermine. Cambridge authors, in refusing to condemn Smith's position and defend the moral economy, were continuing the longstanding position of assaulting the poor with intellectual tools.[15] Although Edward Said never engaged with Cambridge School authors in *Orientalism* or in *Culture and Imperialism*, it is easy to generate accusations of Eurocentrism by looking at intellectual history through Said's lens. In focussing on the original intentions of elite, male, European authors, the prejudices of the past are passed on to the present. The voices of minorities, especially women, and the oppressed, especially from non-European cultures, are neglected. Most intellectual historians who have worked in academic faculties today will recognise such criticisms. We are not seen to be doing things of direct relevance to the contemporary world. We are not reconstructing the life histories of the oppressed or revealing hidden scandal and injustice. We are not directly supporting a New Left, or New Right for that matter. As such, colleagues sometimes see us as aloof and sometimes as purposeless antiquarians, interested in books that no one would read today, and issues that most people have forgotten, or could only understand after several hours of explanation. In a monetised world where everything is valued against a utilitarian calculus putting a priority upon immediate results, and where sustained engagement with something that may be only of indirect relevance is discouraged, what is the place of the intellectual historian?

One of the great achievements in recent decades that has made intellectual-historical research valued today has been Quentin Skinner's research into the history of liberty, and the restoration of a definition of freedom as non-domination, which can be applied directly from past to present, and employed as a tool evaluating the health of a societies with regard to liberty across the globe. Many of us will have had enquiries from potential students who have been inspired by Skinner's research into the history of ideas about liberty, and who want to apply the model to their own national histories. Skinner's work and its remarkable influence is the most successful refutation of the claim that there is no relationship between intellectual history and contemporary politics.

---

14 Antonio Gramsci, *Quaderni del Carcere, vol. 1: Il Materialismo Storico e la Filosofia di Benedetto Croce* (Turin: Giulio Einaudi, 1966), 174–175.

15 E. P. Thompson, *Customs in Common: Studies in Traditional Popular Culture* (London: Merlin Press, 1991), 274–285, 350–351.

Another point to make is that if historical research is associated with the recovery of lost voices, then intellectual history has done more than any other branch of historical learning to do this. Canonical figures in the history of philosophy are no longer studied, at least outside philosophy departments that have turned against history, as if the tallest trees from Plato and Aristotle to Aquinas, Hobbes and Rawls were engaged in a dialogue with one another, concerning eternal problems that only their works can be said to have truly illuminated. Perhaps the greatest achievement of intellectual history has been to shatter the canon, by showing the benefit of reading a text within its ideological context, and using the texts of innumerable forgotten authors who were considered brilliant and relevant in their own time, to work out the meaning of the better-known texts whose reception was more fortunate. In expanding vastly the range of texts and authors that need to be studied in order to understand the past, intellectual historians are especially suited to the age of Google.

What about the argument that Cambridge school intellectual historians teach scepticism, and a particularly elitist form of scepticism associated with the collapse of the British empire and of British influence abroad, being themselves the product of an elite culture in decline? One of the benefits of beginning with the local, or starting with particular facts and seeing the world from the vantage point of a specific historical actor, is that the distinctiveness of such actors becomes quickly apparent, and the falsity of commonplace generalisations underlined. With this in mind, let us look in more detail at the case of John Pocock.

John Pocock's Approach

Pocock was born in London and has retained his British citizenship. But he moved at the age of three to New Zealand because his father, Lewis Greville Pocock, was appointed professor of classics at Canterbury College. After graduating MA from Canterbury himself, Pocock moved to Cambridge in 1948, where he completed a PhD under the supervision of Herbert Butterfield in 1952. After holding academic posts at Otago, at St John's College, Cambridge, and at Canterbury, Pocock moved to Missouri in 1966 as the William Eliot Smith Professor of History, and then on to Johns Hopkins, where he became professor of history in 1974. Pocock was shaped by a childhood and early adulthood spent in New Zealand, still considers himself an outsider in North America, despite having spent most of his life there, and is as far from being a member of the British Establishment as it is possible to be. Nor is he a member of the liberal establishment, as his recent note underscores in the *London Review of Books*, telling readers not to be so afraid of Brexit.[16] Pocock has spent his intellectual life telling new stories about the past, and challenging the way history has traditionally been perceived in the process.

In 1957 Pocock's *The Ancient Constitution and the Feudal Law* showed the extent to which English lawyers, addicted to a notion of immemorial common law and an immemorial constitution, were inhibited in their historical investigations by comparison with their French counterparts. English lawyers in the sixteenth and seventeenth centuries were obsessed with history, but their approach to the past was essentially unhistorical. For the French, such as the monarchomach François Hotman, whose work on feudal landholding appeared in 1572 (*De Feudis*), the contrast between the legacy of Roman Law and the customary law of the French provinces facilitated a comparative study of laws through time. Pocock charted the revolution that followed the appearance of Sir Henry Spelman's *Glossarium Archaeologicum* (1626), which traced the rise and fall of feudal tenures, and in turn facilitated the new kinds of political thinking that could be found in James Harrington's *Oceana* (1656), where land ownership determined the operation of political structures. In revealing that perspectives on the past both shaped and limited political theorising in early-modern times, Pocock supplied the most detailed illustration of the fact that new kinds of history were being produced.[17]

In his *The Machiavellian Moment* (1975), Pocock supplied a history of the Aristotelian impulse to live a civic life in a free city as a citizen from early-modern to modern times, charting the foundation of the philosophy called civic humanism in the warring communities of Renaissance Italy. Small states that thrived in central and southern Europe from the eleventh century onwards began to assert their independence against marauding princes, and against the imperial aspirations of Popes and of the Holy Roman Emperor. They also fought one another. The result was a ceaseless speculation concerning the means of maintaining cities in a state of liberty. It was this issue that concerned Machiavelli above all others. The Machiavellian moment denoted Machiavelli's appearance as a political thinker and actor but more particularly the consequences of his speculations concerning the foundation and formation of a republic, and the point at which the life of the republic became precarious. The creation of the republic

---

16 J. G. A. Pocock et al., "Where are we now?," *London Review of Books* 38 (2016): 8–15 and "Deconstructing Europe," *London Review of Books* 19 (1991): 6–10.

17 J. G. A. Pocock, *The Ancient Constitution and the Feudal Law: A Study of English Historical Thought in the Seventeenth Century: A Reissue with a Retrospect* (Cambridge: Cambridge University Press, [1959] 1987).

was always associated with crisis, and it generated controversies about the origins and possibilities of politics.[18]

The history of Machiavelli's speculation about the prolongation of the life of the republic and of its natural death was extended chronologically and geographically, describing James Harrington's adaptation in the mid-seventeenth century of Machiavelli's perspective on the history of Rome, according to which the practice of arms and inheritable landed property were the precondition for the enjoyment of liberty and the exercise of civic virtue. Pocock went on to detail the controversy over this perspective in the eighteenth century, in the very different context of ideas about liberty and autonomy that accompanied the end of the wars of religion and the rise of large and competing commercial monarchies in Europe. Maintaining these new forms of state required the development of standing armies and public credit; these were defended by association with modern forms of politeness, and praised by such men as Daniel Defoe alongside consumption and financial independence, in societies organised in accordance with the division of labour. 'Neo-Harringtonians', as Pocock termed them, such as Andrew Fletcher, favoured ancient virtue, protected and sustained by militias and an elite of landowners, whose interest in the state ensured their political wisdom and the moderation of their laws. The neo-Harringtonians despised modern politeness, believing it to entail the corrosion of masculinity, the growth of forms of corruption accompanying the rise of parties and the specialist politician, and far greater uncertainty in civil society and in politics, exemplified by the reliance of the state upon the expertise of the stock-jobber.

The clash between 'ancient' and 'modern' ideas about liberty occurred across the Atlantic world through concerns about the likely stability of real and of moveable property, and was in turn complicated both by the domestically uncertain identity of composite states comprised of different 'nations', and by discussions in Protestant and Catholic states of the likely consequences of commercial society for religious belief, some of which questioned the compatibility of different forms of Christian worship with a polity competing for survival by commerce and by war. This state of affairs in turn generated an influential literature of jeremiad that was particularly marked in the writings of historians, politicians and philosophers in the late eighteenth century. Pocock's central claim was that it was absolutely vital to distinguish between political discourses founded on ideas about rights, being inspired by jurisprudential speculation,

18 J. G. A. Pocock, *The Machiavellian Moment* (Princeton, NJ: Princeton University Press, 1975), 554.

and those that were founded on the aspiration of restoring virtue and the capacities deemed necessary to human flourishing in societies. How to maintain free states had become a commonplace of political argument in late medieval times, and Pocock revealed that they always rested on ideas about the historical development of liberty, whether liberty had been established in the ancient world and rediscovered, or whether ideas about liberty had only been established after the decline of Rome, by the barbarian tribes that brought down the Empire, in part by asserting their own right to create sovereign nations.

The on-going debate entailed the definition of Europe as a continent composed of a multitude of sovereign powers seeking to live in harmony with one another, or the basis of a new empire, on the grounds that empires alone were capable of bringing peace to a world marred by ceaseless war since the beginning of the 'Christian Millennium' that began with the conversion of the Emperor Constantine. For Pocock political thought in Europe has been pervaded by jurisprudence, contributing to what he has termed 'the ideology of liberal empire'. By contrast, historiography, the writing of grand historical narratives, has been concerned with the story of the transformation of the republic into the empire or of the story of the incompatibility of liberty and empire.

Rather than being purely antiquarian, Pocock has always contended that such issues remain identifiable in the political cultures of modern states. The fears that the lone individual who relied upon himself to assert his liberty would lapse into barbarism, or that the individual who had numerous capacities but refused to bring them together in public activity for the freedom of the whole society, would become corrupt and ultimately subject to a tyrant, could be found across modern political cultures. His contention that the legacies of civic humanism or classical republicanism can be discerned particularly within the political languages of the North American Republic has been one of the reasons for the controversial reception of his work, with numerous attacks charting 'liberal' rather than 'republican' origins of the American state.[19]

Pocock's *Barbarism and Religion* series of six volumes describes Gibbon's intellectual journey from his Swiss exile as a young man and criticisms of the *Encyclopédie* to the growth of his historical interests through his reading of the 'Enlightened Narrative' of Western historical development in the work of such authors as Giannone, Voltaire, Hume, Robertson, Ferguson and Adam Smith

19 Joyce Appleby, "Republicanism and Ideology," *American Quarterly* 37 (1985): 461–473; "Republicanism in Old and New Contexts," *William and Mary Quarterly* 43 (1986): 20–34; "Recovering America's Historic Diversity: Beyond Exceptionalism," *Journal of American History* 79 (1992): 419–431; *Liberalism and Republicanism in the Historical Imagination* (Cambridge, MA: Harvard University Press, 1992).

among others. Pocock is as concerned with what Gibbon might have written as with what he actually did write. As such he underlines the extent to which Gibbon is misunderstood when he is presented as a classical humanist rhetorician. Rather, Gibbon is revealed as the historian of 'Afro-Eurasia', encompassing regions that can be described as Chinese, Arab-Iranian in addition to Greco-Latin. Pocock has explained why it is necessary to study sacred history, erudition, patristics, Christology and ecclesiology if we are to understand Gibbon's world. Pocock is arguing that Gibbon's *Decline and Fall* was not written with the intention of rejecting belief in the Christian revelation. Gibbon was rather responding to what in the parlance of today would be called a global cultural heritage.

Pocock has revealed that historical narratives more often than not combine a story about the origin of the community in question in addition to a narrative about the continuity of the community. These narratives are challenged, revised and challenged again in an endless cycle.[20] In Pocock's view, such narratives form an element of the personality of an individual that is as important as traditional definitions of personal identity. Pocock has been concerned in recent years that the process he identified in the enlightenment era is accelerating today because of the loss of sovereignty that has accompanied the growth of federal relationships across Europe and elsewhere. It is unsurprising that Pocock is especially interested in the collapse of identities and their consequences. Exactly this occurred in 1973 when the British abandoned New Zealand and other members of the longstanding Commonwealth to their own fate when it joined the European Common Market. For decades now Pocock has been demanding that British history be perceived from the broad perspectives generated by perceiving it as a sometime empire, the peripheries of which are as revealing as its Little England centre-point. Pocock has been concerned particularly to emphasise the importance of Britain within what he termed the 'Atlantic archipelago'. For Pocock, the approach generates the always-contested narratives of dominion, subject-status and sovereignty when reflections on history and national identity occur. His own journey has turned him into the rarest of breeds, in Colin Kidd's words a 'liberal Eurosceptic intellectual'.[21] His historical writing, culminating in *Barbarism and Religion*, has attacked the notion of Europe as a continent, arguing that it was never anything more than a sub-continent, a peninsula of the gargantuan Eurasian land-mass.

---

20 J. G. A. Pocock, "The Politics of Historiography," in J. G. A. Pocock, *Political Thought and History: Essays on Theory and Method* (Cambridge: Cambridge University Press, 2009), 257–271.
21 Colin Kidd, "Europe, what Europe?," *London Review of Books* 30 (2008): 16–17.

In contemporary historiography Pocock attacks what he has called a 'post-historical culture' which, especially when influenced by post-modern narratives about the death of the author or the inaccessibility of knowledge about past or present, abandons historical narratives altogether. Pocock has asked whether what he has termed 'post-historical ideology', characterised by the view that all history is invention on the part of the author, marks the final break up of the historical personality?[22] At the same time he reminds his readers 'that the contest continues and is not over yet'.[23] The liberal polity where multiple identities are intermixed and respected is the ideal for Pocock, sustained by historical narratives that are always being rejected and revised. Pocock states that the task of establishing such a polity has only increased in difficulty at a time when means of communication and information are being transformed, causing further shifts of identity in turn. Given his belief that the self will never dissolve and that history is unlikely to end, the process of creating historical narratives will continue.

Intellectual History as a Global Enterprise

Does this mean that in the hands of John Pocock intellectual history can be considered the archetypal form of global history or its enemy? Pocock has recently engaged with this question directly in the article 'The Unglobality of Contexts', where he has accepted the Eurocentric character of Cambridge School labours:

> The beginnings of the "global" critique are well known and may as well be accepted as common ground. They reduce to the assertion that "Cambridge" scholarship in this field is "Eurocentric"; that is, that it has dealt exclusively with the "political thought" generated in the Greco-Roman Mediterranean, transmitted to medieval and modern Europe, and taken up in the Euro-colonized Americas and a world (or "globe") subjected to European or "western" domination. This is obviously true and calls for reformation.[24]

The solution to the problem of Eurocentrism, however, is to reaffirm rather than to reject the Cambridge method. Pocock argues that the method 'is in principle applicable to cultures and histories other than its own, while facing the daunting challenge of learning languages (Chinese, Arabic) other than those of Euro-West-

22 J. G. A. Pocock, "Conclusion: History, Sovereignty, Identity," in J. G. A. Pocock, *The Discovery of Islands: Essays in British History* (Cambridge: Cambridge University Press, 2005), 293.
23 J. G. A. Pocock, "Gaberlunzie's Return," *New Left Review* 5 (2000): 41–52.
24 J. G. A. Pocock, "On the Unglobality of Contexts: Cambridge Methods and the History of Political Thought," *Global Intellectual History* 4 (2019): 99–109.

ern derivation. Here it must invoke the ideal of a "global", in the sense of "cosmopolitan", "republic of letters" in which pluralised and multi-cultural discussants instruct each other and themselves." Pocock goes on to argue that this pluralist method is vital if we are to avoid some of the worst excesses of globalisation; the latter exist, firstly, in the form of a turn against the past because it is derided as an anti-global area of injustice and exploitation and secondly, because any criticism of global processes is increasingly rejected. As Pocock puts it, the danger is of emptying "the political, and in that sense the historical, of their capacity to act upon a globalised economy and culture's power to generate new "contexts" more rapidly than we can control them or even call them by that name."

What would Pocock's version of a global intellectual history of political thought look like. One answer is a lot like the work of the late Istvan Hont. Hont saw scepticism, crisis and uncertainty about the future during the enlightenment era and drew direct parallels with the present. The history of ideas mattered in the seventeenth and eighteenth centuries because it was unclear how far existing large states in Europe were doing something altogether new in history, in pursuing commerce, war, luxury and empire, or whether they were straightforwardly reliving the history of Rome, finding themselves on the edge of an abyss representing the inauguration of a new dark age. The capacity of individuals in the modern world to be deluded by the pursuit of baubles or trinkets, by projects that promise a heaven upon earth, by evangelical schemes of social or global transformation, or by the self-interested promises of captains of industry or politicians, was evident by the seventeenth century.

Hont revealed in his book *The Jealousy of Trade* that in the hands of someone like David Hume or Adam Smith, the history of ideas combined with economic histories of the rise and fall of states, resulted in a comprehensive analysis of modern Europe and its prospects.[25] For Smith, luxury unleashed by commercial development had undermined both the Roman Empire and the polities of feudal Europe. When Rome fell, however, several Roman cities devoted to commerce survived and maintained their long-established trade routes to the east. It was the addiction of the feudal elites in large monarchies to luxury consumption, supplied from the east, which undermined their social and political authority. Crucially for Smith, Renaissance republicanism was not the source of European liberty. The Italian cities had developed economically, and promoted the aristocratic regime of self-government in consequence, only because they trans-

---

25 Istvan Hont, *The Jealousy of Trade: International Competition and the Nation-State in Historical Perspective* (Cambridge, MA: Harvard University Press, 2005).

ported the armies of the monarchies of Europe during the Crusades. Smith's doleful conclusion was that European liberty was not the product of political liberty. Commerce rose only because the economic needs of warfare created military elites who valued civil liberty. The spread of civil liberty across Europe was a consequence of luxury and war together. Smith, following Hume, destroyed the illusions about the history of European liberty and the presumption of its connection to ancient traditions of liberty, or to modern forms of political liberty. Significantly, one of Hont's plans for *The Jealousy of Trade* was to present it as a history of globalisation. In his papers now held in St Andrews there is an outline introduction to a book entitled 'Jealousy of Trade: Sovereignty, Competition and The Wealth of Nations' which is worth citing in full:

> This book is about theoretical responses to globalisation. It is also an inquiry into the past of political economy, chiefly in the eighteenth-century. It rests on the assumption that the two are intimately connected. The word globalisation is new and it is often asserted that it describes an intensity of interconnectedness of individuals and nations which surpasses anything that went on before. Even the partisans of this position, however, depict it as a long-term process and finger the sixteenth and seventeenth centuries as its proximate starting point. If globalisation has a long history, it must have been observed, theorised and critically reflected upon from its very beginnings. Hegel's pithy comment that Minerva's owl flies at dusk, that humans understand the history in which they participate only when it has unfolded, is now a commonplace. Nonetheless it is often misunderstood. Hegel's own *Rechtphilosophie* is arguably one of the most interesting reflections ever written about globalisation and indeed it is frequently believed (even if falsely) to be the most solid foundation in political theory for twenty-first century reflections on the subject. Famously, Hegel also grand-fathered (although unintentionally) the most enthusiastic theoretical work written on globalisation ever, Karl Marx's *Communist Manifesto*. This is only possible if the dialectic of globalisation was very well visible indeed by Hegel and Marx's time, or, alternatively, that the human imagination (at least at its best) has the ability to diagnose tendencies in history and project them ahead in an interesting and significant fashion. I believe both to be true and in fact it is difficult to see how any significant work of political theory could have ever been written without facing the future. I argue in the book that globalisation pervasively penetrated the political imagination at least from the beginning of the seventeenth century and that it was a central, or perhaps even obsessive, preoccupation of the eighteenth, vulgarly called the Enlightenment. The salient structures of the process were noticed, diagnosed and theorised in an interesting fashion, generating projections of mankind's moral, social and economic trajectory that have remained the foundations of our thinking on the same issues today. Kant, although he might hate to be on it, no doubt would easily comprehend the import of the fact Concorde gets faster to the New York than even the fastest ship sailing from a nearby Baltic port. But it is by no means clear that the globalisation theorist flying on Concorde and contemplating the 'compression of time' would necessarily be able to comprehend what Kant said about the meaning and prospects of globalisation in his famous 1795 essay on *Eternal Peace* (not to mention what he said about time and space in his *Critique of Pure Reason)*. The evidence to the contrary is actually overwhelming, and motivated me to write the essays in this book. It is per-

> fectly conceivable that Hume, Smith and Kant (in addition to Hegel and Marx) are better guides to today and tomorrow than the books that roll off the presses (or posted globally on web-pages) today.[26]

Hont remained convinced to his death that eighteenth and nineteenth-century authors are better guides for those who determine our future than the pontifications of economists, journalists and civil servants who have not been schooled in intellectual history. At the same time, Hont was under no illusion that a world where intellectual history came to prominence as a discipline in any general public sphere was likely to become a reality.

26 Istvan Hont Papers, Special Collections, University of St Andrews.

Part I Inclusion and Exclusion in the History of Ideas

László Kontler

2 Inventing "Humanity": Early-Modern Perspectives

Introduction

This essay addresses a crucial chapter in the development of the modern concept of humanity (mankind, *humanité*, *Menschheit*) in European culture.[1] Rather than an empirical study based on primary research, it is an attempt to sketch an analytical framework for approaching and understanding a broad array of specific historical topics and phenomena within the parameters of an encompassing theme. The methodological assumption at its heart is trivial; our concept of "humanity" is not an intrinsic one, but a contextually defined cultural product shaped by processes of philosophical, historical, social-anthropological, and political self-reflection, and of encounter with "others" in modern times, which all raised important and disturbing questions about the *differentiae specifica* of the human kind. In tackling some of these questions and significant answers to them from the sixteenth to the nineteenth centuries, I focus on early-modern versions of three important intellectual frameworks that determined the consideration of the diversity *versus* unity, and diversity *within* unity, of mankind. These are, first, the temporalisation of human difference: the notion that such difference is largely a matter of patterns in the development of human faculties and relations both among men and between them and their environment across (virtual) time. Second, the historicisation of nature: the study of nature on the basis of the collection and ordering of data about phenomena as they actually exist in space as well as in time. Third, the naturalisation of man: the study of humans without the ascription of a special status to them, with the approach of the naturalists, as coequal from the methodological point of view with any other product of the Creation.

1 Earlier versions of this paper were delivered at Babeş-Bolyai University in Cluj (18 May 2017); in the summer school on "Comparative and Transnational History of Europe" at the European University Institute (12 September 2017; and as a keynote talk at the conference "Inclusion and Exclusion in the History of Ideas" (Helsinki Centre for Intellectual History, 14–15 December 2017). It also builds on experience gained in a course with graduate students at Central European University in 2016 and at the University of Cambridge in 2018. Thanks for the stimulation to everyone involved, especially Marcell Sebők, with whom we designed the course at CEU.

https://doi.org/10.1515/9783110679861-003

Generalities and the "Columbian Moment"

Regarding the subject of human diversity – the real or alleged difference of some human individuals or groups in physical appearance, physiological mechanisms, psychological properties, socio-cultural and moral standards, etc. from others – it is important to observe that such diversity is not only a matter of humanity's geographic dispersal all over the planet, as it is most often understood. The question underlying inquiries into it can also be meaningfully framed in temporal terms: how different are we from our forebears? Historians taking a multi-disciplinary approach to evolution, also deriving their cues from "big history," have called attention to the importance of this manner of setting the problem, with important consequences to our understanding of the history of humanity itself. They propose that while we tacitly take it for granted that evolution "stopped" with the rise of modern humanity, and that slow and long biological evolution was "replaced" with rapid cultural development from the Neolithic era onwards, this is erroneous. Dietary change of several millennia, public health interventions of several centuries, toxic environment exposures of several decades are only a few among so many factors serving as reminders that people themselves have been constantly changing the conditions in which all organisms, including their own, exist. Evolution itself and the identity of "humanity" across time are thus placed in a different light for the historian of our days; does, then, "mankind" have "a" history at all?[2]

Arguably, this temporal dimension in discussing human diversity first became salient at the level of reflexivity familiar to us in the context of the massive encounter with human groups formerly unknown to Europeans in the early-modern period. The problem arose as a cognitive one. How were these groups to be inserted in the existing European system of knowledge, and how were they to be related to on the basis of this system? That this question is by no means a trivial one is vividly illustrated by an example presented in a recent analysis dedicated to the "Columbian moment."[3] Suppose that a group of Neanderthalers which survived the extinction of their fellows elsewhere tens of thousands of years ago were suddenly discovered today among the secluded mountains of Mongolia. Especially since we now know with a fair degree of certainty that Nean-

2 John L. Brooke and Carl Spencer Larsen, "The Nurture of Nature: Genetics, Epigenetics, and Environment in Human Biohistory," *American Historical Review* 119 (2014): 1500 – 1513; Edmund Russell, "Coevolutionary History," *American Historical Review* 119 (2014): 1514 – 1528.

3 David Abulafia, *The Discovery of Mankind: Atlantic Encounters in the Age of Columbus* (New Haven and London: Yale University Press, 2008), 5.

derthalers mingled with *homo sapiens* before their disappearance, and possibly for other reasons, it would be problematic to deny their human status. But would they not be subjected to scientific examinations which, if applied to "modern" humans, would be rejected as dehumanising? Could they be integrated into our modern system of labour, of social welfare, of education, of human rights – would they be eligible for suffrage?

The dilemmas perplexing Europeans upon the "discovery" of (native) Americans were not indifferent in kind and gravity from these ones, even though for them the questions arose immediately and explicitly in terms of the grounds for dominion over indigenous peoples. The answers, which have been explored in now classic studies,[4] can be summarised as follows. None of the templates familiar from Western Christians legal traditions regarding how to relate to "pagans" were applicable to the case of Amerindians. Therefore, Christian claims to sovereignty over them had to be established not on supposed juridical rights of the conquerors, but on the nature of the people conquered; sixteenth-century Thomist philosophers reached back to Aristotle's theory of natural slavery defining a category of man (as distinct from civil slavery, which was an institution of punishment or inflicted on captives of just war). Natural slavery allegedly originated in the psychology of the slave in which, of the two poles of the duality in the human psyche, reason has failed to achieve proper mastery over the passions. This failure apparently undermined the slave's capacity for making deliberate choices, i.e., for moral action and thus for being a virtue-seeking, political animal. Slaves were located outside the civil community, at the bestial end of humanity, with a function of *being* slaves; their freedom would thus be a violation of the natural order, even harmful for themselves. The relationship between Spaniards and Indians was proposed to be determined not by human but by natural and universal law.

One problem with this explanation was posed by the lack of any recognisable and substantial difference between Europeans and Amerindians in physical shape, and that the allegation that one of them was "inferior" *as a species* would have even violated the belief in the perfection of the creation as well as the Aristotelian theory of habituation (*ethismos*). The solution lay in the conflation or identification of "slaves" and *barbaroi* whose culture and society is insufficient and inferior, so that in the case of Indians "a great labour is necessary before

---

4 Anthony Pagden, *The Fall of Natural Man: The American Indian and the Origins of Comparative Ethnology* (Cambridge: Cambridge University Press, 1982); cf. several studies in Joan-Pau Rubiés, *Travellers and Cosmographers: Studies in the History of Early Modern Travel and Ethnology* (London: Routledge, 2007).

they can be brought to the faith and to the practice of good customs".[5] This was a crucial moment, and the element of emphasis in this statement is the word *before*. The project of improvement requires considerable effort and implies serious hazards, but it is feasible because the difference between the civilised conquerors and the savage or barbarous natives is presented as a matter of location on a temporal axis. In this approach, human diversity is historicised, with reference to the natives' primitive modes of subsistence, property, knowledge, standards of intercourse, etc., which made them "live in the past."

This manner of discussing the topic was already quite prominent in its emblematic sixteenth-century treatments. In *A Brief Account of the Destruction of the Indies* (1542, pub. 1552) Bartolomé de las Casas elaborated on the indigence, imbecility, incapacity for hard labour, and lack of ambition in the Amerindians. However, he also emphasised that they were capable of morality and of receiving the Gospel, and that they were not at all averse to civility – i. e., to progress, and the enhancement of their own humanity. Las Casas may also have been the first to object to the disparaging of the "primitive" customs and manners of indigenous peoples with reference to the existence of similar practices among the ancestors of "civilized" Europeans.[6] Similarly, José de Acosta, in his *The Natural and Moral History of the Indies* (1590), painted a vast canvas of barbarians and savages, some of them virtuous while others less so, most of them living in societies marked by relatively low levels of specialisation (distinction of functions), primitive laws and customs, rudimentary political organisation and cultural attainments (with a special emphasis on the lack of alphabetical writing as a versatile means of fluent communication, record keeping and cultivating collective memory) when compared to contemporary Europe.[7] However, Acosta, too, had no doubt that the gulf separating "them" from "us" arose from differences in socio-cultural development across historical time, but certainly not one of kind.

5 This formulation derives from Bernardo de Mesa, later bishop of Cuba, at the junta – debate of theologians, civil and canon lawyers – of 1512 in Burgos, as cited in Pagden, *Fall of Natural Man*, 50.

6 Bartolomé de las Casas, *A Brief Account of the Destruction of the Indies*, Project Gutenberg EBook edition (2007), http://www-personal.umich.edu/~twod/latam-s2010/read/las_casasb2032120321-8.pdf , 3, 12, 21. Accessed May 15, 2018.

7 Joseph [sic] de Acosta, *The Natural and Moral History of the Indies* (London: The Hakluyt Society, 1880), II. 396, 404–406, 409–413, 421–422.

The New Science and Modern Natural Law

At this point, it is important to remember that well into the early-modern period *historia* was understood not merely as the narrative record and evaluation of human events and deeds that have occurred, but also more broadly as an approach: as knowledge based on the collecting and rendering of first-hand observational data or "facts" about objects, including human ones – about natural as much as civil history. Bacon's "inductive method" – the injunction that laws and regularities in the operation of the universe and its creatures ought to be inferred, instead of pre-assigned assumptions about "essences," on the basis of data ascertained by experience and observation – was a methodical reformulation of this approach. In turn, as it became established as the manner of procedure characteristic of naturalists, the human phenomenon was also found eminently susceptible for being studied through this lens. There are thus two intersecting developments that need to be taken into account as underlying the rise of the modern notion of mankind: the historicisation of nature, and the naturalisation of man. The one regarded nature as an assemblage of "things", including events as they happen or have happened, to be studied as they are, with properties peculiar to them, and to be ordered or classified according to the degrees of affinity and compatibility (or, contrariwise, distance and difference) among them. The other tended to locate the human animal firmly within the order of such "things."

It is true that until the nineteenth century, when history became institutionalised as a university discipline and those ushering in this development decided that nature has no part in it, a long tradition anchored in classical antiquity had regarded civil and natural history to be mutually incomprehensible without constant reference to one another.[8] In this sense, there was nothing really new in the early-modern manifestations of the historicisation of nature and the naturalisation of man. And yet, there was an equally old tradition, potentially at odds with the developments just described, which ascribed to man a privileged status in the order of creation by virtue of being endowed with the soul. This representation received strong stimuli from the ancient paradigm of the Great Chain of Being, especially as it reverberated in Christian thought. Thanks to the soul, in especially eloquent statements of the "dignity of man," such as the one put forward in Giovanni Pico della Mirandola's famous eponymous treatise of 1486 (pub. 1496), this dignity was proposed to consist in the capacity of ascension:

8 Joyce E. Chaplin, "Ogres and Omnivores: Early American Historians and Climate History," *The William and Mary Quarterly* 72 (2015): 26.

lifting oneself above the temptations of the flesh and the achievement of a quasi-angelic elevation. This interpretation, while it took account of the animal side of human nature, posed a barrier to engaging the relevant phenomena with the methodology of the naturalists because it was preoccupied with precisely those features of man that enabled him to participate in a transcendental – superhuman – communion with the higher spheres.[9] It was also compatible with old stoic notions about the ultimately shared moral outlook of all mankind as based on "innate ideas" and a propensity to acknowledge and respect universal laws of nature.

Several aspects of the sixteenth and seventeenth century European experience tended to undermine these assumptions. Even among themselves, Christians were seen to disagree about the most suitable manner of attaining what supposedly all of them regarded as the supreme good – salvation – to an extent that led them break out in mass physical violence. This spoke strongly against the allegation of a shared set of principles of conduct, and common subordination to natural laws, among them. The simultaneous inundation of information about the enormous disparities of religious belief, ideas and practices of morality, social and civil institutions, etc. among men in other geographic regions – opened to the gaze of Europeans by voyages of exploration and military, commercial and missionary penetration – only amplified the effects of domestic experience. An important intellectual effect was the rejuvenation of philosophical ideas of scepticism, especially regarding the above-mentioned stoic notions concerning the universality of certain fundamental moral precepts. The thrust of scepticism was to suggest that if there was anything "universal" in human behaviour *as it is* according to observed evidence in real time and space, it is obedience not to abstract laws demanding ethical conduct, but to the natural urge of preserving oneself – by extension, to obtain and retain, and to perform all that is necessary for self-preservation.

No serious discussion of the laws of nature after Michel Montaigne[10] could afford avoiding engagement with this proposition, and as a further consequence,

---

9 Giovanni Pico della Mirandola, *On the Dignity of Man: On Being and the One: Heptaplus*, trans. Charles Glenn Wallis, Paul J. W. Miller, and Douglas Carmichael (Indianapolis, IN: Hackett, 1998), 3–34, esp. 9–10.

10 Especially Michel de Montaigne, "Of Cannibals," "Of custom, and not easily changing an accepted law," "Apology of Raymond Sebond (section "Man can have no knowledge")," in *The Complete Essays*, trans. Donald M. Frame (Stanford: Stanford University Press, 1958), 77–89, 150–158, 420–442.

the very understanding of natural law underwent an important transformation.[11] The contemplation of the overwhelming inconsistency of cultural behaviour across the widening space known to Europeans led to the questioning of the idea of primary and universally binding laws of nature. The seventeenth-century classics, from Grotius through Hobbes to Pufendorf and Locke, continued to believe in such laws, but for them they were not metaphysically given. The evident, empirically ascertained centrality of self-interest to human nature led them to assert that self-preservation – the minimal expression of self-interest, justifiable in all circumstances – must be acknowledged as a universal natural right, and universal laws of nature guiding human conduct exist in so far as they proceed from the obligation to mutually recognise this right in one another.

The point of contact with what has been advanced about the historicisation of nature and the naturalisation of man above is that on these grounds it was meaningful to distinguish, more clearly than in earlier contributions to the tradition, an initial natural state of mankind from a subsequent civil state. While even in the first one, individuals were obliged to seek peace as long as there was a chance to obtain it, once this did not *seem* viable, so that they *felt* their security under threat, it was legitimate for them to resort to violence to defend themselves. Given both the weakness of human faculties in attaining full certainty of judgement regarding situations of insecurity, and the fact that in the state of nature they were indeed the sole judges of such situations as they affected them, that state was one of ubiquitous conflict over resources, and of general instability. In the state of civil society, order and mutual security is provided by the translation of natural laws into positive laws specific to the particular community, and submission to a mutually accepted public authority wielding the monopoly of defining and sanctioning types of behaviour that constitute a threat to mutual safety, thus invested with the power of making and executing the laws. Seventeenth-century natural law thus fully embraced temporality and integrated as one of its organising concepts the notion of progress over a historical continuum from one state or stage to the other, and remained a strong inspiration for much further reflection along the same lines in other fields.

Perhaps nowhere do these threads intersect so succinctly, yet so poignantly as in a well-known clause in the second of John Locke's *Two Treatises of Government* (1689): "in the beginning the whole world was America."[12] Locke's classic

11 On "modern" natural law as a response to skepticism by integrating its central tenets, see generally Richard Tuck, *Philosophy and Government 1572–1651* (Cambridge: Cambridge University Press, 1993).

12 John Locke, *Two Treatises of Government*, ed. Peter Laslett (Cambridge: Cambridge University Press, 1988), 301. Importantly, Locke highlights the retardation of American development by

defence of constitutional government and civil liberty in the later sections of the Second Treatise was firmly established, among many other things, on a philosophical history of the rise of private property through appropriation from common enjoyment via "mixing one's labour" with the things of nature.[13] In Locke's account, improvement – as emergence from the "[native] American" condition – began and status distinctions among men arose already in the pre-civil state, and the voluntary transfer into civil (political) society was explained by him precisely with reference to the widely shared desire of preserving men's "lives, liberties and estates" (the latter term denoting both status and property) – and the consequent willingness to suppress the passion of pursuing self-interest in the hope of a greater good. It was primarily thanks to the – however rudimentary – analysis of the civilising process of conquering the violent passions and submitting them to rational control necessary for arriving at the decision of entering political society that seventeenth-century students of natural law went beyond their predecessors in infusing if with a historical dynamics. Especially Locke and Pufendorf among them did not cease to appreciate man's inherent sociable drive. But for a full account of sociability, and more widely of the human capacity of "elevation" above mere animal instinct, they were willing and able to rely on an ingenious analysis of the operation, including the full spectrum of cognitive-psychological consequences, of the natural and self-regarding urge of seeking the satisfaction of bodily and other needs.

These initiatives supplied a great deal of social and moral philosophical depth to the explanation of human difference as a matter of "virtual time" emerging in the literature launched and hallmarked by figures like Las Casas and Acosta, on which seventeenth-century natural jurisprudence relied heavily for its empirical underpinnings. Among the authors of this tradition, Locke was also distinguished by the fact that an emphasis on the lack of a consistent

pointing to the lack of cultivation of its potentially rich lands in a passage that anticipates Adam Smith's explanation of the advantages of the division of labour: "a King of a large and fruitful Territory there feeds, lodges and is clad worse than a day Labourer in England." Ibid., 296–7. Hobbes accounted for the "brutish manner" in which the "savage people in many places of America" lived with reference to the rudimentary form of government among them. Thomas Hobbes, *Leviathan* (Harmondsworth: Penguin, 1981), 187. On Hobbes's "natural condition of mankind" in conjunction with the opening chapters of the Genesis, American Indians and the savage ancestors of civilized nations, cf. Ioannis D. Evrigenis, *Images of Anarchy: The Rhetoric and Science in Hobbes's State of Nature* (Cambridge: Cambridge University Press, 2014), esp. Ch. 7.

13 Locke, *Two Treatises*, 288, 296.

pattern in moral views across mankind also permeated his epistemology.[14] In *An Essay Concerning Human Understanding* (1690), Locke put forward a comprehensive criticism of the notion of innate ideas as identical principles implanted in and “born” with every human individual, and famously asserted that the mind is a “blank sheet of paper” on which ideas arise in response to experience and sense perception. The cornerstone of Locke’s argument in support of these claims was a kind of common sense empiricism. For a principle to claim innate status, he insisted that it must be shown to enjoy universal agreement among all sensible men, without a single exception. Besides offering a critique of the various accounts of how innate ideas arise (whether spontaneously with the acquisition of reason, or through consent upon their first presentation),[15] Locke referred to the unfathomable dimensions of actually existing moral diversity among human communities. Different societies, he pointed out, reconcile very disparate actions with words like justice, reverence, etc.,[16] and the sources where this is documented relate to “primitive” peoples as well as “polite” ones: some of those classified among the latter are equally marked by disturbing practices ranging from the murder of children and aging parents through cannibalism to revenge – so that these are not to be written off as customs of mere barbarians and savages. The ultimate test was the idea of God and the idea that the Deity should be worshipped,[17] which were regarded as innate by representatives of the rival tradition (in Locke’s time, e. g., the Cambridge Platonists). Locke challenged the innateness of these ideas with reference not only to accounts of “savage” societies (such as the Tupinamba of Brazil, or other “whole nations” at the Cape of Good Hope), but also lettered societies (like Siam and China), which demonstrated that not only immoralists and lawbreakers but entire peoples engaged in such “transgression.”[18] If God had intended to endow man with innate ideas, he would have begun with the notion of himself, and the “generally allowed breach” of this supposedly fundamental principle was a proof against innateness.

The relevance of these propositions to the problem of ‘mankind’ as a distinct and unitary category is put into sharp relief by the controversies which they eli-

---

14 For a comprehensive discussion, see David Carey, *Locke, Shaftesbury, and Hutcheson: Contesting Diversity in the Enlightenment and Beyond* (Cambridge: Cambridge University Press, 2006), 34–68.

15 John Locke, *An Essay Concerning Human Understanding*, ed. Peter H. Nidditch (Oxford: Oxford University Press, 1975), 48–49.

16 Ibid., 84–85.

17 Ibid., 87.

18 Ibid.

cited. One of Locke's critics, Edward Stillingfleet, bishop of Worcester objected that Locke's account of natives "makes them not fit to be a standard for the Sense of Mankind, being a People so strangely bereft of common Sense, that they can hardly be reckoned among Mankind." Locke's response was unhesitating: "all the use I made of them was to show, that there were men in the world that had no innate idea of God ... you go near denying those Cafers to be men: what else do these words signify?"[19] Besides the substantive aspects of inclusion versus exclusion in this exchange, the methodological implications are noteworthy. The debate between Stillingfleet and Locke highlights the central importance of the approach to choosing the criteria of the "human." Stillingfleet, believing in the possibility of a stringent definition – the possession or lack of an (innate) idea of God – was led to a firm denial of human status to many whom Locke's position, recognising the arbitrary, culturally determined nature of the standard, included in that category. In the latter perspective, scepticism as a philosophical position was intertwined with the method of natural history adopted by the Baconian adherents of the new science in the Royal Society. In the case of Locke, continuing in the tradition of Las Casas, Acosta and others, flexibility in regard of the criteria allowed for a broad diversity within the overall category of "the human" and for explaining variation with reference to cultural (and other) environment. We shall see, however, that the exact reverse of the Stillingfleet-Locke casting in regard of stringency versus flexibility and their consequences was equally feasible.

The Eighteenth Century: Taxonomy, Stadial History, Scientific Travel

Natural history continued to provide powerful incentives, inspiration and empirical material for thinking about the social in the framework of the eighteenth-century "science of man."[20] This new-old field of inquiry came to embrace subjects as diverse as language, moral psychology, and political economy, the study of all of which was established on the historical analysis of progress through stages defined in terms of "modes of subsistence" and the concomitant development in the sophistication of manners and institutions. What is more, these foun-

---

19 Cited in Carey, *Locke, Shaftesbury, and Hutcheson*, 59–60,

20 On these imbrications, see Robert Wokler, "The Gaze of Natural History," in *Inventing Human Science*, ed. Christopher Fox, Roy Porter, and Robert Wokler (Berkeley and Los Angeles: University of California Press, 1995), 112–151.

dations were also shored up with new advances in physical anthropology and taxonomy, i.e., systems of classification of the whole of the natural order. It is helpful to begin this section with a brief consideration of the two most influential works in the latter area, *The System of Nature* (1735 and several later, revised and expanded editions and elaborations in the author's lifetime until the three-volume twelfth edition of 1766–1768) by Carl von Linné, and the *Natural History, General and Particular* (36 volumes, 1749–1789) by Georges-Louis Leclerc, Comte de Buffon, focusing on the element highlighted in the case of the Locke-Stillingfleet debate: the centrality of criteria for establishing categories, or the grounds on which specimens are identified as belonging to genera and species.

In a somewhat old-fashioned manner, but in a way also compatible with the Cartesian and Leibnizian emphasis of the faculty of reason, man was generally acknowledged by Linné to be "the last and best of created works, formed after the image of his Maker, endowed with a portion of intellectual divinity."[21] Nevertheless, within the genus of "homo" he established, first, two human species – *homo sapiens* and troglodyte – and then introduced in the former further subdivisions according to morphological traits, such as the shape of organs of reproduction, and generally of the body, the limbs, the skull, facial features, teeth, skin colour, etc. He also determined psychological characteristics (supposedly) accompanying the physical ones, and even assigned the groups thus defined peculiar socio-cultural habits and dispositions. There was the European: "Fair, sanguine, brawny. ... Hair yellow, brown, flowing; eyes blue; gentle, acute, inventive. Covered with close vestments. Governed by laws." By contrast, the "Black" was characterised as "phlegmatic, relaxed. Hair black, frizzled; skin silky; nose flat; crafty, indolent, negligent. Anoints himself with grease. Governed by caprice."[22] Besides two other groups identified by skin colour (red Americans and yellow Asians), there were some further categories, including *homo monstrosus* and *homo ferus*. As for the troglodyte or orang-utan, Linné was following the anatomist Edward Tyson's *Orang-Outang, sive Homo Sylvestris: or, the Anatomy of a Pygmie Compared with that of a Monkey, an Ape, and a Man* (1699) where the body and organs of some apes – Tyson's "Orang-Outang or Pygmie" was actually a chimpanzee –, even the brain, was described as nearly the same as those of

---

21 Carl von Linné, "*Homo* in *The System of Nature*," in *Race and the Enlightenment: A Reader*, ed. Emmanuel Chukwudi Eze (Oxford: Blackwell, 1997), 12–13. Cf. Gunnar Broberg, "Homo sapiens: Linnaeus's Classification of Man," in *Linnaeus: The Man and His Work*, ed. Tore Frängsmyr (Berkeley and Los Angeles: University of California Press, 1983), 156–194.
22 Linné, "*Homo*," 13–14.

humans.[23] What is noteworthy is that in spite of the lip service to humans' (apparently common) participation in divine intelligence, the meticulous presentation of and emphasis on such subdivisions in Linné's system without equally strong and clear standards for what *unites* humanity as a species raised three problematic interpretive possibilities. The first one of these was the establishment of hierarchies within the species with reference to different morphological qualities and the consequent psychological properties as inherent or "genetic" in these groups. Second, it enabled claims about the permeability, or even the questioning of the boundary between some human groups at the "lower" end of the scale and morphologically similar non-humans (apes). Third, with reference to the differences among human groups as intrinsic and constant, it encouraged speculation about "polygenesis":[24] the origin of these groups of mankind from several pairs of ancestors created by God through multiple acts, further accentuating the sense of separation among them.

Buffon, on the other hand, chose the element of procreation as the cornerstone of classification: according to him, it was the capacity for having fertile offspring that identified two specimens as belonging to the same species. If the mule defined the horse and the donkey as belonging to two different species, by implication the same was incontrovertibly the case with man and monkey, too, while all individuals demonstrably capable of producing fertile human offspring were to be members of "humanity," in spite of the great and obvious differences in physical appearance. These were asserted by Buffon to spring from climate, nourishment, air, soil and other factors in the environment that, over several generations, nurtured the development of inheritable features. As he concluded,

---

23 It is important to add that the apparent blurring of the boundaries was, for Tyson himself, not incompatible with the "dignity of man." See Nicole Mennell, "'The Dignity of Mankind': Edward Tyson's *Anatomy of a Pygmie* and the Ape-Man Boundary," in *Seeing Animals after Derrida*, ed. Sarah Bezan and James Tink (New York: Lexington Books, 2018), 87–106.

24 This term was not consistently used until after it appeared as a counterpart of "monogenism/monogenist" in the work of the Philadelphia school of anthropology in 1857. However, the idea itself had been in currency for several centuries, even without necessary regard to global human diversity: the notion of "pre-Adamite man," occasioned by the consideration of Cain's encounter of human creatures after his expulsion because of the fratricide, belongs to this tradition, too. Cf. Isaac la Peyrère's *Pre-Adamitae* (1655), with sixteenth-century antecedents including the work of Paracelsus, Water Raleigh and Giordano Bruno. See Claude Blanckaert, *Monogénisme et polygénisme*, in *Dictionnaire du darwinisme et de l'évolution*, ed. Pierre Tort (Paris: PUF, 1996), II. 3021–3037

> [u]pon the whole, every circumstance concurs in proving, that mankind are not composed of species essentially different from each other; that, on the contrary, there was originally but one species, who, after multiplying and spreading over the whole surface of the earth, have undergone various changes by the influence of climate, food, mode of living, epidemic diseases, and the mixture of dissimilar individuals; that, at first, these changes were not so conspicuous, and produced only individual varieties; that these varieties become afterwards specific, because they were rendered more general, more strongly marked, and more permanent by the continual action of the same causes; that they are transmitted from generation to generation [...].[25]

The concurrence of nature and history in Buffon's system resulted in a novel concept of species as the unceasing succession of similar – or even fairly dissimilar – individuals who are able to reproduce.

In a parallel tradition, the temporalisation of human difference and its analysis with a view to the human engagement with nature evolved into a fully fledged theory of the progress of societies from rudeness to refinement. Eighteenth-century stadial history was thoroughly indebted to the aspects of Lockean (and Pufendorfian) natural law highlighted above, as well as to the kind of geographic, climatic and cultural determinism found in Montesquieu's *The Spirit of the Laws* (1748), where "national characters" were explained as relative to circumstances. Its distinctive contribution was its systematic insistence on, and methodical application of the idea that the diversity observed among human groups in any historical moment ought to be largely attributed to the stage they have attained in a universal pattern of development in their mode of subsistence – or the different pace of progress from one stage to the next – beginning with hunting-gathering, through stockbreeding-pasturing and agriculture (with the rise of the division of labour as a decisive moment), to commerce. The main methodological assumptions (including "conjecture": reasonable inferences made on the basis of sociological comparison in order to make up for the lack or unreliability of empirical data in "original" testimonials) are succinctly illustrated in this sentence from one of the classics, William Robertson's *History of America* (1777): "A tribe of savages on the banks of the Danube must very nearly resemble one upon the plains washed by the Mississippi. Instead then of presuming from this similarity, that there is an affinity between them, we should only conclude, that the

---

25 Georges-Louis Leclerc, Comte de Buffon, "From *A Natural History, General and Particular*," in Eze (ed.), *Race and the Enlightenment*, 27. Of the vast literature, see for a concise introduction Jacques Roger, *Buffon: A Life in Natural History* (Ithaca, NY: Cornell University Press, 1998), Ch. 9–11.

disposition and manners of men are formed by their situation, and arise from the state of society in which they live."[26]

There was a considerable amount of disagreement among the practitioners of stadial history – including philosophers and historians of the Scottish Enlightenment, French physiocrats, Rousseau, and many more across Europe and its colonial extensions – about the direction and the benefits of progress. This, in turn, heavily depended on their judgement about the most fundamental features of humanity in its "original state" and the triggers of emerging from it. A major fault-line separated Rousseau from the Scots. The former believed in animal-like self-sufficiency as an ultimate human characteristic, which enabled primitive or pre-social man – Tyson's orang-utan/pygmy and Linné's orang-utan/troglodyte[27] – to exist as an independent and free agent, a condition lost as a result of the operation of "perfectibility": an *a priori* distinguishing feature of humans which enabled them to raise themselves to more sophisticated levels of existence, but also demolished the bulwarks of individual integrity by nurturing needs that could only be satisfied by resorting to what others had to offer. The resulting inter-subjective relations, non-existent in the original state, catalyzed natural inequalities and transformed them into social inequality.[28] In his emblematic critique of Rousseau, Adam Smith, and in his wake most figures of the Scottish Enlightenment, dissented exactly in their judgement of human nature: according to them, humans were distinguished from the animal world by their original and constant dependence on the assistance of their fellows for the satisfaction of even basic needs. This predicament was alleged to feed an interest-based sociability: a propensity to "truck and barter", evoking an endless succession of human interactions in which the parties are increasingly compelled to act in ways that make others interested in their own well-being, mitigating antagonism and fostering fellow-feeling.[29] It has recently been pointed out that in spite of such disagreements, the analysis of morality and politics in modern

---

26 William Robertson, *The History of America* (London: Routledge/Thoemmes Press, [1777] 1996), II. 30.

27 Silvia Sebastiani, "L'orang-outang, l'esclave et l'humain: une querelle des corps en régime colonial," *L'Atelier du Centre de recherché historiques* 11 (2013), 32, http://journals.openedition.org/acrh/5265, last accessed 21 May 2018.

28 Jean-Jacques Rousseau, *Discourse on the Origin and Foundation of Inequality among Men*, Preface and Part I, in *The Basic Political Writings*, trans. and ed. Donald A. Cress (Indianapolis, IN: Hackett, 1987), 33–60.

29 Adam Smith. "A Letter to the Authors of the Edinburgh Review," in *Essays on Philosophical Subjects*, ed. W. P. D. Wightman and J. C. Bryce (Indianapolis, IN: Liberty Fund, 1982), 251–254; cf. idem., *An Inquiry into the Nature and Causes of the Wealth of Nations*, ed. R. H. Campbell, A. S Skinner, and W.B. Todd (Indianapolis, IN: Liberty Fund, 1981), I. 26.

commercial society by Rousseau and Smith had much more in common than usually acknowledged.[30] For the purposes of this essay, it is important to remember that the commonality extends to another important issue: "mankind," just as in Buffon's vision in the natural-physical aspect, was seen in their gaze uniformly as emerging socially as a product of time.

Many of these works did engage directly or indirectly Linnean and Buffonian natural history, occasionally also pointing out their inconsistencies (in which regard it is important to remember that both works themselves developed over several decades). In some cases, like James Burnett, Lord Monboddo's *Of the Origin and History of Language* (1773) and especially and explicitly Henry Home, Lord Kames's *Sketches of the History of Man* (1774), the thrust of these critiques was a reassertion of the multiplicity of humanity. They pointed out the weaknesses of climate theory (and thus the proposition of the development of inheritable features under the impact of environmental factors) on empirical grounds, and challenged the argument from procreation; with reference to differences in physical appearance, they maintained the possibility of polygenesis, or at least irreparable disarray upon the convulsion of Babel which consolidated the division of humans into separate "kinds" or "races"; and they identified "pre-social man" in apes.[31]

As far as the empirics of these contributions are concerned, while taxonomical patterns derived from natural history and theories of progress put forward by the sciences of man were central to the mental equipment of "scientific travellers", their accounts, in turn, provided an immense wealth of material to the former throughout the eighteenth century.[32] This often took place in a shape already subjected to a primary procedure of "ordering" and analysis *en route*, all the more because the authors of the reports were usually highly qualified naturalists and social philosophers whose pursuit of fieldwork was informed by a thorough familiarity with and participation in the ongoing intellectual debates, and a confident mastery of the relevant scientific paradigms. They were generally also enlightened citizens of the world whose attitude to indigenous peoples around the globe was marked by a blend of enthusiastic curiosity and generous philanthropy. Two especially famous ones among them, father and son, Johann Reinhold

30 István Hont, *Politics in Commercial Society: Jean Jacques Rousseau and Adam Smith*, ed. Béla Kapossy and Michael Sonenscher (Cambridge, MA: Harvard University Press, 2015).

31 James Burnett, Lord Monboddo, *Of the Origin and Progress of Language*, 2nd. ed. (Edinburgh: Balfour, London: Caddell, 1774), I. 270–280; Henry Home, Lord Kames, *Sketches on the History of Man*, ed. James A. Harris (Indianapolis: Liberty Fund, 2007), I. 17–24, 46–51.

32 Harry Liebersohn, *The Traveler's World: Europe to the Pacific* (Cambridge, MA: Harvard University Press, 2006), Introduction.

and Georg Forster, companions of James Cook on his second voyage (1769 – 1772), should suffice here to illustrate the perplexity, and the ways of coping with it, which the contemplation of indigenous populations and their cultures across the Pacific caused to this type.

Both Forsters published extensive and rich accounts of their experiences. In Johann Reinhold's *Observations Made during a Voyage round the World* (1778), the "Varieties of the Human Species" (as the relevant, bulky section is entitled) in the Pacific archipelago are explained predominantly with reference to different levels of social development – "manners" (sociability, taste, "amiability", etc.) as related to the level of material well-being and the sophistication of social organisation: these are occasionally made to account even for differences in physical features among the various groups of islanders, besides environmental factors. While the elder Forster made efforts to reconcile Linné and Buffon, in emphasising the ultimate unity of humanity he evidently drew on the latter:

> [in spite of the Biblical position of common descent,] [s]ome divide mankind according to its colours into various species, instead of being contented with bringing all men under one kindred, choose to extend the human species even to ouran-outangs [...] indeed, if we are at once to make a sudden transition from the contemplation of the fairest beauty of Europe to that of a deformed negro; the difference is so great, and the contrast so strong, that we might be tempted to think them of a distinct species; but if we examine the insensible gradations, in the form, habit, size, colour, and some external differences, we shall find that they are by no means so widely remote from each other in the scale of beings, as to form separate species. [...] For considering that if the most remote tribes of mankind cohabit together, they always procreate children similar to their parents, and capable of procreating others, the difference cannot be so material [...].[33]

To be sure, disparaging overtones abound in these descriptions of indigenous peoples, and within the large family of humankind some appear to be grossly inferior to others even in the representation of a self-styled champion of the equal dignity of all men, such as the future revolutionary radical, the younger Forster was. This is how he wrote in his *Voyage Round the World in His Britannic Majesty's Sloop, the Resolution* (1777) about the inhabitants of the Tierra del Fuego: they have a "vacant stare which is the characteristic of the most consummate stupidity"; they are "dull, hungry, deformed savages [...] having their mental faculties reduced to that miserable situation which places them next to

33 Johann Reinhold Forster, *Observations Made during a Voyage round the World*, ed. Nicholas Thomas, Harriet Guest and Michael Dettelbach (Honolulu: University of Hawaii Press, 1996),172, 174.

brutes."[34] However, it must be stressed that in this account these qualities are described as unequivocally arising not from genetic features, but from cultural distance, possible to bridge through improvement. They are even presented as an inverted proof of the merits of progress:

> [i]f ever the pre-eminence of a civilized life over that of the savage could have reasonably been disputed, we might, from the bare contemplation of these miserable people, draw the most striking conclusions in favour of our superior happiness. Till it can be proved, that a man in continual pain, from the rigour of the climate, is happy, I shall not give credit to the philosophers, who have either had no opportunity of contemplating human nature under all its modifications, or who have not felt what they have seen.[35]

Forster, the philanthropist, appears to be resorting here to the discourse of the civilising process indebted to stadial history as an antidote to inferences which – under the dramatic and disturbing impact of first-hand exposure to human "otherness" – offered themselves via the approach of natural history in its Linnéan guise.[36] In must be added that this use of the two paradigms was specific to Forster, as it was generally contingent; both stadial history and natural history were capable of inclusionist as well as exclusionist uses.

Public-Political Stakes and the Nineteenth-Century Legacy

The public-political cause intertwined with such experiences, theories, and debates of the later eighteenth and nineteenth century was, of course, slavery and the slave trade. An especially salient contribution in this regard was the *History of Jamaica* (1774) by Edward Long, lieutenant-governor of Jamaica. Reading Buffon, Linnaeus and Tyson through Monboddo's lens, Long advanced an argument in which the orang-utan was humanised, while the "Hottentot" (classified

---

34 Georg Forster, *A Voyage Round the World in His Britannic Majesty's Sloop, the Resolution, commanded by Capt. James Cook, during the Year 1772. 3, 4, and 5* (London: White, Robson, Elmsly and Robinson, 1777), II. 507, 606.

35 Ibid., II. 503. Without being mentioned by name, Rousseau is obviously the targeted "philosopher."

36 For an argument about the four-stage theory as a barrier against racialization, see Roxann Wheeler, *The Complexion of Race: Categories of Difference in Eighteenth-Century British Culture* (Philadelphia: University of Pennsylvania Press, 2000), 182–190.

in the "monstrous" category of man by Linnaeus) became bestialised.[37] Here is a gist of Monboddo's take on the much-vaunted subject of the orang-utan:

> When they are clothed, they immediately walk erect; and they play very well upon the pipe, harp, and other instruments. The females among them have monthly courses; and the males have great desire for women. [...] when they are young, they learn to perform all domestic offices, and, particularly, to carry water; and, if they let fall, and break the vessel, they fall a crying. [...] if they were not men, they had the docility belonging to our species [...] they were entirely of the human form, and their action was, for the greater part, that of a man [...] They were sensible of their captivity, and appeared, on that account, melancholy. [...] these apes [...] seem to have more wit than men in certain respects.[38]

This excerpt contains most of the common stereotypes in popular contemporary accounts about African tribes, from the centrality of the topics of menstruation and excessive sexual desire among them to their specific manner of expressing sentiments[39] – here, however, applied to apes. To the often raised objection that apes ought to be distinguished from humans on account of their lack of the capacity of language, Monboddo retorted that, contrary to allegations, language is "not essential to man's nature", but a cultural product – thus, he concluded, "I believe it will be very difficult, or rather impossible, for a man [...] to draw the line betwixt the Orang Outang and the dumb persons among us."[40] Long, for his part, took these observations as a starting point for approaching the conflation of apes and Hottentots from the other end, summarily styling the latter as "a people certainly very stupid, and very brutal", appending a long list of negative attributes that in his view made them "one of the meanest nations on the face of the earth." In particular, they were alleged to be "almost incapable of making any progress in civility and science" and having "no plan or system of morality." Long asked the – to him – rhetorical question: "Has the Hottentot from this portrait a more manly figure than the orang-outang?", only to answer that the latter had "a much nearer resemblance to the Negro race, than the latter bear with White men."[41]

---

37 Cf. Silvia Sebastiani, *The Scottish Enlightenment: Race, Gender, and the Limits of Progress* (Houndmills: Palgrave Macmillan, 2013), 104–108 and Ch. 4 in general; cf. idem, "L'orang-outang, l'esclave et l'humain"; Suman Seth, "Materialism, Slavery and the History of Jamaica," *Isis* 105 (2014): 764–772.

38 Monboddo, *Of the Origin and Progress of Language*, I. 276–279, 297.

39 Cf. Londa Schiebinger, *Nature's Body: Gender in the Making of Modern Science* (New Brunswick: Rutgers University Press, 1993), esp. 75–114.

40 Monboddo, I. 297.

41 Cited in Sebastiani, *Scottish Enlightenment*, 106.

While the criticism of slavery was on the rise in Europe and America from the 1750s onwards, in response performances like Long’s presumed to bestow a philosophical and scientific guise on the literature which justified slavery with reference to the inferiority of Blacks to Whites. To be sure, the assertion of such inferiority did not necessarily imply a complete exclusion of black slaves from mankind, though certainly and explicitly the ascription of a far less dignified degree of humanity to them. In these defences, slavery was hailed as a “mild and benevolent institution” offering Blacks the best chance of improvement and education they could possibly have: work, starting them on the path to civil society. Thus it was in their inferences, not their general approach that polemicists employing this argumentative strategy differed from philanthropists, who established their position on the universalist principle of the uniform history of humankind. As the philosopher and poet James Beattie suggested in *An Essay on the Origin and Immutability of Truth* (1771), even if the racist assertions (specifically those advanced by David Hume) were true, “they would not prove the point in question, except it were also proved, that the Africans and Americans, even though arts and sciences were introduced among them, would still remain unsusceptible of cultivation. The inhabitants of Britain and France were as savage two thousand years ago, as those of Africa and America are at this day.”[42] That they would never become civilised is like claiming that a child would never become a man – as Beattie rehashed an old metaphor in order to point to the absurdity of the racist and pro-slavery argument.

New advances in physical anthropology during the same period also lent support to the idea of a single human species, though not inevitably to anti-racist and anti-slavery polemics. The works of Peter Camper, Eberhard August von Zimmermann, and Friedrich Blumenbach in the 1770s laid down the foundations of modern physical anthropology, including its distinctive principles of racial classification. According to them, the close study of the structure of the body and comparative anatomy undermined the assumption of several, originally separate human species, and demonstrated the existence of an insurmountable divide between man and animal in the organs – e.g., of speech, the subject of a 1779 article by Camper published in the *Philosophical Transactions of the Royal Society*. Others, investigating the causes of the differences in skin colour, found these in the structure of the skin: “in the skin of the black race there is [...] a particular apparatus, which is altogether wanting in the man of the white race, and apparatus composed of two layers, the external of which is

---

42 James Beattie, *An Essay on the Origin and Immutability of Truth, in Opposition to Sophistry and Scepticism* (Philadelphia: Wieatt, 1809), 318–319.

the seat of the *pigmentum* or colouring matter of the Negroes."[43] These developments strongly worked against the credibility of the indefinite fragmentation that marked polygenism. Blumenbach defined five large groups or "races" (Caucasian, Mongolian, Ethiopian, American, Malay)[44] on the basis of skin colour, shape of the head, proportions of the cranium, sensory organs, teeth, etc., understood as varieties within one and the same human species. To some commentators, both Buffon's argument from reproduction and Blumenbach's assertions on physiological difference and commonality confirmed the scriptural teaching about the unity of mankind.[45]

All these positions were caught up in the debates around the abolition of the slave trade, culminating in the 1807 acts in Britain and the United States, and then the British Abolition of Slavery Act of 1833. Even after that date, they were kept on the agenda by the illegal slave trade and the continuation of slavery in the American South. A compelling argument has been put forward, according to which opposition to slavery and the slave trade was in fact the "sacred cause" for Charles Darwin which made him embark on his search for the true *Origin of the Species* and the *Descent of Man*.[46] These seminal works certainly marked a new beginning, and this is not the place to enter even a most rudimentary assessment of all the specific innovations brought by this new beginning into the discussion of the present subject. Two general observations, however, are important to make. First, in spite of the paradigm-shift inaugurated by Darwin, his "system" was not possible without, and was still deeply anchored in, the early-modern developments, outlined above, in the naturalisation of man and the historicisation of nature. Approaching these texts not with the hindsight gained from the revolutionary changes triggered by evolutionary theory, but from the vantage point of the eighteenth century, they read very much like latter-day contributions to the "natural history of mankind" in the style of the Enlightenment. Darwin's analysis of "the causes which lead to the victory of civilised nations

---

43 Marie-Jean-Pierre Flourens, "On the Natural History of Man," *Edinburgh New Philosophical Journal* 27 (1839), originally *Annales des Sciences* (December 1838), republished in *Race: The Origins of an Idea 1760–1850*, ed. Hannah Franziska Augstein (Bristol: Thoemmes Press, 1996), 182–183.

44 Others worked with fewer of more categories.

45 Marcel de Serres, "On the Unity of the Human Species," *Edinburgh New Philosophical Journal* 39 (1845), originally *Bibliothèque Universelle de Genève* no. 107 (1845), republished in Augstein (ed.), *Race*, 195–202.

46 Adrian Desmond and James Moore, *Darwin's Sacred Cause: Race, Slavery, and the Quest for Human Origins* (Chicago: University of Chicago Press, 2011).

[over savages]"[47] could have been written by Robertson. His reminder that "the Dutch families [...] have not undergone the least change of colour, after residing for three centuries in South Africa"[48] echoes Kames's reservations about Buffon's climate theory. Darwin's comments on "the half-art and half-instinct of language" and "the development of moral qualities", with the subsequent discussion of the topics of sympathy, happiness, and virtue,[49] sound like an engagement of arguments from Rousseau, Monboddo and Smith. With the rejection of the idea of God[50] as innate, even Locke lurks in the text. The last two paragraphs of the *Descent of Man* are distinctly Forsterian:

> The astonishment which I felt on first seeing a party of Fuegians on a wild and broken shore will never be forgotten by me, for the reflection at once rushed into my mind – such were our ancestors. [...] Man may be excused for feeling some pride at having risen [...] to the very summit of the organic scale; and the fact of his having thus risen, instead of having been aboriginally placed there, may give him hopes of a still higher destiny in the distant future.[51]

Naturally, the grafting of "selection in relation to sex" on these traditions as a universal principle of the evolution of all species was a path-breaking contribution, but it is also one that helps in further integrating Darwin with the argument pursued in this article. It serves as a powerful reminder that it is highly context-dependent whether the crossing of the animal/human boundary via classification criteria results in a vision of humanity that is inclusive of all humans, or excludes and dehumanises some. Buffon's insistence on the unequivocal separation of the whole of humanity as a unitary species from the rest of the animal world by the focus on procreation inspired striking expressions of Enlightenment cosmopolitanism concerning the equal dignity of all men. At the same time, the obliteration of the same boundary in other contemporary discourses entailed both the humanisation of (some) animals and the animalisation of (some) humans. Darwinism introduced a change in this casting; in that context, it was the assertion of the shared ancestry of all humans *and* animals that had an emancipatory force in establishing the equality of all humans as part of "one

47 Charles Darwin, *The Descent of Man and Selection in Relation to Sex* (London: Murray, 1871), I. 238–240.

48 Ibid., I. 242.

49 Ibid., II. 390–393.

50 Ibid., II. 394.

51 Ibid., II. 404–405.

family."[52] In every aspect, then – substantively and methodologically – the quest for "humanity" remained a thoroughly contingent pursuit, and "mankind" an unstable notion, over more than three centuries of intense European engagement with the subject; a sobering conclusion to draw at the beginning of the twenty-first century, when the concept is, once again, deeply contested.

52 Undeniably, Darwin's texts also had their ambiguities and lent themselves easily to eugenicist and other problematic inferences and uses. Cf. "There should be open competition for all men; and the most able should not be prevented by laws and customs from succeeding best and rearing the largest number of offspring." Ibid., II. 403.

Eva Piirimäe

3 Human Rights and their Realisation in the World: Herder's Debate with Kant

What is the meaning and historical provenance of the concept of human rights? Are human rights basic moral entitlements that humans hold simply by being human or political and legal constructs that regulate the relationship between governments and citizens? And what are the purposes that they serve – are they genuine ethical idea(l)s and normative standards or empty slogans, perhaps even clever instruments for achieving particularist goals (e.g. the promotion of national interests or Western (neo-)colonialism)? Does one understanding even necessarily rule out another? From a historical perspective, it is clearly important to trace the different uses of this concept and the various kinds of goals that have been pursued through them. From a normative perspective, however, one might still insist on distinguishing a concept's "abuses" from its legitimate uses. As intellectual historians, we might also opt to reconstruct different theorists' accounts of human rights as ethical ideals, while also asking in what way they have seen these ideals identified and realised in the actual world. This is what I propose to do in this essay; it includes examining their views about the potential abuse(s) of this concept.

In so doing, I take inspiration from James Tully's 2012 Oxford Amnesty lecture on human rights. In this lecture, Tully defines "human rights as tools or equipment for getting things done by individuals and groups in the multiplicity of relationships in which they live and act".[1] Tully proposes that there are two ways of thinking about human rights that both go back roughly to the Enlightenment period.[2] The first he calls the "High Enlightenment tradition", associat-

The research for this paper has been funded by the Estonian Research Council grants IUT20–39 and PUT PRG942. This article is a modified and expanded version of my keynote lecture given at the conference "Inclusion and Exclusion in the History of Ideas," Helsinki, 14–15 December 2017. I would like to thank Edward Castleton, Wolfgang Proß, Michael Sonenscher and the editors of this volume for their valuable comments on this paper.

1 James Tully, "Rethinking Human Rights and Enlightenment: A View From the Twenty-First Century," in *Self-Evident Truths? Human Rights and the Enlightenment*, ed. Kate Tunstall (New York: Bloomsbury, 2012), 3–35, 3; see also James Tully, *Public Philosophy in a New Key*, 2 vols. (Cambridge: Cambridge University Press, 2008).
2 Tully, "Rethinking Human Rights," 3–35.

https://doi.org/10.1515/9783110679861-004

ing it, most prominently, with Immanuel Kant's moral and political philosophy.[3] The second he labels the "democratic tradition", locating its – retrospectively assembled – early origins in the thought of the Quakers, John Locke, Jean-Jacques Rousseau, and a few nineteenth- and twentieth-century thinkers. The most full-bodied representation of this tradition, Tully suggests, can be found in Mohandas Gandhi's thought.[4] According to Tully, these two traditions have contrasting views of the origins of human rights. While the High Enlightenment presents human rights as "self-evident" and hence as authoritatively stated and declared by states or international organisations, the democratic tradition treats them as proposals that humans make to each other, and that they accept in a democratic way. These two understandings also accordingly translate into two very different visions of their realisation in the world. For the High Enlightenment tradition, "human rights presuppose and are exercised in a universal set of modern legal, political and economic institutions", which potentially allows for their coercive imposition upon other peoples. The democratic tradition, by contrast, emphasises that human rights can be realised in a plurality of legal, political and economic institutions, which all "gain their legitimacy from being open to the contestation of self-determining persons and peoples who are subject to them".[5] Furthermore, while the High Enlightenment accepts that the progressive realisation of human rights is a process that is necessarily destructive of historical social and ecological relationships, the democratic tradition emphasises humans as forming part of a wider community of human as well as non-human life.[6] Tully's own preference is clear here.

Tully's retrospective historical reconstruction – "a view from the twenty-first century" as he calls it in the title of his essay – has not been greeted with unequivocal acclaim.[7] This is not surprising, considering the high status of Kant among contemporary philosophers and the fact that recent historical studies of Kant's thought have demonstrated his anti-imperialism and critique of colonial exploitation in the 1790s.[8] Indeed, Kant's late moral and political philoso-

---

3 Ibid., 6–12; cf. James Tully, *Public Philosophy in a New Key*, vol. 2, *Imperialism and Civic Freedom*, 127–165.

4 Tully, "Rethinking Human Rights," 20.

5 Ibid., 4–5.

6 Ibid., 25–27.

7 See Christopher Brooke, "A Response to James Tully," in *Self-Evident Truths? Human Rights and the Enlightenment*, ed. Kate Tunstall (New York: Bloomsbury, 2012), 35–42.

8 See, e.g., Sankar Muthu, "Conquest, Commerce, and Cosmopolitanism in Enlightenment Political Thought," in *Empire and Modern Political Thought*, ed. Sankar Muthu (Cambridge: Cambridge University Press, 2012), 199–231, 220–231.

phy has been influentially interpreted as a prime example of a philosophical outlook that contains resources for thinking not only about the possible ways in which inter-state antagonism could be overcome, but also about how the negative cultural, political and environmental impacts of globalisation could be dealt with.[9] From a different perspective, Samuel Moyn has lamented that Tully does not give us much detail concerning the arguments presented by the representatives of the democratic tradition. In Moyn's view, Tully – just like all other advocates of the Enlightenment origins of human rights – has disregarded "the statism – even nationalism – of [human] rights until recently".[10] Understood as an international and transnational agenda of the legal protection of individuals against the state, Moyn argues, human rights have a remarkably short and recent history, one that did not properly start before the 1960s or even the 1970s. For Moyn, human rights are "entitlements that might contradict the sovereign nation-state from above and outside", whilst the Enlightenment's rights of man were to be achieved through the construction of spaces of citizenship in which rights were accorded and protected.[11]

My goal in this article is to show that Tully's distinction does in fact have more of a historical basis than he was able to show in his short lecture. I suggest that we can identify a relatively clear-cut debate within the Enlightenment between two thinkers representing two very different ways of thinking about the ideal of humanity and human rights, which in turn are combined with very different understandings about the ways in which the latter can be seen to be realised in the world. This is not to claim that this reconstruction can do justice to, or that this opposition is in any way representative of, the entire period's views about human rights. Tracing the legacies of these two ways of thinking must also be left for another occasion. All I would like to show here is that Kant's erstwhile student Johann Gottfried Herder presented a penetrating critique of Kant's philosophy of history and an insightful alternative to Kant's ideas about the promotion and realisation of humanity and human rights. Herder's philosophy of

---

9 See, e.g., Sharon Anderson-Gold, *Cosmopolitanism and Human Rights* (Cardiff: University of Wales Press, 2001).

10 Samuel Moyn, "Afterword. The Self-Evidence of Human Rights," in *Self-Evident Truths? Human Rights and the Enlightenment*, ed. Kate Tunstall (New York: Bloomsbury, 2012), 256.

11 Samuel Moyn, *The Last Utopia: Human Rights in History* (Cambridge, MA: Belknap Press of Harvard University Press, 2010), 13; cf. idem, "Imperialism, Self-Determination, and the Rise of Human Rights," in *The Human Rights Revolution: An International History*, ed. Akira Iriye et al. (Oxford: Oxford University Press, 2012), 159–178.

humanity, in turn, shows remarkable structural affinity with what Tully has described as the core ideas of the democratic tradition of human rights.[12]

Herder is not typically seen as an author relevant for the discussion of human rights, as he is still widely characterised as a romantic nationalist whose emphasis on the value of cultural identity stands in tension with his commitment to humanity. Indeed, Tully himself, in his *Public Philosophy in a New Key*, presents Herder as a cultural pluralist who posits unrealistic (and hence potentially oppressive) "billiard-ball picture" of internally uniform cultures.[13] However, as a vast body of excellent scholarship has shown, Herder's approach is much more nuanced than merely cherishing distinct cultural identities. Herder presented a comprehensive natural philosophy that included a philosophical history of mankind. As I hope to show in this contribution, he insisted on the value of human self-determination at various levels (individual and collective), while also identifying a fundamental ethical rule as the basis of human rights' claims. Accordingly, Herder's position regarding the term "human rights" was that it needs to be replaced by a different word: "The word *human rights* [*Menschenrechte*] cannot be uttered without *human duties* [*Menschenpflichten*]; both relate to each other and we are looking for One word [*Ein Wort*] for both".[14] The word that Herder proposed for this purpose was *Humanität* (humanity) – a term that he had first systematically introduced in discussing the vocation of humanity in the first volume of his *Ideas for a Philosophy of History of Mankind* (1784), and that he further fleshed out in his later writings on moral and political philosophy.

---

12 For a different approach to the topic of Herder and human rights, see Michael N. Forster, "Herder and Human Rights," in *Herder: Philosophy and Anthropology*, ed. Anik Waldow et al. (Oxford: Oxford University Press, 2017), 224–239.

13 Tully, *Imperialism and Civic Freedom*, 27–29; this is also the way in which contemporary Kantians still tend to see him; see e.g. Sharon Anderson-Gold, "Kant and Herder," in *A Companion to the Philosophy of History and Historiography*, ed. Aviezer Tucker (Oxford: Wiley, 2008), 457–467. Anderson-Gold's short presentation of Herder's views in this article is greatly indebted to the, by now, highly controversial reading of Herder developed by Friedrich Meinecke and Isaiah Berlin; for a critique of this received view in the light of recent developments in specialised Herder scholarship, see Eva Piirimäe, "Introduction. Herder on Empathy and Sympathy: Historicism, Stoicism and Contemporary Perspectives," in *Herder on Empathy and Sympathy/ Einfühlung und Sympathie im Denken Herders*, ed. Eva Piirimäe et al. (Leiden: Brill, forthcoming).

14 Johann Gottfried Herder, *Briefe zu Beförderung der Humanität, Werke in zehn Bänden*, ed. Jürgen Brummack Martin Bollacher, 10 vols (Frankfurt am Main, 1985–2000), vol. 7, ed. Hans Dietrich Irmscher (Frankfurt am Main, 1991), 147; see also ibid., 344. (Unless otherwise indicated, all translations are mine – E.P.)

Altogether, Herder's debate with Kant can be divided into two main periods, the first conducted in the successively published four volumes of the *Ideas* (1784–1791) and answering Kant's early writings, the second concerning Kant's mature views in the early 1790s (until 1795) and conducted in Herder's *Letters for the Advancement of Humanity* (1792/1793–1797) and *Adrastea* (1800–1803).[15] Since Kant's views are much better known, my main focus is on Herder. Nevertheless, I will seek to capture the evolution of the views of both thinkers, so as to show why and how Herder picked up exactly those points in Kant's theories that he did. The ways in which Kant sought to answer Herder's criticisms in his later works cannot, however, be examined here; nor will I attempt to evaluate whether Herder's critique of Kant was justified or not.[16]

I

Herder provided a grand systematic account of humanity's place in nature in the first volume of *Ideas*. Kant responded with a highly critical review of this volume and introduced an alternative view in his *Idea for a Universal History with a Cosmopolitan Aim* (1784). Herder responded to Kant in the second part of his *Ideas*, raising a number of critical points about Kant's critique and vision. Kant answered with a further review and essay,[17] while Herder came back to Kant's ideas in the subsequent volumes of the *Ideas*.

From a systematic point of view, the differences between Herder's and Kant's approach to the "philosophy of history of mankind" were manifold, which does not mean that Kant had not influenced his former student. The teacher and stu-

---

15 Herder's specific answers to Kant's late works (*Metaphysics of Morals* (1797) and *Contest of Faculties* (1798)) cannot be traced here. As Marion Heinz has recently shown, the second volume of Herder's *Metacritique* (titled *Calligone*) (1800) can also be read as not only a response to Kant's aesthetic theory (its ostensive purpose), but also to his natural and moral philosophy as a whole, Marion Heinz, "Sympathie. Zur Palingenesie stoischen Denkens in Herders *Kalligone*," in *Herder on Empathy and Sympathy/ Einfühlung und Sympathie im Denken Herders*, ed. Eva Piirimäe et al. (Leiden: Brill, forthcoming).

16 The overview draws on my "State-Machines, Commerce and the Progress of *Humanität* in Europe: Herder's Response to Kant in *Ideas for the Philosophy of History of Mankind*," in *Commerce and Peace in the Enlightenment*, ed. Béla Kapossy et al. (Cambridge: Cambridge University Press, 2017), 155–181, and Chapter Six of my book manuscript *Patriotism, Cosmopolitanism, and Nationalism: Herder and the Enlightenment*.

17 "Conjectural beginning of human history". An excellent reconstruction of this essay can be found in Michael Sonenscher, *Sans-Culottes: An Eighteenth-Century Emblem in the French Revolution* (Princeton, NJ: Princeton University Press, 2008), 195–201.

dent disagreed about the relationship between nature and culture, happiness and virtue, as well as the very methodology of philosophy of history. Most fundamentally, Kant was a dualist on body and soul as well as on nature and morality, while Herder was a radical naturalist.[18] As Nigel DeSouza has recently shown in fascinating detail, Herder's radical naturalism was both deeply indebted to Kant's pre-critical metaphysics as well as also going far beyond it.[19] In the *Ideas*, Herder posited forces operating in an analogous manner at all levels of nature. For Herder, there was fundamentally just one force, that of God, which permeated nature (the created world) and diversified itself into various modifications of different degrees of complexity, from the forces of attraction and repulsion to those associated with the elasticity of fibres, irritability of muscles, and sensitivity of nerves. In so doing, these modifications of the divine force also took the most various ascending forms of inanimate and animate organisation through the scale of beings all the way up to human beings. For Kant in the critical period, Herder's naturalism was "metaphysics, indeed even a very dogmatic one".[20]

Herder's and Kant's radically different views on human self-determination were also grounded in these disagreements. For Kant, famously, freedom of the will could not be proven in the natural world (the realm of causal determination), it was not a *phenomenon*, but a *noumenon* (something posited by our reason). As rational beings, humans for Kant were able to determine themselves, and determining ourselves on the basis of the moral law inherent in our reason was in turn the core of morality for him. Human nature (belonging to the realm of nature) and reason for Kant were separate, and our self-legislating and -binding reason was not supposed to draw on our natural drives.[21] Herder's radical naturalism implied a fundamentally different understanding of natural laws (the latter included also teleological relationships) and of the relationship be-

18 On Herder's "radical naturalism", see Wolfgang Proß, "*Ideen zur Philosophie der Geschichte der Menschheit*," *Herder Handbuch*, ed. Stefan Greif et al. (Paderborn: Wilhelm Fink, 2016), 171–215.

19 Nigel DeSouza, "Herder's Theory of Organic Forces and its Kantian Origins," *Kant and His Contemporaries*, ed. Corey Dyck et al., vol. 2 (Cambridge: Cambridge University Press, 2018), 109–30.

20 Immanuel Kant, "Review of J. G. Herder's *Ideas for the Philosophy of the History of Humanity. Parts 1 and 2*," in idem. *Anthropology, History and Education*, ed. Günter Zöller et al. (Cambridge: Cambridge University Press, 2007), 124–142, 132.

21 For the central tenets of Kant's philosophy of life, and its relationship to Herder's ideas, see John Zammito, *The Genesis of Kant's* Critique of Judgement (Chicago: Chicago University Press, 1992).

tween nature, morality and freedom.[22] As DeSouza has aptly put it, for Herder there were also ascending degrees of "interiority" and freedom in nature, human beings having the highest degree of both, in the form of self-consciousness and conscience.[23] Since human beings had the greatest complexity of forces and drives, and even had "forming power" like God, they also created the most intricate secondary worlds of culture and tradition, while in so doing they could also err against nature. Yet this kind of complexity and self-awareness also allowed for the greatest degree of self-determination and -formation both individually as well as collectively. The highest degree of self-determination for Herder was to knowingly determine oneself according to, not against nature.

How exactly does Herder describe human self-determination in the first volume of the *Ideas?* On the one hand, he grounds this idea in his metaphysics and vitalist philosophy of nature, according to which the complexity of the external phenomenal form and organisation reflects the internal complexity of force, while at the same time enabling a respective degree of complexity in its sensuous and representative capabilities. The form and organisation of a being, further, already reveals the purposes that it should serve. This is what Herder has in view, when he argues:

> I wish I could extend the word humanity [*Humanität*], so as to comprise in it every thing I have thus far said on the noble formation [*Bildung*] of man for reason and freedom, finer senses and impulses, the most delicate, yet strong health, the population and the rule of the Earth; for man has not a more dignified word for his destiny, than what expresses himself, in whom the image of the Creator lives imprinted as visibly as it can here. We need only delineate his form [*Gestalt*], to develop his noblest duties.[24]

In Herder's scale of beings, humans represent the most developed life form on earth, essentially a "middle ring" between animals and divine beings. On the one hand, they share a number of fundamental features and desires with animals, among them, most importantly, the fundamental desire of preserving

---

22 For Herder's understanding of "natural laws," see Wolfgang Proß, "Die Begründung der Geschichte aus der Natur – Herders Konzept von 'Gesetzen' in der Geschichte," in *Wissenschaft als kulturelle Praxis*, ed. Hans Erich Bödeker et al. (Göttingen: Vandenhoeck and Ruprecht, 1999), 187–225.

23 DeSouza, "Herder's Theory of Organic Forces," 125.

24 Johann Gottfried Herder, *Outlines of a Philosophy of History of Man*, trans. T. Churchill (London, 1800), ix (henceforth abbr. as *Outlines*), 249, and Johann Gottfried Herder, *Ideen zur Philosophie der Geschichte der Menschheit* [1784–1791], in idem, *Werke*, vol. 3/1, ed. Wolfgang Proß (Munich: Carl Hanser Verlag, 2002) (henceforth abbr. as *Ideen*), 142. I have modified the translation – E. P.

one's constitution, which encompasses both the desire of self-preservation as well as the sociable inclinations that help to preserve the species. Humans also share with other sensitive beings a capacity for sympathy grounded in the constitution of their nervous system – the sense of hearing enables them to share in other sensitive beings' feelings, which in all of nature functions best at the intra-species level. As the most delicate beings in nature, humans are also most sensitive to other creatures' pain as expressed in sound. On the other hand, humans relate to their environment with reflective awareness [*Besonnenheit*], which makes it possible for them to develop language and thinking. Combining the sensations of their tactile and visual senses thanks to reflective awareness, humans develop various higher kinds of sympathy. They are able to sense the forming force (soul) in the phenomenal forms, most importantly, other human beings, and are also capable of recognising the image of the divine in the latter. Human cognition is thus never separate from sensation and volition. Reason itself, Herder argues, should be seen as an adaptive capacity enabling humans to preserve themselves and their species.[25]

Herder did not fail to spell out the implications of this view for an account of human morality in the *Ideas*, invoking and developing the insights that he had already developed in his earlier works, most notably *Treatise on the Origins of Language* (1772), *This Too a Philosophy of History* (1774) and *On Sensation and Cognition* (1775 – 1778). Fundamental to all kinds of social interaction was the capacity of sympathy or with-feeling [*Mitgefühl*], which relied on human self-feeling. In adapting themselves to various environments, humans develop complex linguistic and cultural worlds. This leads to their sharing of more specific cultural self-images, on the basis of which they in turn feel attraction and aversion towards other human beings and groups. Human sympathy thus also fosters special relationships as well as binds together cultural communities (drawing greatly on common language). This, however, also has the downside of translating as coldness or, in some cases, even as antipathy in interaction with groups with a radically different kind of culture.[26]

Already in his earlier works, Herder indicated that it was a historical destiny or task for humans to *learn* to determine themselves so as to overcome this kind of antagonism.[27] In the *Ideas*, Herder specified that humans possess a separate

25 For discussion, see Proß, "*Ideen zur Philosophie der Geschichte der Menschheit*," 191 – 192.
26 For an in-depth exploration of these themes, see the contributions in *Herder on Empathy and Sympathy/ Einfühlung und Sympathie im Denken Herders*, ed. Eva Piirimäe et al. (Leiden: Brill, forthcoming).
27 See Eva Piirimäe, "Sociability, Nationalism and Cosmopolitanism in Herder's Early Philosophy of History," *History of Political Thought* 36 (2015): 521 – 559.

disposition, which enables them to regulate these necessarily partial and culturally based sympathies:

> But as the mere with-feeling [*Mitgefühl*] of man is incapable of being extended to everything and could be but an obscure and frequently impotent guide to him, a limited, complex being, in everything remote; his guiding mother has subjected its numerous and lightly interwoven branches to her more unerring standard: this is the "rule of justice and truth" [*Regel der Gerechtigkeit und Wahrheit*].[28]

This disposition, Herder argues, is grounded in humans' specific bodily constitution and organisation (erect posture), which creates unity from the symmetry of the two ears and two eyes.[29] Humans can reflectively recognise fundamental similarities as well as distinguish between true and false, which translates into a rudimentary sense of justice in their dealings with each other. The essence of the "great law of equity [*Billigkeit*] and reciprocity [*Gleichgewicht*]" written in all human hearts is thus: "Do not unto others what they should not do unto you; but what others should do unto you, do unto them too".[30] "All [natural] right [i.e. laws] of humans, nations and animals [*alles Menschen-, Völker- und Tierrecht*]", he stipulates, is based on the "similarity of sentiment, unity of design among different persons, and equal loyalty in an alliance".[31]

By invoking the rule of equity, Herder was clearly drawing on the early-modern natural law tradition, which in turn harked back to ancient Stoic and Ciceronian discussions of *oikeiōsis*.[32] However, it is important to note that in contrast to early-modern natural lawyers he stipulated the uniform foundations of "all [natural] right of humans, animals and nations". True, early-modern natural lawyers also often quoted various ancient authors to support arguments about human natural sociability, referring not only to animals' desire of society, but also to their special relationships with, and avoidance of harm to, members of their own species. For example, when developing his defence of human natural sociability, the natural lawyer Hugo Grotius cited among others Marcus Terentius

28 Herder *Outlines*, 102; *Ideen*, 147.

29 For discussion, see Proß, "*Ideen zur Philosophie der Geschichte*," 194–197.

30 Herder *Outlines*, 101–102; *Ideen*, 147. I have modified the translation here, so as to bring out the juridical origins of this term and the connection to Hugo Grotius's notion of *aequitas*, as highlighted by Wolfgang Proß in "Anmerkungen," in idem, *Werke*, vol. III/2, 301–304; "*Ideen zur Philosophie der Geschichte*," 195; "Kolonialismuskritik aus dem Geist der Geschichtsphilosophie: Raynal, Herder, Dobrizhoffer und der Fall Paraguay," in *Raynal – Herder – Merkel: Transformationen der Antikolonialismusdebatte in der europäischen Aufklärung*, ed. Mix York-Gothard et al. (Heidelberg: Winter Verlag, 2017), 17–73.

31 Herder, *Outlines*, 103; *Ideen*, 148.

32 See also Piirimäe, "Introduction. Herder on Empathy and Sympathy," 14–18.

Varro's reference to an old proverb that "a Dog will not eat Dog's Flesh" and Juvenal's remark that "Tigers live peaceably together, and that the wildest Beasts spare those of their own Species".[33] For Grotius, too, these were examples of a rudimentary desire of society common to humans and animals, but he took care to underline that humans had a separate "Faculty of knowing and acting, according to some general Principles, so that what relates to this Faculty is not common to all Animals, but properly and peculiarly agrees to Mankind".[34] To this, Grotius's most prominent eighteenth-century commentator Jean Barbeyrac further added a clarification that this does not mean that humans and animals follow the same kind of natural law ("a Right common to humans and animals").[35] Herder, however, affirmed exactly that. Characteristically, Herder emphasised the analogous principles underlying the interactions between natural beings, while still seeking to highlight the distinctive features of human cognition and volition.

In Herder's view, thus, non-human animals possess an instinctive understanding of the fundamental similarity and thus equality of all members of one's species, one that informs a further sense of reciprocity. Humans have this understanding inscribed in their natural sentiments as much as in their reason (a developed capacity), distinctively developing a reflective understanding of equity, which enables them to "become sincere brothers and associates" for each other.[36] Humans, however, may deviate from nature due to various kinds of imaginary ideas they develop, up to a point at which they would be prepared to eat the flesh of another human being. Yet even an "inhuman monster who eats the flesh one's brother", Herder argues, still demonstrates a rudimentary sense of reciprocity, expecting to be "eaten in turn".[37] The fundamental disposition towards equity thus never fully disappears in humans, even though it may be overrun by false ideas and misguided education. It is the task of a developed form of

---

33 Hugo Grotius, "The Preliminary Discourse," *The Rights of War and Peace*, ed. and with an Introduction by Richard Tuck, from the Edition by Jean Barbeyrac (Indianapolis: Liberty Fund, 2005), § 7, 82.

34 Ibid, § 7, 84–85.

35 In a note, he argued: "[...] our Author only affirms that the Principle of Sociability has so real a Foundation in the Nature of Man, that we find some faint Tracks of it even amongst irrational Animals, in regard to those of their own Species. He does by no means pretend either that there is any Right common to Men and Beasts, or that any certain Consequences can be drawn from the Actions of Brutes, for proving any one particular Thing conformable or contrary to the Law of Nature". Ibid., § 7, 83, fn.2.

36 Herder, *Outlines*, 102; *Ideen*, 148. See also Proß, "Kolonialismuskritik," 68.

37 Ibid.

human reason to lead human beings back to their own internal voice of equality and reciprocity between themselves.

Herder's substantive understanding of justice is closer to the Stoics than to Grotius. However, here too, the footnotes that Grotius provided seemed to support the idea that Grotius was continuing in the same tradition. For Grotius, sociability was the foundation of "strict justice" specifically: This Sociability [...], Grotius famously argued, "is the Fountain of Right, properly so called; to which belongs the Abstaining from that which is another's, and[xviii] the Restitution of what we have of another's, or of the Profit we have made by it, the Obligation of fulfilling Promises, the Reparation of a Damage done through our own Default, and the Merit of Punishment among Men.'[38] Yet in a footnote, he also referred to Seneca's much broader account of reciprocity.[39] Seneca, he argued, made an "excellent application" of this principle by describing the human urge and duty to reciprocate good offices with gratitude, and characterising the entire social interaction as an exchange of mutually beneficial offices for the sake of maintaining society between equals.[40] Grotius also referred to Marcus Aurelius's similar understanding of the desire of society.[41] Encouraging reciprocity both in terms of abstaining from harm as well as mutual love, Herder's formula of equity clearly echoes those of Seneca and Marcus Aurelius and goes beyond "justice properly and strictly called" in the Grotian sense. For Herder, human justice entailed much further-going duties than Grotius's account of natural right. We will return to Herder's ideas about how this kind of equity can be promoted in the world below.

II

In his earliest response to Herder, published in January 1785, Kant lashed out at Herder's "hypothesis of invisible forces", dogmatic "metaphysics" and the method of analogy he used for creating his system.[42] Yet he had already proposed his own alternative philosophy of history in November 1784 in his *Idea for a Universal History.* I can only state briefly his key ideas in this essay. Kant sought to pro-

---

38 Grotius, "The Preliminary Discourse," § 8, 85–86.
39 Ibid., § 8, 86, fn. 2. Grotius refers to Seneca's *De beneficiis*, Bk. IV, ch. XVIII..
40 See Hans Blom, "Sociability and Hugo Grotius," *History of European Ideas* 41 (*Sociability in Enlightenment Thought*, ed. Eva Piirimäe et al.) (2015): 589–604 for an argument about the way in which sociability was a remedy to the original elitist tendencies in Grotius's early views.
41 Grotius, "The Preliminary Discourse," § 7, 84, fn. 6.
42 Kant, "Review of J. G. Herder's *Ideas*," 132–133.

vide an idea for writing universal history. Such a history, he hoped, might serve to encourage humans to continue their efforts to improve things, even despite the apparent meaninglessness of history (which caused moral despair). While Kant came to lay out the purely rational source of the supreme principle of morality in the *Groundwork of the Metaphysics of Morals* (1785), he already gave a hint in *Idea* that even though freedom of the will as the basis of morality is not demonstrable in the phenomenal world, it had to be *possible* there. This justified trying to develop an argument of natural teleology about history. Humans, Kant suggested in this argumentative mode, were destined by nature to develop reason and exercise freedom of the will, which constituted morality.[43] While animals could reach their destiny as individuals, humans could reach it only as a species, collectively. Reason could only be developed cumulatively. Yet Kant also ventured another hypothesis about the actual mechanism of human antagonism that "nature" used for achieving this destiny. This mechanism for Kant was sustained by what he famously called human "unsocial sociability", humans' fundamentally antagonistic disposition, which led to conflict between them. It could, however, yield positive results when law and order were guaranteed by the sovereign.[44] In a civil society, humans would be able to exercise and practice skill and discipline – the two key aspects of Kant's notion of culture – whereby they would further develop "taste" and "progress in enlightenment".[45] As a result of these developments, a beginning is made towards the foundation of a mode of thought which can with time transform the crude natural predisposition to make moral distinctions into determinate practical principles and hence transform a *pathologically* compelled agreement to form a society finally into a *moral* whole.[46]

Over time, as members of civil societies, humans would thus also arrive at an increasingly correct understanding of the nature of the "just civil constitution" guaranteeing equal freedom (i.e. rights) to all and the methods of implementing it in practice. They would come to see that the development of reason and morality required the establishment of such a constitution, which in turn de-

43 For a concise overview of the interpretative debates about the consistency of Kant's philosophy of history with his critical philosophy as a whole, see Anderson-Gold, "Kant and Herder," 460–462.
44 Immanuel Kant, "Idea for a Universal History with a Cosmopolitan Aim," in idem, *Anthropology, History, and Education*, ed. Günter Zöller et al. (Cambridge: Cambridge University Press, 2007), 111–112.
45 Ibid., 112–113; 117. Compare also Kant's famous discussion of enlightenment in "What is the Enlightenment?" published in the same year (1784) as *Idea*.
46 Ibid., 111.

pended on achieving lawful order and peace at the international level. "The human being", Kant famously argued, "is an *animal which*, when it lives among others of its species, *has need of a master* [...] who ... necessitates him to obey a universally valid will with which everyone can be free. But where will he get this master? Nowhere else but from the human species. But then this master is exactly as much an animal who has need of a master".[47] The only secure way to achieve lawful order and international peace, Kant argued, was to establish an international federation of states [*Völkerbund*] with coercive powers.[48]

A philosophical history, Kant suggested, could trace the gradual improvement of the "civil constitution and its laws and [...] the relations of states" over different periods.[49] He argued that there were already several indications that states might also enter into new kinds of relationships among themselves. First, thanks to the ever-greater importance of commerce as a source of revenue for the states, rulers were increasingly compelled to leave their subjects as much freedom as possible, while the inevitable progress of Enlightenment in such conditions led the public to press for reforms. At the same time, however, rulers were forced to extract ever more revenue from society in order to sustain the increasingly expensive warfare, which would at some point lead towards a general situation of exhaustion. The mounting public debt, further, would make rulers regard wars as increasingly dubious enterprises.[50] Thus, Kant argued, it was not entirely groundless to cherish a "chiliastic" expectation that "the purpose of nature is at least fairly well safe-guarded (if not actually furthered) even by the ambitious schemes of various states".[51] It was also to be expected, Kant did not forget to add, that "our part of the world" – in which this improvement was most visible – would also "someday give laws to all the others".[52]

When Herder read Kant's *Idea for a Universal History*, he was outraged. Partly, he felt that Kant had stolen his own key idea of applying a form of natural teleology to history, even though with qualifications (as a hypothesis and guideline for writing history, rather than as part of a broader natural philosophy). Even more importantly, he resisted what Kant had turned this idea into. In letters to his friends Johann Georg Hamann and Friedrich Heinrich Jacobi in early 1785, Herder argued that Kant's central thesis was not just ridiculous, but also detest-

47 Ibid., 107–121, 113.
48 Ibid., 114.
49 Ibid., 118–120.
50 Ibid., 118.
51 Ibid., 116–118.
52 Ibid., 119.

able. Explaining the development of human forces [*Kräfte*] and ultimately, morality, through "political antagonism and the most perfect monarchy, indeed, the co-existence of many most perfect monarchies that are ruled by pure reason in corpore", Herder argued, Kant's essay breathed "wretched ice-cold, slavish enthusiasm".[53]

For Herder, Kant's analysis of the mechanism of natural antagonism read as a legitimation of the military rivalry and ruthless colonial imperialism of European monarchies. In his *This Too A Philosophy of History* published in 1774, Herder had already sharply mocked the remarkable hypocrisy of modern Europeans in spreading light and freedom to vanquished peoples,[54] now it was his own teacher who was complicit in this. In subsequent years, Herder sought to work out his critique of Kant in the various draft versions of his *Ideas.* Only some of this critique, however, came to be included in the final, published version. In a recent article, I have tried to reassemble this critique piece by piece.[55] One of Herder's key points, I suggest there, was that Kant's argument was inconsistent: at the domestic level, what concerned the nature of authority within the state was fundamentally Hobbesian, while he sought to combine the Hobbesian argument with the Abbé de Saint-Pierre's optimistic international solution (which presupposed different, less Hobbesian, foundations). Kant described the subjects of modern monarchies as self-seeking antagonistic "animals" fundamentally unable to govern and rule themselves; they needed a "master" to break their will. They were capable of questioning established authorities and reasoning about religion and political constitutions, yet unable to master themselves. At the same time, Kant also hoped that the "masters" (i.e. rulers) would develop the necessary "good will" to establish and maintain a lawful constitution in their states, suggesting that modern commercial interests would force them to do so to a great degree. Yet, what about commercial interests pressing for an ever-expanding number of colonial conquests? What kind of "rights" would be granted to those thereby "included" in the civilised world? And, indeed, if a perfectly lawful domestic order could only be established once a "master of masters" was set up, what would guarantee its good will and equal justice towards its members?

---

53 Herder to Hamann 14. February 1785, in Johann Gottfried Herder, *Briefe. Gesamtausgabe*, ed. Wilhelm Dobbek and Günter Arnold, 18 vols. (Weimar: Hermann Böhlaus Nachfolger, 1977–2016), vol. 5 (September 1783–1788) (1979), 106; Herder to Jacobi, 25. February 1785, in Herder, *Briefe. Gesamtausgabe*, 109.

54 See Piirimäe, "Sociability, Nationalism and Cosmopolitanism," 521–559, 533–537.

55 Piirimäe, "State-Machines".

Herder's own vision of politics, which he laid out in subsequent volumes of the *Ideas*, was in many ways exactly the opposite, drawing on much more optimistic moral psychological foundations. This is best captured in Herder's famous retort to Kant in Book Nine of the *Ideas:*

> The maxim that "man is an animal who needs a master when he lives with others of his species, so that he may attain happiness and fulfil his destiny on earth", is both facile and noxious as a fundamental principle of a philosophy of history. The proposition, I feel, ought to be reversed. Man is an animal as long as he needs a master to lord over him; as soon as he attains the status of a human being he no longer needs a master in any real sense. Nature has designated no master for the human species, brutal vices and passions render one necessary.[56]

Individual happiness is nature's aim, Herder emphatically argued, and has to be achievable in all cultures. The abstraction of the "happiness of mankind", by contrast, encouraged inertia, submissiveness and lack of responsibility. Instead of monarchs, individual human beings were to be trusted. Although constitutional mechanisms for defending the people against the abuse of power by rulers were necessary, human beings had a natural disposition to engage in mutually beneficial activities and joint ventures, ultimately making the state redundant. Modern monarchies, the origins of which Herder located in the Germanic tribes' conquest of Roman imperial territories were, in his view, "state-machines" grounded in, and still geared towards, conquest. They were elaborate edifices of artificial roles and honours, which at the same time excluded the people from active participation in public life. To expect such machines to come to achieve a stable balance of power among them, or indeed, join a universal league of states with coercive powers, was naïve, and attempts to force them into such a league, imperialistic.[57]

Kant responded to the second part of Herder's *Ideas* with another review (November 1785). One of his key points in this second review was to reassert his belief that nature's purpose lies in developing the capacities of the species:

> But what if the genuine end of providence were not this shadowy image of happiness, which each makes for himself, but rather the always proceeding and growing activity and culture that is put in play by it, whose greatest possible degree is only the product of a state constitution ordered in accordance with concepts of human right [my emphasis – E.P.], and consequently something that can be a work of human beings themselves? [...]

56 Herder, *Ideas*, 323 (I have extensively modified the translation.); *Outlines*, ix, 249; *Ideen*, 336–337.

57 Piirimäe, "State-Machines," 176–177.

> Does the author really mean that if the happy inhabitants of Tahiti, never visited by more cultured nations [*gesittetere Nationen*], had been destined to live for thousands of centuries in their tranquil indolence, one could give a satisfying answer to the question why they exist at all, and whether it would not have been just as good to have this island populated with happy sheep and cattle as with human beings who are happy merely enjoying themselves?[58]

For Herder, this completely ignored the fact that all human beings were moral and cultural beings seeking self-preservation and self-constitution, in accordance with what was possible for them in their "time and place".[59] Happiness was connected with the natural exercise of the active forces of the mind and a simple sensation of existence accompanying it. This did not rule out pursuing ever purer and nobler forms of humanity by developing, and critically engaging with, the local traditions.[60] Kant's argument entailed that happiness could only be achieved in states with a distinct kind of "constitution ordered in accordance with concepts of human right", while the entire human history and interactions between nations were to be measured according to their contribution towards the progress of such a constitution. In Herder's view, this perspective disregarded the value of self-determination for all human beings and undermined the notion of their equal worth. Instead of positing a linear progress in political constitutions, it was necessary to understand that all humans possessed resources for recognising each other as equals. In the Third Part of *Ideas*, in Book Fifteen, Herder thus responded to Kant by holding up the idea of humanity as a guiding principle for each individual and nation, and through that, humanity in general. This fundamental ethical principle, Herder suggested, was reinforced by humans' evolving understanding of the "natural laws" of human history. Instead of glorifying the progressive development towards a certain form of political organisation and thereby establishing new hierarchies among different nations and cultures, history could teach moderation and reciprocity with others. Insofar as all humans have *Billigkeit*, a kind of "practical reason" that teaches them the "measure of the actions and reactions of similar beings for the general security", humans could also come to understand that erring against reciprocity is bound to have consequences for everyone involved. "Human nature" itself, Herder maintained, "is constructed on this principle, so that no individual can suppose himself to exist for the sake of another or of posterity".[61] The history of human-

58 Kant, "Review of J. G. Herder's *Ideas*," 141–142.
59 Herder, *Outlines*, 438–442; *Ideen*, 580–585; for discussion, see Piirimäe, "State-Machines," 165–168.
60 Piirimäe, "State-Machines," 180–181.
61 Herder, *Ideen*, 613; *Outlines*, 464.

kind, in turn, could be seen as the field in which the Goddess of justice – *Nemesis* – was ruling, punishing those who violated the law of equal respect and reciprocity. Indeed, by understanding the realm of history as ruled by *Nemesis*, humans could also increasingly correct the excesses of their imagination about the differential worth of different individuals, social groups and nations, and reflectively clarify the implications of the rule of justice for concrete human and intersocietal relationships.[62]

III

In subsequent years, Kant worked out the basics of his moral philosophy and continued to engage with questions of philosophy of humanity, whereas the issues of legal and political philosophy became prominent for him in the 1790s. It is thus also important to emphasise that it was only in his *On the Common Saying: 'This May be True in Theory, but Does not Apply in Practice'* (1793), written in the wake of the French revolution, that Kant first developed his political theory along explicitly republican lines and revisited his theory of how the problem of antagonistic "masters" was to be solved at the international level.[63] He elaborated on these ideas in *Perpetual Peace* and his writings of the late 1790s.[64] In this

62 Herder, *Ideen*, Book XV, particularly 581, 584, 585–595. On the idea of *Nemesis* in Herder's thought, see Wolfgang Proß, "Geschichtliches Handeln und seine Nemesis: Visionäre der Geschichte im Zeitalter der Französischen Revolution," in *Die Gestaltbarkeit der Geschichte*, ed. Kurt Bayertz et al. (Hamburg: Meiner, 2019), 81–116.

63 Immanuel Kant, "On the Common Saying: That May be Correct in Theory, but It is Of No Use in Practice," in idem, *Practical Philosophy*, trans. and ed. Mary J. Gregor (Cambridge: Cambridge University Press, 1996), 273–310.

64 Idem, "Toward Perpetual Peace," and "The Metaphysics of Morals," in *Practical Philosophy*, trans. and ed. Mary J. Gregor (Cambridge: Cambridge University Press, 1996), 311–352 and 353–604. In *Perpetual Peace* Kant continued to claim that the only *rational* way of solving the problem of war at the international level was the creation of an *international state* with coercive powers, but argued that this state was only to be achieved gradually. As a first step, only its negative substitute – an "enduring and gradually expanding pacific federation" or voluntary league of states – was practicable. In such a league, Kant argued, humans would have an opportunity to cultivate morality, and hence improve their conception of international right. Finally, on this basis, it could be hoped that they would decide to create what he called "the international state," in which it would also be possible to achieve the widest conceivable realisation of moral agency, i.e. the highest good of a "moral world," the world in which all agents act morally, for discussion, see Pauline Kleingeld, *Kant and Cosmopolitanism: The Philosophical Ideal of the World Citizenship* (Cambridge: Cambridge University Press, 2013), 51; cf. Reidar Maliks, *Kant's Politics in Context* (Oxford: Oxford University Press, 2014), ch. 5.

period, Kant came to suggest that republics – he meant here modern representative and commercial republics, which could very well be also ruled by monarchs — were the most stable, self-maintaining systems of government.[65] The practice of freedom in republics created possibilities for the cultivation of morality. He also put forward a theory of republican peace, combining moral and empirical arguments. The Republican state, he argued, is instituted in order to guarantee individual rights and property, but in so far as it has no property outside its territory, it can wage war only in self-defence.[66] Furthermore, the people, when allowed to determine the foreign policy of their country, would abhor war. Also, it was only in *Perpetual Peace* that Kant clearly spelled out the idea that no state could legitimately force other states to join the federation of states, and hence underlined both the voluntary nature of this federation and the value of national autonomy.[67] He now also coined the novel conception of "cosmopolitan right", but limited it to the one of visiting foreign countries and proposing commerce (trade and exchange of ideas). In so doing he did not advocate "rampant commercial exploitation" as Tully, for example, has suggested.[68] Although continuing to highlight the instrumental value of both commerce and war (national animosity) in pushing mankind towards the republican and cosmopolitan condition, he specified that commerce could not be forced upon foreign peoples: it was perfectly legitimate for the latter to close themselves off from international trade, if the major trading powers and particularly, private companies, were offering it on unacceptable, unfair, terms.[69]

While fleshing out his account of moral virtue and philosophy of right, Kant maintained his interest in discussing universal history. It was not a theoretical

---

65 For a discussion of whether, in Kant's view, these self–maintaining systems would come about automatically, or would require a benevolent legislator to establish them, see Paul Guyer, *Kant on Freedom, Law, and Happiness* (Cambridge: Cambridge University Press, 2000), 13. Guyer suggests that Kant must have distinguished between the motives of the subjects in adhering to a constitution, and those of a ruler in establishing one. While it is perfectly possible for the subjects of a just state to be ruled solely by self-interest, such a state can only be instituted and maintained by what Kant in *Perpetual Peace* calls "moral politicians." Paul Guyer, "The Crooked Timber of Mankind," in *Kant's* Idea for a Universal History with a Cosmopolitan Aim: *A Critical Guide*, ed. Amélie Oksenberg Rorty et al. (Cambridge: Cambridge University Press, 2009), 129 – 149, 131.

66 Arthur Ripstein, *Force and Freedom: Kant's Legal and Political Philosophy* (Cambridge, MA: Harvard University Press, 2009), 228 – 230; Maliks, *Kant's Politics in Context*, 162 – 166.

67 On this issue, see Kleingeld, *Kant and Cosmopolitanism*, 47 – 58; Maliks, *Kant's Politics in Context*, 154 – 158 and 162 – 167.

68 Tully, "Rethinking Human Rights".

69 Kant, "Toward Perpetual Peace," 329 – 331; for discussion, see Muthu, "Conquest, Commerce, and Cosmopolitanism in Enlightenment Political Thought," 220 – 231.

interest (in so far as nothing conclusive could be proven about history), but a practical interest and, indeed, his whole perspective on history was thus a "regulative" one, providing moral orientation – which, indeed, he believed, human beings necessarily needed. This is best captured in this quotation from hislate work, *Anthropology from a Pragmatic Point of View* (1798):

> The character of the species, as it is known [*kundbar*] from the experience of all ages and by all peoples, is this: that, taken collectively (the human race as a whole), it is a multitude of persons, existing successively and side by side, who cannot *do without* being together peacefully and yet cannot *avoid* constantly being objectionable to one another [*das friedliche Beisammensein nicht entbehren und dabei dennoch einander beständig widerwärtig zu sein nicht vermeiden können*]. Consequently, they feel destined by nature to [develop], through mutual compulsion under laws that come from themselves, into a *cosmopolitan society* (*cosmopolitismus*), that is constantly threatened by disunion but generally progresses toward a coalition. In itself it is an unattainable idea but not a constitutive principle (the principle of lasting peace amid the most vigorous actions and reactions of human beings). Rather, it is only a regulative principle: to pursue this diligently as the destiny of the human race, not without grounded supposition of a natural tendency towards it.[70]

Nevertheless, in the early 1790s, Kant did not as yet provide clear answers to the questions about the relationship between the ethical duties of humanity, on the one hand, and the "mechanism of nature" contributing towards the establishment of a cosmopolitan society, on the other. How exactly could individuals influence the progress towards a cosmopolitan society? Was it only through public debate about the best practices and forms of political institutions and legislation that it was possible to do so? Kant rejected the "right of resistance", but approved of the French revolution in retrospect. Was he thus encouraging submission or resistance? He also celebrated wars as instrumental in spreading humankind all over the globe as well as fostering contacts between societies. Did he not

---

70 Immanuel Kant, "Anthropology from a Pragmatic Point of View (1798)," in idem, *Anthropology, History and Education*), ed. Günter Zöller and Robert B. Louden (Cambridge: Cambridge University Press, 2007), 227–429, 427. For discussion, see Georg Cavallar, *Kant's Embedded Cosmopolitanism: History, Philosophy, and Education for World Citizens* (Berlin/Boston: De Gruyter, 2015), 14. Drawing on Robert Louden's various studies, Cavallar proposes "vocation" as the unifying element of all Kant's cosmopolitanisms, 13. Cf. Robert B. Louden, *Kant's Human Being: Essays on his Theory of Human Nature* (Oxford: Oxford University Press, 2011); idem, "Cosmopolitan Unity: The Final Destiny of the Human Species," in *Kant's Lectures on Anthropology: A Critical Guide*, ed. Alix Cohen (Cambridge: Cambridge University Press, 2014), 211–229; cf. Sharon Anderson-Gold, *Unnecessary Evil: History and Moral Progress in the Philosophy of Immanuel Kant* (Albany: State University of New York Press, 2001).

thereby tacitly approve of them? And what about wars to bring about republican constitutions guaranteeing equal rights, including individual property rights?[71]

In 1792, Herder initially welcomed Kant's ground-breaking moral philosophy in the second half of the 1780s: "What if", he asked, "[Kant's] *Critique of Practical Reason* and the *moral Philosophy* based on it laid the foundation for a natural right [Recht] and right of nations, which – when recognised generally [the unusual sentence format is Herder's – E.P.]? When generally practiced?"[72] Yet among the great number of thinkers discussed in the published version of his *Letters for the Advancement of Humanity*, Kant was perspicuously absent. In outlining his understanding of humanity in the *Letters*, Herder instead turned to the ancient Stoics such as Marcus Aurelius or to their early-modern admirers such as Frederick the Great. In the Tenth Collection of the *Letters*, he explicitly invoked Hugo Grotius as his [Herder's] "Anti-Machiavelli",[73] while also naming Algernon Sidney, Locke, Shaftesbury, Leibniz and even Rousseau among the "peaceful minds" to which one would like to return from the "tumults of these [his own] times".[74]

As we saw above, already in the *Ideas* Herder drew on, and radicalised, the insights of the ancient Stoics and Grotius in specifying the fundamental principles of "all [natural] right of humans, animals and nations". Now in *Letters*, Herder was specifically interested in Grotius' law of nations. While Frederick the Great had sought to refute Machiavelli, but had still "lived and died as a king", Grotius had genuinely worked towards uniting humankind. In sharp contrast with Kant's dismissive remark in *Perpetual Peace* (1795) about Grotius, Pufendorf and Vattel as "sorry comforters" whose philosophical and legal codes

71 For debates about Kant's evolving philosophy and Kant's answers to his critics, see Maliks, *Kant's Politics in Context*. For an argument that Kant's *Contest of Faculties* (1798) was able to provide an answer to such questions, see, Sharon Anderson-Gold, *Unnecessary Evil: History and Moral Progress in the Philosophy of Immanuel Kant* (Albany: State University of New York Press, 2001).

72 Johann Gottfried Herder, "Entwurf der Humanitätsbriefe," in idem, *Werke in zehn Bänden*, ed. Jürgen Brummack and Martin Bollacher, 10 vols (Frankfurt am Main, 1985–2000), VII, ed. Hans Dietrich Irmscher (Frankfurt/Main, 1991), 761–806, 800.

73 Herder, *Briefe zu Beförderung*, 343.

74 Herder also approvingly quoted from August Ludwig Schlözer's *Allgemeines Statsrecht und Statsverfassungslehre* (Göttingen, 1793), 161 to buttress his point about the primacy of human duties [*Menschenpflichten*] over human rights [*Menschenrechte*]: "Heil den Predigern der *Menschenrechte*, sagt ein neuerer Lehrer des Staatsrechts; aber versäumen sie ja nicht, vorher *Menschenpflichten* zu lehren. Um jene in ihrem ganzen heiligen Umfange einzuführen, müssen wir erst eine Majorität der Menschen haben, die fähig sind, diese in ihrem ganzen Umfange ausüben", Herder, *Briefe zu Beförderung*, 344. In making this claim, Schlözer was rejecting the radical revolutionary understanding of popular sovereignty.

have served to legitimate, rather than restrain military aggression,[75] Herder celebrated Grotius as the first author to embrace an open and eclectic spirit conducive to mutual understanding and peace of human beings from different periods and cultures. Thus, even though he had been unable to "unite religions", he had "united human principles", so that "what has been written about the right of peoples [*Recht der Völker*], about natural and rational right [*Natur- und Vernunftrecht*] ever since follows in his footsteps".[76] Grotius's *De jure belli ac pacis* had lain open on the Swedish king Gustavus Adolphus's table in his tent in camp, at the very moment the king himself was killed on the field of battle. Indeed, the fact that "a number of the noblest men in Sweden, France, Holland and Germany had also loved and honoured him [Grotius]" gave hope that one day the "entire European posterity would become his ally and confederate [*Verbündete und Verbundene*]".[77] The gradual rediscovery of these principles, which originated in human nature, was the result of humanity's learning process. There were good signs in the air, as peoples had come to communicate and trade with each other, the barbaric military spirit was receding and the rapacious colonial and commercial imperialism of European powers was increasingly harming also those very powers which pursued it.[78]

Acknowledging human fallibility and a natural sense of equity at the same time, Herder rejected both the doctrines of human dignity as well as original sin. He granted that humans were necessarily prone to delusion [*Wahn*] and prejudices grounded in self-love and self-interest, while their sympathy with distant others was rather weak and motivationally unreliable.[79] While our sense of equity and indeed, sense of humanity [*sensus humanitatis*] could help us identify the cases in which anyone had erred, imagination and enlargement of mental horizons via sympathy were needed to really transform us.[80] In a fictitious continuation of the dialogue between Ernst and Falk originally written by Gotthold Ephraim Lessing, Herder called for the combined efforts of poetry, philosophy and history to educate human beings. Poetry was to incite human imagination, philosophy to teach them firm principles and history to provide them maxims as to

---

75 Kant, "Toward Perpetual Peace," 326.
76 Herder, *Briefe zu Beförderung*, 342–343.
77 Herder, Ibid., 344.
78 Herder, *Briefe zu Beförderung*, 101–106, 116.
79 Ibid., 244.
80 I elaborate on this idea in Chapter Six of my *Patriotism, Cosmopolitanism and Nationalism*. I have previously discussed some of these issues in Eva Piirimäe, "Herder and Cosmopolitanism," in *Critique of Cosmopolitan Reason: Timing and Spacing the Concept of World Citizenship*, ed. Rebecka Lettevall and Kristian Petrov (Oxford: Peter Lang, 2013), 198–207.

how to apply them. Yet all of them in turn were to be moved by one and the same drive [*Antrieb*] of humanity:

> ME: *Humanity.* By giving this concept its full strength, and by showing it in the entire scope of its effects, and laying it on ourselves and others at heart as a duty, an unavoidable, universal, first duty, all prejudices of reason of state, inborn religion, and the stupidest prejudice of all, that of rank and estate would [...] HE: Disappear? Here you are deceiving yourself. ME: Not disappear, but suppressed, limited, made harmless. [...] Don't you know better than me that all such victories over the prejudices can be achieved only from the inside, not the outside?[81]

As authors offering examples of such a history, Herder listed "*Las Casas, Fénelon,* [...] two good St. *Pierres* [the Abbé de Saint-Pierre and Bernardin de Saint-Pierre – EP], many an honest *Quaker, Montesquieu, Filangieri*"[82] – each of whom had characteristically sought to lay bare the various kinds of atrocities and injustices that had been committed towards individuals and whole peoples in Europe and elsewhere. These thinkers, Herder argued, had written *humane history* guided by a human feeling [*Menschengefühl*] and the rule of right and wrong [*die Regel des Rechts und Unrechts*].[83]

Herder did not fail to indicate that his *humane* history was profoundly different from the kind of universal history envisioned by Kant. First, Herder explicitly rejected the "hypothesis of the radical evil" of human nature that Kant had invoked in his *Religion within the Boundaries of Mere Reason* (1793), arguing that virtue was never to be understood as a suppression of our nature.[84] He also saw no use in Kant's strict separation of respect for moral law and moral sentiments and vehemently rejected the idea that only in modern states could education for morality truly begin. This also had profound implications for historiography and indeed, politics.[85] Herder even went so far as to warn against the possible abuse of a Kantian "history of constitutions" and enthusiasm towards the ideal as a pretext for republican imperialism – a very pertinent warning in an age of French revolutionary wars.[86] While a certain recovery from the basest

81 Herder, *Briefe zu Beförderung*, 140.

82 Ibid., 689; idem, "Tenth Collection," 386.

83 Herder, *Briefe zu Beförderung*, 733, cf. 688; idem, "Tenth Collection," 411; cf. ibid., 386.

84 Herder, *Briefe zu Beförderung*, 746 – 753; idem, "Tenth Collection," 420 – 424.

85 Herder, *Briefe zu Beförderung*, 735 – 727; cf. ibid., 750; idem, "Tenth Collection," 415; cf. ibid., 423.

86 Kant himself talked about the impartial onlookers' sympathy with the French republicans' enthusiasm in the pursuit of "the rights of the people to which they belonged" in his "Contest

kind of "reason of state" was palpable in the public opinion of modern Europe, he argued, a new "dazzling phantom" was rising in history, namely, "*the calculation of undertakings towards a future better republic, towards the best form of the state, indeed of all states*".[87] This phantom was particularly dangerous since it seemingly introduced "a nobler yardstick of merit" in history and blinded "with the names of 'freedom,' 'enlightenment'", "highest happiness of the peoples".[88] "The happiness of one single people", Herder insisted, "cannot be imposed on, talked onto, loaded onto the other and every other. The roses for the wreath of freedom must be picked by a people's own hands and grow up happily out of its own needs, out of its own desire and love".[89]

In the Tenth Collection of the *Letters*, Herder famously discussed Native American peace arrangements.[90] It is very likely that this discussion was a direct response to Kant. Kant had ironically argued in *Perpetual Peace*, "the difference between the European and the American savages consists mainly in this: that whereas many tribes of the latter have been eaten up by their enemies, the former know how to make better use of those they have defeated than to make a meal of them, and would rather increase the number of their subjects, and so too, the multitude of their instruments for even more extensive wars, by means of them".[91] Instead of hastening to leave such a condition of lawless freedom, Kant continued, "each *state* [in Europe] puts its majesty [...] just in its not being subject to any external lawful coercion at all".[92] For Herder, this comparison was demeaning to the American "savages", insofar as the latter had in fact been the first to create a long-lasting institutional solution to the problem of war, while it was the Europeans who had not only been unable to do so, but who had also been responsible for destroying the Native American peace settlement.[93]

Instead of focusing on political constitutions and portraying humans as mere "critics" participating in public ratiocination,[94] universal history had to narrate human actions and uncover the various kinds of *opinions and principles*

---

of Faculties," Kant, *Political Writings*, ed. H. P. Reiss (Cambridge: Cambridge University Press, 1996), 171–190, 183.

87 Herder, *Briefe zu Beförderung*, 734; idem, "Tenth Collection," 413.

88 Ibid.

89 Ibid.

90 Herder, *Briefe zu Beförderung*, 714–719; idem, "Tenth Collection," 400–404.

91 Kant, "Towards Perpetual Peace," 326.

92 Ibid.

93 Herder, *Briefe zu Beförderung*, 716; idem, "Tenth Collection," 403.

94 Herder, *Briefe zu Beförderung*, 736–737; 750, translation from idem, "Tenth Collection," 415, 423.

guiding them.[95] As a next step, the latter were to be evaluated in the light of "moral sense" [*moralische Sinn*]. This evaluation involved (1) meticulous study and lively imagination of the actual historical circumstances and overall situation in which the agents found themselves, as well as (2) impartial empathetic consideration of the motivations of historical actors as well as the consequences of their actions to others, including the imaginative reconstruction of the sentiments of the victims; (3) an assessment of these sentiments, morals and principles based on an inborn awareness of the fundamental rule of equality and reciprocity regulating the interaction of human beings and societies.[96] A new "spirit of the age", Herder argued in *the Letters*, was already identifiable in Europe, expressing itself in most different domains of life, from the ways in which war was conducted on land and sea, as well as in the ways in which prisons and hospitals were run, the police was organised, judicial processes were conducted, or indeed, life at home was organised.[97] While remaining suspicious about states' self-proclaimed commitment to cosmopolitan or humanitarian goals, he nevertheless mused about the possibility that modern citizens would turn their states into self-governing political communities that would also collectively seek to promote humanity in a non-violent manner, by supporting human agency:

> If the state is, what it must be, an eye of the general reason, the ear and heart of universal equity and goodness, it will hear all of these voices [of different individuals – E.P.], and awaken and encourage the activity of human beings according to their various kinds of inclinations, sentiments, weaknesses and needs.[98]

Most importantly, as a result of a broader historical education, humans could also be hoped to develop new "dispositions of peace". As such dispositions, Herder listed and described "horror of war", "reduced respect for heroic glory", "horror of false statecraft", "purified patriotism" in the sense of self-contained, stable national self-respect, a "*common feeling* so that every nation feels

95 Herder, *Briefe zu Beförderung*, 339.
96 Herder writes in *Adrastea:* "Why does the evaluating *Nemesis* look into the breast [of an agent]? It is because its yardstick, the feeling of self-respect, compassion and fellow-feeling with others is there." (the translation is mine – E.P.) *Adrastea* (*Auswahl*), in idem, *Werke in zehn Bänden*, vol. 10, ed. Günter Arnold (Frankfurt am Main: Deutscher Klassiker Verlag, 2000), 142. See also Johannes Schmidt, "Herder's Political Ideas and the Organic Development of Religions and Governments," in *Herder on Empathy and Sympathy/ Einfühlung und Sympathie im Denken Herders*, ed. Piirimäe et al. (Leiden: Brill, forthcoming).
97 Herder, *Briefe zu Beförderung*, 103.
98 Herder, *Briefe zu Beförderung*, 131.

itself into the position of every other one", and finally, and positively, "love of useful activity" in promoting human well-being.[99] With the view to colonial and imperialist legacies of European states, Herder also emphasised the Europeans' responsibility with regard to contributing to removing the causes of unhappiness everywhere: "We cannot be happy or entirely worthy and morally good as long as, for example, a single slave is unhappy through human beings' guilt, for the vices and bad habits that make him unhappy have effect on us as well or derive from us".[100]

IV

Herder's ideas about the realisation of the ethical ideal of humanity in history show remarkable parallels with James Tully's account of the democratic tradition of human rights. Briefly fleshed out, the main features of this tradition, according to Tully, include the following. First of all, the tradition is strongly anti-legalist, viewing human rights as preceded and enabled by human duties.[101] Second, all its characteristic values are also clearly different from those of the High Enlightenment tradition: 1) instead of High Enlightenment's market liberalism, the democratic tradition emphasises economic self-reliance and democratic self-government; 2) instead of regarding land and environment as regular commodities in market relations, it portrays the "human family" as part of a world community that includes all forms of life, human and non-human; 3) instead of antagonism, it views cooperation as the primary factor in human and ecological evolution. All in all, according to Tully, the democratic tradition portrays human rights as:

> tools for conviviality within cooperative relationships; relationships that we have responsibilities to uphold and improve. Rights-bearers are caretakers of the pre-existing relationships in which they live and evolve, and human rights are tools of cooperation and nonviolent contestation within them.[102]

I hope that my interpretation has shown Herder's affinity with this view of human rights in all three aspects. (1) As we have seen, one way to make sense of Herder's understanding of humanity is through tracing his reworking of the

99 Herder, *Briefe zu Beförderung*, 720–726; idem, "Tenth Collection," 404–409. For discussion, see Piirimäe, "Herder and Cosmopolitanism".
100 Herder, *Briefe zu Beförderung*, 116, 749–750; idem, "Tenth Collection," 423.
101 Tully, "Rethinking Human Rights and Enlightenment," 30–31.
102 Ibid., 25, 26, 28.

Stoic and early-modern traditions of natural law. Herder rejected the more severely individualist and contractarian arguments and emphasised the Stoic strands in Grotius and early-modern natural-law tradition in general. For Herder, human rights were inseparable from human ethical duties, while he in turn saw them best realised in self-governing communities; (2) At the same time, Herder reinterpreted the Stoic strands in early-modern natural law in a vitalist idiom, erasing a strict borderline between the laws of humans and animals, and viewing all living beings as demonstrating a number of functional similarities in the ways in which they relate to themselves, the members of their species and those of other species. As we have seen, Herder proposes that human beings need to be understood as part of a broader family of living beings, while also emphasising adaptation to the environment as a universal feature of any kind of life. Sensitive to the well-being of other living beings and capable of the highest degree of self-determination, humans were to develop reason and determine themselves in line with the "laws of nature", not against them. This entails a certain understanding of land and environment as common heritage essential for sustaining traditional ways of life, and not as regular commodities in the market relationships. (3) What particularly appealed to Herder in Grotius was the latter's syncretism and call for the reunification of mankind in the form of a common agreement on the fundamental principles of a law of nations, which Herder, again, viewed as part of the unified system of natural law. While Grotius himself presented only strict justice (and perfect rights as they were later characterised by Samuel von Pufendorf) as "Right properly understood", Herder sought to emphasise the consistency of Grotius's understanding of natural law with the Stoic (and Christian) ideas, viewing mutual help and beneficence as also directly derived from the rule of equity. Here, indeed, he seems to have constructively ascribed a much greater continuity with Stoicism to Grotius's system than Grotius himself had actually wanted to establish.

Given Herder's own critique of the term "human rights", it is admittedly somewhat anachronistic to characterise him as being representative of a certain "tradition of human rights". Similar critique has been raised against Tully's claiming of Mohandas Gandhi as an avatar of the democratic tradition.[103] In some sense, clearly, we should guard against constructing new "tunnel histories" tracing direct lineages across long timespans. However, these authors themselves searched for common ground among different philosophies and religions. While

103 See Samuel Moyn, "Imperialism, Self-Determination, and the Rise of Human Rights"; cf. Karuna Mantena, "On Gandhi's Critique of the State: Sources, Contexts, Conjunctures," *Modern Intellectual History* 9 (2012): 535–563.

emphasising the need for the education of human sentiments and the inseparability of human duties and rights, they also called for the establishment of appropriate institutions to guarantee the latter. Furthermore, Herder's critique of Kant and his own alternative view of the promotion of the ethical ideal of humanity serve as powerful counter-examples to Moyn's view concerning the universal "statism" of the Enlightenment thinkers. Herder raised a number of important criticisms of Kant's alternative rationalist ethics and his legalistic and strongly (although not exclusively) state-centric conception of human rights, pointing out possible abuses to which such conceptions have been and can be submitted. Advocating for international sympathy and solidarity with the victims of crimes against humanity across the globe, he also insisted on self-determination as a fundamental individual and collective value.

Does this historical exposition help us provide an answer to the philosophical questions posed at the beginning of this essay? Only in an indirect way. By delving into the thought of past individuals and the debates between them, we can deepen our engagement with contemporary issues.[104] Too often we tend to posit rigid oppositions between different positions that need not mutually exclude each other, or view historically contingent connections between ideas as those of logical necessity. Herder did not believe that declaring human rights as rigorous normative standards would preclude their abuse by states as pretexts for imperialism or colonialism, just like his insistence on human rights as grounded in ethical duties did not prevent him from regarding the institutions that guarantee them as democratic constructs. As his philosophy of humanity and critique of Kant reveal, the problem of the abuse of human rights had already been identified in the Enlightenment period, while he also put forward an alternative comprehensive vision of human duties and rights as grounded in a broader natural law and philosophy of life. Yet we should also ask and think why this vision was largely forgotten or transformed beyond recognition subsequently. As Tully himself admits in his essay, the two ways of thinking about human rights "overlap and criss-cross in complex ways historically and in the present".[105] Indeed, it would be a fascinating task for future research to trace the afterlife of the two Enlightenment visions of human rights outlined here.

---

104 For interesting reflections on this theme, see Richard Whatmore, "The State of Intellectual History: Local and Global," in *Passions, Politics and the Limits of Society*, ed. Heikki Haara, Mikko Immanen, and Koen Stapelbroek (Berlin: de Gruyter, 2020), 5–26.

105 Tully, "Rethinking Human Rights," 4.

Justin Begley

4 Pierre Gassendi and the Humanist Case for a Vegetarian Diet

Introduction: A Learned Vegetarian

The French priest, mathematician, historian, and philosopher, Pierre Gassendi (1592–1655), was one of the most influential and well-respected thinkers of his day.[1] While the linguistic and conceptual complexity of his Latin tomes largely excluded him from the philosophical canons that were formed during the nineteenth century, historians have begun to appreciate just how central his ideas were to early-modern intellectual life.[2] However, recent studies of Gassendi have consistently bypassed a significant feature of his moral and physiological reflections: his defense of a plant-based diet.[3] Conversely, because the relevant passages from Gassendi's work are buried deep within his six-volume *Opera Omnia*, published posthumously in 1658, historical surveys of vegetarianism have mostly neglected his arguments.

When historians have discussed mid-seventeenth-century vegetarianism, the emphasis has typically been placed on intellectual outsiders and specifically associates of radical English Civil War sects such as John Robins, Roger Crab, and

---

1 A version of this paper was originally given at the conference "Inclusion and Exclusion in the History of Ideas" at the University of Helsinki in 2017. An adapted and extended version is forthcoming as a chapter in *Animal Theologians*, ed. Andrew Linzey (Oxford: Oxford University Press, 2020/1).

2 On some aspects of Gassendi's reception in England, see Dmitri Levitin, *Ancient Wisdom in the Age of the New Science: Histories of Philosophy in England, c. 1640–1700* (Cambridge: Cambridge University Press, 2015), 330–397.

3 The most notable studies of Gassendi include, Lynn Joy, *Gassendi, the Atomist: Advocate of History in the Age of Science* (Cambridge: Cambridge University Press, 1987); Barry Brundell, *Pierre Gassendi: From Aristotelianism to a New Natural Philosophy* (Dordrecht: Reidel, 1987); Antonia Lolordo, *Pierre Gassendi and the Birth of Early Modern Philosophy* (Cambridge: Cambridge University Press, 2007); Margaret Osler, *Divine Will and the Mechanical Philosophy: Gassendi and Descartes on Contingency and Necessity in the Created World* (Cambridge: Cambridge University Press, 1994); and Lisa Sarasohn, *Gassendi's Ethics: Freedom in a Mechanistic Universe* (London: Cornell University Press, 1996). On Gassendi and animals, see the discussion in Guido Giglioni, "Life and Its Animal Boundaries: Ethical Implications in Early Modern Theories of Universal Animation," in *Ethical Perspectives on Animals in the Renaissance and Early Modern Period*, ed. Cecilia Muratori and Burkhard Dohm (Florence: SISMEL edizioni del Galluzzo, 2013), 111–137 (especially 114–123).

https://doi.org/10.1515/9783110679861-005

George Fox.[4] While Gassendi was a fierce critic of the Scholastic tradition in his own right, he was thoroughly embedded within the institutions of his day as Professor of Mathematics at the Collège Royal in Paris and Provost of Digne Cathedral. Writing from these positions of authority and channeling the full gamut of humanist apparatuses, Gassendi made it his mission to render Epicurean (instead of Aristotelian) philosophy the mainstay of the university curricula. To this end, he endeavored to distance Epicurus from his association with excess, atheism, and debauchery as reflected in the widespread use of the vernacular labels "epicure" and "épicurien" to castigate those who lived for physical, and especially gastronomic, pleasure.

The standard seventeenth-century conceptions of Epicurus were principally an outgrowth of the pedagogical centrality of Cicero who was famously antagonistic towards this philosopher, and discounted him in *De finibus bonorum et malorum* as a hedonist who did not "even understand what Good there can be or where it can be found, apart from that which is derived from food and drink, the delight of the ears, and the grosser forms of gratification."[5] Echoing the sentiment of this ancient pagan, Church Fathers from Origen of Alexandria to Jerome likewise condemned Epicurus for his alleged intemperance.[6] Yet, turning to more sympathetic sources on Epicurus, especially Diogenes Laërtius's *Vitae Philosophorum* and Lucretius's *De rerum natura*, and situating their representations of his thought in relation to the ideas of other ancients including Aristotle, Plutarch, Galen, and Porphyry, Gassendi sought to demonstrate that the garden philosopher not only championed frugality but also a plant-based diet. By exploring Gassendi's case for vegetarianism, this article aims to show that early-modern defenses of abstention from meat did not always take the form

4 See Keith Thomas, *Man and the Natural World: Changing Attitudes in England, 1500–1800* (London: Allen Lane, 1983), especially 287–301; Robert N. Watson, "Protestant Animals: Puritan Sects and English Animal-Protection Sentiment, 1550–1650," *English Literary History* 81 (2014): 1111–1148; Rick Bowers, "Roger Crab: Opposition Hunger Artist in 1650s England," *The Seventeenth Century* 18 (2003): 93–112; James Vigus, "'That Which People Do Trample Upon Must be Thy Food': The Animal Creation in the Journal of George Fox," in *Ethical Perspectives on Animals*, 193–212; Tristram Stuart, *Bloodless Revolution: Radical Vegetarians and the Discovery of India* (London: HarperPress, 2006); Diane Kelsey McColley, *Poetry and Ecology in the Age of Milton and Marvell* (Aldershot: Ashgate, 2007), 171–196; Colin Spencer, *The Heretic's Feast: A History of Vegetarianism* (London: University Press of New England, 1995), 201–251.

5 Quintus Tullius Cicero, *De finibus bonorum et malorum* (Cambridge, MA: Harvard University Press, 2014), II.7.

6 For an overview of antagonistic views towards Epicurus among Church Fathers, see Richard Jungkuntz, "Fathers, Heretics and Epicureans," *The Journal of Ecclesiastical History* 17 (1966): 3–10.

of sectarian reactions to the intellectual mainstream, but could just as easily flow from the pen of a major institutional figure in his efforts to understand and adapt ancient philosophical ideas.

The present article focuses on two places in Gassendi's *Opera Omnia* that most explicitly grapple with the topic of vegetarianism. In the first section, I home in on a chapter of *Syntagma Philosophicum* – the main body of the *Opera Omnia* – titled "On the Faculties and Organs that Carry Nutrition" that contains an extended deliberation on abstention from meat.[7] In the second section, I turn to a 1629 epistle, also contained in the *Opera Omnia*, in which Gassendi attempted to persuade the prominent Flemish physician, Jan Baptista van Helmont, of the virtues of vegetarianism.[8] As we will see, Gassendi strove to convince his readers and especially this eminent medical reformer that a herbivorous diet would not only improve human health but even constitute a major step on the path towards reclaiming the fullness of our God-given natures.

The Virtue of Pleasure

In *Syntagma Philosophicum*, Gassendi made the case that just as every species has a unique shape and structure, each one likewise has its proper sustenance.[9] Setting aside the fact that humans had long been accustomed to feasting on a wide range of comestibles, he returned to this fundamental question: what is the appropriate diet for beings made in God's image? While he proceeded to summon scriptural authority to augment his view that a plant-based diet is most suitable for humans, Gassendi supposed that this conclusion could equally be derived from a careful examination of human anatomy and physiology.

Inspired by Plutarch's monumental essay "On the Eating of Flesh," Gassendi observed that carnivores such as lions and wolves are outfitted with long and sharp teeth, whereas human teeth are short and flat, akin to those of herbivorous

7 See Pierre Gassendi, "De facultatibus, ac organis quibus Nutritio peragatur," in *Opera Omnia* (Lyon, 1658), vol. 2, 296–302.

8 Pierre Gassendi, "Viro Clarissimo, & Philosopho, ac Medico expertissimo *Joanni Baptistæ Helmontio* amico suo singulari," in *Opera Omnia*, vol. 6, 19–24.

9 "Dicendum heic aliquid foret de varietate alimentorum, quibus Animalia nutriuntur; verùm res manifesta est, cùm & constet non posse eadem idonea esse omnibus, propter varietatem temperamentorum, ex qua est, ut quæ his gratissima sunt, illis nauseam pariant, neque ab ipsis attingantur." Gassendi, *Opera Omnia*, vol. 2, 301.

horses, oxen, and sheep.[10] For all of his dissatisfaction with Aristotle, Gassendi maintained, like the Stagirite, that God did not create any superfluity in nature, but rather devised everything to fulfill a natural purpose.[11] Based on this premise, he reckoned that God formed humans with teeth that are perfectly suited to the food that they are meant to consume and that He would have furnished them with claws or a beak that could tear flesh if He had intended for them to hunt other animals.[12] Humans instead had to invent tools and train species with superior senses such as dogs to help them hunt, all to sustain a diet that was unnecessary for continued existence. Additionally, Gassendi noted that in contrast to vegetables and fruits meat is "a burden to the stomach" and can hardly "be distributed through the parts of our bodies," necessitating the arduous task of cooking.[13] These considerations led him to conclude that humans would be very different animals were they designed to feed on flesh. Responding to claims that vegetables alone could not afford the energy required for vigorous manual or intellectual labor – an argument that still circulates today – Gassendi further perceived that the "strength of the bull and the swiftness of the deer" must be attributed to their plant-powered diets.[14] As he saw it, fruits and herbs possess the proper balance of liquid and solid parts that a human diet requires, while "grains, honey, and especially wine" contain the sharp *aqua vitae* that can vivify the spirits of individuals with cold constitutions who might be tempted to turn to

---

10 "Siquidem cùm inter terrestreis, gressileisque animanteis constituerit nos; non taleis nobis tribuit denteis, qualeis iis, quæ ex sua natura vesci debuerunt carnibus, ut sunt leones, lupi, & aliæ, ideò vocatæ carnivoræ; sed qualeis iis, quæ vesci herbis, variisque fructuum generibus, ut sunt equi, oues, & aliæ, quæ non carnivoræ habentur." Gassendi, *Opera Omnia*, vol. 2, 301. See Plutarch, *Moralia*, vol. 12, trans. H. Cherniss and W. Helmbold (Cambridge, MA: Harvard University Press, 1957), 12.995a–b.

11 See Aristotle, *Parts of Animals. Movement of Animals. Progression of Animals*, trans. and ed. E. S. Forster and A. L. Peck (Cambridge, MA: Harvard University Press, 2014), 1.1.639b and Aristotle, *Physics*, trans. and ed. F. M. Cornford and P. H. Wicksteed (Cambridge, MA: Harvard University Press, 2014), 2.3.195a. On Gassendi and final causes, see Margaret Osler, "From Immanent Natures to Nature as Artifice: The Reinterpretation of Final Causes in Seventeenth-Century Natural Philosophy," *Monist* 79 (1996): 388–407. For the persistence of teleological accounts in contemporary discussions of animal ethics, see Bernard Rollin, "Animal Pain: What It Is and Why It Matters," *Journal of Ethics* 15 (2011): 425–437.

12 Gassendi, *Opera Omnia*, vol. 6, 21.

13 "Potest insuper *tum* ex eo, quòd non est herbarum, fructuúmque usus ita stomacho onerosus, ut caro: siquidem cibus levior est; cùm caro Animalium ex parte ipsorum pinguiore facta, compactâque, difficiliùs longè exsolui, ac distribui per parteis nostri corporis possit." Gassendi, *Opera Omnia*, vol. 2, 302.

14 "taurorum robur, & ceruorum pernicitas, & dotes aliorum Animalium similes, ex alio victu non deducantur." Gassendi, *Opera Omnia*, vol. 2, 302.

meat.[15] These, Gassendi insisted, were the victuals that humankind was intended to consume.

A belief that it was possible to strip back layers of societal baggage to arrive at an image of a truly "natural" human partially underpinned Gassendi's vindication of vegetarianism. Taking seriously Lucretius's pronouncement that "each living body seeks its own food untaught" and generating a line of reasoning that Jean-Jacques Rousseau later recycled in his 1762 *Emile*, Gassendi pointed out that young children, with more physically pure bodies than adults, almost invariably prefer fruit to meat.[16] Far less optimistic than Rousseau, however, he proposed that the milk of a mother who regularly consumed meat might, in its own right, condition carnivorous inclinations in her infant.[17] A far cry from Romantic notions of youthful innocence, Gassendi's appeal to this childhood predilection was rooted in his reading of the Epicurean position (which he extracted from Plutarch) that a newborn instinctively seeks pleasure and avoids pain.[18]

In his broader project to Christianize Epicurus, Gassendi construed the pleasure principle as God's way of providentially directing the natural world, and its diverse beings, without the need for constant intrusion.[19] While this endowed cognizance of what it is natural to enjoy with the utmost ethical and even theological import, it also suggested that humans were similar to other animals (or natural objects, for that matter) in their possession of certain desires or inclinations. Harboring an Aristotelian outlook on the "will," Gassendi was of the opinion that when a rock is dropped from a high place and falls spontaneously, that rock can be said to "will" or "desire" to go downwards, just as a child of a certain age naturally reaches, without conscious self-reflection, for fruit instead

15 "Indicio porrò maximo est, quòd res unaquæque tanto sit magis alimentitia, quantò ex ea elicere maiorem huiusmodi aquæ, sive spiritus aquam licet; indéque sit, cur omnia grana, cur mel, cur vinum maximè nutrient." Gassendi, *Opera Omnia*, vol. 2, 301.

16 Lucretius, *De rerum natura*, trans. and ed. W. H. D Rouse and Martin F. Smith (Cambridge, MA: Harvard University Press, 1982), 158–159. Gassendi claims that "omneis pueros præferre perdicibus poma, esséque universe amantissimos non carnium, sed fructuum." *Opera Omnia*, vol. 2, 302. On Rousseau and vegetarianism, see David Boonin-Vail, "The Vegetarian Savage: Rousseau's Critique of Meat Eating," *Environmental Ethics* 15 (1993): 75–84.

17 "Quodammodo, inquam; nam si puer foret & formatus ex semine, & nutritus lacte parentum, qui ipsi abstinuissent à carnibus; aut si saltem dimisso lacte pastus carnibus, jusculisque carneis, non esset, ferretur haud-dubiè in fructus impensiùs." Gassendi, *Opera Omnia*, vol. 2, 302.

18 Plutarch, *Moralia*. vol. 14, trans. B. Einarson and P. de Lacy (Cambridge, MA: Harvard University Press, 1967), 14.1122d–e. For Gassendi's adaptation, see *Opera Omnia*, vol. 2, 701.

19 On Gassendi's broader effort to Christianize Epicurus, see Margaret Osler, "Baptizing Epicurean Atomism: Pierre Gassendi on the Immortality of the Soul," in *Religion, Science, and World-view: Essays in Honor of Richard S. Westfall*, ed. Margaret Osler and Paul Farber (Cambridge: Cambridge University Press, 1985), 163–83.

of meat.[20] To provide a more proximate example, Gassendi would deem it morally acceptable for a lion to chase, kill, and consume a gazelle since the lion's pursuit of her prey is a natural act of self-preservation that occurs almost as spontaneously as the falling of a rock. He realized, however, that adult humans differ from animals, plants, and inanimate objects in their possession of reason in addition to will, which meant that they are capable, on the one hand, of controlling and suppressing unnatural yearnings, and, on the other, of conjuring ever more innovative ways to obtain pleasure.

Rather than spurning the human pursuit of pleasure or denying that the garden philosopher was a hedonist of sorts, Gassendi set out to prove that the Epicurean view of pleasure was wholly compatible with Christian ethics. To this end, he posited a four-tiered hierarchy of pleasures. First he described the instinctive desire for immediate physical gratification, which children share with other animals. Then came the calculated search for increased pleasure that goads rational but unenlightened individuals.[21] The latter, for Gassendi, was the level at which most historical actors (especially non-philosophers) operated, and it was at this stage, he held, that humans began to delight in creophagy, having outstripped their childish preference for fruits, herbs, and vegetables. Yet the other two kinds of pleasure reinstated a vegetarian diet. Taking a cue from Epicurus, Gassendi next discussed a variety of pleasure that was based on tranquility and lack of pain, which was the ultimate pleasure that could be achieved in this lifetime, and which animated all wise individuals. Finally, he identified the sublime pleasure of the beatific vision of God that is only fully attainable in the afterlife.[22]

Putting Gassendi's notion of the beatific vision to one side for the moment, his understanding of pleasure as tranquility requires more attention, given that it was the instantiation that he discussed at the greatest length. In so doing, he affirmed the essential doctrine of Epicurus's moral philosophy that virtue is a necessary adjunct to pleasure, and, with a stress on temperance and prudence, he followed Aristotle's definition of virtue as a habit of the mind that inclines humans towards just and honorable actions.[23] It was in the course of fitting Epicurus's ethical injunction against killing and consuming animals to an Aristotelian

---

20 Gassendi, *Opera Omnia*, vol. 2, 824.

21 For Gassendi's four-tiered hierarchy, see *Opera Omnia*, vol. 2, 659–735. This discussion of Gassendi's notion of pleasure relies on Sarasohn, *Gassendi's Ethics*, 51–75.

22 Don Cameron Allen, "The Rehabilitation of Epicurus and His Theory of Pleasure in the Renaissance," *Studies in Philology* 41 (1944): 1–15.

23 For a relevant discussion, see Veronica Gventsadze, "Aristotelian Influences in Gassendi's Moral Philosophy," *Journal of the History of Philosophy* 45 (2007): 223–242.

framework that Gassendi laid out the criteria that made meat-eating unnatural. In the tradition of virtue ethics, each virtuous act is a mean between two extremes. If humans were natural omnivores – a category that did not in fact exist at the time – then the mean is to consume meat in moderation. By contrast, if a study of the human body leads one to classify humans as herbivores, then any creophagy at all is gratuitous and should be avoided. Drawing the latter conclusion, Gassendi conceived of a vegetarian diet as not only natural and pleasurable but also virtuous.

Gassendi periodically expressed sympathy towards animals, but, as the preceding discussion already indicates, he was not predominantly concerned with the suffering of other species in the sense that the pain caused by killing animals outweighs the maximum amount of pleasure that could be gained by eating them. Rather, the pleasure that Epicurus and Gassendi advocated was known as *katastematic* pleasure, which is passive and includes not only the absence of pain (or *aponia*) and lack of disturbance of the mind (or *ataraxia*) but also resistance to surplus physical effort.[24] *Katastematic* pleasure as a stable, mental state was juxtaposed in the ancient world with *kinetic* pleasure, which was associated with the body, and was the result of an activity (such as creophagy or sexual intercourse).[25] In making the case that a plant-based diet was most consistent with Epicurus's conception of the good, Gassendi was prompted by Porphyry, who concluded that all Epicureans should be vegetarians insofar as this squared with their belief that the best way to achieve *katastematic* bliss is to eschew all excesses by obtaining and consuming only that which is necessary for continued existence.[26]

Shaping his stance in accordance with this understanding of pleasure, Gassendi maintained that the energy expended in unnatural and time-consuming exploits such as hunting and cooking inevitably detracted from an individual's pursuit of more noble and virtuous undertakings – chiefly, philosophizing.[27]

24 See Peter Preuss, *Epicurean Ethics: Katastematic Hedonism* (Lampeter, Wales: Mellen, 1994) and David Wolfsdorf, *Pleasure in Ancient Greek Philosophy* (Cambridge: Cambridge University Press, 2012), 144–81.

25 This distinction is perhaps most clearly spelled out in Porphyry, *On Abstinence from Killing Animals*, trans. Gillian Clark (London: Duckworth, 2000), 1.110.32–115.3.

26 See Porphyry, *On Abstinence*, 1.88.1–1.54.6.

27 As regards the view that hunting and cooking is unnatural and unnecessary, Gassendi writes: "Potest item tum ex eo, quòd cùm nobis arma, seu instrumenta naturalia dilacerandis, dissecandisque carnibus non suppeterent, excogitare, usurpatéque artificialia oportuerit, cultros scilicet, quibus animantes carnibus alioquin vescentes non egent: tum ex eo, quòd cùm carneis crudas auersemur, oportuerit varie illas coquere, ut suauiores efficerentur, quem apparatum quæ animantes carne vescuntur, non requirunt." Gassendi, *Opera Omina*, vol. 2, 302.

But the liberty that God granted humans by equipping them with reason, which allowed them to outstrip their natural inclinations, paradoxically left most human beings enslaved by unnatural and detrimental desires.[28] After the Fall, meat had become the fruit of a tree from which nearly all humans were too easily lured into eating.

The Chymical Challenge

Gassendi initially rehearsed many of the arguments that made their way into *Syntagma Philosophicum* in his epistle to van Helmont, which continues a conversation that the pair had in Brussels, and offers a point by point response to a brief disquisition that van Helmont penned as he reflected upon the Frenchman's arguments. While Gassendi calls on much of the same anatomical evidence here as he did in the *Syntagma*, this compelling letter also dwells on theological questions at greater length and underscores just how deeply entangled medical and ethical issues were during the early-modern period.

Before diving into the particulars of the epistle, it is notable that Gassendi was an assiduous reader of Galen's field-shaping works, against which van Helmont so forcefully reacted. Both Galen and his seventeenth-century beneficiaries typically advised their patients to abstain from overindulging on animal flesh, especially when they were ill. The prominent English herbalist and physician Nicholas Culpeper recorded in his 1652 translation of Galen's *Ars medica*, for instance, that melancholics, phlegmatics, choleric-melancholics, melancholic-cholerics, phlegmatic-sanguines, and phlegmatic-cholerics should all "beware of overfilling themselves with meat."[29] Only straightforward cholerics were permitted to "eat meats hard of Digestion, as Beef, Pork, &c."[30] In framing his physiological views, Gassendi embraced an essentially Aristotelian-Galenic conception of digestion as the concoction that occurred as heat in the stomach worked upon the foodstuff consumed. Yet, drawing on Plutarch, he went even further than the Galenists who were happy to recommend meat, in moderation, to young and healthy individuals. He reasoned that if humans habitually adhered to a vegetarian diet then there would be far less illness in the first

28 On Gassendi and freedom, the best discussion remains Osler, *Divine Will and the Mechanical Philosophy*, especially 80–101.
29 Nicholas Culpeper, *Galen's Art of Physick* (London, 1652), 64.
30 Ibid., 54.

place.[31] In early-modern medicine, there was an entrenched distinction between therapy (the cure of disease) and hygiene (the prevention of disease).[32] By shifting vegetarianism from a therapeutic treatment to hygienic prevention, Gassendi aspired to make a plant-based diet the ordinary practice for individuals in good health.

In their efforts to supplant established medical practices, however, Helmontians sought to discredit the Galenic physician's hands-on approach to balancing individual humors, and consequently deemphasized the longstanding *regimen sanitatis* that was centrally concerned with dietary regulation. As a rule of thumb, learned (Galenic) medics holistically attended to individual patients, whereas empirics and chymists aimed to directly combat diseases as they were manifested in shared symptoms.[33] Largely indifferent towards dietary matters, van Helmont and his disciples commonly advised patients to eat what they pleased, supposing that whatever satisfied the palate must be suitable for the body, and that a content patient was more likely to experience a swift recovery than one who was forced into a strict and often unpleasant regimen. The Irish Helmonian, Thomas O'Dowde, thus urged a patient "to be kind to himself, and (without regard to Dietory Prescriptions) to eat Roast Beef and drink Sack."[34]

In contrast to van Helmont and his votaries, Gassendi denounced the abandonment of dietary considerations as a dangerous course, not least because, taken to an extreme, such neglect could erode the barriers that stood before the practice of cannibalism. This issue of anthropophagy was especially pressing at the time that Gassendi was writing, with the recent European discovery that the consumption of fellow humans was an accepted custom among certain peoples in the New World. Addressing specific travelers' tales about the anthropophagy of indigenous Brazilians – and recapitulating a sentiment from Michel de Montaigne's essay "Of Cannibals" – Gassendi culminates his discussion in "On the Faculties and Organs that Carry Nutrition" with the claim that these can-

31 Gassendi, *Opera Omnia*, vol. 2, 302. For Plutarch's similar argument, see *Moralia* 12.995c–d. On early modern ideas about digestion more generally, see the essays in *Studies in History and Philosophy of Biological and Biomedical Sciences* 43 (2012), especially Justin Smith, "Diet, Embodiment, and Virtue in the Mechanical Philosophy," *Studies in History and Philosophy of Biological and Biomedical Sciences* 43 (2012): 338–348 and Antonio Clericuzio, "Chemical and Mechanical Theories of Digestion in Early Modern Medicine," 329–337.

32 See Heikki Mikkeli, *Hygiene in the Early Modern Medical Tradition* (Helsinki: Academia Scientiarum Fennica, 1999), especially 125–140.

33 See Andrew Wear, *Knowledge and Practice in English Medicine, 1550–1680* (Cambridge: Cambridge University Press, 2000), 399–434.

34 Thomas O'Dowde, *The Poor Man's Physician, or The True Art of Medicine* (London, 1665), 22–23.

nibals assumed themselves "to be following nature as their guide" as much as Europeans who feasted on animals.[35] While it may now seem like a stretch to link the ingestion of human flesh with that of other species, such a comparison had ancient precedents in pagan thinkers such as Plutarch and Porphyry along with Christian ones including Clement of Alexandria, all of whom averred that killing and eating animals had a desensitizing effect that could make one more open to killing and consuming humans.[36]

At the same time, opposition to cannibalism was also firmly grounded in seventeenth-century notions of digestion and nutrition.[37] In particular, Galenic physicians tended to maintain that foodstuff that was most dissimilar to the matter making up the human body took more work to assimilate and was therefore more nutritional, meaning that plants, and especially green vegetables, were widely regarded as more salubrious than meats. As Gassendi pointed out, eating meat, by contrast, was akin to sticking flesh to flesh.[38] But if the medical consensus became that food most similar to the human body (such as animal flesh) was best assimilated – or if this process was simply passed off as irrelevant to human health – then there would be far less reason to consider anthropophagy taboo. Insofar as the transgression of other ethical norms could be attributed to humoral imbalances that a diet of human flesh might serve to neutralize, cannibalism could even be ethically justifiable in select instances.

All of this is not to say that van Helmont was a champion of dietary decadence (never mind cannibalism). On the contrary, he frequently recycled the biblical dictum that "abstinence and sparingness, are the best meanes in the Diet-

---

35 "tum ex eo, quòd non est opponendum inventos esse Brasilianos, Hurones, aliósque feros Homines carnibus vescenteis; quasi illi Naturam ducem insequuti esse videantur; cùm ex hoc capite natura tam in illis potuerit, quàm in cæteris depravari, ac tantò magis, quantò minùs humanitatis retinuerunt, ut pote, qui non carnivori simpliciter, sed etiam Anthropophagi specialiter evaserint." Gassendi, *Opera Omnia*, vol. 2, 302.

36 See Plutarch, *Moralia*, 12.996a; Porphyry, *On Abstinence*, 1.23.1–1.24 and Clement of Alexandria, *Stromateis. Book 1–3*, ed. John Ferguson (Washington, D.C.: Catholic University of America Press, 1991), 2.18.

37 For fuller discussions of early modern ideas about cannibalism, see Cătălin Avramescu, *An Intellectual History of Cannibalism* (Princeton, NJ: Princeton University Press, 2009), especially 162–182. See also Louise Noble, *Medicinal Cannibalism in Early Modern English Literature and Culture* (New York: Palgrave Macmillan, 2011) and Cecilia Muratori, "Animals in the Renaissance," in *Animals: A History*, ed. Peter Adamson and G. Fay Edwards (Oxford: Oxford University Press, 2018), 163–186.

38 "Neque enim quòd carnem fieri ex carne vulgò dicitur, id fit carnem carni, ut gypsum gypso agglutinando." Gassendi, *Opera Omnia*, vol. 2, 302.

ary part."[39] Moreover, it is not clear whether van Helmont wholeheartedly embraced the conceits that he had defended in his disquisition, since Gassendi implied that his epistle resumed a friendly spar, in which van Helmont had been pleased to play devil's advocate.[40] In any case, Gassendi grasped that the Flemish physician was at the forefront of medical reform, and he undoubtedly apprehended that convincing van Helmont of vegetarianism's advantages for human health could have wide-reaching and concrete effects on the diets of his contemporaries and even subsequent generations. There was also at least one solid reason within the framework of Helmontian medicine to suppose that creophagy could harm both body and soul. That is, van Helmont held that the chief agent of digestion was the divine *archeus* or an immaterial principle that was suffused throughout the natural world and was densely compact in human bodies.[41] He lamented, however, that the *archeus* had lost much of its power to assimilate food at the Fall (which is why humans now produce feces) and that it was particularly inept at absorbing rich or fatty foods such as meat. On this basis, Gassendi had reason to hope that he could coax van Helmont into recognizing the benefits of a meatless diet.

Unwilling to enforce dietary strictures, van Helmont instead concentrated on the radical possibility of restoring humankind to its former perfections through a mithridate or universal medicine. In his more optimistic moments, he even appealed to an elixir or a "modern tree of life" that would extend the human lifespan and preserve perfect health for upwards of three hundred years.[42] With this in mind, Gassendi attempted to convince van Helmont that vegetarianism was a more plausible and gradual way to restore the human body to some of its former excellences.[43] He maintained, in this regard, that the pristine bodies of Adam

---

39 See Jan Baptista van Helmont, *Van Helmont's Works: Containing His Most Excellent Philosophy, Physick, Chirurgery, Anatomy*, trans. J. Chandler (London, 1664), 70.

40 "Tenuisti tu oppositam viam, sicque mutuis oppositisque contendentes rationibus, jucundissimas exegimus horas." Gassendi, *Opera Omnia*, vol. 6, 20.

41 See Walter Pagel, *Joan Baptista van Helmont: Reformer of Science and Medicine* (Cambridge: Cambridge University Press, 1982), 96–101.

42 See van Helmont, *Van Helmont's Works*, 645–647. On this aspect of van Helmont's work, see Georgiana Hedesan, *An Alchemical Quest for Universal Knowledge: The "Christian Philosophy" of Jan Baptist van Helmont (1579–1644)* (London: Routledge, 2016), 172–192.

43 "Etsi enim fieri videmus, ut ex usu vulgarium ciborum vix Homines possint propagare vitam ad sæculum usque, aut aliquid ampliùs, nihilominus certum esse paratam fuisse arborem in Paradiso terrestri, ex cuius esu homo potuisset immortalis euadere: & aliunde in hac naturæ corruptione probabile fieri, parari posse Elixir, cuius usu homo possit, nisi æternum tempus vivere, tot certè fæcula durare, ut duratio homini possit videri quædam æternitas." Gassendi, *Opera Omnia*, vol. 6, 20–21.

and Eve – who lived peacefully alongside the animals as they feasted on fruit before the Fall – were even more "natural" than those of children and that humans would be most likely to flourish if they adhered to a similar diet. Gassendi's and van Helmont's respective approaches to vegetarianism and its status in scripture accordingly corresponded to their divergent visions of history: Gassendi contended that humans were gradually corrupted after the Fall and could make choices to ameliorate their condition and pave the way for the second coming, whereas van Helmont posited a fundamental transformation from perfection to a fallen state that required a drastic reversal such as the discovery of a supreme universal remedy.

To Gassendi's mind, it was one thing to debate whether Adam and Eve were vegetarians (which the preponderance of divines affirmed) or whether humans consumed meat before the great deluge (which was more controversial). But it was quite another to emphasize medicinal perfectibility and the possibility of the dramatic prolongation of life, which would render diet irrelevant to human health, and therefore strip the prevailing conviction that antediluvian or at least prelapsarian humans were vegetarians of all practical import. This is one sense in which the unorthodox medical and religious search for perfectibility could sit in tension with arguments for abstention from meat. Gassendi, by contrast, was happy to treat ancient philosophy and the Bible as blueprints for behavior, in keeping with the humanist preoccupation with reading for action.[44]

Conclusion: The Beatific Vision

While Gassendi believed that the ultimate pleasure of human communion with God could not be realized in this lifetime, he nonetheless insisted that it should be continually sought.[45] Most significantly for the purposes of this article, he saw the consumption of flesh as a major obstacle on the road to actualizing this beatific vision, since the natural world supported the Bible in suggesting that humankind would not eat meat after the return of Christ, when "men are no longer ignorant of God's ways."[46] In the restored paradise that Gassendi envisioned, the

44 The classic work on this topic is Lisa Jardine and Anthony Grafton, "'Studied for Action': How Gabriel Harvey Read His Livy," *Past & Present* 129 (1990): 30 – 78.

45 Gassendi, *Opera Omnia*, vol. 2, 662 and 717.

46 "Quid quòd etiam post primam labem, cum homines adhuc tam multa superarent fæcula, carnium usum nullum audimus; sed tum demum ille est inductus, cùm iam corruptis hominum viis Deus illum, ut permulta alia, ob duritiem cordis concessit?" Gassendi, *Opera Omnia*, vol. 6, 21.

relationship between humankind and animals would once again be one of peaceful dominion, as opposed to the tyranny that was on display when animals were butchered to satisfy *kinetic* pleasure.[47] As his stress on dominion indicates, Gassendi by no means downplayed the divine nature of humans or their distinct rational capacities, but rather embraced the age-old concept of the *scala naturae.* Consistent with the arrangement of traditional textbooks, he structured the natural philosophical section of his *Syntagma* by working up the scale of nature, and directly stated in his letter to van Helmont that humans stood between animals and angels as natural beings with immaterial and immortal souls.[48] While there has been a scholarly emphasis in recent years on how the early-modern elevation of human reason undergirded the sometimes brutal treatment of other animals, Gassendi held that humans, unlike lower species, had responsibilities towards their fellow creatures not in spite of the fact that they were created in God's image (and could rationally reflect on their behavior) but for precisely this reason.[49]

Not only did Gassendi mobilize arguments from medicine, history, and scripture to bolster his case for a meatless diet, but his focus on eventual communion with God was also derived from the stress on purity as a path to godliness among vegetarians of a Neoplatonic bent including Porphyry and Plotinus, along with Church Fathers such as Tatian and John Chrysostom. Although both of the latter explicitly opposed Epicurus, Gassendi summoned their teachings to substantiate Christian doctrines such as the immortality of the soul, and to show that, despite the historical resistance to Epicurus, his ideas were no less compatible with Christian thought than those of any other ancient.[50] Vegetarianism had been sullied as a concept owing to its association with Pythagoras and his controversial

---

47 "Et tueatur sese Scripturâ, agnoscere tamen bona fide debet, id, quod exinde in animantia mutuatur dominium, post peccari labem ademptum, vel ita refrictum, ut in pauca solùm, eáque innoxia tyrannide dominetur." Gassendi, *Opera Omnia*, vol. 6, 21–2.

48 Gassendi specifically stated: "Angelicam enim naturam, ut supra Mundanam prætereo, concedóque Hominibus, ut Animæ intelligentis & immortalis gratiâ, simileis se Angelis faciant, vel cum Psalte Regio modestiùs, paullò minores Angelis." *Opera Omina*, vol. 6, 21.

49 The most notable instance of this discourse is Erica Fudge, *Brutal Reasoning: Animals, Rationality, and Humanity in Early Modern England* (Ithaca: Cornell University Press, 2019), especially 39–58.

50 On the symbiotic relationship between these pagan thinkers and early Christian ones, see Gillian Clark, "Fattening the Soul: Christian Asceticism and Porphyry on Abstinence," in *Ascetica, Gnostica, Liturgica, Orientalia: Studia Patristica*, vol. 2, ed. M.F. Wiles and E. J. Yarnold (Leuven: Peeters, 2001), 41–51. While there is not yet a full study of Gassendi's uses of the Church Fathers, he evidently knew Chrysostom's writing well: see, for example, Gassendi, *Opera Omnia*, vol. 2, 632.

theory of the transmigration of souls, yet Gassendi supposed that rehabilitating a plant-based diet in light of the Epicurean stress on *katastematic* pleasure and the natural state of the human beings would prove more suitable to the Christian palate than the ancient alternatives.[51] Vegetarianism, in this sense, was crucial in Gassendi's eclectic endeavor to baptise this widely misunderstood heathen.

As a Catholic priest, Gassendi naturally regarded decisions in this lifetime to be of paramount importance in preparing body and mind for the next. He made it clear, however, that his case for vegetarianism was devoid of the dogmatism exhibited by many radical religious sects, and was rather the result of his measured consideration of a gamut of (mostly ancient) arguments, as well as his esteem for the historical virtue and excellence of its practitioners.[52] On his reading of history, advocates of abstention from meat were some of the most enlightened individuals in their respective societies. In this sense, his defense of a plant-based diet was of a piece with his methodological precept that scholars should study, extract, fuse, and follow the best ideas that have been promoted over the course of history. Having discerned the widespread practice of vegetarianism among writers whom he and many of his contemporaries most admired – not least the Epicureans – Gassendi was adamant that if not all humans then at least all *humanists* should be herbivores.[53]

51 On reincarnation and vegetarianism, see G. Fay Edwards, "Reincarnation, Rationality, and Temperance: Platonists on not Eating Animals," in *Animals: A History*, 27–55.

52 "Tum ex eo, quòd non modò Viri Sancti, qui se in solitudines Religionis ergò receperunt, abstinuerúntque à carnibus; verùm etiam Philosophi, qui virtutis moralis gratiâ candem sunt amplexi abstinentiam, vitam & diuturnam, & sanam duxerunt." Gassendi, *Opera Omnia*, vol. 2, 302.

53 For the sense of humanism used here, see Nicholas Mann, "The Origins of Humanism," in *Cambridge Companion to Renaissance Humanism*, ed. Jill Kraye (Cambridge: Cambridge University Press, 1996), 1–19.

Ben Dew

5 Enlightenment Historical Writing and the Expulsion of England's Jews

Introduction

In June 1290, Edward I made the final decision to banish England's Jews. Writs were issued on the 18 July of the same year, and by November the entire Jewish population had been expelled, principally to France.[1] The expulsion – generally regarded as the only act of mass deportation in English history – has been a standard topic in accounts of the reign of Edward I from the thirteenth century to the present. Consequently, Edward's actions and the events leading up to them have been described and analysed in a wide variety of historical genres: medieval and early-modern chronicles; largescale, neo-classical narrative accounts; and more specialist works of economic, antiquarian and Jewish history. This body of work constitutes an important resource for our understanding of attitudes to Jews and Judaism within British culture, as has been demonstrated, perhaps most clearly, by James Shapiro in his seminal 1996 work *Shakespeare and the Jews*.[2] At one level, the overview Shapiro presents emphasises the startlingly diverse range of approaches to the expulsion taken by historians over the last seven hundred or so years. Indeed, his key point is that changing ideas about immigration and constitutional affairs have caused the banishment's meaning within British historical discourse to shift in myriad ways. What gives Shapiro's analysis real focus, however, is his claim that beneath these vacillations lies a consistent underlying meaning. The expulsion is an object of fascination because it enables writers to express deep-seated anxieties about national identity and, through doing so, provide "a satisfying narrative of [England's] national past" to manage those concerns.[3]

This approach, particularly Shapiro's emphasis on issues relating to nation and nationalism, has done much to shape the critical and historiographical agenda and, in doing so, has inspired a number of excellent, more detailed stud-

1 For accessible, modern accounts of the expulsion, see: Robin R. Mundill, *The King's Jews: Money, Massacre and Exodus in Medieval England* (London: Continuum, 2010); Richard Huscroft, *Expulsion: England's Jewish Solution: Edward I and the Jews* (Stroud: Tempus, 2006).
2 James Shapiro, *Shakespeare and the Jews* (New York: Columbia University Press, 1996), 46–55.
3 Ibid., 55.

https://doi.org/10.1515/9783110679861-006

ies of individual aspects of English attitudes towards Jews and Judaism.[4] Shapiro's work, however, contains a significant omission and one that has not been dealt with in any of the subsequent literature: it completely passes over the analyses developed by Enlightenment-era historians.[5] The article that follows aims to fill this gap by providing an account of the contribution to controversies regarding the expulsion made by British writers in the latter half of the eighteenth century. My principal focus is on four works of history, two of which are specifically concerned with economic affairs.[6] Adam Anderson's hugely ambitious *Historical and Chronological Deduction of the History of Commerce* (1764) provided an account of the development of international trade from the earliest times to the present.[7] John Sinclair's *History of the Public Revenue* (1785–1790), meanwhile, was conceived as "the first attempt at financial history on an enlarged scale" and sought to develop a complete analysis of British approaches to taxation.[8] The other two works, while showing a marked interest in commerce and finance, provide more wide-ranging narrative discussions of English history: William Guthrie's *General History of England* (1744–1751) and David Hume's *History of England* (1754–1762).[9]

4 See particularly: Eliane Glaser, *Judaism without Jews: Philosemitism and Christian Polemic in Early-Modern England* (Basingstoke: Palgrave, 2007); Andrew Crome, "English National Identity and the Readmission of the Jews, 1650–1656," *Journal of Ecclesiastical History* 66 (2015): 280–301.

5 Hume's attitude to England's Jews is the only aspect of the topic to receive attention, and the discussion here has been very general. See: Robert Palter, "Hume and Prejudice," *Hume Studies* 21 (1995): 3–23. See also: Richard H. Popkin, "Medicine, Racism, Anti-Semitism: A Dimension of Enlightenment Culture," in *The Languages of Psyche: Mind and Body in Enlightenment Thought: Clark Library Lectures, 1985–1986*, ed. G. S. Rousseau (Berkeley and Oxford: University of California Press, 1990), 405–444. The key account of the complex relationship between Jewishness and the European Enlightenment is: Adam Sutcliffe, *Judaism and Enlightenment* (Cambridge: Cambridge University Press, 2003).

6 The works chosen provide some of the more detailed discussions of Jewish affairs in English historical writing. For reasons of space, I was unable to include the fascinating and often paradoxical analysis of medieval Jewry developed in: Robert Henry, *The History of Great Britain*, 6 vols (London, 1771–93).

7 Adam Anderson, *An Historical and Chronological Deduction of the Origin of Commerce, from the earliest accounts to the present time*, 2 vols (London, 1764), 1: v. On Anderson, see: Mark Salber Phillips, *Society and Sentiment: Genres of Historical Writing* (Princeton, NJ: Princeton University Press), 161–62.

8 John Sinclair, *The History of the Public Revenue of the British Empire*, 2nd. ed. (London, 1790).

9 William Guthrie, *A General History of England*, 3 vols (London, 1744–1751); David Hume, *The History of England*, 6 vols (Indianapolis, IN: Liberty Fund, 1985). Guthrie's discussion of England's Jews comes in the first volume of his history (published in 1744). Hume's account is to be found in what were to become volumes one and two of his history; as Hume wrote his history

An exploration of these accounts has significance for a number of ongoing historiographical debates. Recent work on ideas about Jews and Judaism in the history of political economy by Jonathan Karp has demonstrated that discussions of Jewish identity frequently served "as a barometer of shifting general attitudes toward commerce, money, and credit as a whole".[10] The stakes in such discussions, therefore, were high: the issues being debated were not just the status of a relatively small minority group, but rather the nature of "good" commercial practice, and the relationship between trade and finance and a nation's political interests. To an extent, an examination of eighteenth-century historical literature on the expulsion simply provides further evidence to support this thesis. As is the case in political economy, historians used Jewish themes to discuss economic issues, and, consequently, their analyses of a major event like the expulsion provide a useful way of gauging attitudes to commerce, finance and associated matters. Significantly, however, the nature of history as a literary genre provides a distinctive kind of information for modern scholars. While economic texts are undoubtedly a rich resource, their employment in relation to Jewish debates necessarily involves a high degree of selectivity. The basic criteria for inclusion are straightforward: only accounts which contain substantial discussion of Jewish themes are of relevance. This ensures, as Karp openly acknowledges, that basing a study around such material produces a highly unconventional taxonomy of the history of political economy; canonical writers such as David Hume Adam Smith and David Ricardo are pushed to the margins, while figures conventionally regarded as less significant like Josiah Tucker and Adam Müller take centre stage. Things are very different in historical writing. No medieval historical

"backwards" – beginning with the Stuart volumes and concluding with the pre-1485 volumes – these parts of the text were the last to be published and emerged in 1761 and 1762.

10 Jonathan Karp, *The Politics of Jewish Commerce: Economic Thought and Emancipation in Europe, 1638–1848* (Cambridge: Cambridge University Press, 2008), 19. See also for European examples of a similar phenomenon: Francesca Trivellato, "Credit, Honour, and the Early Modern French Legend of the Jewish Invention of Bills of Exchange," *Journal of Modern History* 84 (2012): 289–334; Francesca Trivellato, "Images and Self-Images of Sephardic Merchants in Early Modern Europe and the Mediterranean," in *The Self-Perception of Early Modern Capitalists*, ed. Margaret C. Jacob and Catherine Secretan (Basingstoke: Palgrave Macmillan, 2008), 49–74. Karp's conception of the role played by commerce and finance in eighteenth-century debates, as he acknowledges, has been shaped by the work of J.G.A. Pocock. See specifically: J.G.A. Pocock, *The Machiavellian Moment: Florentine Political Thought and the Atlantic Republican Tradition*, 2nd. ed. (Princeton, NJ and Oxford: Princeton University Press, 2003 [first published 1975]). See also: Adam Sutcliffe, "The Philosemitic Moment? Judaism and Republicanism in Seventeenth-Century European Thought," in *Philosemitism in History*, ed. Jonathan Karp and Adam Sutcliffe (Cambridge: Cambridge University Press, 2011), 67–89.

work of the period sought to discuss the reigns of Richard I, Henry III and, in particular, Edward I without substantial reference to these monarchs' dealings with England's Jewish population. Moreover, the nature of history writing meant that, when writing about the expulsion, writers constructed their accounts through copying, adapting and disputing the narratives of their predecessors. As a result, the historical literature on the expulsion constitutes an ongoing conversation which stretches from the medieval chroniclers who first documented Edward's reforms, through the major works of humanist-influenced historical writing, among them those of Polydore Vergil, Raphael Holinshed and John Speed, to the national and economic-focused histories of the eighteenth century. An examination of the development of this conversation enables us to see with a good deal of clarity the processes through which new ideas regarding commerce and finance came to shape discussions concerning Jews. Or, to put it another way: if debates about Jewish issues functioned as a kind of economic barometer, just as political economy provides privileged access to the readings that barometer gave, historical literature permits us to see some of the intellectual processes through which it came into existence.

The remainder of this discussion will be divided into three parts. The first delineates, with rather broad brushstrokes, some of the main features of medieval and early-modern historical writing concerning the expulsion and the events leading up to it. The second, in a little more detail, situates the work of my four historians in this context. My conclusion will argue that it was the economic focus of Enlightenment writing which produced a new conception of Jewishness in the eighteenth century. This development had important implications for ideas about English national identity, as well as, more fundamentally, eighteenth-century historical practice.

Medieval Chroniclers and Tudor and Stuart Historians

The earliest discussions of English medieval Jewry are to be found in the chronicles authored by contemporary monks. These works, perhaps most significantly the writing of Roger of Hoveden, Roger of Wendover and Matthew Paris, provided discussions of both the measures used by the authorities to manage the Jewish population, and the various incidents which arose when regulations were flouted.[11] Such accounts, as was customary in the chronicle tradition, were recy-

11 Roger of Hoveden, *The Annals of Roger of Hoveden, Volume 2, part 1*, trans. Henry T. Riley

cled by later authors, and they went on to form the basis of the commentaries contained in the major Tudor and early-Stuart histories.[12] Key to these works was an association between England's Jews and illicit financial practices, most significantly usury. The authors of the Holinshed *Chronicle* (1577, 1587), for example, explained that Jewish usury was practised "to the undoyng of many an honest man", while Speed noted that, in the reign of Edward I, the Jews had "by their cruell usuries had [...] eaten [the King's] people to the bones".[13] Frequent references were also made to the Jews' role as, in the words of Speed, "the ordinary Clippers and defacers of [the King's coyne] and the forgers of seales and Charters".[14] Attempts to palliate such criticisms are generally only to be found when historians compared Jewish practices with those of other pariah groups. Thus, Matthew Paris, a frequent critic of the Church authorities in Rome, observed that while usury was a sin, at least the Jews offered more agreeable terms than the Pope's money-lenders, the Cahorsins.[15] In making such claims, it should be emphasised, Matthew, and those who later utilised his work, were not so much defending the Jews as using contemporary assumptions about their sharp practices for polemical purposes. The fact that, in the words of the militant Protestant John Foxe, "the very Jewes [were] crying out" against the Cahorsins, was conclusive evidence of their treachery.[16]

Considerable attention was also given to Jewish outrages against Christians and Christianity. The most widely reported incidents were the so-called "blood-libels", the accounts of ritualistic attacks on Christian children. Again, Mathew Paris' work is of central importance. His *Historia Major* provided accounts of var-

---

(Felinfach: Llanerch, 1997); *Roger of Wendover's Flowers of History*, 2 vols, trans. J.A. Giles (London: Henry G. Bohn, 1849); Matthew of Paris, *Chronicles of Matthew Paris: Monastic Life in the Thirteenth Century*, ed. and trans. Richard Vaughan (Gloucester: Alan Sutton, 1984); Matthew of Paris, *English History: from the Year 1235 to 1273*, 3 vols, trans J. A. Giles, (London: Henry G. Bohn, 1847).

12 Polydore Vergil, *Anglica Historia*, ed. Dana F. Sutton, philological.bham.ac.uk/polverg/. This edition of the text is based on the 1555 version of the text; John Foxe, *Actes and Monuments of Matters Most Speciall and Memorable, Happenyng in the Church* (London, 1583); Raphael Holinshed, *The First Volume of the Chronicles of England, Scotlande, and Irelande*, 2 vols (London, 1577); *The First and Second Volumes of the Chronicles*, 3 vols (London, 1587); John Stow, *A Summarie of the Chronicles of England* (London, 1575); *A Survey of London* (London, 1598); John Stow and Edmund Howes, *Annales, or a Generall Chronicle of England* (London, 1631). On these accounts, see: Shapiro, *Shakespeare and the Jews*, 46–55.

13 Holinshed, *Chronicle*, (1577) 4: 482; John Speed, *The History of Great Britaine under the Conquests of ye Romans, Saxons, Danes and Normans* (London, 1611),

14 Speed, *History of Great Britaine*, 529.

15 Matthew of Paris, *English History*, 3: 47–38.

16 Foxe, *Acts and Martyrs*, I: 325–326.

ious such incidents including the circumcision and attempted crucifixion of a Christian boy by Norwich's Jews in 1240, the recovery in London in 1244 of the body of a crucified Christian boy whose corpse had been inscribed with Hebrew characters, and the martyrdom of little Hugh, a Christian boy kidnapped in Lincoln and later tortured and crucified.[17] This sort of material was frequently and uncritically repeated by later writers. Vergil labelled the Norwich incident 'a horrible crime committed by the Jews' and went on to describe how:

> that dregs of humanity [...] secretly kidnapped a little boy and fed him for an entire year, so that when Easter came around, as if to disfigure our religion with a new disgrace, they might crucify him. But a few days before they would have shed his innocent blood, these worst of butchers were accused and convicted of their crime and paid the deserved penalty.[18]

Holinshed's version is very similar:

> [The] Iewes of Norwich, [...] had stolen a yoong child, being not past a twelue moneths old, and secretlie kept him an whole yeare togither, to the end that he might (when Ester came) crucifie him in despite of our sauiour Iesus Christ, and the christian religion. The matter as it happened fell out well for the lad: for within a few daies before that those curssed murtherers purposed to haue shed this innocents bloud, they were accused, conuicted and punished, whereby he escaped their cruell hands.[19]

Underlying these accounts, it perhaps need hardly be said, was a belief that the fervent and debased religious beliefs of the Jews rendered them an explicit threat to England's Christian culture.

A concern with Jewish acts of perfidy did much to shape narrative accounts of Anglo-Jewry. Writers did not, however, gloss over the violence that Jews had suffered at the hands of the Christian population. By far the most significant incident was sparked by the coronation of Richard I in 1189. When London's Jews, who had been banned from attending events surrounding the ceremony, attempted to give the new King presents, a riot ensued in which both the persons and property of the Jewish population were attacked.[20] This event prompted a wave of further incidents in Lincoln, Stamford, Norwich and, most tragically,

---

17 For the Norwich incident, see: Matthew of Paris, *English History*, 1: 277. See: Sophia Menache, "Matthew Paris's Attitudes toward Anglo-Jewry," *Journal of Medieval History* 23 (1997): 139–162. The London incident is discussed in Paris, *English History*, 2: 21–22. The martyrdom of 'little Hugh' is to be found in *English History*, 3: 138–40.
18 Vergil, *Anglica Historia*, Henry III, paragraph 17. See also: Foxe, *Acts and Martyrs*, I: 327.
19 Holinshed, *Chronicle* (1587), 6: 219.
20 The key source for the coronation is Roger of Hoveden, *Annals*, 119–120.

York, where the entire Jewish population of around a hundred was wiped out.[21] While some historians saw the Jews' punishment as at least partially merited, most extended sympathy to the victims and criticised their perpetrators.[22] Samuel Daniel, for example, writing in 1618, lamented the "miserable slaughter", while the 1587 edition of Holinshed added a new paragraph which attributed the "great vexation and pitifull distresse" of the Jews to the actions of Richard.[23] Such material was supplemented by repeated censure of the high taxes and arbitrary levies issued by England's monarchs against the Jewish population. For Matthew Paris, the "avaricious thirst" of Henry III ensured that money was "extorted from the Jews to such a degree that they appeared to be entirely and irreparably impoverished".[24] Daniel, meanwhile, maintained that Jewish estates had been "continually ransackt" while Holinshed pithily observed that the King had "fleeced the Jewes to the quicke".[25]

In relation to the expulsion itself, things are a little more complicated. Contemporary chroniclers generally dealt with the incident in a single sentence, providing neither praise, criticism nor explanation for the King's actions. Many later writers took the same approach. Holinshed, for example, observed: "It was also decreed, that all the Iewes should auoid out of the land, in consideration whereof, a fifteenth was granted to the king, and so héervpon were the Iewes banished out of all the kings dominions, and neuer since could they obteine any priuilege to returne hither againe".[26] Similarly, John Stow commented that Edward "banished all the Jewes out of England, getting them to beare their charges til they were out his Realme, the number of Jewes then expulsed, were xv.M [15,000] parsons".[27] In her discussion of thirteenth and fourteenth-century accounts, Sophia Menache has attributed this approach to the chroniclers' complex relationship with the Jews.[28] While these authors were willing to propagate anti-Jewish stereotypes, they were aware of the financial benefits which the cheap mortgaged property obtained through Jewish connections brought their monasteries. As a

21 For the York incident, see: Hoveden, *Annals*, 137–139.

22 Speed, for example, saw the action against the Jews as "a presage, that this *Lion-hearted* King (as his by-name *Ceur-de-Lion* did import) should be a specall destroyer of the enemies of our Saviour." Speed, *Historie*, 530.

23 Samuel Daniel, *The Collection of the Historie of England* (London, 1618), 96; Holinshed, *Chronicle* (1587), 6: 119.

24 Paris, *English History*, 3: 340.

25 Daniel, *Collection*, 140; Holinshed, *Chronicle* (1587), 6: 252.

26 Holinshed, *Chronicle* (1587), 6: 285.

27 Stow, *Summarie*, 229.

28 Sophia Menache, "Faith, Myth, and Politics: The Stereotype of the Jews and Their Expulsion from England and France," *Jewish Quarterly Review* 75 (1985): 351–374 (357–358).

result, they showed a reluctance to fully vindicate Edward's actions. In relation to Tudor historians the situation seems more straightforward. Given the multiple tales of usury, coin-tampering and child murder writers employed prior to discussion of the expulsion, the implication of such accounts was clear: despite the oppressions they had suffered, Jewish crimes merited such a response from Edward. A number of writers went on to make such claims directly. Polydore Vergil conceived of the Jews' removal as an act of religious purification, whereby Edward had sought to separate the "sheep" from the "goats".[29] Vergil's only regret was that the Jews had not been persuaded to leave their literature behind which, he claimed, was vital for the preservation of Christian secular life. For Speed the expulsion was a part of Edward's more general plan to undermine corruption and revive England's fortunes. The Jews were expelled "to purge England [...] from such corruptions and oppressions, as under which it groaned".[30] Within medieval and early-modern writing, therefore, it is possible to identify a spectrum of opinion ranging from the ambivalence of the earliest accounts to the implicit and explicit support for Edward's actions shown by later historians. However, while some discussions drew attention to the avaricious concerns which led Edward to act, the extant literature offers very little criticism of the expulsion itself.[31]

The Eighteenth-Century Debate

Enlightenment-era historians utilised medieval and early-modern chronicles extensively in their accounts.[32] The writing of the period, however, was also shaped by new approaches to both source material and historical narrative. In relation to the former, the key development was the publication of a series of antiquarian

29 Polydore Vergil, *Anglia Historia*, Edward I, paragraph 7.

30 Speed, *Historie*, 650.

31 For discussions which emphasise Edward's avarice, see: Speed, *Historie*, 160; Daniel, *Collection*, 160.

32 On Jews in eighteenth-century England, see: Todd M. Endelman, *The Jews of Georgian England, 1714–1830: Tradition and Change in a Liberal Society* (Ann Arbor, MI: University of Michigan Press, 1999 [first published 1979]); David M. Katz, *The Jews in the History of England, 1485–1850* (Oxford: Clarendon Press, 1994). The central issue in Jewish debates was, of course, the Jewish Naturalisation Act of 1753. Discussions of medieval Jewry did feature in debates concerning this measure, perhaps most notably Josiah Tucker's *A Second Letter to a Friend Concerning Naturalizations* (London, 1753). However, while Tucker's preoccupations have something in common with those of Hume, none of the four eighteenth-century writers discussed here engage directly with naturalisation issues.

accounts based, in whole or part, on England's state archives. Three such works were to exert a longstanding influence on ideas about medieval Jewry: William Prynne's *Short Demurrer on the Jews* from 1656, a highly polemical account written to oppose the plans developed by Oliver Cromwell to readmit Jews to England; Thomas Madox's *History of the Exchequer* (1711), chapter six of which was devoted to the "Exchequer of the Jews", the body charged with regulating the taxes and legal affairs of the medieval Jewish population; and D'Blossiers Tovey's 1738 *Anglia Judaica*, the first complete published history of England's Anglo-Jewish community.[33] Such texts, as we shall see, encouraged methodological innovations and provided important information for later writers regarding the practices of medieval government. With regard to narrative, the most important shift was an increased concern with processes of long-term cultural change. As J.G.A. Pocock has argued, eighteenth-century historians came to structure their work around "the enlightened narrative": the story of the transformations through which the "shared civilization of manners and commerce" that characterised contemporary Europe had emerged out of the "barbarism and religion" of the medieval age.[34] Such a focus meant that commerce was increasingly conceived of as the key marker of modernity, and as a result, assessing the level of commercial development achieved by past societies became one of the historian's key tasks. Moreover, whereas earlier writers had understood commerce as an aspect of statecraft, a series of actions performed by a monarch to promote or retard trade, the historians of the eighteenth century viewed it as a social phenomenon.[35] As such, economic advancement was conceived of as a product of a "commercial spirit" which, at some point in Europe's modern history, had come to shape the moeurs and manners of the populace.

To an extent the antiquarian approaches and the "narrative of Enlightenment" could work in concert with one another. Indeed, Enlightenment ideas

---

33 William Prynne, *A Short Demurrer to the Jewes*, 2nd edn (London, 1656); Thomas Madox, *The History and Antiquities of the Exchequer of the Kings of England, in two periods* (London, 1711), 150–178; D'Blossiers Tovey, *Anglia Judaica: or the history and antiquities of the Jews in England* (London, 1738). For Prynne, see: Glaser, *Judaism without Jews*, 121–129; Avrom Saltman, *The Jewish Question in 1655: Studies in Prynne's Demurrer* (Jerusalem: Bar Ilan University Press, 1995). For a useful discussion of Prynne's views on history: J.G.A. Pocock, *The Ancient Constitution and the Feudal Law: A Study of English Historical Thought in the Seventeenth Century, A Reissue with a Retrospect* (Cambridge: Cambridge University Press, 1987 [first published 1957]), 156–161.
34 J.G.A. Pocock, *Barbarism and Religion, Vol. 2: Narratives of Civil Government* (Cambridge: Cambridge University Press, 2001), 20. For L.P. Hartley, see: *The Go-Between*, ed. Douglas Brooks-Davies (London: Penguin, 2004).
35 On this issue, see: Ben Dew, *Commerce, Finance and Statecraft: Histories of England, 1600–1780* (Manchester: Manchester University Press, 2018).

of economic development were, in many ways, a direct product of the methodological innovations of seventeenth-century antiquarians. One of the key effects of serious research in antiquarian affairs was a growing awareness of the fundamental "otherness" of the past. These ideas are neatly summarised by Thomas Madox in a passage which foreshadows the more famous observations of L.P. Hartley:

> When a Man, though a Native of this Island, comes fresh to peruse a systeme of Antiquities, or a piece of Ancient History of the same Island, he is like one newly landed in a Strange countrey. He finds himself in another climate. He observeth many things strange and uncouth in Language, Laws, customs, and manners.[36]

This conception of the past helped to transform attitudes to Jewish history. A modern historian, it came to be believed, could not simply accept the word of the strange and uncouth monks who had authored the chronicles; rather he needed to carefully weigh up which elements of the accounts from contemporary observers could be considered trustworthy. In relation to medieval Jewry, this ensured that while the records of anti-Jewish riots were still taken seriously, accounts of supposed crimes committed by Jews were not. Thus Hume referred to the idea that Jews had "crucified a child in derision of the sufferings of Christ" as an "improbable and absurd accusation", while Anderson noted that "they were accused of, and sometimes cruelly treated for, Crimes which it is probable they never committed, occasioned by the Violence of a bigoted Clergy, [and] the Ignorance of the Laity".[37] Accusations concerning Jewish financial practices were treated in a similar manner. What is perhaps most noteworthy here is the philological emphasis on the changing meaning of the term usury. Anderson, observed that "it is needless again to note here, that the Word *Usury* in those Times, and long after, meant no more than barely the *Use* or *Interest* taken for the *Loan* of Money".[38] Hume agreed arguing that it was "the prejudices of the age [that] had made the lending of money on interest pass by the invidious name of usury".[39] The high interest rates of the period meanwhile, Hume contended, were a product not of the greed of Jewish money-lenders, but "the barbarism of the times and men's ignorance of commerce".[40]

36 Madox, *History of the Exchequer*, vi-vii.
37 Hume, *History*, 2: 69; Anderson, *Deduction*, 1: 133.
38 Anderson, *Deduction*, 1: 93.
39 Hume, *History*, 1: 378.
40 Ibid., 2: 68.

Such discussions of the guiltlessness of the Jewish population were supplemented by new and more detailed accounts of the failings of England's monarchs. Antiquarian archival research had uncovered multiple new examples of the various extortions exacted upon the Jewish population, particularly by Henry III and Edward I. Madox's work was key here, but even William Prynne, a relentless critic of all aspects of Jewish life, noted that England's monarchs had proved to be the Jews' "most unsatiable, merciless, perfidious, tyrannical Exactors, Fleecers, Oppressors, Taxmasters, Tormentors".[41] As a consequence, he concluded, "*England* was little better than a second *Aegypt*, and our Kings and their griping Officers nothing else but so many new *Phaeroahs* and Aegyptian Tax-Masters".[42] Later writers developed this theme with a good deal of enthusiasm. Guthrie maintained that Henry III's attitude to Jewish taxation was fundamentally "void of humanity", while for Anderson the English court had "fleeced" the Jews at pleasure.[43] Hume labelled such measures "barefaced acts of tyranny and oppression" and provided seven separate examples from Madox's Jewish chapter to support his claim.[44] Taken in sum, therefore, the key effect of Enlightenment-era accounts was to alter the balance of narratives regarding medieval Jewry. While references to Jewish greediness are still to be found, discussions of Jewish crimes were generally downplayed, and through an engagement with antiquarian sources, increased attention was given to examples of monarchical extortion.

These ideas were supplemented by new claims about the nature of Jewish economic life. The chroniclers, as we have seen, maintained that the medieval Jews derived their wealth from usury and coin-clipping. In the eighteenth century, however, the Jew was increasingly conceived not as a petty moneylender, but rather as a successful international merchant. This suggestion was first formulated with, it should be emphasised, no reference to archival sources, by D'Blossiers Tovey:

> For, as the *Jews* understood Trade better than our own Merchants, (from the general Correspondance they held with their Brethren, in all Parts of the World,) and (from managing

41 Prynne, *A Short Demurrer*, 2: 128. Prynne's point here was that the Jews were "aliens" who in legal terms existed outside of the constitution. As a consequence, they were subject to non-constitutional forms of royal prerogative, the exercise of which in England threatened the liberties of the whole population. On this issue, see: Karp, *Politics of Jewish Commerce*, 38.

42 Prynne, *A Short Demurrer*, 2: 132.

43 Guthrie, *General History*, 1: 768; Hume, *History*, 1: 133.

44 Hume, *History*, 1: 483.

> their Traffick as it were by a *common* Stock) were able to under-sell them; no one car'd to by [sic] anything of a Christian.[45]

Similar claims were then taken up and expanded by numerous other writers. Guthrie argued that: "the experience of the Jews in foreign countries opened channels of commerce, which few or no English of those times had either genius of spirit to attempt".[46] Sinclair, meanwhile, imagined an international Jewish network which had dominated the trade of northern Europe "from the period of the Norman invasion, to the establishment of the Hanseatic league".[47]

It is not difficult to establish the origins of this sort of argument. From the latter part of the sixteenth century onwards Jews had come to play a key role in international commerce entering, as Jonathan Israel has shown, into "into several crucial east-west transit, colonial, and precious-metal trades".[48] Such successes led to the emergence of what Benjamin Broad has labelled "the myth of the Jewish economic superman", the idea that the cosmopolitan-connections of the Jews had enabled them to achieve complete dominance over international trade.[49] At one level, therefore, eighteenth-century writers simply took a contemporary stereotype about Jewish economic practices and projected it back into the twelfth and thirteenth centuries. However, what is most noticeable here is not the otherness of the Jews, but rather the striking resemblance of Jewish practices to the values that, as eighteenth-century writers conceived of things, underpinned European commercial modernity. Indeed, the medieval Jews were, in a sense, not so much supermen, but rather conventional modern Englishmen. In Hume, this idea is implicit. "this people", he argued, had gained possession of England's "ready money" as a result of their "industry and frugality".[50] These qualities, which contrasted sharply with the "idleness and profusion" of the rest of the populace, had, Hume contended, been key to England's economic development.[51] As he noted in his 1752 essay "Of Interest", a low interest rate was "a sign almost infallible of the flourishing condition of a people" and that it

45 Tovey, *Anglia Judaica*, 80.
46 Guthrie, *General History*, 1: 576–577.
47 Sinclair, *History of the Public Revenue*, 1: 26.
48 Jonathan Israel, *European Jewry in the Age of Mercantilism, 1550–1750* (Oxford: Clarendon Press, 1985), 256.
49 Benjamin Braude, "The Myth of the Sephardi Economic Superman," in *Trading Cultures: The Worlds of Western Merchants: Essays on Authority, Objectivity and Evidence*, ed. Jeremy Adelman and Stephen Aron (Turnhout: Brepols, 2001), 163–191. See also: Francesca Trivellato, "Images and Self-Images of Sephardic Merchants," 66.
50 Hume, *History of England*, 1: 378.
51 Ibid.

"must proceed from an encrease of industry and frugality, of arts and commerce".[52] In the work of William Guthrie, the association of the Jews with English commercial modernity was dealt with explicitly. The Jews were: "perhaps the main, though secret, causes of that uncommon affluence of coin which then prevailed in England, and that universal spirit of commerce which afterwards distinguished her".[53]

Such examples demonstrate the synchronicity between the emergence of new forms of commercial and financial history, and the growth of a more sympathetic attitude towards England's Jews. It is, however, necessary to add a caveat to such an argument, which constitute what might be labelled a "limit" on economic arguments for toleration. Of the four writers surveyed, Hume is the only one to develop a specifically economic case against the expulsion. His key assumption was that the expulsion had been designed to reduce usury. Such a move, however, was pointless – borrowing was a necessary part of any culture – and ill-managed; ultimately, the practices of the Italians who took over the money-lending trade were less "open and unexceptionable" than those of the Jews.[54] The incident, as a result, was evidence that, despite Edward I's merits as a lawmaker, his commercial statecraft had been shaped by "the prejudices of the times".[55] Sinclair was also critical of the banishment, but conceived of it not as a product of Edward's economic ignorance, but rather of his personal moral failings. Indeed, for Sinclair, in expelling the Jews the King had prioritised personal financial gain over any other consideration. As such, the incident "impresses us with no very favourable idea of [his] humanity".[56] Guthrie, despite his considerable praise for Jewish commerce, focused his account around an attempt to exonerate Edward of any real crime. The Jews he argued, were, most probably, not expelled; rather the increasing regulation of their financial practices led them to petition to be allowed to leave.[57] Moreover, the King's decision to seize the fleeing populace's moveable goods was "necessary" as it it "prevented a great part of the nation's wealth from falling into the hands of those, who were

52 David Hume, "Of Interest," in *Essays: Moral, Political and Literary*, ed. Eugene F. Miller (Indianapolis, IN: Liberty Fund, 1985), 303, 299.

53 Guthrie, *General History*, 1: 576. Guthrie does not provide any explanation of the means by which these processes took place.

54 Hume, *History of England*, 2: 77.

55 Ibid., 2: 76.

56 Sinclair, *History of the Public Revenue*, 66.

57 In making such a claim, Guthrie is drawing on the work of Edward Coke: *The Second Part of the Institutes of the Lawes of England* (London, 1642), 506–507.

thenceforth to be deemed foreigners".[58] Such details "took off the odium" from an act which might, on first reflection, appear "inexcusable".[59] Anderson, meanwhile, was broadly supportive of Edward's actions. While he remained sceptical about claims regarding Jewish coin-tampering, and drew attention to the Jews' expertise in commerce, he concluded that the Jews "brought on [their] banishment" through their "insatiable Thirst of Gain".[60] Taken in sum, therefore, these accounts demonstrate that positive representations of Jewish economic life did not necessitate a negative view of the expulsion. Indeed, the concern for the economic interests of the English state that underpin all the accounts discussed could be used to show the benefits of both greater and lesser degrees of toleration.

Conclusion

I would like to conclude by reflecting on the significance of Enlightenment-era histories for debates concerning Jewish identity and eighteenth-century historiography. Historical accounts of the expulsion, as we have seen, have generally been read within the context of debates concerning English national identity. The focus in such analyses has been on the antithetical relationship between Jewishness and Englishness. As Shapiro has argued: 'Englishness would not be the same as it is without the existence of Jewishness, even as it would not be the same without the existence of Irishness, Scottishness, Welshness, Frenchness, or Spanishness.'[61] "This is especially so", he continues, "because the first and only story of mass deportation of people from England – what has come to be known as 'the expulsion of the Jews in 1290' – has meant that Englishness has in part defined itself by the wholesale rejection of that which is Jewish".[62] Among the four principal historians discussed in this article, it is only Guthrie who developed an account based on this sort of rejection. Underpinning his work was the conventional early-modern notion that Edward I had played a key role in establishing the institutional framework which was to underpin the modern English state.[63] Such a premise made it necessary to present the expul-

58 Guthrie, *General History*, 1: 910.
59 Ibid.
60 Anderson, *Deduction*, 1: 133.
61 Shapiro, *Shakespeare and the Jews*, 4.
62 Ibid.
63 In the "character" of Edward I which concludes Guthrie's narrative of his reign it is noted: "Under Edward the English constitution and civil polity was regenerated from the pollutions

sion either as an uncharacteristic blot on Edward's record or to integrate it into a narrative of national development. While Hume was to take the former option, Guthrie opted for the latter and, as a consequence, his account implies that Edward's expungement of England's Jewish constituted an element in the emergence of modern forms of Englishness. This is not, however, the end of the story. In all four accounts surveyed, the failure of English monarchs to understand the benefits provided by Jewish economic practices is presented as evidence of the ignorance and backwardness, particularly with regard economic affairs, of England's Angevin and early-Plantagenet government. Given these works are grounded in the basic assumption that the modern English state is fundamentally commercial in character, the Jewish interlude functions within them as a marker of the gulf between medieval and contemporary Englishness. Implicit in these narratives, therefore, is the notion that English history has, in part, been the story of the gap between the Jewish and the English people narrowing as the English became more commercial and, as such, more Jewish in character.[64] In this sense, for Enlightenment historians, contemporary Englishness is premised not on a rejection, but an absorption, of Jewish values.

Eighteenth-century commentaries on the expulsion also have significance for our understanding of Enlightenment-era historiography. The latter part of the eighteenth century has generally been seen as the period in which a narrow, classical notion of history based around the study of "the public actions of public men" was challenged as historians incorporated a range of "new" subjects into their commentaries.[65] These included, as Mark Salber Phillips has argued, "commerce and navigation [...]; the history of literature, of the arts and sciences; of manners and customs [...]; of opinion and sentiment", and an engagement with such issues resulted in an "enlargement of the boundaries of the historical".[66] In general terms, this thesis is a compelling one and it provides a useful way of conceptualising the distinctiveness of Enlightenment writing. Discussions of England's Jewish population, however, reveal another, and in many ways op-

contracted under former reigns. It was he who repaired, enlarged, and strengthened the laws of England. Under him, that is, in less than five-and-thirty years, they acquired a greater degree of perfection from the state in which he found them, than perhaps they have since done from that state in which he left them" (Guthrie, *General History*, I: 959).

64 As a consequence, Enlightenment examples provide evidence in support of the thesis developed by Yuri Slezkine that "modernisation is about everyone becoming Jewish." Indeed, the treatment of Jewish themes in Enlightenment writing demonstrates the deep historical roots of ideas regarding Jews and ideas of commercial modernisation. See: Yuri Slezkine, *The Jewish Century* (Princeton, NJ and Oxford: Princeton University Press, 2004), 1 (and passim).

65 Phillips, *Society and Sentiment*, xii.

66 Ibid., 17.

posite, tendency. Eighteenth-century accounts increasingly came to present the Jews not as the adherents of a faith, but rather as the followers of a particular approach to commerce. Consequently, the distinctiveness of Jewish religious and cultural practices which had been dealt with – albeit mainly pejoratively – in earlier accounts was ignored, as the actions and significance of England's Jewish population came to be understood in almost entirely economic terms.[67] Such an approach was a consequence of both a more rigorous and more critical approach to historical sources – material from medieval chronicles came to be conceived as fundamentally untrustworthy – and, even more importantly, the challenges of dealing with new types of commercial practice within a historical framework. The need to provide an account both of the economic backwardness which had characterised England's earlier history and the processes through which it had transformed itself into a major commercial power gave economic issues a new centrality. While writers like Hume and Guthrie were never guilty of economic reductivism – commerce is always treated as a phenomenon that shapes and is shaped by multiple political and social factors – the desire of these writers to foreground a coherent narrative of commercial development made it necessary for other historiographical issues to slip into the background or to vanish entirely. The treatment of Jewish material provides a useful example of this preoccupation with economic analysis and its consequences, and, as such, a reminder that Enlightenment historiography could result not just in a broadening, but also, on occasions, a narrowing of perspective.

---

67 The classic account of Jewish economic identity is Werner Sombart's, *The Jews and Modern Capitalism*, tr. M. Epstein (New Brunswick and London: Transaction Books, 1982), first published as *Die Juden und das Wirtschaftsleben*, 1911. The movement towards an "economic" conception of Jewishness. For an illuminating discussion of Sombart's work and its relationship with earlier attitudes to Jewishness, see: Adam Sutcliffe, "Anxieties of Distinctiveness: Walter Sombart's *The Jews and Modern Capitalism* and the Politics of Jewish Economic History," in *Purchasing Power: The Economics of Modern Jewish History*, ed. Rebecca Kobrin and Adam Teller (Philadelphia: University of Pennsylvania Press, 2015), 238–258.

Tatiana Artemyeva

6 The Encyclopedism of the Russian Enlightenment in the History of Ideas

The history of encyclopedism is an important part of intellectual history and helps us understand philosophical foundations of research and thinking. The encyclopedic look at the world was an outcome of new epistemological principles and the separation of science into a specific sphere of knowledge. Initial attempts to systematise knowledge in Russia were presented through linguistic dictionaries, which acted as a substitute for universal encyclopedias in the Enlightenment period. Russian scholars, however, did not follow famous examples like Zedler's *Universal-Lexicon*, *Encyclopaedia Britannica*, or even *Encyclopédie, ou Dictionnaire raisonne des sciences, des arts et des métiers*, despite the fact that many texts from the *Encyclopédie* were translated into Russian and the authors were supported by many prominent Russian aristocrats, including Empress Catherine the Great herself. French philosophers such as Voltaire, Diderot, D'Alembert, Rousseau, and Montesquieu were never studied systematically in connection with the specificity of the encyclopedic discourse. The birth of the phenomena of encyclopedism as an epistemological ideal or a form of universal knowledge in the Enlightenment epoch signaled the emergence of an encyclopedic thinker like Christian Wolff. Wolff's philosophical method was adequately grasped by Russian thinkers, who used it in the process of assimilation and classification of new knowledge. His method proved to be most valuable for natural sciences, as it allowed the separation of physical, chemical, mathematical, and other studies from socio-political and ideological problems, thus separating philosophy and science. His method formed a whole generation of Russian scholars and formulated scientific thinking in Russia, creating a system of encyclopedia principles which later developed into a new type of rationality that gradually encompassed science, philosophy, history, philology as well as political and economic theories. This "encyclopedic" view of the world emphasised the universality of method that made it possible to work out new knowledge when required and to bring it into correlation with other branches of knowledge. However, Wolffianism was interpreted and modified to fit the requirements of the Russian Enlightenment.

https://doi.org/10.1515/9783110679861-007

Dictionaries as Encyclopedias: a Way to the Universal Knowledge

The quest for universality and systematisation of accumulated knowledge has been typical for all stages of human development. This desire has manifested itself most actively at points of "cultural bifurcations", language and epistemological displacements. Various types of knowledge were presented, with their specific forms of encyclopedic generalisations. These forms were mainly dictionaries, especially dictionaries of foreign terms, which fixed the paradigm shift and tried to relate it to the logic of language development. The first dictionaries of "un-understandable words" appeared in Russia in the thirteenth century. They were named *Azbukovnik* (ABC-dictionary). Essentially explanatory dictionaries, they explained fragments from the Holy Scripture. In 1627, the famous lexicographer Pamva Berynda (1550/70s–1632) issued the *Lexicon slavenorossky* (The Slavonic-Russian Lexicon) along similar lines, and it was only in the eighteenth century that encyclopedic publishing more generally became systematic. The characteristic feature of Russian encyclopedism of that time was an absence of universal encyclopedias but a plurality of special ones: geographical, mineralogical, historical, linguistic, etc. One could argue that linguistic dictionaries, primarily dictionaries of foreign words, were a substitute for universal encyclopedias, because they contained detailed entries about various subjects.

In 1700, Ilia Kopievskij (1651–1714) published *Nomenklator* in Amsterdam (reissued in Russia in 1718 and 1732 under the names *Vocables or Speech of Slavonic, German and Latin Languages* and *Latin-Russian and German Verbal Book*).[1] *Nomenklator* was modeled after European educational dictionaries. Words were divided into thematic groups. The first group contained general philosophical and theological concepts (God, the Virgin, an angel, the heaven, the soul). The second, "About the World, elements and heaven", was ontologo-cosmological. The third, "About times and holidays", was temporal and socio-cultural. There were additional sections: "About waters", "About earth and lands", "About man and parts of his body", "About illnesses and ailments". Some sections

1 Ilia Fedodrovich Kopievskij, *Latina grammatica in usum scholarum celeberrimae gentis Sclavonico-Rosseanae adornata* [Latin grammar in frequent scholarly use among Slavonic-Russian people] (Amsterdam, 1700); Ilya Fedodrovich Kopievskij, *Vokabuly ili rechi na slavenskom, nemeckom i latinskom yazykah* (St. Petersburg, 1718); Ilya Fedodrovich Kopievskij, *Latinorossiiskaya i nemeckaya slovesnaya kniga* (St. Petersburg, 1732). All translations are mine unless otherwise indicated.

were devoted to the concept of life in villages and town, of school, boating, war, arts, politics, etc.[2]

In 1704, the *Lexicon of Three Languages* by Fedor Polikarpov-Orlov (d. 1731), was published.[3] This dictionary also had a systemic character. The section titled "About Science" included theology, philosophy, grammar, poetics, rhetoric, logic, physics, geometry, and music. Sometimes words were interconnected (bird, wing, feather, beak, tail, nail). The reason for this construction was very practical. Memorising words with close meanings (and not in alphabetical order) was easier for students who had to learn 10 to 15 words in Latin and Greek in every class.[4] In the Petrine era, special attention was paid to technical dictionaries that included naval terms. According to Peter the Great's personal instructions, a handwritten *Lexicon of New Words* had been drafted and corrected by Peter himself.[5]

In 1769, Nikolai Kurganov's "Multi-language dictionary or thesaurus of Hebrew, Greek, Latin, French, German, and other foreign words used in Russian and some Slavic languages" helped to explain the meanings and use of such foreign words to people who "do not know their meaning and use them wrong".[6] The dictionary was reprinted five times and was followed by Vasilii Tatishchev's small *Lexicon of Russia: Historical, Geographical, Political, and Civil.*[7]

Classifications were oriented to external, not internal characteristics. In the *Mineralogical Dictionary*, one could find such "minerals" as bricks, stones, "moss from trees", "roots", "bones, nails, nests of birds", "painted stones", "stones representing town ruins", etc. Such a "liberal" approach to the classification

---

2 Yulia Yakimovich, *Deyateli russkoi kul'tury i slovarnoe delo* [Agents of Russian culture and dictionary making] (Moscow: Nauka, 1985), 319–325.

3 Fedor Polikarpov-Orlov, *Leksikon treyazychnyi, sirech' rechenii slavenskih, ellinogrecheskih i latinskih sokrovishe* [Lexicon of three languages or the collection of Slavic, Greek, and Latin phrases] (Moscow, 1704).

4 Irina Kuznetsova, "Ob istochnike Nomenklatora na russkom, latinskom i nemeckom yazyke Il'i Kopievskogo" [On the source of nomenclator in Russian, Latin, and German of Ilya Kopievskii], in *Materialy chtenii, posvyashennyh pamyati professora Iosifa Moiseevicha Tronskogo* (St. Petersburg: Nauka, 2009).

5 *Leksikon vokabulam novym po alfavitu.* See Vladimir Dubichinskii, *Leksikografiya russkogo yazyka* [Lexicography of the Russian language] (Moscow: Nauka, Flinta, 2008), 21–28.

6 Nikolaii Gavrilovich Kurganov, "Slovar raznoyazychnyi, ili tolkovanie evreiskih, grecheskih, latinskih, francuzskih, nemeckih i prochih inozemskih upotreblyaemyh v russkom yazyke i nekotoryh slavyanskih yazykah slov (Russkii slovotolk)", in *Rossiiskaya universal'naya grammatika, ili vseobshee pis'moslovie* (St. Petersburg: Morskoi kadetskii korpus, 1769), 381–416. Citation on page 381.

7 Vasilii Nikitich Tatishchev, *Leksikon rossiiskoi istoricheskoi, geograficheskoi, politicheskoi i grazhdanskoi* (St. Petersburg: Tipografiya Gornogo uchilisha, 1793).

could be explained by the closeness of the notions of "sciences" and "arts". Both were included in "the artificial", i.e., created by humans, contrary to "the natural", created by God. "Sciences and arts" were believed to be synonymous with "civilization" and "culture", and to be the criteria for social development and enlightenment.[8]

For example, the *Mineralogical Dictionary* presents theories for the origin of various fossils found during mining, prevalent in the Age of Enlightenment. The first theory suggests that they had been created together with the earth, and the second one states that they were formed in the bowels of the earth gradually, as crystals. Proponents of the second theory saw in nature a force that "for amusement" could create prints of plants, shells, animals or even quaint ruins of towns. This phenomenon was called "nature's fun". Nature pursued a whim to create various forms arbitrarily and accidentally. An educated scientist should understand this and know that it is not possible to find prints of shells on the top of a mountain. Therefore, this "strange" classification of the eighteenth century actually does not reflect the "poetic license of the originator", but the epoch's version of rationality.

The entry of Russia into the European intellectual space made the need for various types of dictionaries urgent. Even authors of scholarly books tried to explain the epistemological status of their research with the help of micro-dictionaries as was done in the first Russian manual on philosophy, published in 1751 by Grigory Teplov, *General Philosophical Knowledge for Those Who Cannot Read Foreign Books on This Subject*, in which he explained principal terms in accordance with Christian Wolff's system.[9]

Linguistic dictionaries were, therefore, very important in Russia in the epoch of Enlightenment, and they sometimes played the role of universal encyclopedias due to the following reasons:

1. The Russian Empire was a multinational and multilingual country, as many areas were incorporated into it during the eighteenth century (both voluntarily and involuntarily).
2. The Russian intellectual and political elite used French for international as well as internal communications.
3. The Russian intellectual (academic) elite, including representatives of church schools, used Latin (sometimes German) because their representa-

---

8 *Slovar' mineralogicheskii* (St. Petersburg: Imperatorskaya akademiya nauk, 1790).

9 Grigory Nikolaevich Teplov, "Znaniia, kasaiushchiesia voobshche do filosofii, dlia pol'zy tekh, kotorye o sei materii chuzhestrannykh knig chitat' ne mogut, sobrany i iz'iasneny Grigoriem Teplovym", *Filosofskii vek, Al'manakh* 3 (1998): 207–289.

tives were mostly from various German universities or influenced by German authors.

Next, Catherine the Great's project, 500 copies of a dictionary of "all languages and dialects" with the ambitious subtitle *Linguarum totius Orbis vocabularia comparativa*, was published in 1787–1789.[10] The method for compiling the dictionary was worked out by an academician of the St. Petersburg Academy of Science, Peter Simon Pallas (1741–1811). A questionnaire was published as *Modèle du vocabulaire qui doit servir à la comparaison de toutes les langues* and sent to Europe, Brazil, China, and Northern America.[11] Many eminent intellectuals were involved in the project. The dictionary was based on materials received from governors of Russian regions, ambassadors, and foreign scholars.

This project emphasised the idea that there had existed just one primordial language. Special attention was paid to the languages of Inner Asia. Pallas thought that it was the cradle of humankind. Regarding this project, John Walter (1738/9–1812), the founder of *The Times* newspaper, wrote to Benjamin Franklin from London in May 1784:

> I have corrected the Outlines of a grammatical Dictionary for a universal Language, so digested, that the same Writing and Character, shall be perfectly understood in the Latin, Greek, Hebrew, English, French, Italian, Spanish, Portuguese, German, Russian, Swedish, Danish, and Turkish Languages; with Blank Columns for the Inserting of any other Language, and that each may be alternately translated into the other, by being acquainted with one Language only.[12]

The Marquis de Lafayette wrote to Benjamin Franklin from Paris on 10 February 1786:

> Enclosed, My dear Sir, I send You a Vocabulary which the Empress of Russia Requests May Be filled up with Indian Words. You Know Her plans of a Universal dictionary. I Have thought You Might Send me the Delaware and languages with some others. Your Commissioners for Indian affairs, Col Harmar, or Gnl. Butler will Be able to superintend the Busi-

10 *Linguarum totius orbis vocabularia comparativa: augustissimae cura collecta. Sectionis primae, linguas Europae et Asiae* [A comparative vocabulary of languages of the whole world: collected with the highest permission. Section one, Asian and European languages] (Petropoli, 1786–1789).

11 *Modèle du vocabulaire qui doit servir à la comparaison de toutes les langues.* [A model of vocabulary that should serve as a comparison for all languages] (St. Petersburg, 1785).

12 Walter to Franklin, May 1784, in The Papers of Benjamin Franklin, https://franklinpapers.org/framedVolumes.jsp.

> ness Which it is important to Have Well done as the Empress, altho I think to very little purpose, sets a Great Value By it.[13]

The project of the dictionary had greater ideological than linguistic significance. Foreign words were written in Cyrillic letters, far from the real pronunciation (phonetic transcription had not yet been created), data collection was conducted hastily and often by non-specialists, and contained many errors and distortions in the transmission of sound words.[14]

The project united languages of Russia (including those of illiterate peoples who had no written language) and languages of other nations of the world, proclaiming that the "residence" and the "capital" of Russia were part of the Enlightenment, along with the entire country. It also proclaimed the cultural mission of the Russian Empire as one among "natural" nations and became an indirect example of the legitimacy of the policy of "internal colonization". Catherine the Great was very sensitive to her status as the Empress of a large multicultural empire. Her visit to Kazan in 1769 was accompanied by a solemn celebration with poems dedicated to her in various languages, including languages of the Russian Empire: Russian, Latin, Greek, Mari, Chuvash, Udmurt, Tatar, and Mordovian.[15]

A principal role in Russian encyclopedic discourse was played by the publication of the *Dictionary of the Russian Academy.*[16] The Russian Academy was a special research centre for Russian language and literature, separate from the Academy of Sciences. It was established in 1783 following the example of the Académie française.[17] Princess Catherine Dashkova (1743 – 1810) was the founder and first President of the Russian Academy. Whereas the French Academy took more than fifty years to compile their *Dictionary*, Catherine Dashkova and Cath-

13 Fayette to Franklin, 10 February 1786, in https://franklinpapers.org/framedVolumes.jsp.

14 Anna Muradova, Slovar' vseh yazykov: Puteshestviya vokrug sveta [Dictionary of all languages: a journey around the world] 33 (2003), accessed October 11, 2019, http://archive.li/l9hc#selection-163.0 – 165.

15 *Duhovnaya ceremoniya proizvodivshayasya vo vremya vsevozhdelenneishago prisudstviya eya imperatorskago velichestva velikiya gosudaryni premudreishiya monarhini i popechitel'neishiya materi Ekateriny Vtoryya v Kazane* [A liturgical ceremony partaken in the time of the highest presence of her majesty great ruler, monarch, and caring mother Catherine the Second in Kazan] (St. Petersburg: Pri Imperatorskoi Akademii nauk, 1769).

16 *Slovar' Akademii Rossiiskoi* (St. Petersburg: Imperatorskaya akademiya nauk, 1789 – 1794).

17 Mikhail Smilievich Fainshtein, *"I slavu Francii v Rossii prevzoiti": Rossiiskaya akademiya (1783 – 1841) i razvitie kul'tury i gumanitarnykh nauk* ["And to overcome the fame of France and Russia": Russian Academy (1783 – 1841) and development of culture and humanities] (St. Petersburg: Dmitrii Bulanin, 2002).

erine the Great facilitated the production of the Russian Dictionary. Russian language became, for the first time, an object of careful study, with many eminent scholars, writers, representatives of the political elite, and theologians taking part in the dictionary project; it became much more than a simple linguistic dictionary. Analytical explanations of linguistic meanings, with lexical and etymological analysis, made the edition especially important for research in physics and metaphysics. Every entry had plenty of examples from literature, official documents, and folklore, as well as from philosophical, religious, or scientific texts. It became not only a *Dictionary of Russian Language*, but a "Dictionary of Russian Discourses".

Nikolai Yanovsky's (d. 1826) three-volume *New Explanatory Dictionary* occupies a special place among dictionaries. It contained more than ten thousand entries on astronomy, mathematics, medicine, anatomy, physics, chemistry, jurisprudence, commerce, mining, music, military arts like artillery and fortifications, and many other subjects.[18]

Foreign words (terms) had a special significance in the Enlightenment in Russia, and ideas were borrowed together with their linguistic forms. Thus, the Russian vocabulary was oversaturated with foreign terminology. Naval and military terms came from Dutch; physical, metaphysical, and national from German and French. Many words came from Latin and Greek. *The New Explanatory Dictionary* became a model for future dictionaries of foreign words and encyclopedias, because it contained many informative entries and analyzed scholarly approaches under a categorical system of sciences and humanities, and was in this sense a real encyclopedia.

Ideology played an important part in the development of encyclopedism in the Enlightenment, and Russia was no exception. The formation of state identity in the eighteenth century associated Russia with the system of cosmological and geographical coordinates. The spatial uniqueness and magnitude of the Russian Empire was an object of pride for the Russian rulers.

This was clearly expressed in the literature of the period. An *Atlas of the Russian Empire* stated with conscious superiority that "the Russian Empire has more than 130 degrees, but the terrestrial globe contains 360".[19] A *New and Complete Geographical Dictionary of the Russian State* noted that "Russia occupies more than one-seventh of the known dry land, or nearly one-26th of the entire surface of the globe". And further: "there is no, and even in ancient times there had

18 Nikolai Maksimovich Yanovsky, *Novyi slovotolkovatel', raspolozhennyi po alfavitu* [New thesaurus in alphabetical order] (St. Petersburg: Imperatorskaja akademija nauk, 1803–1806).
19 Ivan Kirillovich Kirilov, *Atlas Vserossiiskoi imperii* (St. Petersburg, 1731).

never been any, state under one rule, which could be compared with Russia in its extensiveness".[20] *The Instruction for a New Law Code* (1767), a principal political document of the epoch written by Catherine the Great, noted: "The Possessions of the Russian Empire extend upon the terrestrial Globe to 32 Degrees of Latitude, and to 165 of Longitude". It validated the form of government because "the Extent of the Dominion requires an absolute Power to be vested in that Person who rules over it. It is expedient so to be, that the quick Dispatch of Affairs, sent from distant Parts, might make ample Amends for the Delay occasioned by the great Distance of the Places".[21]

These ideas were also reflected in Feodor Polunin's *Geographical Lexicon of the Russian State*, in which information was collated about the latest Russian conquests during the Russo-Turkish Wars of 1735–1739 and 1768–1774.[22] *Dictionnaire géographique des Gaules et de la France* was used here as a pattern.[23] The editor of the publication, academician Gerhard Friedrich Müller (1705–1783), wrote in his preface that the next editions of a *Dictionary of History, Policy, and Geography of Russian State* should remedy its incompleteness. He discussed an alphabetic system of encyclopedic entries that was good for history, because it "consisted of names", but bad for science because it disrupted the logic of theoretical description. The edition was organised alphabetically, but every entry had detailed accounts of the history and economics of places and of the personal roles played by various important historical persons such as apostle Andrei, Peter I, or Catherine II.

The next edition of the *New and Complete Geographical Dictionary of Russian State, or Lexicon*, expanded by Lev Maksimovich in six volumes, included the newest conquests of the Russian Crown.[24] The *Geographical Dictionary of the Russian State* was represented as an ambitious plan to demonstrate encyclopedic descriptions of the Russian Empire, including its geography, hydrography, history with genealogy and heraldry, social structure, education, policy, agriculture, domestic industry, population, ethnology, religious situation, and church life.

---

20 *Novyi i polnyi geograficheskii slovar' Rossiiskogo gosudarstva*, Part III. (Moscow: N. I. Novikov, 1788), 173.

21 *Nakaz o sochinenii proekta novogo Ulozheniya*. See William Fiddian Reddaway, trans., *Documents of Catherine the Great: The Correspondence with Voltaire and the Instruction of 1767 in the English*, (Cambridge: Cambridge University Press, 1931), 216–217.

22 Feodor Afanasievich Polunin, *Geograficheskii leksikon Rossiiskago gosudarstva* (Moscow: Napechatano pri Imperatorskom Moskovskom universitete, 1773).

23 *Dictionnaire géographique des Gaules et de la France* [Geographical dictionary of Gauls and France], 6 vols. (Paris: Desaint et Saillant 1762–1770).

24 Lev Maksimovich Maksimovich, *Novyi i polnyi geograficheskii slovar' Rossiiskago gosudarstva* (St. Petersburg 1788–1789).

It also contained entries about peoples of the Russian Empire according to their social-political status ("Zaporozhian Cossacks"), ethnicity ("Kalmyks", "Samoyedic peoples"), religion ("Uniat"), as well as places such as monasteries, churches, palaces, and fortresses. All kinds of historical events, including historical myths, were included in these entries. The *Geographical Dictionary* made Russian history a history of the regions of Russia. Again, this example shows how dictionaries and lexicons of the Russian Enlightenment are clearly not merely records of lexical meanings of concepts and terms, but also important sources for studying the epoch's history of ideas.

Encyclopedism as a Form of Universal Knowledge

In spite of the absence of universal encyclopedias, learned Russian society was very sensitive to the way of thinking they developed. Encyclopedism as a form of universal knowledge or as a universal epistemological approach was a result of a new type of rational vision. Thinkers were sure that the right method gave them comprehensive knowledge and, as a consequence, understanding of the absolute truth, so they tried to find a universal method to study sciences and humanities. Systematisation of the already accumulated knowledge was considered the next step in that process.

Principal lessons in the encyclopedic way of thinking were taught by the German intellectuals Leibniz and Christian Wolff, who were very popular in Russia in the Enlightenment. Peter I met Leibniz several times while travelling abroad (Leibniz never visited Russia), and in 1712 he took Leibniz into Russian service, paying him one thousand talers per year. Presumably, it was Leibniz who prompted Peter with the idea of a "cultural cycle". In a letter to the Russian emperor he wrote: "Apparently, according to its divine destiny, science has to go round the world and now come also into Scythia, and so it has chosen Your Majesty to be its instrument, because You can [. . .] acquire the best and improve in the right way what was created in both parts of the world". Leibniz proposed projects to transform Russia and "to be from outside a Solon of Russia". Leibniz believed that Russia could avoid the mistakes made by the West and create an ideal society ruled by the wisest, like Bacon's New Atlantis. In an essay written for Peter, he recommended the handing over of the administration of education, industry, and economy to the learned. Leibniz advised Peter to establish the "Collegium of popular education and social prosperity".[25] The Academy of Sci-

25 Vladimir Ivanovich Chuchmarev, *Leibnits i russkaia kul'tura: Iz istorii mezhdunarodnykh*

ences, in his opinion, should have more power and be independent of the state. Peter listened cautiously to Leibniz. There is no doubt that the tsar was not going to bring about a Baconian epistemological utopia in Russia, nor to share his power with anybody. Besides, Leibniz died in 1716, at the height of the Petrine educational reforms. From that moment on Christian Wolff became the main Western authority to advise Peter in the sphere of science and education.

The first serious steps began with the studying of the Western experience. In 1721 Johann Daniel Schumacher, a librarian and councilor of the academic office and one of the first organisers of Russian scientific institutions, was sent abroad. Peter wrote an instruction for him entitled "Points of what the librarian Schumacher while traveling through Germany, France, England, and Holland should do".[26]

He was ordered to study the organisation of science in other countries, visit their museums and libraries, and buy books, various devices, and instruments for scientific research. Schumacher had also to invite "a mathematician" from Halle, Ch. Wolff, to work in Russia. On 10 July 1722, Schumacher wrote to Wolff that Peter was inclined to establish a society of scholars in Petersburg who would work to develop arts and sciences, and Wolff was proposed as the organiser and vice-president of this society.[27] Wolff did not give his direct consent to move to Russia, but took a very active part in the creation of the Petersburg Academy of Sciences. Wolff, in his letter from 26 June 1723, doubted that it was possible to create the academy straight away and recommended they begin with some "usual universities" to educate personnel.[28]

Peter I valued Wolff highly and asked for his recommendations on various scholarly problems. For instance, wishing to buy a "perpetuum mobile" invented by Orffyraeus (whose real name was Johann Ernst Elias Bessler, 1680 – 1745) and to be assured of its authenticity, the Tsar appealed to Wolff's expertise. Peter asked the President of the Academy, Laurentius Blumentrost, to correspond with Wolff about the issue. Wolff answered that there was no fraud in Orffyr-

---

nauchnykh i kul'turnykh sviazei [Leibniz and Russian culture: from the history of international scholarly and cultural connections] (Moscow: Vysshaya shkola, 1968), 19 – 20, 41.

26 Nina Nevskaia, ed., *Letopis' Rossijskoi Akademii nauk* [Chronicle of the Russian Academy of Sciences] (St. Petersburg: Nauka, 2000), 34.

27 Schumacher to Wolff, 10 July 1722. Cited in Alexander Timofeev, "Khr.Vol'f i sozdanie rossiiskoi Akademii nauk" [Chr. Wolff and the foundation of the Academy of Sciences in Petersburg in the history of world's academies], in *Peterburgskaia Akademiia nauk v istorii akademij mira. Materialy Mezhdunarodnoi konferentsii.* T. IV (St. Petersburg: Nauka, 1999), 85.

28 Wolff to Schumacher, 26 June 1723. Cited in Timofeev, "Khr.Vol'f i sozdanie rossiiskoi Akademii nauk," 85.

aeus's invention because he had received a certificate from "mister landgrave". However, the engine did not produce enough power, so it had no practical value.[29]

Insistent invitations to Wolff to come to Russia came to nothing. In 1725, the management of the Academy thought of a compromise. In the *Minutes* of the Academy on 19 March 1725, there was mention of the following: "L. Blumentrost wrote to A. Golovkin that the Empress ordered to establish the title of honourary member of the Academy for eminent scholars. It was proposed that Wolff be made an honourary member and a representative of the Academy in Germany with a salary of three hundred rubles per year. On 26 April Wolff informed the Academy of his acceptance".[30]

Wolff's support for the organisation of Russian science was great and many projects were accomplished due to his professional competence and participation. He sent his books to Petersburg and discussed various theoretical problems. At the Academy meetings his opinions on problems of natural law, botany, cosmology, etc. were discussed. Thus, the universal, encyclopedic character of the thinker's knowledge was often referred to by Russian academics.

Wolff's help in collecting personnel for the Academy was invaluable. From 1725 to 1726, he wrote about 30 invitation letters to foreign scholars. Some of them, for example Leonard Euler, Jacob Hermann, Georg Bernhardt Bülfinger, he recommended personally. In the Academy archives, there is a note preserved that testifies that Bülfinger was invited as a philosopher rather than as a mathematician. Bülfinger was summoned as a philosopher-Wolffianist, as was Christian Martini from Wittenberg. President L. Blumentrost was himself Wolff's student and attended his lectures in Halle in 1706.[31]

The "state-bound" character of the science organisation had certain merits. In a very short time, a major scientific centre was created with an observatory, a physical cabinet, a botanic garden, an anatomy theatre, a printing press, a library, a chemical laboratory, and tool-making shops. When young Euler, also recommended by Wolff, was invited to enter the Academy, Wolff wrote him: "You are going to a paradise of scholars, and I wish most of all that you would preserve

---

29 Timofeev, "Khr.Vol'f i sozdanie rossiiskoi Akademii nauk," 85.

30 Nevskaia, *Letopis' Rossijskoi Akademii nauk*, 38–39.

31 M. V. Mandrik, "Lavrenti Lavrentyevich Blyumentrost," in *Aktual'noe proshloe: vzaimodejstvie i balans interesov Akademii nauk i Rossijskogo gosudarstva v XVIII – nachale XX v.*, Part 1 [Actual Past: interaction and balance of interests of the Academy of Sciences and Russian State in the eighteenth to the beginning of the twentieth century], ed. I. V. Tunkina (St. Petersburg: Renome, 2018), 3.

your good health in this voyage, and would be satisfied as long as possible by your stay in Petersburg".[32]

Some promising Russian students, M. Lomonosov, D. Vinogradov, and G. Raizer, were sent to Wolff at Marburg University in September 1736 to be educated in chemistry and mining and be taught sixteen subjects: logic, philosophy, natural and national law, politics, geography, chronology, astronomy, mathematics, theoretical physics, mechanics, optics, hydraulics, military and civil architecture, and pyrotechnics. Thus, the Russian students could learn from the eminent scholar's erudition to take an encyclopedic look at the world.

Being an experienced teacher, Wolff appreciated the talent of young Lomonosov straight away. It was Wolffian training that, in my view, formed the genius of Lomonosov, who became equally conversant in physics, chemistry, philology, and history. In a letter to the president of the Academy, Johann Albrecht von Korff, in September 1737, Wolff wrote: "Mr. Lomonosov, it seems, has the smartest head among them".[33] Lomonosov promoted Wolff's doctrine in Russia and recommended his books for reading at Russian schools, considering them the last word of European science. He praised Wolff highly for his clear and accurate thinking. He underlined Wolff's method as the main merit of his doctrine, pointing out that the most important thing for Russia was a Wolffian combination of scientific thinking and teleology. Crucial was the Wolffian belief that scientific cognition did not contradict the truths of the Holy Scripture, but supported them and allowed man to serve God by doing science. This conviction made Lomonosov an outstanding scientist and he made many interesting theological propositions in his spiritual odes.

A researcher of the German Enlightenment, V. A. Zhuchkov, remarks that "Wolffian philosophy was special in its underlined orientation to enlightenment. This trend contrasted with the rather elitist character of eighteenth-century philosophical thought or the so-called 'age of geniuses'".[34] Wolff's use of his national language also shared affinities with similar schools of thought in Russia during this period. I propose that the teaching of philosophy at Moscow University in Russian was at least in part inspired by Wolff's example. Leibniz, who preferred to use Latin and French in his works, thought that German was "non-philo-

32 Wolff to Euler. Cited in Rüdiger Thiele, *Leonard Euler* (Kiev: Vishha shkola, 1983), 26.

33 Wolff to von Korff, September 1737. Cited in Timofeev, "Khr.Vol'f i sozdanie rossiiskoi Akademii nauk," 86.

34 Vladimir Zhuchkov, "Metafizika Vol'fa i ee mesto v istorii filosofii Novogo vremeni" [Wolff's metaphysics and its place in modern history], in *Khristian Vol'f i filosofiia v Rossii* (St. Petersburg: Russkaya hristianskaya gumanitarnaya akademiya, 2001), 11.

sophical", whereas Wolff showed clearly in his writings that German could deal perfectly well with all shades of metaphysical discourses.

Wolff's example inspired many Russian thinkers to create philosophical terminology in their native language. Grigory Teplov, a Russian Wolffianist, wrote:

> Cicero was a man of great eloquence, but he was ashamed of his Latin words, when he translated them from Greek for the first time, and some of them he could not translate and left them in philosophy in Greek. The same happened in our time with French and especially with German. Professor Wolff was ridiculed by many for his translated words, especially those at Leipzig University, but now nowhere as much as at Leipzig University are the words of his translation used. The same is happening also in the Russian language.[35]

Wolff and his works were very well known in Russia. Translations of his works into Russian and the great number of copies of his books in Russian libraries testify to this. The Department of Rare Books of the Library of Academy of Sciences alone now preserves more than a 100 volumes of Wolff's works (about 50 titles) published in the eighteenth century. The St. Petersburg Branch of the Academy Archives owns many documents on Wolff, the main part of which consists of his letters to Schumacher and Blumentrost. Information about Wolff can also be found in Euler's correspondence. The Archives also keep Wolff's manuscript *Philosophia moralis dire Ethica* (B/d. R. III. Op. 3. D. 12). It is interesting to note that the translated works were not "philosophical". The only philosophical work translated was Wolff's *Deutsche Metaphysik.*[36] Other editions were about fortification, mathematics, and physics.

Philosophy was studied rather through Friedrich-Christian Baumeister, whose works *Logic*, *Metaphysics*, and *Moral Philosophy* were translated and printed repeatedly in Russia. This fact was connected with the popular character of his books and with his use of "Wolffianism". An example will illustrate the ambiguous usage of Wolff's doctrine. It is well known that Wolff was a supporter of pre-established harmony, and in the corresponding parts of his works he used just this model to explain the connection of mind and body. In Baumeister's *Metaphysics*, however, one may find mention of the traditional models: of the ancient (Aristotelian) theory of "physical influx", of the system of occasional causes by Descartes and Malebranche, or the model of pre-established harmony by Leibniz and Wolff. Baumeister remarked: "Which of these opinions is closer to the truth, I do not know, and even if I knew, I would not dare to define this. Every reader can without any obstacle make his own judgment. Our duty consists

---

35 Teplov, "Znaniia, kasaiushchiesia voobshche do filosofii," 219.
36 Christian Wolff, *Razumnye mysli o silah chelovecheskago razuma* (St. Petersburg, 1765).

only in proposing philosophical opinions, but not to say how they should think".[37]

The system of occasional causes and pre-established harmony were not accepted by Russian thinkers. They were rejected first of all for moral reasons. The main shortcoming of all these systems was a peculiar justification of evil that became objective and inevitable. Mechanism, a consequence of the Cartesian-Leibnizian pneumatological scheme, led the thought out of morality, and Russian philosophy refused to go there. D. S. Anichkov (1733–1788), a Wolffianist and Professor of Logic, Metaphysics and Mathematics at the University, became critical of these doctrines. He analyzed in detail both the methodological and ethical bases of the problem in *A Discourse on Various Ways to Explain the Union between Body and Soul* and *A Discourse on Human Understanding and the Measures which Preserve the Mind of a Mortal from Various Errors*. Placing itself between logic and morals, Russian metaphysics chose the latter, contrasting a kind of dualism with monistic mechanism and deism.[38] The most appropriate way to explain the mind-body problem was the peripatetic theory, rejected in Europe, of "physical influx", which did not counterpoise but joined them together. The Leibnizian-Wolffian doctrine of theodicy and freedom of will, very actively discussed in Russia after the famous earthquake in Lisbon in 1755, was rejected.

In the first Russian manual of philosophy, Grigory Teplov's *General Philosophical Knowledge for Those Who Cannot Read Foreign Books on This Subject* – written as a presentation of the Wolffian system – the main point of emphasis was on problems of epistemology and classification of various ways of cognition. Teplov paid considerable attention to the Wolffian differentiation of cognition into historical, philosophical, and mathematical modes. In his book, he interpreted and explicated the entity and the nature of cognitive processes, explaining how fruitful the right method could be. However, he wholly ignored the concepts of pre-established harmony and monadology, taking just what he thought useful for him and his compatriots.[39]

The philosophy taught at Russian schools was also positioned as Wolffianism. Wolffianism became the official system taught at Moscow University, found-

---

37 Friedrich Christian Baumeister, *Khristiana Baumeistera Metafizika/ Perevod s latinskago [Aleksandra Pavlova] vnov' vysmotren i na mnogikh mestakh ispravlen professorom Dmitriem Sin'kovskim* (Moscow: Universitetskaya tipografiya u Novikova, 1789), 206.

38 Dmitry Sergeevich Anichkov, *Slovo o raznyh sposobah, tesneishii soyuz dushi s telom iz'yasnyayushih* (Moscow: V Universitetskoi tipografii u N. Novikova, 1783); Dmitry Sergeevich Anichkov, *Slovo o svoistvah poznaniya chelovecheskago i o sredstvah predohranyayushih um smertnago ot raznyh zabluzhdenii* (Moscow: Pechatano pri Imperatorskom Moskovskom universitete, 1770).

39 Teplov, "Znaniia, kasaiushchiesia voobshche do filosofii," 207–289.

ed in 1755. The manifesto "About the Foundation of Moscow University" clearly said: "None of the professors should of his own free will choose a system or an author to teach his discipline to his students, but everybody should follow the order and the authors prescribed by the assembly of professors and curators".[40]

This rule was strictly observed and dissenting opinions mercilessly banned. Even in the beginning of the nineteenth century, Wolffianism was set against both French and German (Kant, Schelling, and Fichte) philosophy. In the manuscript, "Opinion about Teaching of Philosophy", a member of the General School Administration, I.M. Murav'ev-Apostol, remarked that he preferred the Wolffian system to any other. Wolffianism was for him an example of a didactic and systematic discourse spared from the destructive freethinking of French authors.[41] The same situation prevailed at church schools, where Wolffianism replaced scholasticism and Aristotelianism in the second half of the eighteenth century. The interest in Wolffianism resulted from the general academic tradition of attention to German philosophy and in part from the impact of Protestantism upon Orthodox hierarchs. Many of them were influenced by German philosophy, especially Wolffianism. For example, Bishop Damaskin (D. Semenov-Rudnev) was a publisher of Lomonosov's works and one of the first Russian bibliographers educated in Göttingen University. In the seminary at Nizhny Novgorod, Damaskin sponsored theological debates using the experience he acquired in Göttingen. The bishop of Byelorussia, Georgy Konissky, who had graduated from Kievo-Mogilianskaia Academy and was its rector, wrote to Timofey, the metropolitan of Kiev, that he regretted that he had lost much time reading Aristotle and had not studied and taught Wolff's philosophy, which he found to be "well-grounded, sound, clear".[42]

The organisers of spiritual education were, most of all, afraid of the anticlerical tendencies of the French Enlightenment. Thus, they found that the solid German systems of Leibniz and Wolff were the best to philosophically support religious truths. The ontological notions of Wolffianism seemed to provide the general foundation for all the rational arguments used to confirm the key theses of any dogmatic religious system. Thus, Wolffianism was quite naturally included in the system of Orthodox theology. The Wolffianism studied in church

---

40 *Polnoe Sobranie Zakonov Rossiiskoi Imperii.* [Full codex of laws of the Russian empire] T. XIV. (St. Petersburg, 1830), 290.

41 Tatiana Artemyeva, "Kak prepodavat' filosofiyu? Mnenie universitetskogo chinovnika" [How to teach philosophy? The opinion of a university official], *Filosofskii vek, al'manakh* 30 (2005): 67–80.

42 Petr Vasilievich Znamenskii, *Dukhovnye shkoly v Rossii do reformy 1808 goda* [Religious schools in Russia before the reform of 1808] (St. Petersburg: Letnii Sad., 2001), 748.

schools, however, differed from Wolff's philosophy, being more inclined to Baumeister's variant in certain interpretations.

The tendency was clearly stated by the archimandrite Gavriil in his history of philosophy. In his article on Wolff titled "An Editor of Leibniz", Gavriil criticised Wolff not only for monadology and pre-established harmony, but also for his mathematical method, entirely "subjected to the cobweb of formalism". Besides, Wolff's maxim "do the good and avoid the evil", Gavriil believed, "breathes with vanity, and thus is hostile to the nature of human reason that obliges us to strive for the improvement of others, sometimes even to our own detriment".[43] Wolff's system was approved by officials because he never linked his method with any possibility to reform society, but only with its cognition. Social problems he treated from the point of view of ethics (the science of will, as logic, was the science of reason) and Wolffian ethics had "natural" rules that had, in turn, the status of general principles. Thus, social problems were treated as secondary, of minor importance, in contrast to the doctrines of French eighteenth-century philosophers, who always pushed social problems and their attitude to the church to the foreground.

Hence, Wolffianism was interpreted, modified, and distorted to fit the requirements of various figures of the Russian Enlightenment. Wolff became an official philosopher in Russia. At the same time, what was used was not his entire philosophy, but only those parts that corresponded to the logic of the Russian Enlightenment processes.

However, Wolff's method proved to be most valuable for natural sciences, because it allowed the objects of physical, chemical, mathematical, and other studies to be made independent of socio-political and ideological problems. Thus, it helped to separate philosophy and science. This secularisation promoted natural sciences and met the needs of newly-founded scientific institutions, like the Academy of Sciences and the Moscow University. It is evident that the didactic potential of Wolff's system, his rigid methodology, and the strictness of his deductive reasoning made his doctrine attractive to Russians. Just these very qualities later provoked Heinrich Heine's romantic irony reproaching Wolff for having built a system that looked like a wardrobe where the shelves were well-situated, well-filled, and well-inscribed. Russian thinkers of the Enlightenment saw nothing nasty in ordering systems. "Poetical disorder" may be attractive to poets, but not to scholars.

43 Gavriil Arkhimandrit, *Istoriia filosofii v 6 chchastiakh.* Ch. III. (Kazan': V Universitetskoi tipografii, 1839), 190.

It is unlikely that this striving to classify, order, systematise, complete, and scrupulously calculate phenomenological and speculative entities was accidental or senseless. For example, A. Baumgarten, a Wolffianist, studied a special sphere of philosophical cognition, namely aesthetics, which he clearly recognised, and which later overgrew its Wolffian frames. The "encyclopedic look at the world" was an outcome of new epistemological principles and of the separation of science into a specific sphere of knowledge. This was attractive to Russian scholars who considered Wolff as their instructor. Thus, it was not the metaphysical content of Wolff's doctrine but his philosophical method that was adequately grasped by Russian thinkers and used by them in the process of making, assimilation, and classifying new knowledge.

The idea to create a universal system of scientific knowledge, "scientia generalis", based upon strict logical laws, had already been expressed by Descartes and Leibniz. Wolff brought it to life.

It may be said that this method formed a whole generation of Russian scholars and influenced the formulation of scientific thinking in Russia. It created the system of encyclopedic principles later developed into a new type of rationality that gradually seized the sciences, philosophy, history, philology, and political and economic theories. The main feature of the "encyclopedic look at the world" was not the plenitude of knowledge, but rather the universality of method that permitted the working out of new knowledge, when required, and to bring it into correlation with other branches of knowledge. Wolff called this method mathematical (as distinct from historical and philosophical). Today we would call it scientific. It was much later, in the twentieth century, that scientism was criticised, its universality called into question, and the groundlessness of its claims to universality proved. In the epoch of Enlightenment, it was an epistemological breakthrough based on a belief in human reason.

In various epochs, the idea of entire and final knowledge was based upon the belief in the boundless abilities of reasoning (divine or human) that possessed the universal cognitive method equally applicable in various spheres of being. Thus, the phenomenon of encyclopedism was born as an epistemological ideal or a form of universal knowledge in the epoch of Enlightenment. Thus, the type of the encyclopedic thinker emerged, and Christian Wolff undoubtedly belonged to this type.

Why, then, did the Wolffian model of encyclopedic discourse that consisted in his ordering method come to dominate in Russia? In that era, there were two other excellent models, the French and the British.

The French encyclopedia collected around itself an entire constellation of French philosophers and scientists.[44] Besides Diderot and D'Alembert, Holbach, Voltaire, Marmontel, Rousseau, Turgot, Montesquieu, and others also participated in the edition. The *Encyclopédie* (at first planned to be a mere translation of Ephraim Chamber's *Cyclopaedia*[45]) aimed to throw new light upon all possible tendencies and manifestations of "sciences, arts and crafts". It has become a historical monument of the past. The *Encyclopaedia Britannica,* intended by Edinburgh publishers Andrew Bell and Colin Macfarquhar as a national and commercial edition, on the contrary, turned into an international reference edition, one of the most authoritative in the modern world. The *Encyclopédie* formed the epoch, but went down in history. The *Encyclopaedia Britannica* had a modest start, but gradually created a stable and leading position for itself in the learned world. The *Britannica* incorporated borrowed and translated articles with ease, aiming at fundamentality, not originality. These principles defined its success.[46]

This historical example confirmed the main principle of the encyclopedic approach: not to invent the new, but rather to regulate the old. At a certain stage of scientific development, ordering and systematisation are essential to move on. Moreover, in any epoch, this principle is a significant component of science.

However, both the French and British types of encyclopedism were never accepted in Russia. This may seem paradoxical, especially where French encyclopedism is concerned. Texts from the *Encyclopédie* were translated into Russian, and the authors were supported by many outstanding Russian aristocrats, including the Empress Catherine the Great herself (she even proposed transferring its publication to the Russian Empire, to Riga).

Although many French philosophers, such as Voltaire, Diderot, D'Alembert, Rousseau, and Montesquieu, were very popular among the noble intellectual elite in Russia, they were never studied systematically. They were interesting as persons, social philosophers, anti-clerics, and political thinkers, but not in connection with the specificity of encyclopedic discourse. Russian readers paid much more attention to the ideas expressed by the French philosophers than to how their texts were organised. Thus, the very type of encyclopedic dis-

---

44 *Encyclopédie, ou Dictionnaire raisonne des sciences, des arts et des* métiers [Encyclopedia or reasonable dictionary of science, arts, and trades] vols. 1–35 (Paris, 1751–1780).

45 Ephraim Chambers, *Cyclopædia*, (London: Printed for D. Midwinter, W. Innys, 1741).

46 Tatiana Artemyeva, "Nauki o cheloveke v pervyh izdaniyah Britanskoi enciklopedii" [The human sciences in the first editions of the Encyclopaedia Britannica], *Chelovek* 6 (2003): 670–685.

course proposed by Diderot and D'Alembert was a secondary, optional one for the Russian reader.

The ideas of the *Encyclopaedia Britannica* were scarcely known in Europe. The reception of British, especially Scottish, philosophy in Russia was implicit, non-demonstrative, and mostly restricted to the social philosophy of Adam Smith, David Hume (who was known in eighteenth century Russia primarily as a historian), and Adam Ferguson. Besides, up to its third edition (1788–1797) the *Britannica* had been a modest compilation that could neither fascinate its reader with a large-scale plan nor with a high level of performance. Encyclopedism as a form of universal knowledge was mainly connected with natural sciences and their strict methodology, and in this sphere the influence of German scholars was beyond comparison. By turning to Wolffianism, one of the most developed and advanced systems of that time, the Russian Enlightenment showed that it carefully selected the authorities whom it would make its teachers. Possibly it was the Wolffian model of encyclopedism as the use of the universal method that led to the situation in Russia, where there were many scholar-encyclopedists, but no serious attempt to create an encyclopedic edition emulating the famous European patterns.

Çağlar Çömez

7 David Hume, Immanuel Kant, and the Possibility of an Inclusive Moral Dialogue

Introduction

Immanuel Kant and David Hume developed moral theories that diverged from each other in many respects. Hume famously claimed that reason is the slave of passions and it cannot provide a motive for the human will to attain an end. Kant explicitly rejected this view and equally famously argued that pure reason can be practical and determine the will independently of our passions. Besides the power of reason to determine the will, the two philosophers also disagreed about the nature of moral judgment. Hume believed that our moral judgments arise from feelings of approbation and disapproval. According to him, when a moral agent reflects on an action, she develops certain sentiments about its moral value and thereby makes a moral judgment. Kant, on the other hand, thought that because there is a moral law we can appeal to in order to identify the moral value of an action regardless of our inclinations, we can make moral judgments that do not reflect our sentiments.

My first main aim in this chapter is to show that Hume's sentimentalist theory of moral judgment faces an important problem. Hume's account leads us to a point where a moral dialogue in which moral agents with conflicting sentiments about a morally significant situation can be included is impossible. I argue that Hume's sentiment-based theory of moral judgment fails to lay the basis for an inclusive moral dialogue for moral agents who do not share the same set of sentiments with respect to a moral issue due to differences in their social contexts of upbringing and education. On a model of moral dialogue based on Hume's account of moral judgment, the members of different societies who are socialised to have conflicting feelings about the same morally significant issue are not capable of engaging in a moral dialogue on social problems.

I also present two responses to this objection against Hume's theory of moral judgment. The first response is based on a distinction between two types of sentiments and emphasises the idea that when Hume argues that our moral judgments arise from sentiments, he is referring only to *moral* sentiments that are the products of what Hume calls "the common point of view". According to this response, once moral agents take this point of view, they have a basis for

https://doi.org/10.1515/9783110679861-008

a moral dialogue in which one can be included regardless of one's non-moral sentiments. I show that even though this response looks promising, it is actually incompatible with Hume's idea that moral judgments are not conclusions of causal reasoning that express matters of fact. The second response appeals to the idea that Hume provides not only a psychological explanation of how we make moral judgments, but also a theory of moral language. This response suggests that, in order to make a moral judgment, one has to use the moral language by satisfying requirements such as universalisability and impartiality. I argue that if we accept the idea that there are criteria such as universalisability and impartiality, which we all have to satisfy to make a moral judgment, this would entail certain factors that guide and determine our moral judgments regardless of our sentiments. However, in developing his sentiment-based account of moral judgment, Hume explicitly rejects this.

My second main aim in this essay is to show that Kant's principle-based moral philosophy provides us with a common basis for engaging in moral dialogues with each other regardless of our socially-shaped, subjective feelings about human action. This basis is the categorical imperative. Although the categorical imperative does have the form of an imperative, it is actually a description of how a purely rational agent would act, and it demands that a moral agent justify her actions only on the basis of considerations that can be endorsed by each and every rational agent. For this reason, according to Kant, as long as one is rational, one justifies one's actions on mutually endorsable terms without appealing to any sentiment or feeling that may work as argument-stoppers in our moral dialogues.

Hume's Sentiment-Based Ethical Theory and the Possibility of an Inclusive Moral Dialogue

Sentiments play a series of central roles in Hume's ethical theory. One role concerns how we acquire moral knowledge and make moral judgments. In a famous passage, Hume states that "the distinguishing impressions, by which moral good or evil is known, are nothing but particular pains or pleasures".[1] Hume here states his well-known epistemological view that our moral knowledge and judgments are products of sentiments. According to him, when we make a moral judgment by applying a certain moral notion (such as virtuous or vicious) to a

1 David Hume, *A Treatise of Human Nature*, ed. David F. Norton and Mary J. Norton (Oxford: Clarendon Press, 2007), 303.

particular morally significant object, that judgment and the relevant moral classification arise from the feeling of approbation or disapproval that the situation invokes in us.

Kenneth R. Westphal makes an important distinction between two ways in which sentiments can have a place in our moral judgments. On the one hand, according to what Westphal calls the *weak thesis*, "sentiments are a necessary component or basis of moral judgment".[2] The idea that our moral sentiments are the *media* through which we acquire moral knowledge and make a moral judgment is compatible with this thesis. Since he thinks that "the distinguishing impressions, *by which* moral good or evil is known, are particular pains and pleasures", Hume is committed to this thesis and he believes that sentiments of approbation and disapprobation are at least our moral media.[3] This thesis does not entail, however, that an action or a character is a virtuous action or virtuous character *because* it arouses in us certain feelings of pleasure or approval.

On the other hand, according to the *strong thesis*, "sentiments form the sole and sufficient basis of moral judgments (or classifications)".[4] Westphal rightly argues that in his ethical theory Hume goes beyond the weak thesis and endorses the strong thesis. Hume states that "an action, or sentiment, or character is virtuous or vicious; why? *because* its view causes a pleasure or uneasiness of a particular kind [...] to have the sense of virtue, is nothing but to *feel* a satisfaction of a particular kind from the contemplation of a character".[5] And just after claiming that the feeling of satisfaction constitutes our positive moral attitude towards a character, Hume continues by arguing that we go no further than this feeling "nor do we enquire into the cause of the satisfaction".[6] He also states that "moral distinctions depend *entirely* on certain particular sentiments of pain and pleasure, and that whatever mental quality in ourselves or others gives us satisfaction, by the survey of reflection, is of course virtuous; as everything of this nature, that gives us uneasiness, is vicious".[7]

The strong thesis implies that our moral judgments and our moral classifications of actions and characters into moral categories derive entirely from sentiments. According to the strong thesis, when I make a moral judgment and think that an action is virtuous, it is because I have a feeling of approbation with re-

2 Kenneth R. Westphal, *How Hume and Kant Reconstruct Natural Law: Justifying Strict Objectivity without Debating Moral Realism* (Oxford: Clarendon Press, 2016), 43.
3 Hume, *Treatise*, 303 [emphasis mine].
4 Westphal, *Natural Law*, 43.
5 Hume, *Treatise*, 303 [emphasis mine].
6 Ibid.
7 Ibid., 367 [emphasis mine].

gard to that action. Similarly, when an action is virtuous, it is virtuous because it creates a certain feeling in me. Hume argues that it is impossible to find vice in an action that we take to be vicious when considered in itself and claims that "you never can find it, till you turn your reflection into your own breast, and find a sentiment of disapprobation, which arises in you, towards this action".[8]

The strong thesis creates a serious problem for Hume's ethical theory. Suppose that you are in a discussion on a moral topic with a friend and she makes a moral judgment about an action. Suppose further that she was raised and educated in a culture in which the action in question is considered considerably differently from in your own culture. Even though you consider the judgment and the action carefully, you do not understand why she is making that judgment and classifying the action as an instance of vice or virtue. Suppose further that the judgment your friend makes is also in the form of a call for action. In other words, the judgment is of the form *we ought to do A*. When we encounter cases like this, as practically rational beings we do not simply act on the moral judgment another person makes. Before we act, we want to understand why that moral judgment constitutes a sufficient basis for action. And if Hume's account of moral judgment and the strong thesis is correct, the person will explain why her moral judgment is a reasonable moral judgment by indicating that she has a feeling of approval towards action A.

It would be safe to think at this point that the culture in which one is raised and educated has a considerable impact on the moral feelings one experiences towards at least some actions.[9] So given that your culture considers the action significantly differently from your friend's culture, we may assume that you have a moral sentiment about it, which leads you to a conflicting moral judgment. And when you are asked why your moral judgment is the reasonable one to make, according to Hume's account of moral judgment and classification, you would say that you have a contrary feeling towards action A. The problem here is that if we preserve Hume's thesis that sentiments are the sole and sufficient basis of our moral judgments and classifications, then we have no way to determine whose sentiments are superior to others except by appealing back to sentiments themselves. This means that once the parties in a moral dialogue disagree with each other by making conflicting moral judgments on the basis of their feelings of approval or disapproval, they can go no further than telling

8 Ibid., 301.
9 An important social factor here is religion. For instance, in societies where Islam is the dominant religion, the moral significance of consuming alcoholic drinks is very different from countries where the dominant religion does not prohibit consuming alcoholic drinks.

each other these feelings or sentiments and end up at a point where there is hardly any prospect for moral discussion and dialogue.

One might grant that we recognise that sentiments do work as argument-stoppers in our moral dialogues and argue that appealing to a feeling or a sentiment to explain why a moral judgment is a reasonable one is not something we usually do. For instance, when we observe a child being hit by her parent and make the moral judgment that hitting the child is not a virtuous action, we justify our judgment not by saying that we have a feeling of disapproval toward the action but by appealing to something like "children are not moral agents who are responsible for their actions". But does Hume's theory of moral judgment allow us to explain why our moral judgments are reasonable by appealing to moral considerations like this? If it does, then there is still a good prospect for further discussion in our scenario above.

One of the most peculiar aspects of appealing to considerations like "small children are not moral agents who are responsible for their actions" as an explanation of why a moral judgment is reasonable is that, by such an appeal, one commits oneself to a moral judgment regardless of one's or any other person's feelings towards the action that brought about the judgment. Explaining why a moral judgment is a reasonable one on the basis of moral considerations without appealing to our feelings entails that one will be committed to one's moral judgment as a conclusion of these considerations, independently of what one's feelings are. However, Hume's sentimentalist anti-rationalism does not allow this because he believes that moral distinctions are not conclusions of reasoning but "depend *entirely* on certain peculiar sentiments of pain and pleasure".[10] For this reason, according to Hume's theory, the only possibility for the person in our scenario to explain why her moral judgment is reasonable is to appeal to her feelings of approval and disapproval towards action A.

In our scenario, if the other person has sentiments that converge with yours, then you can agree on your judgments based on sentiments and discuss what practical measures must be taken to execute the action about which you have feelings of approbation. Therefore, if Hume's theory of moral judgment is correct, moral agents with the same kind of sentiments towards an action can engage in a moral dialogue and can also include another person who has the same sentiment in their moral conversation. However, if another moral agent has a conflicting sentiment about the same action, she is excluded from the conversation the moment she is asked why her judgment is reasonable.

---

10 Hume, *Treatise*, 367 [emphasis mine].

Whether a moral theory makes it possible for us to engage in a moral dialogue without encountering argument-stoppers depends largely on the basic elements in terms of which it characterises moral judgment.[11] If a moral theory selects subjective states of awareness such as sentiments to characterise moral judgment, then whether we can make moral judgments that could address different individuals depends on which subjective states of awareness these individuals happen to have, but these subjective states of awareness vary significantly across historical periods and regions. Closely tied to this point, an important function that we expect moral philosophy to fulfill is to provide us with a basis on which we can deal with moral problems that concern different societies with different cultures.[12] However, on a theory of moral judgment that appeals to subjective states of awareness that vary culturally and historically, it is hardly possible to deal with these social problems. There are morally pressing social problems that concern different social groups who have strong tendencies to develop conflicting sentiments about them. If Hume's sentiment-based account of moral judgment is correct, we simply have no way to address and solve them through dialogues that include not only those who happen to share our feelings of approbation but all concerned parties.[13]

The Common Point of View as a Ground for Moral Dialogue

What are some ways to save Hume's ethical theory from this objection? I shall now present two Humean responses against it. The first is based on Rachel Cohon's interpretation of Hume's notion of the common point of view. This response is extremely important and needs to be addressed because of the centrality of the notion of the common point of view in Hume's moral philosophy.

Cohon's reading makes a distinction between two types of sentiments. She calls the sentiments that arise when we reflect on a morally significant situation "from our ordinary, individual perspective" without taking a general point of

11 Westphal, *Natural Law*, 73.

12 One can argue that this is not a *requirement* that each moral theory should satisfy. However, we may at least reasonably think that a moral theory that fulfills this function is superior to another one which cannot.

13 For another criticism of Hume's sentiment-based ethical theory, see Westphal, *Natural Law*, 39–67. Westphal argues powerfully that sentiments are not sufficient to identify and justify basic moral principles. My objection here in this section draws upon and confirms Westphal's criticism of Hume's ethical theory by showing that sentiments are insufficient in yet another regard.

view which we can share with other moral agents *situated sentiments*.[14] Situated sentiments reveal our particular points of view when we consider an action or a character. Our situated sentiments might be influenced by self-interest or other non-moral factors. Therefore, situated sentiments are not *moral sentiments*. Moral sentiments arise in us when we reflect on a morally significant situation from a *steady* and *general* point of view. As Hume argues, in moral judgment "we fix on some *steady* and *general* points of view; and always, in our thoughts, place ourselves in them, whatever may be our present situation".[15] We have moral sentiments and can make moral judgments only if we take a common point of view. According to Cohon, the sentiments that arise from our ordinary, individual point of view can also be corrected by the sentiments we have when we reflect from a general and steady common point of view but, as Hume himself points out, "the passions do not always follow our corrections".[16] For this reason, it might be the case that "we feel two sentiments toward the same character trait".[17] When this is the case, the two sentiments produce two different judgments. However, Cohon argues that "the one that arises from imagining oneself occupying the common point of view is the source of moral judgment".[18]

Moreover, on Cohon's reading of Hume's notion of the common point of view, Hume thinks that when one takes the common point of view and has a moral sentiment, the interest or pleasure that is taken into account is "that of the person himself, whose character is examined, or that of persons who have a connexion with him".[19] This is why, Cohon thinks, the common point of view is the same for every reflective moral agent.[20] In other words, according to Hume, the common point of view leads each and every person to the same moral judgment.

One can respond to the objection I raised above against Hume by indicating that it takes each and every sentiment we have when we reflect on a morally significant situation as a moral sentiment without making the required distinction that Cohon's reading makes between situated sentiments and properly moral sentiments. According to this response, Hume does not treat every point of view in which we have some sentiment as a moral point of view. There is a

14 Rachel Cohon, "The Common Point of View in Hume's Ethics," *Philosophy and Phenomenological Research* 57 (2007): 834.
15 Hume, *Treatise*, 372.
16 Ibid., 374.
17 Cohon, "The Common Point of View," 836.
18 Ibid., 837.
19 Hume, *Treatise*, 377.
20 Cohon, "The Common Point of View," 840.

moral perspective we each take to make moral judgments. Therefore, Hume's ethical theory is capable of providing us with a ground on the basis of which we can engage in moral dialogues whatever our situated sentiments are. The common point of view constitutes exactly this ground for inclusive moral dialogues. One could also continue by arguing that since the common point of view is the same for each person: if the disagreeing parties in a moral dialogue take the common point of view, they will reach the same moral judgment and resolve their disagreement. For this reason, you and your friend in our scenario above should take the common point of view if you are to make moral judgments; and when you take it, you will resolve your disagreement.

The first point to note about this response is that two individuals may take what Hume thinks is the proper moral point of view, but still disagree with each other by making contrary moral judgments. To see this, remember Hume's idea that when one takes the common point of view, one reflects on the effects that a particular character has on the person who possesses it, or on those who have some direct relationship with that person. If we grant the idea that "once we do adopt the common point of view, our moral sentiments respond to what we imagine", by taking the common point of view, one might imagine that an action has a great negative impact on those around the individual who performs it, while another person imagines that the same action is extremely beneficial both to the individual herself and to her social group.[21] For instance, consider gay marriage. Reflecting on this question and imagining its possible effects, someone might conclude that gay marriage is evil because it has a destructive influence upon the institution of the family and thus the people around those who are in a gay marriage will be influenced negatively. However, another person may form the judgment, from the common point of view, that gay marriage would be beneficial and produce pleasure not only for individuals who want the right to gay marriage but also for those who have a relationship with gay couples, since gay marriage may be taken as an expression of freedom and societies that allow gay marriage tend to create a tolerant atmosphere for their members.

More importantly, given the fact that individuals who take up the common point of view might disagree with each other, how can they engage in an inclusive moral dialogue and discussion without encountering argument-stoppers? It might be argued, on the basis of Cohon's reading, that individuals who disagree with each other in a moral dialogue can discuss the effects of a certain action on the person who undertakes it, or on the people around that person, because the common point of view focuses on these effects and they can avoid any appeal to

21 Ibid., 846.

situated sentiments that lead to argument-stoppers. Therefore, one of the disagreeing parties in a moral dialogue can point out to the other party that the action they reflect on would have a negative or positive effect on the person herself and those around her and convince him by indicating the possible consequences of the action. The other party can accept that judgment or reject it by arguing that the action would not have the predicted consequences. In this way, one can argue, we can engage in a moral dialogue without argument-stoppers and try to resolve our moral disagreements even though our initial sentiments conflict with each other.

Hume's ethical theory may enable us to engage in a moral dialogue and try to resolve our disagreements by reflecting on the effects of an action from the common point of view. However, this response is actually incompatible with Hume's explicit anti-rationalist thesis that our moral judgments are not conclusions of reason but arise from sentiments. One reason why Hume thinks that moral judgments are not conclusions of reason is that moral judgments do not reflect matters of fact, which are the proper objects of causal reasoning. According to the model of moral dialogue engendered by this response, individuals who disagree on a morally significant situation reflect on the consequences of an action on a particular person or group of persons and make causal inferences about the possible effects of the action in question. Therefore, their moral judgments are products of causal reasoning. This flatly contradicts Hume's basic idea that "vice and virtue are not matters of fact, whose existence we can infer by reason".[22]

Speaking the Moral Language as a Requirement of Moral Dialogue

Another response to my objection against Hume's theory of moral judgment can be developed on the basis of Henning Jensen's interpretation of Hume's moral theory. In this reading, Hume is presented as a theoretician of moral language who is "extremely preoccupied with the disagreements which occur in our sentiments and beliefs".[23] Jensen criticises the view that the sole aim of Hume's ethical theory is to provide a psychological account of the nature of our moral judgments. He thinks that if this narrow reading of Hume's ethical theory is rejected and a broader view is adopted, we see that "the broader concerns of [Hume's]

22 Hume, *Treatise*, 301.
23 Henning Jensen, "Hume on Moral Agreement," *Mind* 86 (1977): 499.

ethical theory forced him at key points [...] to deal with issues which go beyond a purely psychological approach and which relate to problems involving conceptual analysis and moral language".[24] In other words, according to Jensen, in addition to providing a psychological account of how we make moral judgments, Hume also develops a theory of moral language.

One of the key elements of the theory of moral language that Jensen attributes to Hume is the idea that we must use the moral language to make a moral judgment. For this reason, the requirements of the moral language also set limits to what can be considered a moral judgment. Jensen argues that, according to Hume's theory, "to employ moral language is to be committed to setting restrictions on what we are prepared to regard as a moral term or moral judgment".[25] Jensen's reading seems reasonable. For instance, Hume states the following:

> When a man denominates another his *enemy*, his *rival*, his *antagonist*, his *adversary*, he is understood to speak the language of self-love, and to express sentiments, peculiar to himself, and arising from his particular circumstances and situation. But when he bestows on any man the epithets of *vicious* or *odious* or *depraved*, he then speaks another language, and expresses sentiments, in which, he expects, all his audience are to concur with him.[26]

On the basis of passages like this, Jensen argues that Hume has a theory of moral language and he articulates some of the requirements that this language involves. The crucial point for our purposes is: if we accept that Hume does have a theory of moral language which must be used to make moral judgments, we may think that, in a moral dialogue where the parties disagree on a morally significant situation, one of the parties may not be using the moral language at all. In such a dialogue, the other party may note to her that she is not making a moral judgment because the language she uses is not the moral language, and that if she uses the moral language by satisfying its criteria, then she can be included in the moral dialogue and the dialogue can proceed within the boundaries and rules of the moral language. Therefore, one can respond to my objection against Hume's ethical theory by arguing that Hume has a theory of moral language with a set of restrictions on what is to be considered a moral judgment, and this can provide a ground for an inclusive moral dialogue between individuals who have a moral disagreement.

---

24 Ibid., 500.
25 Ibid., 502.
26 David Hume, *An Enquiry Concerning the Principle of Morals*, ed. Jerome B. Schneewind (Indianapolis, NJ: Hackett, 1983), 75.

Jensen believes Hume's theory of moral language has the following requirement. Jensen argues that to make moral judgments "our judgments must be universalizable. And in so judging we are required to be impartial [...] Finally moral language is described as employing certain terms such as 'virtue', 'vice', and 'justice' whose very function is to express praise or blame".[27] Hence, in order to make a genuine moral judgment, one needs to make universalisable judgments with notions such as virtue from an impartial point of view. It seems reasonable to say that the requirements that Jensen puts forward as the requirements of the moral language are among the requirements that we are generally committed to when we make or criticise moral judgments. We often reject moral judgments because they reflect a partial perspective or because they are not universalisable in the sense that they express "purely private sentiments occasioned by some particular circumstance at some particular time".[28] However, the problem for Hume's ethical theory here is that the requirements of the moral language seem to be authoritative regardless of our sentiments or how we feel about a morally significant situation. If Jensen's reading is correct, Hume articulates a conception of moral language which has a series of requirements that must be met in order to make moral judgments, whatever sentiments or feelings we have. For instance, whether a moral judgment has the character of universalisability and is made from an impartial perspective is totally independent from what anyone feels about the object of that judgment. A partial moral judgment does not simply become impartial when we develop negative feelings about its object. This shows that at least an important part of the basis of our moral judgments is completely independent of how we feel or what our sentiments are. However, as we saw above, according to Hume's sentimentalist anti-rationalism, "moral distinctions depend entirely on certain peculiar sentiments of pain and pleasure"[29] and "the very *feeling* constitutes our praise or admiration".[30]

There are also other interpreters who read Hume's theory of judgment in similar ways. For instance, Gabriele Taylor states the following:

> The [moral] epithets we apply are then not just a function of the sentiments we feel, for they do not always vary in accordance with the intensity of our feelings. But if so then there must be something in the light of which we correct either our feelings or our judgment. If we can have doubts about the appropriateness of our feelings, as we must, if we can

27 Jensen, "Moral Agreement," 502.
28 Ibid., 502.
29 Hume, *Treatise*, 367.
30 Ibid., 303.

> modify our judgments irrespective of them, then we must operate with some *norm* telling us what responses are appropriate or natural in what situations, and whatever the basis of such a norm (majority view, consensus of interests) it provides us with some standard for judging emotional reaction.[31]

This reading is even more obviously problematic for the same reason. If we grant that there are norms for moral judgment which we can and should use to modify our emotional reactions towards morally significant situations, and which are independent of these reactions, then we need to disregard Hume's sentimentalism about moral judgment and distinctions. It is also noteworthy that Taylor develops his reading against Peter Jones, who thinks that there is only limited opportunity for rational discussion and dialogue in Hume's theory of moral judgment. According to Jones' interpretation, Hume believes that there is a causal process at the basis of moral judgment and the first component of this process is constituted by sense impressions of external states of affairs.[32] These sense impressions cause sentiments, which in turn cause moral judgments. Jones argues that, on Hume's theory, moral judgment, rational discussion and dialogue can take place only at the first stage of the causal process, where sense impressions about a morally significant object are formed. The rest of the process does not have any room for rational discussion. We might believe that a theory of moral judgment which has an extensive space for rational dialogue is superior, and think that the theory represented by Taylor's reading is more promising than Jones', but the problem is that Jones' reading seems to better represent Hume's sentiment-based moral theory.

Turning back to the first response, a model of moral dialogue that is based not on the notion of a moral language but on that of the common point of view faces the same problem. As I mentioned, one might argue that, in order to make a genuine moral judgment, one has to take the common point of view. This would entail certain requirements that our judgments need to meet in order for us to make a moral judgment, because taking the common point of view demands a certain way of reflecting on morally significant situations. And we know that Hume argued that the common point of view is a perspective that is *steady* and *general*.[33] Therefore, according to Hume's notion of the common point of view, generality and steadiness are among the criteria that a judgment needs

31 Gabriele Taylor, "Hume' Views of Moral Judgments," *Philosophical Quarterly* 21 (1971): 65 [emphasis mine].
32 Peter Jones, "Another Look at Hume's Views of Aesthetic and Moral Judgments," *Philosophical Quarterly* 20 (1970): 59.
33 Hume, *Treatise*, 372.

to satisfy in order to be considered a moral judgment. In other words, when we make a moral judgment, we make it in the light of certain standards that reflect the character of a certain type of judgment. However, this entails that we are guided by our concern with taking a certain point of view in our moral judgments by fulfilling its criteria of generality and steadiness, even if we have no sentiment about that point of view nor its requirements. This means again that at least part of how we make moral judgments is to be accounted for independently of sentiments.

Kant's Principle-Based Ethical Theory and the Possibility of an Inclusive Moral Dialogue[34]

A moral theory based on a principle that specifies a procedure through which we can give and demand reasons for our moral judgments, regardless of our feelings, does not face the objection I raised against Hume's sentiment-based theory. By following such a principle, a moral theory recognises a fundamental fact about our moral lives. In our moral lives, we convince each other and make moral judgments by critically discussing our reasons for or against possible courses of action in different situations without appealing to how we feel about them. Therefore, a moral theory based on a principle by which these practices can take place satisfies a demand created by our daily moral interactions. As I argued above, Hume's ethical theory does not provide us with a ground that we can use to engage in a moral dialogue independently of our feelings, as he construes these judgments as being based on feelings that may significantly vary among individuals and cultures. In this section, I argue that Kant's moral philosophy does not face this problem since it omits justificatory appeals to subjective affective mental states such as sentiments, and develops a principle by which moral agents can give and ask for reasons for their moral judgments.

The central question to my argument is: what kind of a moral agent is a *rational* moral agent? In addressing this question, I appeal to Kant's idea of a purely rational will, which enables me to point out some of the essential characteristics of a rational moral agent. Identifying these essential characteristics will in turn allow us to figure out the moral principle that actual rational agents should follow in their moral dialogues. In a passage on the "fundamental law of practical reason" Kant says the following:

34 My interpretation of how Kant approaches moral judgment in this section is based to a large extent on Kenneth R. Westphal's reading. See Westphal, *Natural Law*.

> pure *reason, practical of itself,* is [...] immediately lawgiving. The will is thought as independent of empirical conditions and hence, as a pure will, as determined *by the mere form of law,* and this determining ground is regarded as the supreme condition of all maxims. The thing is strange enough, and has nothing like it in all the rest of our practical cognition.[35]

Here Kant begins by telling us one of his major claims about moral motivation. Practical reason can provide us with sufficient motivational grounds for action. Practical reason has this motivational power because it is capable of generating a pure *a priori* moral law, but this moral law is a *formal* moral law. The idea of a formal law is based on Kant's distinction between the form and matter of a practical principle. Kant thinks that the matter of a practical principle is the representation of an object of an affective state such as desire.[36] He believes that the fundamental principle of morality is not a principle with a material component. It only has a formal component. The moral law does not assume any empirically given object that can be desired by a moral agent.

Pure practical reason generates its practical law by excluding any empirical affective state. The reason for this exclusion is that a purely rational moral agent is an agent who "omits all empirical desires, motives, urges, inclinations, or preferences and all considerations of the agent's capacities and resources for achieving ends".[37] In other words, a purely rational moral agent does not determine itself to act on the basis of any empirical factor that pertains to a particular individual agent. Therefore, such a moral agent does not act according to what a desire, inclination, feeling or a sentiment would dictate.

If this is the case, then what exactly is the principle that a purely rational agent acts on? Nothing other than the categorical imperative: "Act only in accordance with that maxim through which you can at the same time will that it become a universal law".[38] Kant thinks that this principle actually takes the form of an imperative when it is applied to beings like us that can be determined to act by empirically-given motives, but when it is understood as the practical law of a purely rational being, it is a descriptive principle. In other words, the fundamental principle of pure practical reason describes how a purely rational moral agent acts. A purely rational moral agent always acts in such a way that he is guided by maxims that can also always count as universal laws. The crucial

35 Immanuel Kant, *Practical Philosophy*, trans. Mary J. Gregor (Cambridge: Cambridge University Press, 1999), 164.
36 Kant, *Practical Philosophy*, 155.
37 Westphal, *Natural Law*, 68.
38 Kant, *Practical Philosophy*, 73.

point here is that in order for a maxim to be counted as a principle of universal legislation, it must be capable of being followed not only by the particular moral agent who holds it but also by all other rational beings that it universally applies to. Therefore, practical rationality demands that action-guiding maxims be capable of being endorsed by all rational agents in the relevant situations.[39]

An essential part of what it is to act on the basis of maxims that can be expected to be followed by all rational beings is to justify one's actions by appealing only to considerations that can be endorsed by other rational beings. In other words, a purely rational moral agent justifies his actions in terms of those considerations that all rational parties can be expected to endorse. This means that a pure rational moral agent is an agent who justifies his actions without making reference to subjective states of awareness, including sentiments, because these states cannot be expected to be shared by all rational moral agents. As mentioned above, it is perfectly possible to have moral agents who have conflicting moral feelings in relation to an action. Their mutual endorsement would occur solely out of contingent factors, including the social context of upbringing.

Now, our question is whether Kant's moral philosophy can provide us with a ground for an inclusive moral dialogue in which no one is excluded because she possesses a contrary feeling. The answer is yes: purely rational moral agents justify their actions on the basis of considerations that every relevant rational party can be expected to endorse. The crucial implication is that, as long as a particular moral agent is a rational moral agent, she justifies her moral judgments by appealing only to considerations that can be expected to be mutually endorsable. Hence, as rational moral agents, when we engage in a moral dialogue involving a conflict between our moral judgments, we follow the principle that we appeal only to reasons that can be expected to be endorsed by each party in the dialogue. This principle rules out appeals to feelings as a ground of our judgments. Feelings and sentiments cannot be expected to be shared by each rational party.

Because it develops a moral principle which omits appeals to feelings by demanding that our moral judgments be mutually endorsable, Kant's moral philosophy lays a common basis for different moral agents who have different social backgrounds and different sets of sentiments towards the same action to engage

---

39 Westphal, *Natural Law*, 85. See also Onora O'Neill, "Kant and the Social Contract Tradition," in *Kant's Political Theory: Interpretations and Applications*, ed. Elisabeth Ellis (University Park: Pennsylvania State University Press, 2012), and Onora O'Neill, *Constructions of Reason* (Cambridge: Cambridge University Press, 1989).

in a moral conversation.[40] According to Kant's moral philosophy, the fact that the parties in a moral dialogue are from different cultures with different moral feelings is in itself simply not relevant. As long as they appeal to mutually endorsable reasons for their claims as rational beings, they are included in the same moral dialogue.[41]

40 It might be argued that even though the presence of a general principle in Kant's theory of moral judgment may provide a basis for rational moral discussion, it actually creates a problem. One can claim that appealing to a general principle such as the categorical imperative in our moral deliberations distracts our moral judgments because general principles cannot account for the distinctive features of the different situations where moral discussion and dialogue take place. In other words, introduction of a general principle as a common ground for moral dialogue seems to have important costs. The crucial point here is that a moral theory assigning a central place to a general principle does not mean that the person who is using the principle to make a moral judgment will overlook the particular features of the situation. She can and we do make our judgments by using a range of prior information about the characteristics of the situations we deal with. Our general principles are used within the context of a series of morally relevant information about the details of different situations and this is not incompatible with Kant's theory of moral judgment. Barbara Herman forcefully develops these points much further by making a distinction between *moral rules* and *moral principles* in Kantian moral theory. See Barbara Herman, "The Practice of Moral Judgment," *The Journal of Philosophy* 82 (1985): 416.

41 Kant's rationalist moral theory and Hume's sentimentalism have been compared in many different respects. In his paper "Moral Rationalism vs. Moral Sentimentalism: Is Morality More Like Math or Beauty?" Michael B. Gill provides a broader historical comparison of the rationalist and sentimentalist traditions in ethics. As he notes, the moral rationalists of early modern philosophy relied on the concept of *self-evidence*. They thought that morality rests on principles that verify themselves without appeal to any further principle (Michael B. Gill, "Moral Rationalism vs. Moral Sentimentalism: Is Morality More Like Math or Beauty?," *Philosophy Compass* 2 (2007): 17). One very interesting aspect of the relation between early modern moral rationalism and Kant's moral rationalism is that the concept of self-evidence does not play the same central role in Kant's moral philosophy. Rationalist moral theories that appeal to self-evidence as the justificatory basis of basic moral principles face the same problem as Hume's theory of moral judgment. David Ross' intuitionism is a good example. Ross argues that "... that an act, *qua* fulfilling a promise, or *qua* returning services rendered, or *qua* promoting the good of others, or *qua* promoting the virtue or insight of the agent is *prima facie* right, is *self-evident*". David Ross, *The Right and the Good*, ed. Philip Stratton Lake (Oxford: Clarendon Press, 2007), 29. The problem with Ross' intuitionism is that appeals to self-evidence works as argument-stoppers in rational discussions where justifications are given and demanded for our basic moral principles. In a moral dialogue, a moral judgment that is taken to be self-evidently true by one of the parties may be rejected by the other party, again with an appeal to self-evidence.

Conclusion

This article is an attempt to show that even though Hume's naturalist account of moral judgment may look like a better approach to moral judgment than the rationalist alternatives, including Kant's, it is incapable of showing how we can engage in moral dialogues given that we are members of different cultures and societies that promote different and often conflicting sentiments about moral problems. If we construe the nature of moral judgment in terms of affective mental states such as sentiments, then we had better give up on the possibility of engaging in moral dialogues about social and political problems that would include all concerned parties from different societies.

As mentioned in the second section, we expect moral philosophy to provide us with a basis on which we can address moral and political problems that concern all of us even though we belong to different societies with different cultures. Kant's rationalist account of moral judgment is much more promising in providing us that common basis. It is in this sense superior to Hume's ethical theory. Because it can provide this basis, Kant's moral philosophy also gives us reason to be optimistic about the possibility of engaging in moral dialogues despite all the differences in our emotional reactions towards moral problems. As a rationalist account, Kant's theory of moral judgment gives a central place to reason and this emphasis on reason is also an emphasis on something that is common to each and every one of us. However, reason is not common to all of us in the same way that sentiments are. Reason is common to all of us in that it is the source of a normative principle that applies to and should be applied by each human being regardless of her affective states. When we follow that principle, we appeal to rational considerations that another moral agent can be expected to endorse, not to affective argument-stoppers.

Fabio Mengali

8 Neither Citizens nor Slaves: The Aporetic Condition of Modern Citizenship

Introduction

"The working man can become a gentleman", asserts Alfred Marshall quoted by Thomas H. Marshall in the introduction to his cycle of classes collected in *Citizenship and Social Class*.[1] T. H. Marshall's point is to legitimise the role of work as a rationale, and a historical lever, by which citizenship progressively becomes universal and inclusive. By defining citizenship as a three-axis status, that is, civil, political, and social, he argues that the inclusion of work within the boundaries of a citizen's rights potentially bestows the full membership of a political community upon each and every inhabitant. This is why, in the twentieth century, all three axes (the possibility to be rightly represented in a judicial court, access to the political decision-making process, the benefit of social rights) were finally reunited after being separated by the early-modern State-nation. At the beginning of Modern history, Marshall continues, there were just a few full members of the Commonwealth in England, all low-class individuals being left aside from political and social rights; they could only benefit from the *habeas corpus* principle and, though not in all cases, the right to residence, that is, the civic axis of citizenship. Yet the civic consideration of labourers and servants stemmed from the need to free labour from its feudal constraints, thus realising the theoretical discourse on compacts and free will of the contractors. A poor labourer could enter an agreement with a master on purpose, i. e. without any violent or authoritarian imposition. In addition, labour was a universal ability within a frame of rising capitalism, therefore it founded a community on a universal basis, overcoming status differences. Marshall identifies the apex of this process in seventeenth-century England, given the historical facts occurred between the Great Rebellion and the Glorious Revolution. The subsequent revolutions and class struggles at the dawn of the Contemporary Age (French Revolution, nineteenth-century urban revolts in Europe) marked this very path.

The gaining of political and social rights can be understood as a fulfilment of the idea of universality, which was practically lacking in the past due to the

1 Thomas Humphrey Marshall, *Citizenship and Social Class* (Cambridge: Cambridge University Press, 1950), 4.

https://doi.org/10.1515/9783110679861-009

exclusion of poor and low classes. Notwithstanding the general tendency, Marshall admits that the increasingly inclusive citizenship dwells on a terrain rife with capitalism and the structure of the class system. The liberating role of labour relies on the following principle: being a dependent worker provides the right to welfare and a minimum for social reproduction, reducing the gulf between classes. Put briefly, the aim of Marshall's proposal is to harmonise the citizenship-capital conflict through labour, upon which all the divergences may coincide. Working activity represents a universal interest, both for gaining a surplus thanks to added value (on the part of capitalists) and for accessing welfare (on the part of workers). "The labourers have nothing to stir them up to be serviceable but their wants", states Marshall, quoting Bernard de Mandeville.[2] It follows that being a citizen – a full member of a community – means being a worker, otherwise he[3] might incur the loss of the whole array of citizenship rights.

It is impossible to deny two elements of Marshall's analysis: on the one hand, the conceptual and material formation of citizenship upon exclusion; on the other hand, the assumption of labour and its pivotal role in the making of the liberal, modern citizen. Currently, in the wake of the political, social and conceptual crises in Europe and Western societies, political theory and conceptual history must make an urgent inquiry regarding the nexus between citizenship and labour. For not only is this link contained in legal and constitutional laws,[4] it is increasingly enhanced by a general tendency in recent measures and policies, at least in Europe.[5] The investigation of this link throughout the ge-

---

2 Bernard de Mandeville, *The Fable of the Bees*, quoted in Marshall, *Citizenship and Social Class*, 79.

3 I opt for the masculine subject when I have to make a comparison between workers and freeman with regard to citizenship, as I take up the historical prejudice of thinkers towards women.

4 As an example, it suffices to say that the first article in the Italian Constitution establishes that "Italy is a Republic founded on labour." For this very reason, in a sense welfare State and citizenship rights are submitted to the potential working activity of all the inhabitants of the peninsula.

5 Italian law, as well as other judicial systems in Europe and outside the continent, guarantees visas to migrants sponsored by an employer, that is, migrants can legally stay in the territory if they demonstrate that they are labourers first; something very similar can be said to happen to refugees applying for asylum: Germany opened its doors in 2015 before the possible income that high-educated migrants could create in the country. Furthermore, more and more laws concerning the educational system (in France and Italy) are introducing mandatory hours for traineeships and stages in high schools and universities, thus rooting even more strictly the education of the future citizen in working activity. Generally speaking, the conception behind the welfare State, as formulated by John Maynard Keynes, for example, rests on the exchange between labour-force and employer. Citizens do not have citizenship rights before being labourers or potential ones.

nealogy of its conceptual birth is both a matter of values and of methodology, the latter being essential to show the occurrence of the inclusion/exclusion device in the history of ideas and concepts.

Marshall's perspective contributes to certain readings of social and intellectual history, in which the course of events has affirmed equality and collective freedom in Europe over time. The evolutionist interpretation of history, then, presumes that after many historical events the dominant class gave up its privileges and extended citizenship rights to other inhabitants. In the first place, this point of view implies that the concepts of labour, freedom, and citizenship as they were conceived in early-modern England are exempt from critical inquiry because, once they are granted to everyone, they enlarge citizenship possibilities. Likewise, the device of exclusion must be nuanced. Not only were workers, poor, and women deprived of the right to be full members of Commonwealth, they were a constant reference for the formation of citizenship itself. Rather than focusing the study on the outsiders' position, it may be profitable to look at these outsiders as a segment of society maintaining an internal relationship with full citizens. It seems that in Modern England dependent labourers, waged or daily-employed, underwent an inclusion/exclusion mechanism, or, better put, a *differential inclusion.*[6] Thus the nexus between labour and citizenship, which is historically determined, may present many contradictions and aporias if not deeply analyzed. I maintain that, in taking labour as the new pillar of universal citizenship, forms of social hierarchies affecting equality and freedom (that is, the essential core of citizenship) are still involved. These hierarchies are not exhaustively explained by the class system and the economic disparity between capitalists and workers.

The "differential inclusion" mechanism readily emerges from an account of the philosophical and intellectual debate in seventeenth-century England concerning citizenship. Critics often misguide the reading of the texts by the authors presented here, stating that republican and liberal thinkers upheld a universal, masculine suffrage to be the new status of citizenship. In particular, this thesis is

---

6 The meaning of the expression can be inferred in various books and courses of Michel Foucault's. To quote some: *Discipline and Punishment: The Birth of Prison*, trans. Alan Sheridan (London: Allen Lane, Penguin, 1977); *The History of Sexuality, Vol. I: An Introduction*, trans. Robert Hurley (New York: Pantheon Books, 1978); *Society Must Be Defended. Lectures at the Collège de France 1975–1976*, trans. David Macey (New York: Picador, 2003); *Security, Territory, Population. Lectures at the Collège de France 1977–1978*, trans. Graham Burchell (London: Palgrave Macmillan, 2007); *The Birth of Biopolitcs. Lectures at the Collège de France 1978–1979*, trans. Graham Burchell (London: Palgrave Macmillan, 2008).

attributed to Locke,[7] whom I will refer to the most in this essay. A recall of the conceptual environment of the time, however, favours more thorough research and avoids the recurrence of the "exclusion interpretations". Accordingly, I shall begin by showing the consideration of labourers in the Putney Debates, where, aside from slight differences, Independents concurred with Levellers on the political status of dependent workers. I shall then move on to a discussion over the specific position of servants and labourers in Algernon Sidney's *Discourses Concerning Government.* Following these reflections, I shall put forward an interpretation of Locke's viewpoint on the same topic. As I shall show, these insights offer an overview of the change of the historical regard towards waged labour, moving from a strict exclusion to a "differential inclusion" for governmental purposes. In conclusion, I will suggest considering dependent workers in these authors' works as, in Isin Engin's words, "strangers" interfacing with full citizens at a *distant proximity.* I believe that, through this lens, it may be easier to detect power relationships, often overlooked by evolutionary theorists of citizenship, between equal members of a community and their perdurance to the present day. Back in seventeenth-century England, dependent workers (as well as women and children) were neither citizens nor slaves: they were entitled to certain judicial protections and freedoms, but they were expected to obey a master, because they were denied personal autonomy, along with political voice. Nowadays, for Western constitutions, we are all equal and free citizens. It does not follow, though, that social hierarchies have disappeared.

The Exclusionary Putney Debates

The Putney Debates should be addressed as an essential source.[8] The interventions of the New Agents, although far from representing a unified voice, advocat-

---

7 I refer to the following works: Willmore Kendall, *Locke and the Doctrine of Majority-Rule* (Champaign: University of Illinois Press, 1960); Richard Ashcraft, *Locke's Two Treatises of Government* (London: Unwin Hyman Ltd, 1987); Id., "Revolutionary Politics and Locke's *Two Treatises of Government:* Radicalism and Lockean Political Thought," *Political Theory* 8 (1980): 429–486; James Tully, *An Approach to Political Philosophy: Locke in Contexts* (Cambridge: Cambridge University Press, 1993); Id., *A Discourse on Property: John Locke and His Adversaries* (Cambridge: Cambridge University Press, 2006); Judith Richards, Lotte Mulligan and John Graham, "Property and People: Political Usages of Locke and Some Contemporaries," *Journal of the History of Ideas* 42 (1981): 29–51.

8 Arthur Sutherland Pigott Woodhouse, ed., *Puritanism and Liberty, being the Army Debates (1647–49), from the Clarke Manuscripts with Supplementary Documents. Part I: The Putney Debates* (Chicago: University of Chicago Press, 1951).

ed parliamentarism and the superiority of the House of Commons, elected by all adult males. As for the historical frame, it suffices to say that the New Agents were bringing about an internal claim in the New Model Army, the defence of the king and the maintenance of the old Parliament being at stake.[9] The Independents' refutation of the Levellers' arguments relied on the tradition recalling the Common Law and the necessity of property, whose absence would throw the kingdom into chaos. Cromwell asked what would happen if the majority of people choose representatives in opposition to the Constitution of the country. According to him, the multitude lacked the "temper" and "spirit" to be accountable for and worthy of full membership. Apart from the contention over the nature of compacts and duty, the Independents' stance was connected with the endangerment of property. If the people contended with the constituted power, i.e. the King and the Parliament, they could overturn the essential agreement of the country: the institution and defence of (Lords') individual property.[10] Referring to the dissolution of ownership, Cromwell said: "take away that, I do not know what ground there is of anything you can call any man's right. I would very fain, gentlemen, or any other do account the right you have to anything in England".[11] The sentence echoed the Hobbesian theory asserting the foundation of property in the State, as opposed to its existence in the state of nature. It should be emphasised that the notion of property stood for individual rights, that is, the distribution of one's own right a person is entitled to depending on their class, gender, and ethnicity. Respect for property corresponded to the exact knowledge of the extent of one's own citizenship agency and freedom. All of this being absent, the State risked coming back to the war of the state of nature. Insofar as social order had to be guaranteed, not everyone could be "equally considered". The Independent Ireton pushed forward another topic to reinforce this argument: that "poor" and "mean" people did not have a "permanent fixed interest"[12] in the country. Countering Colonel Rainsborough,[13] who

9 The New Agents imposed the debates following the publication of a pamphlet, titled *The Case of the Army*, reproaching the leaders of the Army with their practical surrender to the Crown after the negotiation with Charles I. Among the New Agents, there were Colonel Rainsborough and his brother William Rainsborough, John Wildman, Petty, Captain Sexby, and Hugh Peters, together with other rank-and-file soldiers. The most prominent Independents were Ireton and Cromwell.
10 Ireton immediately clarified the principal fear of nobility: "For here is the case of the most fundamental part of the constitution of the kingdom, which if you take away, you take away all by that," Woodhouse, *Puritanism and Liberty*, 115.
11 Woodhouse, *Puritanism and Liberty*, 90.
12 Ibid., 112.
13 What the radical Leveller said: "I desired that those that had engaged in it [might be included]. For really I think that the poorest he that is in England hath a life to live, as the greatest he;

stressed the mandatory elective right for everyone to ensure the trust between the State and its inhabitants, Ireton expressed the English common sense about labourers and servants:

> For my part, I think it is no right at all. I think that no person hath a right to an interest or share in the disposing of the affairs of the kingdom, and in determining or choosing those that shall determine what laws we shall be ruled by here – no person hath a right to this, that hath not a permanent fixed interest in this kingdom, and those persons together are properly the represented of this kingdom, and consequently are [also] to make up the representers of this kingdom, who taken together do comprehend whatsoever is of real or permanent interest in the kingdom. And I am sure otherwise I cannot tell what any man can say why a foreigner coming in amongst us [...] why they should not as well lay claim to it as any other.[14]

The analogy between foreigners living in the country and people with no interest was a very common rhetorical move. Both of them had the right to exist under the law of England, while only the natural English-born person could benefit from the right to residence. Who were the inhabitants deprived of a permanent interest? Dependent workers and the poor, as well as vagrants. Ireton spoke about "freemen without dependence" as the only ones worthy of the privilege of citizenship. The word "freeman"[15] exactly expounded the line drawn in the social space of a community to build up the conception of citizenship. Inasmuch as the full membership had to be "fixed upon a place" and find limitations,[16] a boundary along the discrimination line dependence/independence was needed. Only independent men possessing a freehold or a commerce bound to a corporation were free, meaning that they were "not given up to the will of others" be-

---

and therefore truly, sir, I think it's clear, that every man that is to live under a government ought first by his own consent to put himself under that government; and I do think that the poorest man in England is not at all bound in a strict sense to that government that he hath not had a voice to put himself under; and I am confident that, when I have heard the reasons against it, something will be said to answer those reasons, insomuch that I should doubt whether hee was an Englishman or no, that should doubt of these thing," Woodhouse, *Puritanism and Liberty*, 111.

14 Woodhouse, *Puritanism and Liberty*, 111.

15 Many scholars point out the importance of the historical meaning of the word. For instance, see Marshall, *Citizenship and Social Class*; Crawford Brough Macpherson, *The Political Theory of Possessive Individualism: Hobbes to Locke* (Oxford: Oxford University Press, 1962); Ron Becker, "The Ideological Commitment of John Locke: Freemen and Servants in the *Two Treatises of Government*," *History of Political Thought* 4 (1992): 631–656; Maria Luisa Pesante, *Come servi. Figure del lavoro salariato dal diritto naturale all'economia politica* (Milan: FrancoAngeli, 2013).

16 This was a counter-argument against the Levellers, who recalled natural law and natural equality in order to extend citizenship. The independents held that, in so doing, every human being was supposed to be granted citizenship rights beyond national borders.

cause they had all means to sustain themselves and to enrich the nation. Liberty came with property because being a freeholder meant being "[a man] freed from dependence upon others", [17] no matter how the inequality of property was decided in the threshold passage from the state of nature to civil society. The clarification of the concept of "the English people" demonstrated a commitment on the part of the conservatives to exclude aliens and servants, that is, labourers. The cultural prejudice towards servants stemmed from the assumption based on them being accustomed to submission, hence inept at free choices and decisions:

> If you do extend the latitude [of the constitution so far] that any man shall have a voice in election who has not that interest in this kingdom that is permanent and fixed, who hath not that interest upon which he may have his freedom in this kingdom without dependence, you will put it into the hands of men to choose, [not] of men [desirous] to preserve their liberty, [but of men] who will give it away.[18]

Cromwell restated the point by asserting that "servants, while servants, are not included". The exclusion of servants seemed to be so rooted in the intellectual structures of that time that eventually even the Leveller Petty failed to support his previous stance on male suffrage:

> I conceive the reason why we would exclude apprentices, or servants, or those that take alms, is because they depend upon the will of other men and should be afraid to displease [them]. For servants and apprentices, they are included in their masters, and so for those that receive alms from door to door; but if there be any general way taken for those that are not [so] bound [to the will of other men], it would be well.[19]

A servant did not enjoy a full position among citizens insofar as their will was implied by *paterfamilias*, that is, the landowner who was at the same time husband, father, and master.[20] Of course, servants and daily labourers were considered native-born English, thus they could benefit from *habeas corpus*[21] and the

17 Ireton in Woodhouse, *Puritanism and Liberty*, 134.

18 Woodhouse, *Puritanism and Liberty*, 134.

19 Ibid., 135.

20 Carole Pateman, *The Sexual Contract* (Stanford: Stanford University Press, 1988); Becker, "The Ideological Commitment of John Locke"; Daniela Gobetti, "Sfera domestica e sfera politica nella riflessione del pensiero politico britannico del Settecento," *Annali della Fondazione Luigi Einaudi* 17 (1983): 291–332.

21 It is profitable to recall the origins of the *habeas corpus* principle within England. Articles number 36 and 13 of *Magna Charta* stated that no man could be forced to pay under torture, and even servants were not required to work under unjust circumstances (i. e. to repay an unpaid

opportunity to establish their residence within the realm. Their condition was not tantamount to that of slaves, who were forbidden any rights by the judicial system and political institutions. It is valuable to highlight the frequent employment of such words as "slaves", "slavery", etc. whenever a debater was keen to define Stuarts' absolutism, whereas they never referred to it as servitude. By doing this, the participants in the debate conceived of servitude as compatible with the new political order engendered by the Great Rebellion; by contrast, they reviled slavery and associated it with the long-endured submission of the people to the Crown. The *Agreement of the People*, which can be considered the result of the negotiation in Putney, opened with this reference and continued by establishing that the English people were supposed to elect the representatives by consent of the majority because this prerogative belonged to their native rights.[22] Whom the expression "the freeborn people of England" referred to is ambiguous, even though it is quite plain that, according to the last version of the document, it did not encompass the entire male population. Servants and alms-receivers were explicitly barred from the electorate.[23] The uncertainty lies in whether waged workers and other dependants met citizenship requisites in the eyes of the debaters. Although critics are divided over the solution to this quandary, I hold that by saying "servants" the writers of the *Agreement* (Levellers too) likely meant all those submitting to a master in exchange for a wage or protection, including labourers.[24]

---

tax). Cf. "Full Translation of the Original 1225 Edition of *Magna Charta*," The British Library, published 28 July 2014, https://www.bl.uk/magna-carta/articles/magna-carta-english-translation.

22 "An Agreement of the People, as presented by the Council of the Army (28 October 1647)," Constitution Society, https://www.constitution.org/lev/eng_lev_07.htm

23 The version signed by Levellers John Lilburne, William Walwyn, Thomas Prince, and Richard Overtone, "An Agreement of the Free People of England. Tendered as a Peace Offering to Distress the Nation (1 May 1649)," Constitution Society, https://www.constitution.org/eng/agreepeo.htm: "the Supreme Authority of England and the Territories therewith incorporate, shall be and reside henceforward in a Representative of the People consisting of four hundred persons, but no more; in the choice of whom (according to natural right) all men of the age of one and twenty yeers and upwards (*not being servants, or receiving alms*, or having served in the late King in Arms or voluntary Contributions) shall have their voices; and be capable of being elected to that Supreme Trust those who served the King being disabled for ten years onely."

24 Owing to the great heterogeneity of opinions among Levellers, critics do not agree on their political stance in respect of the electoral franchise. Any attempt to summarize in depth the *status quaestionis* would risk coming short in the context of this paper. It suffices to note that, even if Levellers, in particular John Lilburne, advocated for the political recognition of the birthrights of every "free-born Englishman," there were many ways in which a "free-born Englishman" could forfeit his political privileges. One, for instance, was the stipulation of a labour contract, for it entailed the loss of the worker's independence, that is, his natural liberty. This conceptual

Indeed, the basic strategy shaped by the Putney Debates, with the exception of a few Levellers, stood for the exclusion of servants and dependents. The absence of an interest on the part of those statuses was the argument for the line drawn among the inhabitants of a territory. Besides of this, seventeenth-century politicians seemed to have fully assumed the categorisation of dependents as holders of the minimum liberty of their body. It is interesting to trace a continuous tendency of discourse in the texts examined as to the problem of the integration of low-class people.

The Subject of Government in Sidney

Algernon Sidney's *Discourses Concerning Government*[25] seems to be based on the same premises. The Whig militant wrote his essay after the republication of Filmer's *Patriarcha*[26] with the purpose of demolishing the Tory strategy aimed at giving absolute power to the king. Sidney agreed with male suffrage on the basis that consent among male adults gave life to political government. Each and every one was allowed to speak his mind with regard to the Commonwealth

meaning of labour is the reason why the word 'servant' signified both waged workers and domestic attendants in seventeenth century English. Ellen Meiksins-Wood suggests taking into consideration the only certain evidence on the Levellers' stance that we have: that is, Levellers agreed to extend the franchise to householders. Labourers – every servant and wage worker having exited a lord's/master's household, as Robert Steinfeld puts it – theoretically complied with this status after contracting marriage. But, in the absence of a source of self-subsistence, it was not uncommon that they fell back into the realm of wage dependence. It is no accident that "in such circumstances men fought desperately to avoid the abyss of wage-labour". Christopher Hill, *Change and Continuity in Seventeenth-Century England* (London: Weidenfeld and Nicolson, 1974), 225. Therefore, Levellers were likely to address yeomen and the "middling rank of people" when promoting their idea of the "free-born Englishman". To further study this debate, see Brian Manning, *The English People and the English Revolution. 1640–1649* (London: Heineman Educational Books, 1976); Edmund S. Morgan, *Inventing the People: The Rise of Popular Sovereignty in England and America* (New York: Norton and Company, 1988); Ellen Meiksins-Wood, *Liberty and Property. A Social History of Western Political Thought from Renaissance to Enlightenment* (New York: Verso, 2012); Rachel Foxley, "From Native Rights to Natural Equality: The Agreement of the People (1647)," in *Revolutionary Moments: Reading Revolutionary Texts*, ed. Rachel Hammersley (London: Bloomsbury Academic, 2015), 11–8; Rachel Foxley, "John Lilburne and the Citizenship of 'Free-born Englishmen'," *The Historical Journal* 47 (2004): 849–874; Raffaella Sarti, "Servo o padrone, o della (in)dipendenza. Un percorso da Aristotele ai giorni nostri. I: Teorie e dibattiti," *Scienza & Politica* 2 (2015): 2–249.

25 Algernon Sidney, *Discourses Concerning Government*, ed. Thomas G. West (Indianapolis, IN: Liberty Fund, 1996).

26 Robert Filmer, *Patriarcha or of The Natural Power of Kings* (London: Richard Chiswell, 1680)

had he the exercise of rational freedom, that is, if he had learnt to be "master of himself". Through the practice of virtue, a man became worthy of participating in government of a country. Sidney's operation purported an inversion of the status-biased citizenship put forward by Filmer and the Tories inasmuch as it promoted merit over blood and birth. The author of *Patriarcha* denied the condition of liberty to the extent that he framed citizens as subjects to the sovereign's absolute will. In Filmer's opinion no one was free from the authority of another man, i.e. the hereditary monarch and one's own father.

Although Sidney built up his theory on virtue, thus potentially embracing the possibility for every man to be part of the political life, his concept of equality cracked when he described the modes of participation. Virtue was a gift endowed by God upon men; it was in the order of things for the virtuous man to command and guide the community. The rest of men who were not equally worthy had to rely on the virtuous because

> [t]he equality which is among equals, is just among equals; but such as are base, ignorant, vicious, slothful, or cowardly, are not equal in natural or acquired virtues, to the generous, wise, valiant, and industrious; nor equally useful to the societies in which they live: they cannot therefore have an equal part in the government of them; they cannot equally provide for the common good; and 'tis not a personal, but a publick benefit that is sought in their constitution and continuance.[27]

On the one hand, those who were "slaves by nature" were not equal, and thus did not deserve political rights because of their lack of merit. It would have been unjust to let them decide or even form a government: such a configuration would have violated God's natural order, which put in charge wise, righteous, upright people who knew His laws. On the other hand, an equal by virtue had to possess as much dominium – property and rights – as every other equal.

Sidney's turn was ostensibly plain when he continued his reflection. Quoting Aristotle, he then categorised all kinds of virtues. Intellectual virtues were supposed to lead and command; on the contrary, those who had been gifted with body virtues needed to obey. Furthermore, in approaching the topic of family relations to refute Filmer's patriarchalism, the Whig author introduced his conception of servants. In his interpretation of equality, no contradiction occurred when servants and subalterns were concerned: they did not share the same political, social, and urban space as equal citizens. On the part of servants, claiming an equal distribution of *dominium* would have not been a legitimate action.

27 Sidney, *Discourses Concerning Government*, 80.

"Paria paribus", Sidney stated: "equal things to equals".[28] The difference between citizens and servants was *in specie*, thus any comparison would be a contradiction. This was another reason to criticise Filmer and the equivalence he established between servants' and sons' statuses, both of them being under the absolute power of the father/master: a freeman's son, when he came of age, became as free as his father. The male son was expected to become an actor committed to politics.

Being a citizen equalled being a *dominus*. Everyone could be called *dominus*, not only the king or the nobles, "unless such as are of the vilest condition, or in a great subjection to those who speak to them". While collecting some not so thorough knowledge about other nations' and communities' political legacies, Sidney eventually agreed with the fact that a popular sovereign assembly:

> Comprehended[s] all the freemen, that is, all the people; for the difference between *civis* and *servus* is irreconcilable; and no man, whilst he is a servant, can be a member of a commonwealth; for he that is not in his own power, cannot have a part in the government of others.[29]

In fact, upon the preference for a mixed government with a shade of republicanism,[30] Sidney distanced the condition of *cives* from the mere subjects enduring a status similar to the *incolae*, the inhabitants of territory recently conquered by the Romans, who did not benefit from full citizenship.[31] After all, according to Sidney, mere subjects were not even able to practice a worthy uprising:[32] the "rabble" always deployed its license, as opposed to rational liberty, thus failing to provide the necessary order that even revolts had to respect. Uprisings, contentions, and political struggles were matters for freemen only. Lower classes and servants were reckoned by the disrespectful word "rabble" when it came to evaluating the quality of a rebellion. Servants, indigent people, slaves, etc. were reliant on the multitude's irrational feelings. They always put the whole "body politik" at risk of being corrupted by their vices.

---

28 Ibid., 94.

29 Ibid., 103.

30 For a discussion on Sidney's particular position among republicans, see: Cesare Cuttica, "Il primato della politica: Algernon Sidney commonwealthman," in *Ideali repubblicani in età moderna*, ed. Fiorella De Michelis Pintacuda and Gianni Francioni (Pisa: ETS, 2002), 145–160.

31 Cuttica, "Il primato della politica," chap. II, paragraph 16.

32 Sidney dealt with this topic in the passage where he made allusions to the Roman Republic. He downgraded Spartacus' revolt as a sedition and civil war which had little to do with a legitimate rebellion leading to a revolution.

> But when the people is generally corrupted, such designs seldom miscarry, and the success is always the erection of a tyranny [...]. The ways of attaining it have always been by corrupting the manners of the people, bribing soldiers, entertaining mercenary strangers, opening prisons, giving liberty to slaves, alluring indigent persons with hopes of abolishing debts, coming to a new division of lands, and the like. Seditions raised by such men always tend to the ruin of popular governments; but when they happen under absolute monarchies, the hurt intended is only to the person, who being removed the promoters of them set up another.[33]

Is the absence of virtue in the majority of people a matter of luck and fortune? In section 41 of Chapter III, Sidney seemed to place the matrix of inequality by virtue on free will and subjective choice. When he tackled the magistrate's jurisdiction and powers, the explanation reached the private settlements field concerning submission agreements. In this regard, "the state hath no other cognizance of what passes between me and them, than to oblige me to perform the contracts I make, and not to do that to them which the law forbids".[34] Public authority had no voice as for private relations because they were supposed to be executed by a mutual consent between the parties. The duty of the rule of law was exclusively to make each part fulfil its commitment. The master was obliged not to infringe upon servants' individual decisions – again, the *habeas corpus* principle – but only when it did not affect their service. Yet, to the detriment of any equal conception of agreements, Sidney made very clear the servant's duty: the organisation of his work was under his master's control and will, granting the master himself a regulation "of [his] particular affairs according to his own discretion".[35] This unbalanced relationship was stressed to the point that Sidney ventured himself by stating that a magistrate was like a servant (from which the current expression "public servant"), that is, citizens had the duty to limit his power and to dictate his work.

Sidney's contribution to the Servant-Master debate was not innovative in respect of the Putney debates (except for Rainsborough). The author of *Discourses concerning Government* confirmed the historical prejudice and kept on exempting labourers from full membership, the civic right over their body being the only one enacted. It should be noticed, however, that a certain inclusiveness towards subordinated workers emerged throughout the entire book, not only with regard to the protection of the physical body of their persons, but also in the creation of

33 Sidney, *Discourses Concerning Government*, 229.
34 Ibid., 548.
35 Ibid., 564.

consent and a general interest[36] in the preservation of State institutions among the "body politik". Even if servants were not citizens, political authority ought to find a specific place for them, at least to make them realise that "'tis for their brethren to be guided by [the virtuous]".[37] As for a magistrate's office, the first task to accomplish was to place individuals depending on their talents and inclinations. Therefore, the magistrate was akin to an architect who "conduce[s] to the beauty of the most glorious building" following the wise placement of even the "meanest piece of wood or stone". According to the nature of every inhabitant of a community, magistrates "cleave, carve, or cut" the "pieces of timber or stone", thus "allotting to everyone his proper work".[38] The government had to fulfil a project of growth of richness and population, expansion of territories and commerce, if it desired to survive and to prosper. For this reason, every person living within the territory and born as a native Englishman represented a little brushstroke in a bigger picture, in which everyone had a place. This new conception was ostensive in the analysis of war. To win a war, a government had to create affiliation and affection among its soldiers, making everyone feel like composing the country, both the present and the future one. The question of the *trust* perceived by inhabitants – not only citizens – acquired a great importance. The attainment of such a social situation was possible only through a simultaneous effort. On the one hand, as it has been shown, the allocation of specific positions and work for everyone was essential. On the other hand, it was crucial that the development of virtue within the community be brought about by some righteous ones apt to govern and to control magistrates. The dissemination of virtue brought on a social attitude inclined to "integrity of manners", "sobriety" and "honest contentedness",[39] thus eradicating "mischief", which existed mostly due to the state of privation experienced by the poor and labourers. Excellent magistrates promoted virtuous behaviour by promulgating good laws; therefore, individuals were inclined to act properly since they internalised the values of the government. This was the only way to convert the dangerous

36 I am aware of the great significance of the concept of interest. In my usage of it, I imply neither economic advantage nor personal aspiration, as in desire to improve one's own social rank. Rather, by 'interest' I mean the expression of a rational deliberation oriented to personal survival, which equals the civil state of peace. In this sense, it is of interest for subjects to obey State laws as, by doing so, they dispel the possibility of war. For a discussion on the historical evolution of interest (and passions), see: Albert O. Hirschman, *The Passions and the Interests: Political Arguments for Capitalism Before its Triumph* (Princeton, NJ: Princeton University Press, 1997).

37 Sidney, *Discourses Concerning Government*, 80.

38 Ibid., 83.

39 Ibid., *passim*.

rabble into a convenient resource. Notwithstanding Sidney's view about servants and citizenship, he stood against the vexation of the entire population and those tyrants wanting to suck up all the wealth of the nation. In conclusion, servants were not considered masters of themselves, but they could certainly acquire self-control after a top-down social education.

The very peculiar status of servants blurred its boundaries in Sidney's thought. Subordinate and dependent labourers were neither citizens nor slaves; they were barred from the benefits of full membership, but their possession of their bodies was ensured. They were (at least in a hypothetical condition) free-will agents capable of entering contracts. Their inclusion in terms of becoming a political object and subject in the governmental order was almost a necessity. How could they be assimilated, even if not included in citizenship rights? The assimilation had to come about by means of the diffusion of virtue and political education, by which all the people governed themselves and became functional to the economic growth of trade. In doing so, the members of the people, inhabitants as well as citizens, had to develop a certain interest in the political community – an interest recognisable thanks to virtue, which allowed rational choices and integration, steering them away from mischief and debauchery. Such an interest did not correspond to property and equal opportunities of advantage (the "permanent fixed" one), but it certainly rendered every human being under a government a subject to be taken into account on the part of the ruling, virtuous ones.

The Differential Inclusion of Labour in Locke's Philosophy

Locke brought the discussion to another level of complication and definition. The Whig activist was not so explicit about the republican option as Sidney was, leading many scholars and researchers to make theoretical suppositions. Judith Richards, Lotte Mulligan, John Graham, Willmoore Kendall, Richard Ashcraft, James Tully, and, more recently, Antoni Domènech and Christophe Miqueu[40] all comment that Locke can be associated with republicanism and that

40 Richards, Mulligan and Graham, *Property and People*; Kendall, *Locke and the Doctrine*; Ashcraft, *Revolutionary Politics*; Tully, *Property*; Antoni Domènech, *El eclipse de la fraternidad. Una visión publica de la tradición socialista* (Barcelona: Critica, 2003); Christophe Miqueu, *Spinoza, Locke et l'idée de citoyenneté, une génération républicaine à l'aube des Lumières* (Parigi: Classique Garnier, 2012).

he thought of male suffrage as a tool to develop his theory of government. Conversely, other scholars such as Crawford B. Macpherson, Ellen Meiksins-Wood, John Marshall, Peter Laslett, John Dunn, and Christopher Hill[41] point out the inconsistency of Locke's philosophy with republicanism. It is not an object of this article to enter the long-lasting debate about Locke's political orientation. It is sufficient to say that republicanism is not necessarily consistent with male suffrage or popular government. Sidney's reflections should be a warning against such an assumption. Furthermore, many studies stress the conceptualisation of servants, labourers, households, maids, vagrants, and the poor which can be found throughout Locke's political and philosophical production. In the light of these readings, it can be inferred that the philosopher from Wrington did think that dependants were unfit for citizenship rights. Considering the cultural milieu of Modern England, it looks like nothing new. Locke's authentic sleight of hand concerned the role he gave to labour. Overall, English authors, when talking about dependants, intended to deprecate manual, exhausting labour; at the same time, they explicitly asserted that all the burgesses, upright merchants, and businessmen were to be entitled to citizenship. And their entitlement was due to their professional work, not only because of their bloodline. Nevertheless, the aforementioned texts did not provide for a philosophical discussion of labour. That gap was filled by Locke.

First of all, it is profitable to start off by expounding Locke's most prominent concepts. In his *Second Treatise*[42] he introduced the concepts of state of nature, natural laws, liberty, and reason (further developed in the *Essay concerning Human Understanding*).[43] In effect, Locke dealt with some issues left undisclosed in some of his contemporaries' works through the use of the pivotal concepts of jusnaturalism. If every man was born free and independent from anyone's will, how did it come about that civil society involved inequalities and hierarchies? Sidney tried to explain the problem by grounding social hierarchies on natural differences of virtue that made some men kings and others slaves by nature.

41 Macpherson, *Possessive Individualism*; Meiksins-Wood, *Liberty and Property*; John Marshall, *John Locke: Resistance, Religion and Responsibility* (Cambridge: Cambridge University Press, 1994); Peter Laslett, *Preliminary Study to the Two Treatises* (Cambridge: Cambridge University Press, 1988); John Dunn, *The Political Thought of John Locke* (Cambridge: Cambridge University Press, 1982); Christopher Hill, *The Century of Revolution 1603–1714* (New York: Norton & Company, 1961).

42 John Locke, *Second Treatise of Government*, ed. C. B. Macpherson (Indianapolis, IN: Hackett Publishing Company, 1980).

43 *An Essay Cocerning Human Understanding.* Italian translation: *Saggio sull'intelletto umano*, trans. and ed. M. G. D'Amico and V. Cicero (Milan: Bompiani, 2007).

Locke avoided referring to human nature – although he acknowledged men's natural anthropology. After all, this stance could have justified government without consent if the rest of humanity had not recognised the natural superiority of the virtuous, an argument echoing the critique of patriarchalism, especially the premises for which biological fatherhood gave authority. In addition, every man was perfectly capable of understanding natural laws through the employment of reason: God conferred this faculty to let mankind be aware of His ontological and moral order. Men were able to follow His rules and thus be free in the state of nature, that is:

> A state of perfect freedom to order their actions, and dispose of their possessions and persons as they think fit, within the bounds of the law of Nature, without asking leave or depending upon the will of any other man. A state also of equality, wherein all the power and jurisdiction is reciprocal, no one having more than another, there being nothing more evident than that creatures of the same species and rank, promiscuously born to all the same advantages of Nature, and the use of the same faculties, should also be equal one amongst the other, without subordination or subjection.[44]

As they learned to discern natural laws, individuals did not necessarily undertake clashes, confrontations and invasion of their counterparts. Freedom was attached to natural laws: it was not conceived as license; that conceptual move meant tearing down the Hobbesian theory in which men were sociable only under an *imperium*. As much as any man was moved by self-preservation, God forbade the invasion and detriment of another man's property, that is, "liberty, life and goods". Self-preservation was prescribed to make the goods given by God fruitful, meaning that one was to exercise their natural ability to labour. Labour brought to property, as it left a part of the self in the land they had just worked on. By the very fact that labour was a common, universal ability, everyone was potentially entitled to property.

> Though the earth and all inferior creatures be common to men, yet every man has a *property* in his own *person*. This nobody has any right to but himself. The *labour* of his body and the *work* of his hands, we may say, are properly his. Whatsoever, then, he removes out of the state that nature hath provided and left it in, he hath mixed his *labour* with, and joined to it something that is his own, and thereby makes it his *property* [...]. For this *labour* being the unquestionable property of the labourer, no man but he can have a right to what that is once joined to, at least where there is enough, and as good as left in common for others.[45]

---

44 Locke, *Second Treatise*, § 4, 8.
45 Ibid., §27, 19.

In fact, "man (by being master of himself, and *proprietor of his own person, and the actions or labour of it) had still in himself the great foundation of property*".[46] The ontological condition of mankind resulted in an individual having the ownership over his body by natural law; if the body was freely used thanks to this property, then it could be employed to work and to appropriate an external thing, i.e. a portion of land. The background of the argument at stake assumed that a man who was "master of himself" could work regardless of anyone's will. Freedom of labour concerned both the "labour of the body", i.e. the strain to seed and harvest a field, and "the work of the hands", i.e. an artisan's skilled production.[47] It is not hard to see all the more puritan influences in Locke's thought stemming from the debt he owed to religious reflections about the role of work.[48]

At first glance, it seems that Locke exposed himself by advocating full membership for everyone. Insofar as everyone was equal because of their common belonging to humankind, inequality of political participation and rights would have been exempted from his logical premises. But this was not the case. Ron Becker successfully shows how Locke was very strict in his use of the expressions "free man" and "freeman". Throughout this brilliant article, the difference between being a *free man* in the state of nature and a *freeman* holding a full citizenship is inferred by distinguishing the foundation of "natural" society from the political society from which government institutions are born. From Becker's perspective, every man joined civil society by consent on the grounds that he desired a guarantee for his right to appeal to a judge. However, belonging to civil society, Becker reasons, did not entail full membership for everyone, for government and laws were to be chosen by the entitled ones only. Every free man joined civil society by consent in order to ensure his protection and right to appeal; but only every freeman had the right to be politically involved in law-making processes and the election of government. In fact, civil society preserved private and social relations created within natural society, a concept to be distinguished from civil society:

---

46 Ibid., §44, 27.

47 Here I specifically adopt Arendt's distinction between *homo laborans* and *homo faber*. She explicitly makes reference to Locke in defining work as strain and work as production. Hannah Arendt, *The Human Condition* (Chicago: University of Chicago Press, 1968).

48 Cf. Dunn, *op. cit.*; Hill, "Protestantism and the Rise of Capitalism," in Ibid., *Change and Continuity*, cit.; Franco M. Di Sciullo, *Gestire l'indigenza. I poveri nel pensiero politico inglese da Locke a Malthus* (Roma: Aracne, 2013).

> [Locke] makes a distinction between four terms: the government, the political (civil) society, the society and the state of nature. The state of nature and society are the same in that there is an absence of legitimate political authority. Political authority begins with political society from which a form of government is chosen. The state of nature differs from society in that a society includes interpersonal relations of authority [...] In the state of nature all men (or every one, e.g. II, §13) are equal and free from personal authority. In society this is not so. For Locke, relations of authority naturally develop, like the authority of a father over his children, a master over his servant and a husband over his wife. Although there are relations of authority and promises and compacts in society, in terms of political authority people are still in a state of nature.[49]

As Becker contends, beginning from 1660 the definition of free man referred to those who were not slaves: who could move and dispose freely of their body. Being a free man was a necessary but not sufficient condition to enjoy full membership of the Commonwealth. One was a citizen only by blood or by concession of public authority, i.e. the mayor or the alderman of a city. All the other free men were not equal to freemen or citizens. Locke was clear on this point too:

> Though I have said above *Chap. II "That all men by nature are equal"*, I cannot be supposed to understand all sorts of *equality: age* or *virtue* may give men a just precedency: *excellency* of parts and *merit* may place others above the common level: *birth* may subject some, and *alliance* or *benefits* others, to pay an observance to those to whom nature, gratitude, or other respects, may have made it due: and yet all this consists with *equality*, which all men are in respect of jurisdiction or dominion one over another; which was the *equality* I there spoke of as proper to the business in hand, being that *equal right* that every man hath to his natural freedom, without being subjected to the will or authority of any man.[50]

Equality had indeed an all-encompassing efficacy in Locke's thought. In this regard, Daniela Gobetti[51] observes that equality contained almost a scholastic connotation in its meaning because it invoked respect for everyone's position and agreement. Just as the State was called to execute in civil society, equality had to give people what was theirs within a natural society, that is, what corresponded to their age, virtue, and merit and what had been agreed by explicit consent. Fulfilling one's own duty as a servant, thus submitting one's personal will to another person, would not have been called inequality. Becker reckons that agreements and settlements as human conventions were already possible in natural society, prior to the social contract. On this account, inequalities were engendered before the foundation of government; better put, political hierarchies with-

49 Becker, *op.cit.*, 639.
50 Locke, *Second Treatise*, cit., §54, 31.
51 Gobetti, "Sfera domestica e sfera politica."

in the State were constructed on the basis of these inequalities. When did it occur? In the wake of the introduction of money, an event which allowed a person to owe as many lands as he pleased provided that he exchanged perishable materials with durable steel, that is, gold or silver. As Locke states, “this partage of things, in an equality of private possessions, men have made practicable out of the bonds of society, and without compact, only by putting a value on gold and silver”.[52]

The origins of inequality of possessions implied the deprivation of external properties on the part of many individuals because of their lack of industry or strategy, and natural weaknesses, resulting in the dominance of the most rational and skilful men over some other men. The need for livelihood and protection prompted a person without any means to subject themselves to another person’s will. After all, who could rent his land or employ another’s labour but the man already possessing a surplus external property? Locke presumed that at the origins of the state of nature the person who had strained the most in working, thus mixing up a part of his soul with nature, had the right to own more things or human service. There seems to be a meritocratic criterion that, at the dawn of any civil society, created a hierarchy amidst men, separating those who worked hard with practical intelligence and those who did not do as much.[53] The consequential disparity of possessions resulted in the subordinated dependence of those reckoned idle, lazy, and vicious in the state of nature.[54] As Campbell

52 Locke, Second Treatise, §50, 29–30.

53 Campbell Jones, “The Meanings of Work in John Locke,” in *History of Economic Rationalities: Economic Reasoning as Knowledge and Practice Authority*, ed. J. Bek-Thomsen et al. (Cham: Springer, 2017), 51–62.

54 Critics are not unanimous on this point. James Tully, for instance, has argued that in no way, for Locke, could a man be obliged to sell his labour to another by necessity, i.e. when access to livelihood was denied because of the inequality of possessions. Servants/labourers had to contract their labour in a situation free of all kinds of influence (economic, political, and personal). As voluntary as the contract might have been, no ‘free will’ would have been at stake if the subject had been pushed by other factors to enter the contract. For this reason, Tully holds that the Lockean theory of property primarily concerned the commonality of possessions; or, at the very least, everyone’s right to the surplus products of another’s property for survival reasons (cf. Locke, *First Treatise*, in Id., *Two Treatises of Government and a Letter on Toleration*, ed. Ian Shapiro (New Haven and London: Yale University Press, 2003), §42, 29) and to accomplish the right/duty of self-preservation. In this sense, proprietors would only have the right to use the land they worked on, as opposed to the exclusionary *dominium*. Nevertheless, I maintain that Tully has provided a misguiding interpretation of property, in that the exclusionary possession is much needed by Locke to secure civil peace (the distinction between “mine” and “thine”). Moreover, it is important not to overlook the role of the theory of improvement, according to which private possession increases the general survival chances of everyone. But, in order to achieve improve-

Jones notes, this theory of labour (rather than a theory of property) was valid only within the state of nature: afterwards in civil society, even if a dispossessed and propertyless man worked all day long, he was not supposed to appropriate anything he worked on. In that the inheritance right[55] was introduced, the lawful owner's rights were secured: the poor man did not work autonomously, rather he was a "rational mean" of the owner employing his labour. In the well-known "turf passage", Locke did not mince words: "the turf my servant has cut; and the ore I have digged in any place [...] become my *property*".[56] Since servants contracted their judicial submission to a master by consent,[57] it was assumed that they voluntarily gave up their labour (fruits and service time) and ceded it to their employer.

As much as labour was a universal disposition, being both a right and a duty by God's will, in Locke's philosophy labour became a differentiating device. On the one hand, it referred to the "master of himself", the industrious and successful man, historically embodied by 'improving landlords', rich merchants, and skilled artisans.[58] In accordance with the judicial norms to access citizenship,

---

ment, one has to own a lot of land. Money, in the form of wage payments for services, functions as the exchange means for purchasing commodities (produced by improvement) for one's own survival. If wages are not enough, Christian charity covers for them in aiding the poor. In a nutshell, Locke's property theory is consistent with both inequality in possession and godly laws establishing the universal right/duty of self-preservation. Tully, *Property*, 98–99.

55 Cf. Locke, *Second Treatise*, cit., §45, 29: "the several *communities* settled the bounds of their distinct territories, and by laws between themselves regulated the properties of the private men of their society, and so, by *compact* and agreement, *settled the property* which labour and industry began."

56 Ibid., §28, 19–20.

57 Ibid., §85, 45.

58 In effect, in Locke's social imagination (cf. John Dunn, "Individuality and Clientage in the Formation of Locke's Social Imagination," in John Dunn, *Rethinking Modern Political Theory: Essays 1979–83* (Cambridge: Cambridge University Press, 1985), 13–33) the most industrious landlords, gentry, and the middling rank of people occupied a paramount position in terms of political relevance. Presumably, Locke spoke to these classes when nuancing the concept of labour in his original fashion, thus opposing the feudal thinking of hierarchies. By promoting skilful and industrious labour, he was praising the 'frugal life' of people actually dedicated to working, i.e. yeomen and skilled artisans. Also, he was referring to the landlords (mostly gentry members, but also other high-ranking nobles) who were committed to improving their lands and expanding commerce. Being managerial, this last activity, of course, was different from middle-class jobs; but it denoted a new mentality with regard to the function of the higher classes and nobility, whose power was supposed not only to derive from their family ancestry, but also from their work (as managerial as it might have been). Locke's patron Lord Shaftesbury embodied this very historical figure. Cf. Marshall, *John Locke. Resistance, Religion and Responsibility*, 264–267; 282; Meiksins-Wood, *Liberty and Property*, 275.

Locke concurred that landlords, as well as rich merchants of corporations, benefited from full membership (right to vote and to be elected, freedom of commerce, privileges in the context of trials); presumably, his concept of citizenship also embraced skilled artisans belonging to powerful guilds. In doing so, Locke evidently gave new significance to political membership, by grounding it upon work and merit rather than noble bloodlines.

On the other hand, the concept of labour comprised the forms of dependent work and service agreed by compact. Locke needed to recognise dependants' "labour of the hand" in that they, as stated above, were the masters' rational tools for appropriating the fruits of the lands. At this point, labour actually functions as an inclusive device. Nevertheless, there are at least two reasons to believe that Locke belittled this kind of work, thus upholding the political exclusion of the poor and dependents from full membership. The first reason is the then-ongoing cultural prejudice against dependants not being completely free because of their condition of submission. This opinion perfectly fits in Locke's description of private relationships put in place prior to civil institutions. Second, the evaluation of the conduct of servants and the poor posed the argument on a moral field. Works such as *Some Thoughts concerning Education*, *Some Considerations of the Consequences of the Lowering of Interest*, Locke's journal pages like *On Labour* and his *Draft of a Representation, Containing a Scheme of Methods for the employment of the poor*[59] present the reader with all the bile the author directed at servants and the rabble. In his opinion, vices, ill temper, and misbehaviour were consistent with dependent status.[60] The picture of these subjects introduced by his words often connected their moral deficiency to poor employment of their rational faculties. Locke imagined servants being trapped by their own greedy and voracious desires; thus, it was too much of an effort for them to choose, stop, and project their desires in the future.[61] It was the vile attitude that

---

59 Locke, *Some Thoughts Concerning Education*, in John Locke, *The Works of John Locke in Nine Volumes. Vol 8*, Aalen: Scientia Verlag, 1963); Id., *Some Considerations of the Consequences of the Lowering of Interest*, in John Locke, *The Works of John Locke in Nine Volumes. Vol 4*, cit.; Id., "On Labour," in *John Locke: Political Writings*, ed. David Wootton (Indianapolis, IN: Hackett Publishing Company, 2003); Id., "Draft of a Representation, Containing a Scheme of Methods for the employment of the poor," in *John Locke: Political Writings*, ed. David Wootton (Indianapolis, IN: Hackett Publishing Company, 2003).

60 Cf. Locke, *Some Thoughts*, cit., 53: "As for the ill habits held by servants which could be transmitted to children of upright family: The servants should be hindered from making court to them, by giving them strong drink, wine, fruit, playthings, and other such matters, which may make them in love with their conversation."

61 In the *Essay*, cit., chap. XXI, Locke defined the will as the power to assess ideas and to decide upon the prerogative of one rather than another, in opposition to external influences com-

made them be coerced by the sole movement of their body "from hand to mouth",[62] which exposed them to the risk of following bad inclinations as soon as they could:

> The growth of the poor must therefore have some other cause; and it can be nothing else but the relaxation of discipline, and corruption of manners: virtue and industry being as constant companions on the one side as vice and idleness are on the other. The first step, therefore, towards the setting the poor on work, we humbly conceive, ought to be a restraint of their debauchery, by a strict execution of the laws provided against it; more particularly by the suppressing of superfluous brandy shops and unnecessary alehouses, especially in country parishes not lying upon great roads.[63]

When Locke talked about labourers, with the exception of domestic servants and other full-time services (even though they are prone to greed and lust too), he did not mean something very different from poor people. In Modern England the majority of labourers survived on precarious employment, daily contracted or employed for a certain time period (weekly, monthly or, more rarely, yearly). [64] They were always under the threat of falling into inactivity and, thus, of representing a weight on society's shoulders – and a social danger, given that they were not under surveillance when inactive. Moreover, another important theme emerges in the aforementioned quotation for the discourse hereby drafted. Labour was not a free disposition for every man. Evidently, some people worked because they needed to survive. Conversely, some others worked because they wanted to improve their lives, to accomplish God's right/duty to make natural goods productive and increase the wealth of the community. These people worked for *convenience*, not out of *necessity*. A labourer without land property had no interest in enlarging his possessions because he cared about his survival first; and, as soon as he could, he ceased to work, given that a surplus of effort was of no use to him. Why should the government allow dependants to raise their voice to Parliament? They showed no rational behaviour per se; their existence was marked by the power of a master, thus of another person. And their working activity would have been of no use to the improvement of the State, since, if it had been up to them, they would have not made other additional ef-

---

ing from the senses. A condition without freedom occurred when a subject was unable to act upon the decisions of their will.

62 Locke, *Some Considerations*, 24.

63 Locke, "A Draft of a representation," 447.

64 Robert J. Steinfeld, *The Invention of Free Labour: The Employment Relation in English and American Law and Culture, 1350–1870* (Chapel Hill: University of North Carolina Press, 1991).

forts than those for their preservation. Accordingly, in the *Draft* Locke called for the imposition of work discipline over the poor.

The coercion to work marked two philosophico-historical standpoints that were compatible with each other. Working brought about the development of commerce and wealth, the growth of the nation, and, consequently, its power. The inclusion of people as labourers, although not fully citizens, meant accounting for the particular job everyone was called to do in order to accomplish the mercantilist task – and, indeed, God's command:

> The ground which produces the materials is scarce to be reckoned in as any, or at most, but a very small part of it; so little, that even amongst us, land that is left wholly to nature, that hath no improvement of pasturage, tillage, or planting, is called, as indeed it is, *waste*; and we shall find the benefit of it amount to little more than nothing. This shews how much numbers of men are to be preferred to largeness of dominions, and that the increase of lands and the right employment of them is the great art of the government. And a prince who shall be so wise and godlike as by established laws of liberty to secure protection and encouragement to the honest industry of mankind against the oppression of power and narrowness of party will quickly be too hard for his neighbours.[65]

If the "great art of government" was to put everyone at work, then labour had to become a social habit, to belong to ethics. Far beyond the economic outcomes of national industry, Locke took into consideration the same nuance as A. Marshall (quoted by T.H. Marshall): "[W]e are thinking of the effect that his work produces on him rather than the effect that he produces on his work". To some extent, the incorporation of labourers into the political community entailed the internalisation of a political morality. Labourers learned virtue not only by coercion, but also by absorbing work ethics as a constant exercise on themselves, just like owners and nobles were supposed to do. Labour became an *instrumentum regni* directed at all of the inhabitants of a country, all the more if it was conceived as a universal, common human ability. To sum up, in Locke's eyes labour granted both social "easiness"[66] and economic richness. Locke prescribed this very peculiar medicine even to gentlemen, countrymen, and artisans – the small owners known as yeomen and the small country aristocracy named gentry.

> We ought to look on it as a mark of goodness in God that he has put us in this life under a necessity of labour: not only to keep mankind from the mischiefs that ill men at leisure are

---

65 Locke, *Second Treatise*, §42, 26.

66 That is, the state men strove for in their lives, being them under the constant influence of the external world. Easiness was also the condition yearned after in order to completely dedicate oneself to the salvation of one's own soul in the afterlife. In the absence of easiness, men would not have been inspired to work with the aim of accomplishing this duty.

> very apt to do; but it is a benefit even to the good and the virtuous, which are thereby preserved from the ills of idleness or the diseases that attend constant study in a sedentary life.[67]

Working activity functioned as a remedy deployed to heal vices and as a mould to produce the "useful member of commonwealth".[68]

As for social order, a life dedicated to labour – at least six hours a day even for those who could live without it – was better adapted to a Christian existence. Working was how men could show their fondness and strain to God; they transformed their very existence:[69] men found in labour the reason they lived. Labour was practically the embodiment of the sign of individual salvation. Once one had apprehended God's word by obeying His will through practice – pure faith is of no use – one was adequate to follow the first rules of sociability, that is, natural laws. Hence a good and virtuous labourer could worthily stand in his place without infringing someone else's rights. And, if needed, the process of putting someone at work could be facilitated by miracles and revelations, whose effects let an individual understand natural laws in case they were unable to grasp them. Locke explicitly referred to low-ranked people unable to elevate their thoughts. In a sense, labour (with the aid of revelation) helped to govern the multitude deprived of full reason.[70] Ironically, labour, even if imposed, made a person a free man holding the rational faculties needed to be so – which had nothing to do with the freeman.

On this account, labourers and servants were included both as objects and subjects of governments. The ethical education they had to receive aimed to incorporate them into the community by making them feel part of a universal species, project, and human group. They had to behave socially in conformity with the laws approved by the government and its social order because they consented to laws and rules, thus rendering the rules an expression of their own interest. Dependent workers, poor, servants, etc., were not supposed to be exclusively disciplined by an external authority to be politically compatible with society. As

---

67 Locke, *On Labour*, 440.

68 Ibid., 441.

69 Some of Weber's analyses of puritanism show affinities with Locke's religious conception. Cf. Max Weber, *The Protestant Ethic and the Spirit of Capitalism*. Italian translation: *L'etica protestante e lo spirit del capitalismo*, ed. Giorgio Galli and trans. Anna Maria Marietti (Padua: Bur, 1991).

70 Cf. John Locke, *The Reasonableness of Christianity*, in John Locke, *The Works of John Locke in Nine Volumes. Vol. 6*, cit.. Italian translation: *La ragionevolezza del cristianesimo*, ed. Alfredo Sabetti (Florence: La Nuova Italia, 1976).

Weber wrote with regard to puritans, they had to "feel [their] own pulse", especially when they were far away from the gaze of power and its punishments.

As for the development of an interest, labour and its imposition seemed to perform a prominent function: in the first place, the interest of dependant workers, engendered by their desire to survive; in the second place, dependants had to develop an interest in the salvation of their soul. Through duties and needs, labourers achieved the role conferred by government and natural laws even if they were not aware of doing it. Dependent and subordinated people did not necessarily act with awareness and conscience: the importance of their act was due to accomplishing their function or call, not their understanding. Given that they were not able to lift their thoughts over the concerns of their "hand and mouth", the absence of awareness corresponded to the discrimination within the citizenship field, that is, exclusion from political rights. By contrast, being part of the great interest of government was a kind of inclusion that made dependants specific objects of policies and, overall, active subjects in the space of the city. Because of the work they carried out, dependent labourers were certainly neither citizens nor slaves; still, generally speaking they did not seem to belong to a marginalised environment nor to suffer political carelessness with regard to their activity as inhabitants of public space.

Conclusion: The "Distant Proximity" of Citizenship

"The closure theories that define citizenship as a space of privilege for the few that excludes others neglect a subtle and important aspect of citizenship: that it requires the constitution of these others to become possible".[71] With these words, Isin Engin underlines the simultaneity of the creation of citizens and that of "strangers" and "alienated", the internal and excluded elements within the discourse on full membership. As opposed to "proper" aliens, who do not belong to the same social, political and cultural space (i.e., barbarians for ancient Greeks, slaves in Western societies, and Muslims for Western people today), the stranger/alienated comes up at the same moment as when the citizen is shaped. If this scheme were applied to the Modern English thinkers taken into consideration, it would disclose that freemen required dependants to mould their own identity. Labour and virtue become the device fit for liberation from feudal famil-

---

71 Isin Engin, *Being Political: Genealogies of Citizenship* (Minnesota: University of Minnesota Press, 2002), 4.

iar hierarchies, such as those presented by Filmer and upheld by Tories. The focus on labour leads to a potential universality that endangers social hierarchies, potentially leading to the abolition of property. As has been shown, this was not Locke's intention, since the convergence of parliamentarism and the maintenance of old property rights were the true centre of his intellectual efforts.[72] After all, avoiding a contextualisation of labour within the public sphere suited this purpose: subordination compacts had to remain of private domain, which was not a matter of government. For this reason, dependants were not the absolute excluded: they lived in the city, they slept in the same buildings as their masters, they were more than visible. Servants and masters shared a relationship that flourished from a *distant proximity*. Citizenship always involved those who were not entitled to its rights because it created both subjectivities: as was the case of labour acting on dependants, the subaltern individuals conformed to the ruling socio-political norm; as for those belonging to the ruling class defined as citizens, they acquired an identity shaped in opposition to strangers and the alienated.

The connection between citizenship and labour should be problematised by a historical perspective. The inclusiveness of citizenship has often been seen under the light of the extension of liberal values to previously excluded subjects. I believe that this idea does not accurately render the problem regarding the nexus between labour and citizenship. Behind this rationale dwells the idea that, once the excluded gained as many formal rights as the burgesses throughout the nineteenth and twentieth century, formal equality was attained. Or, to put it in A. Marshall's words, everyone could aspire to be a gentleman. This view overlooks the internal position occupied by subordinated workers, thus failing to give an account of the problematic intertwining of citizenship and labour. In other words, access to political and social rights on the part of waged and dependent workers, even though it is to be considered a political advancement, did not at all demolish the cornerstone of inequality: the existence of a subordinated relationship bounding one's will to another's. Following Maria Luisa Pesante, as short as the period of this submission might have been, its brevity did not erase the fact that another person decided over someone else's body. It is true that since the end of the nineteenth century labour relationships have no longer been under the Master-Servant regulation, by which it follows that waged dependants are regarded as fully autonomous and free agents from a judicial point of view. But all of this does not exempt workers from other subtle and in-

72 Laslett, *Preliminary Study*; Dunn, *The Political Thought of John Locke*; John Dunn, "Justice and the Interpretation of Locke's Political Thought," *Political Studies* 16 (1968): 68–87.

direct impositions outside the realm of laws. Suffice to name the stricter dependence on salary before the general disinvestment in welfare policies and precariousness: a dependence which easily turns into submission to the employer, who, by taking advantage of it, may ask for surplus working hours, engage in blackmail and affect the everyday lives of their employees. The resulting disequilibrium constitutes an aporia of Modern citizenship, which should be founded in equality and freedom for every citizen. Furthermore, the aforementioned approach avoids coming to terms with labour as an *instrumentum regni* acting towards social balance and conservation modelling, thus making the people docile.

All that said, a historical inquiry moving on different premises could bring research and political philosophy to wonder: why do we have to be labourers in order to be citizens?

Part II Natural Law, Political Economy and History: Essays in Honour of Kari Saastamoinen

Markku Peltonen

Preface: Kari Saastamoinen – An Appreciation

The second part of this volume is a tribute to Kari Saastamoinen, from friends and students to mark his sixtieth birthday in February 2019. It is intended to honour both his scholarship in the field of intellectual history and his pivotal role as a teacher and a mentor.

Kari is an extraordinary scholar and teacher, but, whilst there were definite signs of a future career in academia in his undergraduate days at the University of Helsinki, there were equally unmistakable signs of other possible careers as well. As a student, Kari won a history students' beauty pageant. He also starred in a minor but important role as a hard-core rocker in *The Heimola Story* (1984), a Finnish coming-of-age film about student life in Helsinki, directed by Ilari and Markus Nummi. In the end, the temptations of a scholarly life prevailed, and soon Kari's short stardom on stage and screen came to an abrupt end, when he embarked on a career in history.

Samuel Pufendorf, the topic of his PhD thesis, was suggested to him, so Kari tells us in the preface of the published version of the thesis, by his supervisor Matti Viikari. This was, as is often the case in such situations, a life-long assignment, and Kari has established himself as one of the best-known international experts on Pufendorf's moral and political thought. He belongs to those scholars who have saved Pufendorf and his seminal contribution to the history of political thought from the scholarly obscurity, where they had been relegated by nineteenth- and early-twentieth-century scholarship. In his own days and still long in the eighteenth century, Pufendorf was seen as an important, perhaps the most important, figure in the transformation of European moral and political thinking in the seventeenth century. He was, as Kari has pointed out, 'the most prominent developer of the so-called modern theory of natural law and contractual political theory'. He was in fact much more widely read than Hugo Grotius, Thomas Hobbes or John Locke in the late seventeenth- and early eighteenth century, and his works appeared in numerous editions and were translated into all major European languages. His textbook, *De officio hominis et civis* (1673), of which there were more than seventy editions, was widely used in universities all over Europe, so much so that, as Kari has put it, 'knowledge of Pufendorf was regarded as an integral part of all-round education'.

In his work on Pufendorf, Kari has demonstrated how Pufendorf occupied a central place in the transformation of European moral thinking from describing

https://doi.org/10.1515/9783110679861-010

the character of highest human good and the virtues which a person needed to possess to be an excellent human being to seeing the moral domain of consisting of the norms one should follow in interpersonal relations to maintain a peaceful and ordered social life. Instead of Hobbes's 'legal positivism', according to which, right and wrong were dictates of the sovereign, Pufendorf argued that there is a pre-political moral obligation to cultivate peaceful sociability. Underlying this was natural law, which God had ordered on humankind to maintain a peaceful social life.

Kari's scholarly work has always been based on extremely careful reading and thorough knowledge of the primary and secondary sources. In this sense it is intellectual history at its very best. Perhaps he has not been an avid reader of wider pamphlet literature of a period, but his scholarship is firmly based on the historical context of the texts he studies. Kari has always been interested in the historical reconstruction of a text's significance in its own times rather than its putative relevance to our own time. This is not to say, however, that his work can in any way been characterised as a mere antiquarian exercise. By demonstrating the precise historical significance of, say, Pufendorf's works, Kari has at the same time showed their relevance to our own time. To put this another way, Kari's work shows, in an exemplary manner, that the history of political thought has a lot to offer for our own contemporary world. It can demonstrate where certain ideas came from, show their contingencies and the context(s) in which they emerged. The history of political thought can show how embracing certain ideas was itself a choice, that there were other choices and ideas available – other paths, as it were, which were not taken. By examining crucial, though hitherto neglected, aspects of past ideas and providing new historical accounts of their development, the history of political thought offers novel and important perspectives on earlier and present-day civil philosophy and discussions of politics alike.

A brilliant example of the application of these methodological commitments and injunctions is Kari's second book – *Eurooppalainen liberalismi: Etiikka, talous, politiikka* (1998). It is above all a historical study of eighteenth- and nineteenth-century liberalism, including Adam Smith, Benjamin Constant, Alexis de Tocqueville, Immanuel Kant, Wilhelm von Humboldt and John Stuart Mill. At the same time, however, it provides an explicit critique of neo-liberalism of the late twentieth century. The critique is not so much about politics but about history – how some neo-liberalists endeavoured, by a deliberate misreading of history, to hijack earlier liberalists, above all Adam Smith, for their vehemently partisan project. By offering a historically more accurate account of Adam Smith and other early liberalists, Kari has, at the same time, demonstrated that Smith and others cannot unproblematically be ranked as progenitors of right-libertarianism.

One of the hallmarks of Kari's scholarly writings is their distinctive style. No matter how complicated theories he is examining, he organises his material extremely well and always expresses himself with elegance and clarity. These rules also apply to his teaching. Kari is a highly respected and well-liked teacher, who has taught the history of political thought to generations of students. The range of his teaching is no less impressive. It covers all aspects of the history of political thought from Athenian democracy to the nineteenth century and includes both general surveys and special subject classes. In his supervision of research students, he has the rare talent to be both kind and exacting. He is always ready to work together with students to tease out the central argument of their research. Kari is held in the highest regard as a scholar, teacher and mentor. The following contributions seek to reflect the range of his broad interests and the profound impact of his teaching.

Heikki Haara & Tim Stuart-Buttle

9 The Problem of Sociability after Hobbes: Pufendorf and Locke on the Politics of Recognition

Thomas Hobbes's place in the history of modern political thought is somewhat curious. Hobbes is perhaps the most "political" of all political philosophers, focusing as he did primarily on the origins, nature, and authority of the state as an "artificial person".[1] Yet the period ca. 1650 – 1800 witnessed a notable expansion of the scope of the political, with an increased attentiveness to how broader social and economic forces exert themselves on individuals in such ways as to render them susceptible to 'government', understood in a Foucauldian sense as "the conduct of conduct".[2] As Foucault argued, sociability (*socialité*) – how individuals coexist with one another – became a new matter to "police" from the seventeenth century onwards.[3] Hobbes is implicated in this turn away from a narrow focus on the state and its monopolisation of disciplinary power, because to a considerable extent it was undertaken to confront a question that Hobbes had himself made pressing – but one to which his own political theory was held to offer an inadequate solution.[4] This was the problem, in Kant's memorable formulation, of "unsocial sociability".[5] By what means might human beings, with all their antisocial characteristics, be induced to exercise the kinds of self-control required to make large-scale, peaceful, and even prosperous societies possible?[6] Few eighteenth-century philosophers exhibited sustained interest in Hob-

---

1 Quentin Skinner, "Hobbes and the Purely Artificial Person of the State," *Journal of Political Philosophy* 7 (1999): 1–29.

2 Michel Foucault, *The Foucault Effect: Studies in Governmentality*, ed. Graham Burchill, Colin Gordon, and Peter Miller (Chicago: University of Chicago Press, 1991), 48.

3 Michel Foucault, *Security, Territory and Population: Lectures at the Collège de France*, 1977–1978, trans. Graham Burchell and ed. Michael Senellart (New York: Palgrave Macmillan, 2007), 326.

4 John Robertson, "Sacred History and Political Thought: Neapolitan Responses to the Problem of Sociability," *Historical Journal* 56 (2013): 1–6.

5 Jerome B. Schneewind, "Good Out of Evil: Kant and the Idea of Unsocial Sociability," in *Kant's Idea for a Universal History with a Cosmopolitan Aim: A Critical Guide*, eds. Amélie Oksenberg Rorty, and James Schmidt (Cambridge: Cambridge University Press, 2009), 94–111.

6 For a conspectus of the scholarship on the post-Hobbesian sociability debate, see Eva Piirimäe and Alexander Schmidt, "Introduction: Between Morality and Anthropology – Sociability in Enlightenment Thought," *History of European Ideas* 41 (2015): 571–588.

https://doi.org/10.1515/9783110679861-011

bes's theory of the state; but their engagement with the problem of sociability to which that theory was intended as a solution only "intensified and ramified" as the decades passed, as the example of Kant illustrates.[7]

A notable characteristic of much eighteenth-century moral and political philosophy is its attentiveness to our radical sensitivity to the evaluative judgments of observing others.[8] Subjectivity is, on this line of thinking, the product of intersubjective processes to which we are all susceptible because of our deep desire for recognition. Political, critical and moral theorists have in recent years drawn attention to recognition as a fundamental human need, essential to our well-being, and to misrecognition as symptomatic of unjust societies and generative of social conflict and strife. Such theorists agree that recognition first acquired prominence in eighteenth-century philosophy – whether in the writings of Hegel or Rousseau.[9] This is, however, mistaken: for all that they may have done so in unusually powerful and innovative ways, Rousseau and Hegel were intervening in an ongoing conversation about the desire for recognition and its implications that they did not initiate. Insofar as they, like Kant, understood this conversation to be a part of a broader debate over the problem of sociability, its terms were set by Hobbes. As István Hont observes, it was Hobbes who first claimed that the fundamental problems of politics all stem "from the politics of recognition".[10] As much recent scholarship has emphasised, sociability was a *problem* for Hobbes in large part because the desire for recognition generated a further desire: for society – the realisation of which it nonetheless frustrated.[11]

If one accepts Hobbes's interpretation of the desire for esteem as by its very nature generative only of mutual *non*-recognition and conflict, then the problem

---

7 Robertson, "Sacred History," 6.

8 Arthur Lovejoy, *Reflections on Human Nature* (Baltimore: The Johns Hopkins University Press, 1961).

9 Axel Honneth, *The Struggle for Recognition: The Moral Grammar of Social Conflicts*, trans. Joel Anderson (Cambridge: Polity Press, 1995); Frederick Neuhouser, *Rousseau's Theodicy of Self-Love: Evil, Rationality, and the Drive for Recognition* (Oxford: Oxford University Press, 2008). For the pre-Hegelian history of recognition, see now Axel Honneth, *Anerkennung: Eine europäische Ideensgeschichte* (Berlin: Suhrkamp, 2018); and Risto Saarinen, *Recognition and Religion: A Historical and Systematic Study* (Oxford: Oxford University Press, 2016).

10 István Hont, *Politics in Commercial Society: Jean-Jacques Rousseau and Adam Smith*, eds. Béla Kapossy and Michael Sonenscher (Cambridge, MA: Harvard University Press, 2015), 11–12.

11 Gabriella Slomp, *Thomas Hobbes and the Political Philosophy of Glory* (Basingstoke: Palgrave Macmillan, 2000); Julia E. Cooper, "Vainglory, Modesty, and Political Agency in the Political Theory of Thomas Hobbes," *The Review of Politics* 72 (2010): 241–269; Paul Sagar, *The Opinion of Mankind: Sociability and the Theory of the State from Hobbes to Smith* (Princeton, NJ: Princeton University Press, 2018), 27–66.

of sociability appears susceptible only of Hobbes's political solution – one reliant upon both fear of punishment and the political re-education of subjects.[12] If, however, the desire for esteem opens us up to the evaluative opinions of our neighbours in such ways as induce us to exercise the self-control required for sociable living, then the production of disciplined and law-abiding citizens is not (and cannot be) the exclusive preserve and achievement of state politics. In what follows, we illustrate how two of Hobbes's earliest critics, who (like Hobbes) operated within the framework of Protestant natural jurisprudence – Samuel Pufendorf and John Locke – challenged his interpretation of the consequences of the desire for esteem in precisely this way.[13] While all three philosophers agreed that the desire for recognition makes men susceptible to (re-)education, Pufendorf and Locke emphasised that the socio-psychological processes that lead people to adopt the norms of sociable behaviour are not directly controlled by the sovereign. Both offered alternative explanations of how human beings become sociable, morally accountable creatures by living together in society, without invoking Hobbes's "mortal God" or rehabilitating the doctrine of natural human benevolence and sociability. The focus on esteem and recognition in post-Hobbesian natural jurisprudence has, until recently, been ignored by scholars.[14] In what follows, we will recover the intellectual framework in which the questions of recognition and non-recognition were initially formulated in post-Hobbesian natural jurisprudence. This shift of focus will reveal the significant continuities between the responses to the problem of sociability generated from within Protestant natural jurisprudence, and those developed by eighteenth-century philosophers from Rousseau and Smith to Kant and Hegel.

---

12 For the place of both fear and education in Hobbes's solution to the problems generated by the desire for recognition, see Eva Odzuck, "War by Other Means? Incentives for Power Seekers in Thomas Hobbes's Political Philosophy," *Review of Politics* 81 (2019): 21–46.

13 Building on Heikki Haara and Tim Stuart-Buttle, "Beyond Justice: Pufendorf and Locke on the Desire for Esteem," *Political Theory* 47 (2019): 699–723.

14 For notable exceptions see James Tully "Governing Conduct", in *Conscience and Casuistry in Early Modern Europe*, ed. Edmund Leites (Cambridge: Cambridge University Press, 1988), 12–71; Kari Saastamoinen, "Pufendorf on Natural Equality, Human Dignity, and Self-Esteem," *Journal of the History of Ideas* 71 (2010): 39–62; Tim Stuart-Buttle, "'A Burthen Too Heavy for Humane Sufferance': Locke on Reputation", *History of Political Thought* 38 (2017): 644–680; Heikki Haara and Aino Lahdenranta, "Smithian Sentimentalism Anticipated: Pufendorf on the Desire for Esteem and Moral Conduct", *Journal of Scottish Philosophy* 16 (2018): 19–37; Heikki Haara, *Pufendorf's Theory of Sociability: Passions, Habits and Social Order* (Cham: Springer, 2018), 99–136; Haara and Stuart-Buttle, "Beyond Justice"; Tim Stuart-Buttle, *From Moral Theology to Moral Philosophy: Cicero and Visions of Humanity from Locke to Hume* (Oxford: Oxford University Press, 2019); Hannah Dawson, "The Normativity of Nature in Pufendorf and Locke," *Historical Journal*, Online First (2019).

Hobbes: Recognition, Inequality, and the Problem of Sociability

In his first published foray into political philosophy, Hobbes launched a forthright assault on Aristotle's theory of natural human sociability which, he claimed, had misled all subsequent "writers on public Affairs".[15] Aristotle's conclusion that "the Human is an animal born fit [*aptum natum*] for Society, – in the Greek phrase, ζῶον πολιτικόν" was the result of a "superficial view of human nature": one that misconstrued "the causes why men seek each other's company and enjoy associating with each other".[16] Importantly, Hobbes accepted two constitutive elements of Aristotle's theory: that men by nature *do* desire society with others; and that they do so to secure goods that are *not* confined to those required for self-preservation and physical well-being. Yet Hobbes argued that Aristotle's claim that "the human being is a political animal" by nature (*zoon politikon*) was unwarranted, and predicated on a fundamental misunderstanding of the "Good" of "the mind" that leads men to seek company.[17] On Hobbes's interpretation, Aristotle assumed that it was a natural love of others – a desire for friendship – that gives rise to society, and generates relationships characterised by reciprocity and an acknowledgement of mutual equality. Political society, in turn, allows men to consolidate these bonds of fellowship in the *polis*.[18] For Hobbes, in contrast, society "is a product of love of *self*, not of love of friends". The "good" of the mind we seek in society is not friendship, but "reputation and honour" – which is a form of power. *All* mental pleasure, Hobbes argued, "is either glory (or a good opinion of oneself), or ultimately relates to glory".[19]

Friendship is predicated upon an assumption of equality by the parties involved, and it is theoretically available to all. If, as Hobbes held Aristotle to

---

15 Here Hobbes underplayed the nuance of medieval and early modern discussions of sociability: see Annabel Brett, *Changes of State: Nature and the Limits of the City in Early Modern Natural Law* (Princeton, NJ: Princeton University Press, 2011).

16 Thomas, Hobbes, *On the Citizen*, ed. Richard Tuck and trans. Michael Silverthorne (Cambridge: Cambridge University Press, 1998), 1.2.

17 Hobbes, *On the Citizen*, 1.2; Aristotle, *Nichomachean Ethics*, IX.9, 1169b16–23; Aristotle, *Politics*, I.2, 1253a3.

18 Nicholas Gooding and Kinch Hoekstra argue that Hobbes took issue primarily with Aristotle's theory of friendship in the *Nichomachean Ethics* (Books VIII-IX), rather than with his account of man as *zoon politicon* in the *Politics:* "Hobbes and Aristotle on the Foundation of Political Science," in *Hobbes's On the Citizen: A Critical Guide*, eds. Robin Douglass and Johan Olsthoorn (Cambridge: Cambridge University Press, 2019), 31–50.

19 Hobbes, *On the Citizen*, 1.2.

maintain, "man naturally loved his fellow man, there is no reason why everyone would not love everyone equally as equally men". Yet it is evident that, in practice, individuals "seek the company of men whose society is more prestigious and useful to him than to others". This proves, Hobbes argued, that "what we are primarily after" from others is the mental good of "honour", along with the satisfaction of our "sensual" pleasures. Unlike friendship, "honour" assumes inequality between men and is by definition not available to all. It is a positional good, which "is nothing if everyone has it, since it consists in comparison and pre-eminence".[20] Recognition-seeking is, it follows, a zero-sum game. It stimulates competition and conflict and gives rise to relationships characterised by dominion and subjugation – by flattery, not friendship.[21] By substituting the desire for recognition for Aristotle's natural love of others (*philia*), Hobbes was able to show that the desire that leads us to seek society necessarily precludes its realisation. Unlike in *The Elements of Law* and *De cive*, in *Leviathan* Hobbes does not explicitly claim that glory is the most foundational human passion, and maintains that only some individuals (rather than all) are glory-seekers. Nevertheless, even in *Leviathan* the problems generated by glory-seeking underpin Hobbes's claims regarding the necessity of the sovereign state for peaceful cooperation, mutual trust and sociability.[22] The competition for recognition, rather than for scarce material resources is the most important cause of quarrel in mankind's natural condition, as prideful individuals endeavour to extort a good from others (esteem) that they are unwilling to reciprocate.[23] Every man desires affirmation of their value from others – even if, due to temperamental differences, this desire is stronger in some (the proud) than others (the more modest). Yet every man considers himself wiser than others – which ironically "proveth rather that men are in that point equall, rather than unequall" – and thus craves an affirmation of his superiority that others are disinclined to offer (unless coerced to do so).[24]

---

20 Ibid.

21 Daniel J. Kapust, *That Glib and Oily Art: Flattery and the History of Political Thought* (Cambridge: Cambridge University Press, 2018), 64–95.

22 For differences and continuities in Hobbes's treatment of glory across his works, see Gabriella Slomp, "Hobbes on Glory and Civil Strife," in *The Cambridge Companion to Hobbes's Leviathan*, ed. Patricia Springborg (Cambridge: Cambridge University Press, 2007), 181–98.

23 Thomas Hobbes, *Leviathan*, ed. Noel Malcolm, 3 vols. (Oxford: Oxford University Press, 2012), Part 1. Chap. 13; cf. 1.17, p. 258; see Arish Abizadeh, "Hobbes on the Causes of War: A Disagreement Theory," *American Political Science Review* 105 (2011): 298–315.

24 Hobbes, *Leviathan*, 1.13, 188; cf. *On the Citizen*, 1.3.

Society relies, as a condition of possibility, upon its members' mutual acknowledgement of their natural equality as men: equality is for Hobbes a political, rather than a physical, metaphysical or ontological imperative.[25] In their natural condition, (some) men's pride precludes them from this act, thereby generating a "contest for dominion", whereas "it is necessary for the obtaining of peace" that all members of a community "be *esteemed* as equal" (or "*accounted by nature equal to one another*").[26] Only thus will they recognise their obligation to play by the same rules as everyone else. In their immiserated natural condition, recognition-seeking generates unanimity on one point alone: that a superior authority is required, to whose laws every individual recognises himself beholden. Only "men's mutual fear", stimulated primarily by the competition and violence generated by recognition-seeking, and not Aristotle's alleged "mutual human benevolence" can provide the foundation for any "large and lasting society".[27] The Gordian Knot resulting from the opposition between pride and equality is only cut once men promise, one to another, to obey a superior (the Leviathan), to whose authority they are all *equally* subject.[28]

The awful "mortal God" instils fear in those in whom the desire for recognition is strongest, thereby emancipating the more modest from *their* fear of the vainglorious. By means of the penalties of civil law and the monopolisation of the apparatuses of socialisation (the pulpit, universities and printing press), the sovereign constrains and educates subjects to acknowledge their natural equality as *men*. As *citizens*, some individuals might legitimately lay claim to honour from others. Yet Hobbes laboured the point – and his sovereign is required to labour the point – that this claim to esteem is not theirs *by right* on account of their superior endowments or achievements. It is enjoyed solely at the free grace and discretion of the sovereign, the fount of all honour in the commonwealth. As king of the children of pride, Hobbes's Leviathan must carefully superintend the economy of esteem in the commonwealth, with an extent of vision that enables it to monitor the "signes of respect" men "give to one another" *even in* "private meetings".[29] Unlike his celestial archetype, the sovereign need not be able to read men's hearts; but like the prisoners of Bentham's Panopticon,

---

25 Kinch Hoekstra, "Hobbesian Equality," in *Hobbes Today: Insights for the 21st Century*, ed. S. A. Lloyd (Cambridge: Cambridge University Press, 2012), 76–112.

26 Hobbes, *On the Citizen*, 3.13.

27 Ibid., 1.2.

28 Hobbes, *Leviathan*, 1.17; see Joshua Mitchell, "Hobbes and the Equality of the All under the One," *Political Theory* 21 (1993): 78–100.

29 Hobbes, *Leviathan* 2.18, 276–80.

his subjects must always feel his eyes upon them, and regulate their every expression of esteem (for themselves, and for others) according to his will.

On Hobbes's interpretation, then, the desire for recognition as an expression of pride precludes men in their natural condition from acknowledging their mutual equality, and their mutual accountability to a shared law. This law is the law of nature, given to mankind by their Creator and promulgating precepts that include the duty laid out most clearly in the Gospel: to love one's neighbour as oneself. Hobbes argued that recognition-seekers, desirous of dominion over others, refused to acknowledge the reciprocal duties inscribed in natural law. Consequently, the more "modest" and "tractable" were only obligated to adhere to natural law "*in foro interno*" – "he that endeavoureth their performance, fulfilleth them" – but "*in foro externo*, that is, to putting them in act, not alwayes". To act on such precepts might render the "modest" man "a prey to others" who refused to do likewise, and "procure his own certaine ruine" – in contravention of the fundamental duty under natural law of self-preservation.[30] It followed that "the Lawes of Nature [...], in the condition of meer Nature [...], are not properly Lawes", but merely "qualities" that if followed by all would "dispose men to peace, and to obedience".[31] Prior to their promulgation by the sovereign in civil law, natural law lacks the sanctions of reward and punishment that make compliance in the interest of every individual.

But might the desire for recognition, if interpreted in a different light, facilitate rather than preclude men's acknowledgement *in foro interno* of their reciprocal duties under natural law? Might esteem and contempt not be considered as sanctions that also incentivise compliance *in foro externo*, and thus make natural law truly a law in our pre-political condition? Hobbes canvassed both possibilities, only to discount them for reasons already discussed: the "Desire of Praise, disposeth [Men] to laudable actions, *such as please them whose judgment they value*".[32] We only "value" the "judgment" of those more powerful than ourselves – and *not* the judgment of all mankind equally.[33] This means that our desire for esteem induces us to act in ways that are deemed good by particular individuals because such actions conduce to *their* personal benefit, rather than to the mutual benefit of all members of our community. Consequently, the sanctions of praise and contempt might only incite a competition to excel one another in the performance of our reciprocal moral duties – "the most noble and prof-

30 Ibid., 1.15, 240.
31 Ibid., 2.26, 418.
32 Ibid., 1.11, 152: italics added.
33 Ibid., 1.10, 142.

itable contention possible" – within a commonwealth, in which the sovereign determines what is estimable and contemptible.[34] Even here, however, there is no guarantee that the sanctions of praise and contempt will reliably enforce the precepts of natural law. The sovereign might legitimately command us to honour those who, in our view, signally fail to embody these precepts in their conduct and character (this might include the deity, if the sovereign is not a Christian).[35] The price of peace, and a necessary condition for the realisation of sociability, might be hypocrisy: professing our esteem for those for whom, in secret, we have nothing but contempt.[36]

Pufendorf and Locke: Esteem, Interdependence and Sociability

The desire for others' esteem occupies a central role in the accounts of human motivation offered by Pufendorf and Locke. Pufendorf's aim was not to articulate a comprehensive account of human psychology but to demonstrate and systematise the norms and institutions that natural law demands. Therefore, his reflections on the desire for esteem are found scattered throughout his works (most significantly, in the monumental *De jure naturae et gentium* [1672]). With the notable exception of Kari Saastamoinen, scholars have overlooked Pufendorf's analysis of how esteem-seeking and esteem-giving may lead people to adopt the norms of sociability.[37] Locke's explanation of the cognitive and behavioural implications of the desire for esteem is at once more systematic and comprehensive, and his rich private manuscripts offer us privileged access to the development of his thinking on this question.[38] A number of commentators have emphasised Locke's interest in how the desire for recognition shapes our actions and opinions. They have, however, either assumed that Locke considers this to be a bad thing – custom and opinion lead us away from the dictates of reason

34 Ibid., 1.11, 154.
35 Ibid., 1.16, 272.
36 For Hobbes and hypocrisy see David Runciman, *Political Hypocrisy: The Mask of Power, from Hobbes to Orwell and Beyond* (Princeton, NJ: Princeton University Press, 2008), 16–44.
37 Kari Saastamoinen, *The Morality of the Fallen Man: Samuel Pufendorf on Natural Law* (Helsinki: Societas Historica Finlandiae, 1995), 149–158. For Pufendorf's analysis of the reactive attitude of resentment if someone questions our status as a human being, see Saastamoinen, "Pufendorf on Natural Equality," 55–62. For more recent analysis of the desire for esteem in Pufendorf's theory of sociability, see Haara, *Pufendorf's Theory of Sociability*, 99–136.
38 For extensive discussion of the content of those manuscripts see Stuart-Buttle, "A Burthen".

and natural law – or focused upon it to show that the liberalism bequeathed to us by Locke requires a social conformity that bleaches us of spontaneity, moral autonomy and subjectivity.[39] A consideration of Pufendorf's and Locke's interpretations of the desire for esteem as engaging critically with Hobbes's theory yields rather different insights. For both philosophers, as indeed for Hobbes, this desire opens individuals up to the evaluative judgments of their neighbours in ways that might potentially be positive *or* negative, depending on the criteria we use to evaluate merit and worth.

Although their proximity to Hobbes is contested, Pufendorf and Locke both accepted many of his fundamental presuppositions about human nature. In seventeenth-century Europe, no one focused more on the nature, origins and sustainability of sociability in large societies than Pufendorf. Pufendorf assumes in man a natural inclination for society (*appetitus societatis*); but he denies that this prompts them to establish civil society, because man can satisfy this appetite in smaller, pre-political communities "by the friendship whereby he is joined to his equals".[40] Although nature has "established a general sort of friendship between men", people enter society in search of honour and advantage.[41] Moreover, as had Hobbes, Pufendorf observed that the "struggle for honour and dignity" is unique to human beings, and stimulates an "envy, rivalry and hatred" that potentially leads them to transgress even the clearest dictates of natural law (not least that of sociality).[42] In a similar vein, Locke routinely denounced "Pride and Ambition" as generative of "Covetousness", "Rapine", "Discord" and "Contention".[43] Neither denied the Augustinian insight, developed by Hobbes, that pride gives rise to a violent "lust for mastery" [*dominandi libido dominatur*].[44] As Locke observed, none of God's other "Creatures are half

39 For the former approach, see Ruth Grant, "John Locke on Custom's Power and Reason's Authority," *Review of Politics* 74 (2012): 607–29. For the latter, Foucauldian reading see Tully, "Governing Conduct"; and Uday Singh Mehta, *The Anxiety of Freedom: Imagination and Individuality in Locke's Political Thought* (Ithaca, NY: Cornell University Press, 1992).

40 Samuel Pufendorf, *De jure naturae et gentium*, ed. Frank Böhling (Berlin: Akademie Verlag, 2008), 7.1.3/ Samuel Pufendorf, *The Political Writings of Samuel Pufendorf*, trans. Michael J. Seidler and ed. Craig L. Carr (New York: Oxford University Press, 1994), 203–4. The original Latin text is cited first, separated by a forward slash from the translation.

41 Pufendorf, *De jure naturae et gentium*, 2.3.18 (our translation).

42 Ibid. 7.2.4/ Samuel Pufendorf *Of the Law of Nature and Nations*, trans. Charles H. Oldfather and William A. Oldfather (Oxford: Clarendon Press, 1934), 969.

43 John Locke, *A Letter concerning Toleration*, ed. Mark Goldie (Indianapolis, IN: Liberty Fund, 2010), 11, 26, 40.

44 Augustine of Hippo, *The City of God against the Pagans*, trans. Robert W. Dyson (Cambridge: Cambridge University Press, 1988), Preface, 3.

so wilful and proud, or half so desirous to be Masters of themselves and others, as Man".[45] Thus animated by wilful self-love, Pufendorf and Locke agreed with Hobbes that there could be no "Peace without Subjection": the laws of nature required for peace and sociability, and enjoining the reciprocal duties of justice and social virtue, are in many respects "contrary to our natural Passions, that carry us to Partiality, Pride, Revenge, and the like".[46] It was evident to Locke as early as 1659 that if every man were left at liberty to guide his actions according to his own will (or "private morals"), sociable living would be impossible.[47] In *An Essay concerning Human Understanding* (1689), Locke returned to this theme: "Men's Appetites, if left to their full swing" would "carry Men to the over-turning of all Morality".[48] For sociability to be realised, Pufendorf and Locke agreed that an external constraint (law) was required to bridle the recalcitrant passions that otherwise directed men's wills and brought them into conflict. Only thus might mankind live as God decreed that they ought: in peace and mutual fellowship.

While both Pufendorf and Locke recognised that sociability requires obedience to political authority and the rules of justice it promulgates and enforces, they denied that Hobbes's (political) solution was adequate to address the problem that he had identified. The civil law, enforced by civil sanctions, might constrain men to refrain from *harming* one another, but it could not incentivise them to perform the reciprocal duties of social morality that give rise to the deeper ties of affection and kinship upon which social life depends. Like Hobbes, Pufendorf argues that the origin of political society "lay not in the mutual good-will of men, but in their mutual fear". Moreover, like Hobbes, he did not think that men are turned into social and political animals merely through political coercion and the fear of punishment.[49] After the establishment of civil society, the sovereign's duty is to teach subjects to act in conformity to the law of sociability "not so

45 John Locke, *Some Thoughts concerning Education*, ed. John W. Yolton and Jean S. Yolton (Oxford: Clarendon Press, 1989), §35, 139.

46 Hobbes, *Leviathan*, 2.17, 254–6.

47 Locke to William Godolphin, Aug. 1659, in *The Correspondence of John Locke*, ed. E.S. de Beer, 8 vols. (Oxford: Clarendon Press, 1976–89), i, 64–6.

48 John Locke, *An Essay concerning Human Understanding*, ed. Peter H. Nidditch (Oxford: Clarendon Press, 1975), 1.3.13.

49 Pufendorf, *De jure naturae et gentium/ Of the Law of Nature and Nations*, 214. For Hobbes's views on education see S. A. Lloyd, "Coercion, Ideology, and Education in Hobbes's *Leviathan*," in *Reclaiming the History of Ethics: Essays for John Rawls*, ed. Andrews Reath, Barbara Herman, and Christine M. Korsgaard (Cambridge: Cambridge University Press, 1997), 32–65; Teresa M. Bejan, "Teaching the Leviathan: Thomas Hobbes on Education," *Oxford Review of Education* 36 (2010): 607–26.

much from fear of punishments as from habit (*assuetudo*)".[50] While critiquing the Aristotelian notion of *zoon politikon*, Pufendorf nonetheless contended that in a more limited sense man can "be said to be by nature a political animal", because once political societies have been established "men become accustomed in them to live a decent civil life".[51] Pufendorf follows Hobbes by advocating the sovereign's duty to educate his subjects to civil obedience. Yet the important difference between the two philosophers is that, for Pufendorf, processes of socialisation and habituation in many cases lie (and ought to lie) outside of the sovereign's reach. In civil society, people learn to act sociably as a result of their iterative mutual interactions: a process that cannot be understood exclusively in terms of political governance. Justice is a necessary, but not sufficient condition for sociability, as Pufendorf observed:

> It is not enough, however, not to have hurt another, or not to have deprived him of the esteem he is owed: These only remove the just cause for hatred. Something good must also be conferred on the other, at least if the minds of men are to be conjoined by a still closer bond. Someone who has not driven me away from himself by some hostile or ungrateful deed has not discharged the debt of sociality; rather, he should furnish something beneficial so that I am glad that others who share my nature also live upon this earth. And, as well, the affinity and kinship established among men by nature must be exercised by means of mutual duties.[52]

Locke was animated by a similar concern, declaring that

> [w]e must not content our selves with the narrow Measures of bare Justice. Charity, Bounty and Liberality must be added to it. This the Gospel enjoins; this Reason directs; and this that natural Fellowship we are born into requires of us.[53]

On Hobbes's account the law of nature only acquires the status of a law, the precepts of which are obligatory in performance rather than merely endeavour, when promulgated in the form of civil law.[54] Concerned to secure peace, the magistrate necessarily focuses on the enforcement of justice: it is hard to see how, by means of civil penalties, men might be induced actively to do good to one another, rather than merely restrained from doing harm. As the above citation from Pufendorf indicates, a basic respect for one's fellow men as one's equals

50 Pufendorf, *De jure naturae et gentium*, 7.9.4/ *Political Writings*, 242.

51 Ibid., 7.1.4/ 205.

52 Ibid., 3.3.1/ 164–5; cf. Pufendorf, *On the Duty of Man and Citizen*, ed. James Tully and trans. Michael Silverthorne (Cambridge: Cambridge University Press, 1991), 1.8.1.

53 Locke, *Letter concerning Toleration*, 20.

54 Hobbes, *Leviathan*, 2.26, 418.

might be a prerequisite for justice; but it is the desire for preferential esteem from others that animates us to labour for their happiness. Here Pufendorf made an important distinction between two types of esteem: "simple" (*existimatio simplex*) and "intensive" (*existimatio intensiva*).[55] In the domain of simple esteem, an act of recognition means considering the other as a good man who has some value in social life: it implies the right to be treated by others not as "a dog or beast, but as much a man as you".[56] For "affinity and kinship" to be "established among men", however, a more generous and positive act in the realm of recognition – that of "intensive" esteem – is required. This involves the free acknowledgement of another as an individual who has exercised his will in ways the admirer deems worthy of admiration and praise. Pufendorf does not deny that some forms of intensive esteem, such as those signified by honorific titles or public office, will rely on the arbitrary decision of the sovereign. He is nonetheless concerned to create social space for a sphere of intensive estimation that relies on the voluntary judgements of men and lies outside of the jurisdiction of the sovereign. Unlike on Hobbes's interpretation, in seeking preferential esteem we have no choice but to accommodate ourselves to *others'* judgments of our value, rather than coerce others to accept *our* subjective (and inflated) sense of our own worth and merit. It follows that the quest for preferential esteem generates shared norms of propriety to which all men, desirous of esteem, recognise themselves to be beholden – rather than, as for Hobbes, precluding this possibility.

In labouring the point that preferential esteem cannot be coerced from others, Pufendorf explicitly identified Hobbes's treatment of honour in chapter 10 of *Leviathan* as his target. Due to our psychological make-up, "intensive esteem" only matters to us – it only gives us pleasure – to the extent that we recognise it to be sincere. "The mere external signs of honour", Pufendorf declared, "unless they arise from the submission of the mind, are empty things". This "submission of the mind" cannot be "forced from a man" even by "the power of sovereignty" and on pain of death.[57] Whereas Hobbes had no problem basing practices of honour in fear, Pufendorf argued that coerced, insincere esteem is worthless: "things which may be extorted by force have no such power to win the hearts of others, as those which may be denied without fear".[58] In any case, we are incapable of concealing the spontaneous sentiments we experience

55 For the distinction between simple esteem and intensive esteem, see Haara, *Pufendorf's Theory of Sociability*, 101–7.
56 Pufendorf, *De jure naturae et gentium*, 3.2.1/ *Political Writings*, 159.
57 Pufendorf, *De Jure naturae et gentium*, 8.4.14/ *Of the Law of Nature and Nations*, 1249.
58 Ibid., 3.4.6/ 386.

when judging and/or being judged by others, because blushing and other involuntary corporeal signs reveal our true sentiments.[59] As Locke similarly observed, "the Physiognomy of the Mind" renders our sentiments legible to others, even if it is most transparent in children.[60]

Locke extended this logic into the realm of divine worship: for the "*esteem*" we profess in worship to be "pleasing unto God", it must express "the inward and full perswasion of the mind"; otherwise, through our "Hypocrisie" we exhibit a "*Contempt* for his Divine Majesty".[61] The mere pretence of esteem, in religion as in civil life, frustrates the end we seek in offering it: the good opinion of others. We are all acutely sensitive, as Hobbes emphasised, to contempt, due to what Pufendorf termed the "very delicate" character of our "self-esteem" (*sui estimatio*), which leads us to desire affirmation from others.[62] For Pufendorf, it is clear evidence of man's social nature that "every good man takes the greatest delight in distinguishing himself among his fellows by worthy deeds".[63] As Locke observed, this "quick sence of Reputation" explains our acute sensitivity ("Tenderness") to others' opinions of our merit and worth – opinions that, try though they might, they cannot conceal or feign.[64] As Locke reflected in his private journals, it was indisputable that the first question most men ask "in all things he doth, or undertakes" is "how will this render me to my Company, and those, whose esteeme I value?".[65] *If* the sovereign could, as Hobbes implied, to a great extent dictate to men the criteria by which they ought to esteem one another, then this would give him a remarkable power over his subjects.[66] Yet the sovereign both lacked this power in practice, and any claim to it in theory: it was no part of his jurisdiction to impose upon men's consciences in the realms of either

59 Ibid., 1.2.7/ 32.

60 Locke, *Some Thoughts concerning Education*, §101, 206.

61 Locke, *A Letter concerning Toleration*, 13. Pufendorf similarly condemns ambitious individuals who use confessional religious doctrines as a vehicle for political power and refuse to acknowledge that "all Men should allow to others their due Esteem, and not to prefer themselves before the World". Because the essence of true religion consists in the inward persuasion of the mind, it is contemptible to think that "*God* should be any Ways favourable to those who think fit to serve him in a different Manner": Samuel Pufendorf, *The Divine Feudal Law: Or Covenants with Mankind, Represented*, ed. Simone Zurbuchen (Indianapolis, IN: Liberty Fund, 2002), 12–13.

62 Pufendorf, *De Jure Naturae et Gentium*, 3.2.1; cf. Hobbes, *Leviathan*, 1.15, 234.

63 Pufendorf, *De Jure Naturae et Gentium*, 2.3.15.

64 Locke, *Some Thoughts concerning Education*, §113, 217.

65 Bodleian Library, MS Locke c.27, f.30^r (1675).

66 MS Locke f.3, 381–2 (12 Dec. 1678). Hobbes nonetheless acknowledged the limits to the sovereign's ability to dictate what is estimable or shameful, as indicated by his claim that patricide is always a cause of 'infamy and loathing', and individuals might legitimately refuse to perform such 'dishonourable' actions even when commanded to do so: Hobbes, *De cive*, 6.13, 83.

civil *or* divine esteem, because such imposition was unnecessary to secure the end (peace and security) for which authority had been entrusted to him.[67]

Aside from enforcing the rules of justice, for Locke men's consciences did not need to be constrained by political means in the moral realm, because they were *already* subject to discipline by alternative and more powerful constraints. As he noted in the *Essay*, civil law is strictly limited in both its coercive and imaginative efficacy: it cannot regulate men's conduct in private, nor can it compel them to behave in ways that exhibit much consideration for the wishes and needs of others. In the moral realm, it is the desire for esteem that (to borrow from Hobbes) forges "*Unity*" out of "Multitude" and creates a common will (law) to which all men recognise themselves beholden – and *not* their mutual subjection to the sovereign.[68] The pursuit of esteem habituates us into norms of propriety that are produced endogenously within societies on account of their communal utility. To secure esteem one must abide by these norms, encoded in what Locke called the "Law of *Opinion* or *Reputation*". It is *this* "Law" that regulates the realm of social morality and incentivises men to perform their reciprocal "imperfect" duties. As Locke declared, "he who imagines Commendation and Disgrace, not to be strong Motives on Men, to accommodate themselves to the Opinions and Rules of those, with whom they converse, seems little skill'd in the Nature, or History of Mankind".[69] Locke imposed a categorical distinction between the "Hobbist" (civil) law and the "Law of *Reputation*" due not merely to their different modes of operation, but to their discrete jurisdictions. The civil law promulgates and polices the negative ("perfect") duties of justice, whilst the "Law of *Reputation*" disseminates the positive ("imperfect") duties of social morality and enforces them with sanctions that are not physically coercive, and yet exercise the greatest power over men's minds: esteem and contempt.[70] As Locke observed as early as 1675, "Mankinde is supported in the ways of Vertue and Vice by the Society he is of, & the Conversation he keeps; Example and Fashion being the great Governours of this Worlde".[71]

Insofar as the "Law of *Reputation*" issues from and is enforced by all members of society collectively, so it tends "to encourage with Esteem and Reputation

---

67 Locke's early *Tracts on Government* (1660–2) and *Essays on the Law of Nature* (ca.1663–4) are decidedly closer to Hobbes on this point. Just as "it is impossible for anyone to grow rich except at the expense of someone else" (*ELN* 211), so Locke seems to conceive of preferential esteem in similar terms.

68 Hobbes, *Leviathan*, 1.16, 248.

69 Locke, *Essay concerning Human Understanding*, 2.28.12.

70 Ibid., 1.3.5; 2.28.7–10.

71 MS Locke c.27, f.30^{r} (1675).

that, wherein *every one* finds his Advantage; and to blame and discountenance the contrary".[72] It encapsulates a corporate (or public) reason which can identify – as the subjective, self-loving individual could not – what is necessary for the collective well-being of *all* members of society. Viewed in this light, the desire for esteem has, so to speak, been hardwired into human nature by God, and for a purpose: to induce us to acknowledge what, in the opening pages of the *Second Treatise*, Locke calls our "Obligation to mutual Love".[73] Our concern for esteem, as for Pufendorf, makes us inescapably interdependent creatures: we rely upon one another to secure the mental good that all of us recognise to be essential to our happiness. This brings the Golden Rule home to mankind, because what Pufendorf termed our "delicate *self*-esteem" – our self-love – is dependent upon the esteem and love of our neighbours: "If then happinesse be our interest end & business, 'tis evident the way to it is to love our neighbour as our self, for by that means we enlarge & secure our pleasures, since then all the good we doe to them redoubles upon our selves & gives us an undecaying & uninterrupted pleasure".[74] This providential process is likely to be disturbed if the sovereign determines, as Hobbes decreed he ought, to interfere with the "Law of *Reputation*": it is for this reason that Locke advanced what he recognised to be the "strange" doctrine that the civil magistrate "hath nothing to do with moral virtues and vices", nor ought to "prescribe any rules about them, but leave them entirely to the discretion and consciences of his people".[75] "People" here assuredly means the collective body – society – and *not* every individual; and Locke's claim relies upon the conviction that such a "people" *already* have a "rule" to guide them to which they subject their individual wills: the "Law of *Reputation*". If left to operate as it ought, this "Law" will contain moral precepts that are likely to be consistent with those of natural law, given to man by God for their terrestrial well-being as well as His eternal glory. Since "nothing can be more natural, than to encourage with Esteem and Reputation that, wherein every one finds his Advantage; and to blame and discountenance the contrary: 'tis no Wonder, that Esteem and Discredit, Vertue and Vice, should in a great measure every-where correspond with the unchangeable Rule of Right and Wrong, which the Law of God hath established".[76]

72 Locke, *Essay concerning Human Understanding*, 2.28.11.
73 John Locke, *Two Treatises of Government*, ed. Peter Laslett (Cambridge: Cambridge University Press, 1988), II: §§5 – 6.
74 MS Locke c42B, 224 (1692).
75 John Locke, "An Essay Concerning Toleration," in *John Locke: Political Writings*, ed. David Wootton (Indianapolis, IN: Hackett Publishing Company, 2003), 195.
76 Locke, *Essay concerning Human Understanding*, 2.28.11.

On Locke's account, the "Law of *Reputation*" is generated prior to, as well as independent of civil law. This underpins Locke's claim in the *Treatises* that, contrary to Hobbes's assumption, men *do* have a rule to guide them in their natural condition: natural law, as discovered by men through their mutual interactions. This "Law" provides criteria by which to evaluate the merit of people and actions that are not subjective. Through processes of socialisation and habituation, members of a society accept these criteria of good and ill as their own and evaluate their own actions, rather than merely those of others accordingly. There is no Hobbesian distinction between the internal and external forums here. Children, as Locke emphasised in his educational writings, might initially learn to act in particular ways because doing so wins them praise, but they will eventually do so because they consider such actions to be by their very nature good and obligatory.[77] Insofar as the precepts of the "Law of *Reputation*" tend to be consistent with natural law, so they are also in harmony with the moral law contained in the Gospels: upon the reading of which men will discover the true foundation of all morality in God's will and command. If the sovereign interferes with the "Law of *Reputation*", he obstructs the social processes by which the individual is disciplined in such ways as render him a sociable, morally accountable creature, capable of government. This is why, in both the *Essay* and *Treatises*, Locke labours the point that individuals must be left at liberty to esteem one another as they see fit. In direct contradiction to Hobbes's theory (and, to some extent, Pufendorf's), for Locke we retain an inalienable right as members of communities collectively to define standards of moral good and ill. We also retain the right to punish transgressions of these moral norms. Even if we give up to the sovereign our natural right to employ *coercive* force to punish transgressions of natural law, we remain empowered to employ the (powerful) sanctions of esteem and contempt. Citizens "retain still the power of Thinking well or ill; approving or disapproving of the actions of those whom they live amongst, and converse with: And by this approbation and dislike they establish *amongst themselves*, what they will call *Vertue* and *Vice*".[78]

77 On which see Michelle E. Brady, "Locke's *Thoughts* on Reputation," *The Review of Politics* 75 (2013): 335–356.
78 Locke, *An Essay concerning Human Understanding*, 2.28.10.

Conclusion

If Hobbes's solution to the problem of sociability was emphatically political in nature, he was nonetheless keenly aware that society generates other forces that shape and constrain the individual's appetites and desires in complex ways. Hobbes identified the desire for recognition as a primary reason why the individual is so susceptible to these currents; and he maintained that they might act on subjects in ways that reliably conduce to peace – the ultimate aim of Hobbes's political philosophy – only if harnessed and regulated by the sovereign. The sociability debate after Hobbes invites the thought that Hobbes's diagnosis of the problem was considered to be far more compelling, and convincing, than his solution to it.

Pufendorf and Locke, at least, appear to have held this view. They could agree with Hobbes that man is, by nature, animated by self-love, and that it is the desire to have this love affirmed by others (rather than natural benevolence) that induces him to seek society. They could similarly agree with Hobbes that self-love appears to preclude the possibility that individuals might voluntarily choose to benefit others unless they stand to gain by doing so. As Pufendorf observed, "not just anyone has such goodness of character as to be willing to do all the things by which he can benefit others out of humanity or charity alone, without a well-founded hope of receiving an equivalent in return".[79] Yet, for Locke and Pufendorf, there *is* an "equivalent" that attends such other-regarding conduct: the reward of esteem, the most pleasing "good" of all. Such esteem, contrary to Hobbes's claims, cannot be extorted from others by force or fraud: it must be earned, by acting in ways that appear meritorious to the esteem-giver. The desire for esteem makes men inherently interdependent creatures. The mental good they consider to be most essential to their happiness – esteem – requires them to treat others as they would be treated: to love their neighbour as they love themselves. Pufendorf and Locke made no effort to rehabilitate the doctrine of natural benevolence, as Francis Hutcheson would later; instead, they endeavoured to show that self-love can, and must, give rise to friendships characterised by mutual equality and reciprocity. Only thus might we self-loving creatures secure the end – the esteem and love of others – that we seek in entering society.

For Locke and Pufendorf, then, a broadly Hobbesian anthropology demanded not a denial of the very possibility that men are capable of sincere friendship and "mutual Love", but rather a new purportedly (non-Aristotelian) explanation of how they *become* such creatures in the course of their iterative mutual inter-

79 Pufendorf, *De jure naturae et gentium*, 3.4.1/ *Political Writings*, 166.

actions in society. This process, as Locke's writings show most clearly, remains contingent: the criteria by which we learn to evaluate the merit and worth of actions and characters (ourselves included) might all too easily become corrupted in pathological societies. If citizens are encouraged to value one another on the basis of their speculative opinions in religion rather than their moral conduct (as in intolerant "Christian commonwealths"), or to mistake material for moral worth (in advanced commercial societies), the harmony between social esteem and moral performance will assuredly be disturbed. But the cause of any such corruption would need to be found in defective social and political institutions, and not – as Hobbes was held to maintain – in human nature itself. This insight was further developed in the eighteenth century by those philosophers, such as Hume and Smith, who foregrounded the importance of processes of socialisation and habituation in the development of the moral personality.

Mikko Tolonen

10 Pierre Nicole and *amour-propre*

Amour-propre is a central concept for understanding early-modern moral and political thought. Much attention in recent scholarship has been placed on the analysis of *amour-propre* in which the excessive attraction to the self (*amour-propre*) is distinguished from the proper love of the self (*amour de soi*) that can be argued to correlate with the love of God.[1] This is a familiar idea of the juxtaposition between charity as a theological concept and self-love that corrupts it. Scholars are also aware that early-modern authors took different approaches to *amour-propre*, concupiscence, self-love and self-interest and not all of the seventeenth-century authors outright condemned human selfishness.[2] Of the early-modern authors following this line of interpretation Jean-Jacques Rousseau characteristically makes a distinction between proper self-preservation (instinctual) and "excessive, and illusion-ridden attachment to the self".[3] Mi-

Kari Saastamoinen inspired me to broaden my methodological approach during my doctoral studies in the mid-2000s to a closer reading of texts than what I was accustomed to at the time. It is this method of close, philosophical reading that I follow in this paper. Heikki Haara pressed me to contribute to this collection of papers for which I am now thankful. I would also like to express my gratitude to Béatrice Guion for her very helpful comments and criticism on my reading of Pierre Nicole on different occasions. I'm also grateful to Eric Schliesser, Christian Maurer and James Harris for organising workshops in the early 2010s that contributed to my thinking on Nicole.

1 For considerations of different aspects of Rousseau's conception of *amour-propre*, see Nicholas J. H. Dent, "Amour-propre" in his *A Rousseau Dictionary* (Oxford: Blackwell, 1992), 33–36 and Dent, "Rousseau on amour-propre," *Supplement to the Transactions of the Aristotelian Society* 72 (1998): 57–73. See also Timothy O'Hagan, "Rousseau on amour-propre: on Six Facets of amour-propre," *Proceedings of the Aristotelian Society* 99 (1999): 91–107 and Frederick Neuhouser, "Rousseau on the Relation between Reason and Self-Love (amour-propre)," *Internationales Jahrbuch des Deutschen Idealismus* 1 (2003): 221–239.

2 The "arguments for the constructive potential of human corruption" by La Rochefoucauld, Pascal, and Nicole have been studied for example in Ben Rogers, "In Praise of Vanity: the Augustinian Analysis of the Benefits of Vice from Port-Royal to Mandeville" (PhD diss., University of Oxford, 1994).

3 Michael Moriarty, *Fallen Nature, Fallen Selves: Early Modern French Thought II* (Oxford University Press, 2006), 238. See also Pierre Force, *Self-Interest before Adam Smith: A Genealogy of Economic Science* (Cambridge: Cambridge University Press, 2003) and especially Béatrice Guion, "Du traité des passions à l'art de se connaître soi-même: l'écrit moral au XVIIe siècle," in *L'Homme et ses Passions, Actes du XVIIe Congrès international de l'Association Guillaume*

https://doi.org/10.1515/9783110679861-012

chael Moriarty has shown that also Cornelius Jansen was pointing to this division and that there are also other seventeenth-century authors who did not lack conceptual tools to separate natural self-preservation from perverted attachment to self.[4] The interpretation of Rousseau's role in shaping early-modern discussion of *amour-propre* has been particularly great. This same division between *amour de soi* and *amour-propre* has also been extended to concern Adam Smith.[5] The main concept that then emerges from this analysis is of course that of interest.[6] While these major figures and this approach to *amour-propre* have received much attention, what has not been fully exhausted is a nuanced analysis of amour-propre offered in Pierre Nicole's essays where the conceptual tool of interest is not sufficient to grasp the relevance of *amour-propre.*[7] The argument put forward in this essay is that Nicole, as an Augustinian intellectual, formulated a theoretically significant analysis of *amour-propre* that can be seen to differ from the interest-centred analysis explained above that crucially anticipated eighteenth-century British thinking on civil society.[8] Instead of self-interest, the main emphasis in Nicole's theory is on self-esteem and how our conception

Budé, eds. Isabelle Boehm, Jean-Louis Ferrary et Sylvie Franchet d'Espèrey (Paris: Les Belles Lettres, 2016), 643–654.

4 Moriarty, *Fallen Nature, Fallen Selves*, 171–185.

5 Force, *Self-Interest before Adam Smith*, 41–47. Force takes his cue from Rousseau's definition of amour-propre already in Force, "Self-Love, Identification, and the Origin of Political Economy," *Yale French Studies* 92 (1997): 46–64.

6 For classic interpretation putting the emphasis particularly on interest in Jansenist understanding of *amour-propre*, see Marcel Raymond, "Du jansénisme à la morale de l'intrêtêt," *Mercure de France* 1126 (1957): 238–255. For more elaborations on interest, see Marcel Gauchet, "De l'avènement de l'individu à la décoverte de la société," in *Annales E.S.C.* 34 (1979): 451–463; Dominique Weber, "Le 'commerce d'amour-propre' selon Pierre Nicole," *Astérion – Philosophie, histoire des idées, pensée politique* 5 (2007): 169–196. For elaborations of the relevance of interest for eighteenth-century Britain, see Albert O. Hirschman, *The Passions and the Interests* (Princeton, NJ: Princeton University Press, 1977) and Malcolm Jack, *Corruption and Progress: The Eighteenth-Century Debate* (New York: AMS Press, 1989). For a useful further analysis of the relevance of French moralists with respect to the question of formation of modern society, see Johan Heilbron, "French Moralists and the Anthropology of the Modern Era," in *The Rise of the Social Sciences and the Formation of Modernity: Conceptual Change in Context, 1750–1850*, ed. Johan Heilbron, Lars Magnusson, and Björn Wittrock (Dordrecht: Springer, 1998), 77–106.

7 My interpretation is thus not intended as a critical intervention in Nicole studies, but as a contribution on the use and relevance of Nicole's essays in the eighteenth-century British context. For critical scholarship on Nicole and his essays, see Béatrice Guion, *Pierre Nicole, moraliste* (Paris: Honoré Champion, 2002).

8 For a somewhat contrasting interpretation, see Béatrice Guion, "The Fable of the bees: proles sine matre?," in *Bernard de Mandeville's Tropology of Paradoxes: Morals, Politics, Economics, and Therapy*, eds. Edmundo Balsemão Pires and Joaquim Braga (Cham: Springer, 2015), 91–104.

of the self is constructed in reciprocal relationship with our interlocutors. The purpose, in short, is to articulate Nicole's theory of *amour-propre* and to show how Nicole constructed one of the building blocks for the architects of the Scottish Enlightenment. At the same time, Nicole deserves our attention on his own right as one of the great historical observers of human condition.

Light of God and Hobbism

Pierre Nicole's essays were mainly composed in 1670s. The first volume of them was translated into English already in 1680. John Locke compiled his own translations of three of Nicole's essays in 1675–8. By the turn of the century Nicole's essays were widely known in Britain. These essays can be interpreted in various ways. We may read them with a view to a normative doctrine, which spells out in terms of basic Christian principles of toleration, charity and respect. We may even consider Nicole's view of Christian politeness. However, Nicole's essays also include a perceptive, naturalistic analysis of civil society based on an account of the basic principles of human nature. The descriptive account may be seen as independent from the normative side of Nicole's essays. In this article, Nicole's essays are interpreted as a blueprint towards the development of political philosophy in the works of Bernard Mandeville, David Hume, Adam Smith and many others. The discussion will concentrate on this descriptive side of Nicole.

The concept of concupiscence plays a crucial role in the Augustinian moral tradition to which Pierre Nicole belongs.[9] For Pierre Nicole it is a general term referring to the position of the fallen man that has left him in a direct contrast with God. Nicole's argument is geometrical in design. He claims that a man is either motivated through God or this worldly "inclination" that, in short, is a "general propensity of our corrupt nature".[10] Nicole is not attempting to pin

---

9 I find Moriarty, *Fallen Nature, Fallen Selves* as a useful account of Augustinian background for eighteenth-century French thinking. About Pierre Nicole, including his Augustinian background see, Edward D. James, *Pierre Nicole, Jansenist and Humanist: A Study of his Thought* (The Hague: Martinus Nijhoff, 1981).

10 Pierre Nicole, "Of the knowledge of one's self," in *Moral essays, contain'd in several treatises on many important duties*, vol. 3 (London, 1680) 4/ "De la connoissance de soi-même," in *Essais de morale [Document électronique]: contenus en divers traittez sur plusieurs devoirs importans*, (Reprod. de l'éd. de, Paris: G. Desprez, 1701, 1997), III, 4–5. I have compared the quotes that I use with the original French text. If I modify the translation, I give the original French text in the footnote. Otherwise, I only indicate the pages to the French edition that I have used. However, for clarity's sake, I have substituted most of the references to 'self-love' used in the trans-

down the actual concept in all its implications, but points out that all the "sentiments of concupiscence" are "contrary to the law of God and his eternal justice".[11] This, however, does not imply that the outward actions motivated through these sentiments would necessarily be in conflict with God's will.

It is important to notice that concupiscence is characterised as an inclination. We are either drawn towards God or pulled away from him. Nicole explains this dichotomy by writing that in 'the bottom of the heart' we can find two separate and conflicting principles, the love of "God" and the love of "creature".[12] Epistemologically the matter is simple. Either our actions are motivated through the love of God or concupiscence. Only a few live through God's grace and sincerely love God. This is possible only if God's will, placed in the heart, touches the person in a certain way, which in other words means that he has been given efficient grace. Such a person treats other people with charity. Perhaps the easiest way to understand the role of grace is to say that the ones who act through grace have God's will as their motivating principle. Their love of God "spills over" towards other people as charity. The rest are sinners. They have God's light in their heart, but it does not sensibly motivate.

The idea that the soul needs to be sensibly touched by God is important for Nicole. It is, he thinks, perfectly logical to state that God's justice is implanted in every human heart, but only a select few are effectively moved by it. The idea of being touched is important also in other respects. For example, Nicole does not have to revert to an unconvincing argument that God's light or justice would be dim or weak in some people and stronger in others. God is the truth and there cannot be any variations of it. This also explains how most of the people are motivated through another principle. Only from the "insensibility towards" God "springs" our "sensible and lively esteem for creatures". Human soul is a faculty that simply "cannot be without some inclination, and must always fix her self on some object".[13] Thus, if it is not God and our love for him that moves us, it must be something else, which in Nicole's vocabulary is termed concupiscence.

---

lation with '*amour-propre*', if there is no indication that Nicole in that particular point is clearly pointing at the 'self-love' side of *amour-propre*.

11 Nicole, "A discourse, wherein is shown how dangerous conversation is," in *Moral essays, contain'd in several treatises on many important duties*, vol. 2 (London, 1684), 272/ "Discours où l'on fait voire combien les entretiens des hommes sont dangereux," in *Essais de morale*, II, 66–67.

12 Nicole, "Of the knowledge of one's self," in *Moral essays*, III, 118/ "De la connoissance de soi-même," in *Essais de morale*, III, 139–140.

13 Nicole, "Of the fear of God," in *Moral essays, contain'd in several treatises on many important duties*, 3rd. ed., vol. 1 (London, 1696), 83/ "De la crainte de Dieu," in *Essais de morale*, I, 168.

This dichotomy is also the root of Nicole's rigorous Jansenist conception of sin. However, by constructing his theory in this way, Nicole leaves another option open. Also a sinner can be a good Christian by trying to reform the wicked state of his soul and desiring to live according to God's law. Since God's light is implanted in the soul, even when it does not sensibly motivate, everyone is able to know God's eternal law and will. In fact, not even the worst of human beings are able to escape the "penetrating rays of his justice".[14] Thus, everyone who truly desires (and is capable of using the faculty of reason) is able to learn "the law", "the will" and "the order of God".[15] However, for these sinners God's justice is not an intrinsic, motivating principle in the soul and it never will be if God does not change their inner constitution. These men have to strive for the truth by trying to conquer the contrasting inclination, concupiscence, which is also a naturally motivating principle of the heart. Main point of Nicole's normative doctrine is the idea that it is possible that men may consciously carry out good acts (those that God wills us to do and that are in accordance with his law and order) and lead a life of a good Christian, even when they do not have efficient grace and God's will does not efficiently move them.[16]

On most occasions Nicole uses concupiscence as a rather vague, general term referring to man's overall inclination to drift away from God. *Amour-propre*, on the other hand, directly linked to this propensity, is a faculty that is pinned down more precisely. In fact, Nicole's significance as a moral philosopher should perhaps be evaluated as an attempt to analyse this difficult concept and form a logical system of its implications.

For Nicole *amour-propre* is the first principle. The idea of concupiscence might remark the fact that our souls are inclined towards creatures, but it is not really towards all the creatures that we are drawn to. Nicole's way of further unravelling this inclination is with a necessary reference to *amour-propre*. A man is in love with himself instead of God. When describing our fallen state, Nicole remarks that 'we bring into the world with us a will totally taken up with the

---

14 Nicole, "Of the weakness of man," in *Moral essays*, I, 58/ "De la faiblesse de l'homme," in *Essais de morale*, I, 123.

15 Nicole, "Of the weakness of man," in *Moral essays*, I, 54/ "De la faiblesse de l'homme," in *Essais de morale*, I, 76. Nicole, "Of the means to conserve peace amongst men," in *Moral essays*, I, 115/ "Des moyens de conserver la paix avec les hommes," in *Essais de morale*, I, 232.

16 About God, grace and concupiscence see especially James, *Pierre Nicole, Jansenist and Humanist.*

love of itself, and incapable of loving any thing but with relation to our selves'.[17] A man does "not only love himself". He "loves himself without limits, and without measure; loves only himself, and refers all to himself". He simply cannot even desire anything that does not stand in a certain "relation to himself".[18] It is evident that without efficient grace there is no possibility of universal benevolence, but how does Nicole's account differ from Hobbists who also claim that a man is an utterly selfish creature, naturally incapable of other-regarding affection?

Some commentators think that it does not differ at all. Pierre Force has emblematically argued that "Nicole agrees entirely with Hobbes on the description of human nature".[19] I agree that there are passages in Nicole's essays that give the impression that his understanding of human nature is in accordance with what has often been taken as Hobbes's view. It is thus crucial for us to read carefully Nicole's essay *Of charity and self-love*. Nicole argues that we have "a secret inclination to seek all things" for ourselves. A man, Nicole writes, has a natural propensity to "make himself the center of all". This principle is also characterised as 'a natural tyranny' elsewhere.[20] This "tyrannical disposition" to make everything centre in us is irresistibly 'stamped in the bottom of' our "hearts". It "renders" us "violent, unjust, cruel, ambitious, flatterers, envious, insolent and quarrellous". As Nicole dramatically rounds off his argument – it is truly "a monster" that "we harbour in our bosoms".[21]

It might be a monster that we harbour in our breasts, but it is not a Hobbist monster. In a Hobbist system self-love engages men to hurt others is a battle for survival. We may debate whether this was Thomas Hobbes's own first principle, but we have to accept it when we talk about Hobbism. In this theory self-preservation is the beginning and the end. Nicole agrees that all our wrongdoings are caused by *amour-propre*. It certainly "includes the seeds of all the crimes, and of all the misdemeanors of men, from the smallest, even to the most detestable ones".[22] "The love of our selves", Nicole underscores, is the "fountain of all

17 Nicole, "A discourse, wherein is shown how dangerous conversation is," in *Moral essays*, II, 259/ "Discours où l'on fait voire combien les entretiens des hommes sont dangereux," in *Essais de morale*, II, 51.

18 Nicole, "Of charity and self-love," in *Moral essays*, III, 124/ "De la charité et de l'amour-propre," in *Essais de morale*, III, 147.

19 Force, *Self-Interest before Adam Smith*, 77.

20 Nicole, "Of Grandeur," in *Moral essays*, II, 194/ "De la grandeur", *Essais de morale*, II, 218.

21 Nicole, "Of charity and self-love," in *Moral essays*, III, 124/ "De la charité et de l'amour-propre," in *Essais de morale*, III, 147.

22 Ibid., III, 124/ III, 147.

our maladies" and it "gives us a violent inclination for pleasures, for promotion, for all that doth nourish our curiosity" and it "disposes us to procure" our "desires by all sorts of means how unjust and how criminal soever they may be". But Nicole's conception of *amour-propre* is something different than that of Hobbism. First of all, Nicole's idea of what causes us to revert to unjust means is not a struggle to preserve ourselves no matter what. The only reason why our worldly inclinations are so violent is that by centring everything to ourselves we are desperately trying "to fill up" that "terrible vacuity which the loss of our true happiness hath caused in our hearts".[23]

This wretched state of the soul is the characteristic feature of a fallen man. A man cannot "bear the interior reproach" of his "disorder".[24] He does not become aware of his disorder by a conscious process, but feels it ever since the day he is born and thus "inclines continually to fly from himself". It is because of this desperate misery of not being touched by God that we revert to means that are unjust and criminal. "A man without grace" is such "a great punishment to himself" that he "looks" even "upon himself in some sort as his own great enemy".[25] We are unconsciously trying to put ourselves in God's place. Inevitably Nicole thinks that this is an uphill battle. The urge to succeed is so violent that without outward restrictions we might turn to any means necessary. Simultaneously, man's miserable life is uncontrollably swayed by "violent passions" that "spring from an unknown root" and "proceed from a hidden abyss".[26] Nicole does not understand the prevalence of *amour-propre* as mere self-preservation. He is constructing his theory from different perspective. Meanwhile, he has no problem of using and modifying Hobbes's ideas.

When we understand the foundation of Nicole's point of view, another vital aspect of *amour-propre* becomes comprehensible. The inherent need to centre everything around ourselves is called a tyrannical propensity for a reason. The simplest and most primitive way of trying to fill up the emptiness of our soul is to "dominate over" the "fellow-travellers in the same unfortunate road".[27] A fallen

23 Nicole, "Of the knowledge of one's self," in *Moral essays*, III, 64/ "De la connoissance de soi-même," in *Essais de morale*, III, 76.

24 Nicole, "Of the weakness of man," in *Moral essays*, I, 59/ "De la faiblesse de l'homme," in *Essais de morale*, I, 124.

25 Nicole, "Of the knowledge of one's self," in *Moral essays*, III, 4/ "De la connoissance de soi-même," in *Essais de morale*, III, 4.

26 Nicole, "Of the fear of God," in *Moral essays*, I, 80/ "De la crainte de Dieu," in *Essais de morale*, I, 163.

27 Nicole, "A discourse of the necessity of not trusting the conduct of ones life to chance, and of not guiding it by the rules of fancy," in *Moral essays*, II, 134. Nicole, "Discours sur la necessité de se nepas conduire du hazard, et par des regles de fantaisie," in *Essais de morale*, II, 22.

man is never fully cured of this instinctive quality and all men "inevitably" have an inclination "of domineering and lording over" other "men".[28] This desire manifests itself in all the possible aspects of life. A particularly strong feature of human nature is a "desire of domineering over the minds of others".[29] Once a man has obtained some opinion, he is "naturally wedded to" it. Not necessarily because it would be a token of particularly good judgment, but because he is "never free from a desire of lording it over others by all ways possible".[30]

It is clear that the simplest and most inevitable function of *amour-propre* is to covet "sovereignty". Once we are "regarded and looked upon by others as great and powerful" and "we stir up in the hearts of others motions of respect and submission", this grossly supports our secret design to put our own image in the place of God's.[31] This is the part of *amour-propre* that is traditionally described as self-love and derived from Hobbes's account that is couched to material goods and self-preservation. Like Hobbes, Nicole claims that in a society where there is no government, "every one would be master, and tyrannize over others". In this state it would be "a necessity" that "the stronger become lords, whilst the weak remain subject".[32] Pierre Force is correct when he writes that Nicole agrees with Hobbes about the origin of government.[33] Indeed, in his key-essay, *Of charity and self-love*, Nicole follows Hobbes's description of the origin of the government closely. But in order to understand Nicole's argument we have to see what he is doing when he agrees with Hobbes. Nicole's idea is to modify the Hobbist conception of *amour-propre*. In this particular essay he retains parts of Hobbes's account while his concrete point is to criticise the actual theory.

If the idea is to "represent" the "disposition of the hearts of men" towards "one another" in the hypothetical state of nature, we may plausibly state that it is, of course, a "condition of war" and "each man is naturally an enemy to

---

28 Nicole, "Of charity and self-love," in *Moral essays*, III, 133. Nicole, "De la charité et de l'amour-propre," in *Essais de morale*, III, 157.

29 Nicole, "Of the means to conserve peace amongst men," in *Moral essays*, I, 116. Nicole, "Des moyens de conserver la paix avec les hommes," in *Essais de morale*, I, 233.

30 Ibid., I, 114/ I, 232.

31 Nicole, "Of charity and self-love," in *Moral essays*, III, 131–132/ "De la charité et de l'amour-propre," in *Essais de morale*, III, 156.

32 Nicole, "A discourse of the necessity of not trusting the conduct of ones life to chance, and of not guiding it by the rules of fancy," in *Moral essays*, II, 147/ "Discours sur la necessité de se nepas conduire du hazard, et par des regles de fantaisie," in *Essais de morale*, II, 162.

33 Force, *Self-Interest before Adam Smith*, 76–78.

all other men".[34] Nicole carries on in this Hobbist mean. The only way that the "multitude of people", who "only endeavour the ruin of one another", can be rendered into "societies, commonwealths, and kingdoms" is when *amour-propre* "which is the cause of this war" changes its ways and eventually guides people how to "live in peace". A man "loves domination". He "loves to enslave all the world to it", but he "loves yet more life and convenientness, and an easie life more than domination; and sees clearly that others are no ways disposed to suffer themselves to be domineered over".[35] Once men realise the "impossibility of succeeding by force" in their tyrannical designs, they are obliged "to submit ones self to the care of his own preservation" by uniting with other men. "To strengthen this union, laws are made, and punishments ordered for those who violate them. Thus by means of tortures, and gibbets set up in publick, the thoughts and tyrannical designs of every particular mans self-love are withheld". It is indeed true, Nicole thinks, that "fear of death is then the first tye of civil society, and the first check of self-love".[36]

Consequently, after a government and laws have been enforced, the way that self-love side of *amour-propre* operates and our bid for power changes. Since "open violence" is "excluded" from men's options, they "seek other ways" to win the worldly contest. They "substitute craft for force". When men can no longer keep on "tyrannizing over" others, they have no other option but "to content the self-love of those whom they" need.[37] This is a clear expression of the Hobbist idea how justice and self-interested commerce come into the world. The idea is still to overpower everyone else and beat others in the competition of gathering supplies needed for self-preservation. It is not, Nicole reminds his audience, that 'this tyrannical inclination which makes us have a desire to rule and govern by force over others' would be lost after a government and laws have been installed. It is still "lively in the hearts of men". In his darker moments Nicole even hints that men are merely "forced to dissemble it, until they are strengthened by gaining others by sweet ways, to have afterwards the means to bring them

34 Nicole, "Of charity and self-love," in *Moral essays*, III, 125. Nicole, "De la charité et de l'amour-propre," in *Essais de morale*, III, 149.

35 Ibid., III, 126/ III, 150.

36 Ibid.

37 Nicole, "Of charity and self-love," in Moral *essays*, III, 127. I have retained the use of self-love in this particular quote, because Nicole is pointing to this side of *amour-propre* instead of talking about the broader concept in general. Nicole, "De la charité et de l'amour-propre," in *Essais de morale*, III, 152.

to their bent by force".[38] Thus, the only thing that actually has changed concerning the self-love side of *amour-propre* is that means are different and now we have laws and justice that restrict how men act. Obviously the greatest restraint on men is the fear of "the punishment, which the laws threaten to those who have recourse to violent ways".[39] Consequently, since men are "forced" to "obey the laws", they at least momentarily "forget these vast thoughts of domination" because it is "so impossible" for "them to prosper therein".[40]

Self-interest and commerce replace the physical struggle concerning the self-love side of *amour-propre* in a political society. Pierre Nicole is very specific in his description of this interested commerce. He uses the terms "utilities", "interests", "gifts", "mon[e]y", "labours", "toyls", "services", "real goods", "merchandises", "traffick", "trade", and "commerce" when describing interested commerce. According to Nicole, even the exchange of civilities can be seen as part of this interested commerce, if the idea is that for "vain complacencies we obtain effective commodities".[41] It is indeed "by the means and help of this commerce, all necessaries for this life are in some sort supplied for".[42] However, what I find interesting is that for Nicole this self-love side of *amour-propre* is something that has to be accounted for before getting to the actual point he is making in *Of charity and self-love* -essay and what is truly interesting about *amour-propre.*

Self-Love and Pride

As we have seen, up to this point everything seems to be in agreement with a common perception of a Hobbist account of the origin of civil society. But all of a sudden, a rapid change takes place in Nicole's argument in his essay *Of charity and self-love.* After saying all this about laws, justice, self-love and interested commerce, Nicole is quick to point out there are "many people", whose "inclination of making themselves be beloved is stronger than that of domineering and lording over men". Thus, we haven't yet said enough about *amour-propre.* It is only now that Nicole starts to develop an original part of his analysis. The previous observation is the key to Nicole's moral philosophy. Nicole's argument is that *amour-propre* has two different sides – the self-love side, which in the Hobb-

38 Nicole, "Of charity and self-love," in *Moral essays*, III, 129/ "De la charité et de l'amour-propre," in *Essais de morale*, III, 153.
39 Ibid., III, 130/ III, 154.
40 Ibid., III, 127/ III, 151.
41 Ibid., III, 128/ III, 152.
42 Ibid., III, 127/ III, 152–153.

ist theory is more or less accounted for, and another side, which has been forgotten. This theoretical distinction is once more geometrical in design. The self-love side of *amour-propre* makes us want "to be rich and powerful", but this inclination is often overshadowed by another side of *amour-propre*, which takes into consideration the "judgements" of others and makes us avoid their "hatred and aversion".[43] Like self-love, this is a universal propensity and there is not a human being that would "not desire to be loved" and take "great pleasure" when others are "turned towards them" and look favourably upon them.[44]

When examined from this perspective it turns out that Nicole's attitude towards Hobbism and the self-love side of *amour-propre* is in fact uninspired. Nicole freely borrows the idea of the origin of government from Hobbes. He runs fast through it in order to get to his actual point. As an observer of human condition, Nicole is generally fascinated by the idea that we are often completely unaware whether our motives are sincere or not. However, in the case of self-love side of *amour-propre* we often "easily" distinguish "what we do, either through human fear or through gross interest".[45] In other words, there is no real intellectual challenge here for Nicole. The matter is completely "different regarding the subtlety of the love and esteem for men".[46]

This distinction between two different sides of *amour-propre* leads Nicole into a theoretical conclusion about civil society. Because of this division in *amour-propre*, according to Nicole, there are three attributes that ultimately render the existence of civil society possible. Two of these seem to be directly borrowed from Hobbes. First, *amour-propre* hinders us "through fear of chastisement" and death "to violate the laws" and removes us "by this means outwardly from all the crimes". Second, *amour-propre* "comforts the necessities of others" in "the sight of" man's own "proper interest" (thus, the idea of justice and interested commerce). These two principles, in Nicole's understanding, are the quintessence of Hobbes's conception of self-love. But Nicole's point is that in human life "there are many occasions, where neither fear nor interest have any place".[47] Therefore we additionally need to take into consideration a third

---

43 Ibid., III, 133/ III, 157.

44 Ibid., III, 132/ III, 157.

45 Nicole, "Of charity and self-love," in *Moral essays*, III, 135: "absolute interest". Nicole, "De la charité et de l'amour-propre," in *Essais de morale*, III, 160 'un interêt grossier'.

46 Nicole, "Of charity and self-love," in *Moral essays*, III, 135: "it is not"... "the same of love, and esteem for men", Nicole, "De la charité et de l'amour-propre," in *Essais de morale*, III, 160 "il n' en est pas de même de la recherche de l' amour et de l' estime des hommes".

47 Nicole, "Of charity and self-love," in *Moral essays*, III, 135/ "De la charité et de l'amour-propre," in *Essais de morale*, III, 160.

feature of *amour-propre* to form a coherent theory of it. "The most general" passion that "springs from amour-propre" is "the desire of being loved" that Hobbes did not take into consideration.[48] Nicole's insight is that "there is hardly any action" that we would take in order to "please God", "whereunto amour-propre cannot engage us to please men".[49] Out of these three principles it is the third, the inclination that renders us to please others, that is the most effective in upholding civil society. As a feature of *amour-propre* it is "much more extended than the two others".[50] This is the core of Nicole's redefinition of *amour-propre* and his criticism of Hobbism. If the idea is to form a theory of civil society based on human nature and this third feature is missing from our definition of *amour-propre*, it is unsurprising that civility and politeness are not an integral part of the Hobbist understanding of civil science. Simultaneously, it becomes overtly clear that theoretically politeness has little to do with interested commerce.

The reason why "we desire to be belov'd", Nicole emphasises, is "that we may love our selves more". The sole object of this propensity is to support the good opinion that we have of ourselves. "The love which others bear us makes us judge we deserve to be belov'd, and makes us frame of our selves a more lovely idea".[51] For Nicole, people's approval is "the object of our vanity" and "the nourishment of amour-propre". But in fact, Nicole highlights, it is even more than this. It is "the bed or couch whereon our weakness rests", he underlines in *Of charity and self-love*. The same idea is expressed also in *Of Christian civility*. Our opinion of ourselves is laid on such a vulnerable ground that "it cannot sustain it self without being under-propt by the approbation and love of others".[52]

Nicole's more nuanced understanding of *amour-propre* becomes inevitable when we broaden our reading of his essays beyond *Of charity and self-love*. All human beings, except perhaps the ones who have efficient grace, are proud and vain to some extent and eager to entertain a good opinion of themselves. It is unquestionably a token of vanity if we love ourselves instead of God. On several occasions Nicole calls attention to the fact that this self-liking side of *amour-propre* is directly linked to what is commonly called pride. "Pride", Nicole in one of his essays defines, is "a swelling of the heart, by which man dilates and mag-

48 Ibid., III, 133/ III, 158.
49 Ibid., III, 134/ III, 159.
50 Ibid., III, 134–5/ III, 160.
51 Ibid., II, 233/ II, 126.
52 Nicole, "Of Christian civility," in *Moral essays*, II, 233–4/ "De la charité et de l'amour-propre," in *Essais de morale*, II, 127.

nifies himself in his own imaginations". Men have an inherent inclination to overvalue themselves, which "imprints" them with fantastic ideas of "strength", "greatness" and "excellence".[53] The only reason why we additionally so passionately "desire" the "approbation of others" is that when we acquire it "we are settl'd and fortifi'd in the idea we have of our own excellence". It simply persuades us that "we are not mistaken in the opinion we have of our selves".[54] It is the "greatest pleasure of a proud man" to "contemplate the *idea* which he makes of himself", which "is the *origin* of all his vain satisfactions". In human mind practically everything is related to this idea of self and for a proud man "nothing pleaseth him but in proportion as it contributes to puff it up, to adorn it, and to render it more lively".[55] In brief, when "the world looks on us with esteem", we "settle in us a better opinion of our selves".[56] By and large, "the true end and aim of the ambitious and voluptuous man, is but to underprop and hold up his weakness by some externe support".[57]

Inevitably, since the approbation of others is "so necessary to keep up our hearts", "we are naturally inclin'd to seek and procure it".[58] Human weakness might perhaps not be anything to rejoice at, but when judged from the perspective that underlines social cohesion in a secular world, the attitude seems to be much more ambivalent. There is indeed a positive, natural effect of the fact that "we must be flattered and caressed like children to be kept in a good humour" or "in our fashion we fall a crying, as children do in theirs".[59] It is only from the supposition of our weakness that Nicole may conclude that "there is hardly" anything that makes a stronger "impression upon the mind" than "the fear of mens judgements" that "springs only from vanity".[60] It is the insecurity of the opinion of ourselves (for Nicole a human being is always an insignificant being, thus this

53 Nicole, "Of the weakness of man," in *Moral essays*, I, 1/ "De la faiblesse de l'homme," in *Essais de morale*, I, 1.

54 Ibid., I, 2–3/ I, 4.

55 Nicole, "Of the knowledge of one's self," in *Moral essays*, III, 5/ "De la connoissance de soi-même," in *Essais de morale*, III, 6.

56 Nicole, "Of Christian civility," in *Moral essays*, II, 238/ "De la civilite Chrétienne," in *Essais de morale*, II, 131.

57 Nicole, "Of the weakness of man," in *Moral essays*, I, 33/ "De la faiblesse de l'homme," in *Essais de morale*, I, 69.

58 Nicole, "Of Christian civility," in *Moral essays*, II, 234/ "De la civilite Chrétienne," in *Essais de morale*, II, 127.

59 Nicole, "Of the weakness of man," in *Moral essays*, I, 26/ "De la faiblesse de l'homme," in *Essais de morale*, I, 55.

60 Nicole, "Of charity and self-love," in *Moral essays*, III, 173/ "De la charité et de l'amour-propre," in *Essais de morale*, III, 206–207.

insecurity is always apparent) that makes us desirous of other people's approval, which in turn renders us sociable.

Path to Politeness

Nicole reminds his audience in several essays that men have a natural desire to boast their pride and expose it for the world to see. "There is", he writes, "a pleasure in hearing amour-propre speak when it is not disguised at all".[61] In fact, "every one" has "a desire either to disparage others, or to distinguish himself from them".[62] The implication is, of course, that since everyone is affected through these very same drives, *amour-propre* takes a different route.

Nicole calls attention to the fact that we are unable to fully understand the workings of our own *amour-propre* because it cunningly deceives us, yet we are extremely sharp "when we perceive it" somewhere else. In others it "appears" to us "under its natural form, and we hate it by so much more as we love our selves". But why do we hate it? Simply because of the fact that *amour-propre* of "other men opposes all" our own "desires".[63] Consequently, this has a direct impact on the development of civil society. Once men have been living in a society for some time, everyone becomes perfectly sensible that he is not the only one that has the urge to speak freely and to express the sentiments of the esteem that he has for himself. Men learn that "nothing" draws as much "aversion" as this inclination. *Amour-propre* simply "cannot shew it self without exciting it". Men "are not able to suffer" pride when they "discover it". Thus, "it is easie" for them to "judge" that the case will not be any different when others discover their true sentiments.[64] It is this experience of the world that "inclines those who are sensible of the hatred of men" to try "not to expose themselves thereunto". As a result, they withdraw their *amour-propre* "from the sight of others", they "start to disguise and counterfeit it" and from henceforth they never "shew it under its natural shape". The method is simply 'to imitate the behaviour of those who would be intirely exempt from it'.[65] These might be somewhat common notions in seventeenth-century France, but it is Nicole's original contribu-

---

61 Nicole, "Of the knowledge of one's self," in *Moral essays*, III, 10/ "De la connoissance de soi-même," in *Essais de morale*, III, 12.
62 Ibid., III, 2/ III, 2–3.
63 Nicole, "Of charity and self-love," in *Moral essays*, III, 125/ "De la charité et de l'amour-propre," in *Essais de morale*, III, 148.
64 Ibid., III, 135/ III, 161.
65 Ibid., III, 136/ III, 161–162.

tion to moral philosophy that he shows us how the rules of good-breeding and politeness are derived from the self-liking side of *amour-propre* – in a parallel way as laws and justice are derived from the self-love side of *amour-propre*.

The core of politeness is simply that pride should not be visible. It is "this suppression of amour-propre", Nicole stresses, "which makes human civility".[66] Politeness is "but a kind of traffick" of the self-liking side of amour-propre, "wherein we endeavour to" lure "the affection of others by owing a kindness for them".[67] We may easily point out from this quote the connotations to commerce and trade, but we have to be careful not to make the mistake of assuming that there would be some kind of material interest involved in the trafficking of the self-liking side of *amour-propre*. In human civility there are no gross interests involved. Indeed, Nicole wants to point out the analogy between interested commerce (that is the way self-love side of *amour-propre* functions in civil society) and reciprocal nature of politeness. However, he is even more eager to keep these two different institutions apart. There is a good reason why useful and agreeable are separate concepts. Of course, material interest and cupidity can motivate individuals to behave politely, but as we saw earlier, in Nicole's theory this kind of behaviour falls under the realm of interested commerce and self-love, not humane civility and self-liking. If you flatter a person in order to get some money from him, your behaviour is part of the interested commerce (that Nicole looks down with contempt). If you flatter the same person, so that he would approve your character and you may entertain a better opinion about yourself, this is humane civility (towards which Nicole's attitude is much more ambivalent). In practice, it might perhaps be impossible to keep these two spheres from overlapping, but theoretically it is important for Nicole that they are not confused as the same institution.

Nicole also demonstrates how politeness keeps evolving. He points out that "these demonstrations of affection for the most part are false". They "run into excess" and "we make a shew of more love than we have". In fact, "in the room of real love, we substitute a language full of affection".[68] Plainly put, the "discourses of civility", which are "so ordinary in the mouths of men" are far apart "from the sentiments of their heart".[69]

---

66 Ibid., III, 136/ III, 162. 'l' honnêteté humaine'. The idea is also to be found in Pascal's *Thoughts*, to which Nicole also refers to. I would like to thank Béatrice Guion for pointing this out.

67 Nicole, "Of Christian civility," in *Moral essays*, II, 234–235/ "De la civilite Chrétienne," in *Essais de morale*, II, 127.

68 Ibid., II, 235/ II, 127.

69 Ibid., II, 235/ II, 128.

But if the development brings about a custom of flattery and insincerity, moreover, men will soon learn to "keep themselves generally to a distance from all that seems vanity". Hence, the tolerable appearance of "modesty" comes into the world.[70] In fact, "civility" does not merely make men to dissimulate and smooth the appearance of their "base vain glories" (which they actually are so eager to show). Since men in general are so "extremely subtile in discovering the by-ways which may be taken to make manifest in us what we desire to shew", "civility renounces these small crafts, and studies to avoid them". Simultaneously, a new fashion comes about and, at least in theory, soon there is nothing "more simple and humble" than the "discourses" of the world. Because of the nature of *amour-propre*, it is rendered "a general rule" that a man is "never to speak of himself". If he is forced to make a comment on himself, it has to be done "with more coldness and indifferency than of others".[71] However, this does not mean that men who have adopted this new fashion would actually be humble. As Nicole points out, "pride" is "born with man" and it "never abandons him". Therefore, "in the conduct" that seems humble we may often find "a more cunning and delicate sentiment of this pride".[72]

It goes without saying that Nicole's normative position is different from his naturalistic description of politeness. However, I have no interest in the attempt to show Nicole's conception of Christian civility. Additionally, the actual methods how to operate politeness (or laws that protect self-love) and the locus where they are practised are of no concern. The relevant part is to examine the theoretical foundation behind (in Humean terms) artificial moral institutions and how they are derived from human nature. "It is manifest", Nicole clearly points out, that all 'conduct', which falls under the institution of politeness, is in the end aiming "directly" at the self-liking side of "amour-propre", since the idea is to "obtain the esteem of the friendship of men".[73] In my opinion, what is crucial for Nicole is this link between the moral institution and the passion (self-liking side of *amour-propre*) and the idea that this is analogous to justice and the self-love side of *amour-propre*.

70 Nicole, "Of charity and self-love," in *Moral essays*, III, 138/ "De la charité et de l'amour-propre," in *Essais de morale*, III, 164.

71 Ibid., III, 139/ III, 165.

72 Ibid., III, 141/ III, 167.

73 Ibid., III, 150/ III, 179.

Search for Truth, Melancholy and Progress

Interesting fact is that even when Nicole stresses that the expressions of civility are exaggerated and often false, yet the institution compels us "to praise voluntarily what is praise-worthy, to set a value as great as we can on other mens good qualities, and not to refuse even to our enemies our testimonies of esteem which they deserve". If we fail to follow these obvious guidelines, we are very unlikely to meet with approbation from others. We also have to remember that men are not merely judged by single instances but by the overall impression of their character. Nicole goes so far as to claim that "an extreme indulgence for other mens faults", hiding and excusing them as much as possible, "never" condemning anyone, explicating "all to the best", being "easily satisfied" and rather being "deceived" than giving "way to suspicions which are hurtful" to others are all part of civility. For Nicole "all this tends directly" in the end "to amour-propre".[74] Perhaps Nicole is right that this is the only way that *amour-propre* actually "hinders us for passing for proud and presumptuous".[75] At least, if we take Nicole's word for it, it seems that in order to even uphold our self-esteem it takes much more than an empty shell to actually "prosper in the design of making our selves beloved", to "acquire friends", "pacifie our enemies" and to "keep a good correspondence with all the world".[76]

Nicole does not think that a man ever succeeds in his forlorn battle of loving himself as he ought to love God. Our high "opinions" about ourselves "are grounded only upon a voluntary error". For Nicole, it really does not matter what we have achieved in the world. The opinions about ourselves "are never firm and sure", but "always mixed with mistrust, and consequently with melancholy, trouble and molestation". Instead of "pure joy" and "full and entire satisfaction which amour-propre aimeth at, all it can do" is "to suspend for some time the sentiments of sadness, which are nourished at the bottom of the heart".[77] Nicolean man is pathetic, but it is difficult to imagine a civil society more progressive than the one inhabited by these men.

The idea of God's justice and order imprinted in men is a basic Christian doctrine, uninteresting as such. However, Nicole is effectively using it also as part of his naturalistic account of civil society. I think that because of this paradoxical

---

74 Ibid., III, 157/ III, 187.
75 Ibid., III, 158/ III, 189.
76 Ibid., III, 156/ III, 187.
77 Nicole, "Of the knowledge of one's self," in *Moral essays*, III, 26/ "De la connoissance de soi-même," in *Essais de morale*, III, 29.

contrast between the love of God and the love of self, the dynamic nature of Nicole's explanation of human progress appears almost modern. It is the agonising conflict within every individual, who leads a secular life that keeps the world in motion. Men are always in a genuine search after what they can think true and good. According to Nicole, every human being has to believe, at least in some very confused and obscure manner, that what he does and what he is, ultimately is worthwhile. Nicole is very precise that "we can love nothing which we do not think good" and "true".[78] We "cannot" even "enjoy" anything, if we think that it is "false".[79] Thus, even when stirred by base motives and false judgement, "people" have to "justifie in themselves and flatter themselves, that their stubbornness, and their inflexibility in their sentiments, proceed only from the love they have for truth".[80] They "are so fashion'd by nature, that they lay hold on nothing but what is by the understanding presented to them under the appearance of some good".[81]

What, of course, happens is that this seemingly noble quality turns upside down. "The love of truth" is hailed as the first principle by everybody, but it usually unveils as an ill-servant because "the chief and principal use we make" of it "is to persuade us that what we love is true". As it often unfolds, we do not "love" things "because they are true", but "we believe them true, because we love them". Thus, we manage "to add" the "idea of truth" into our "inclinations", which only fixes us "more firmly" in our meaningless ways.[82] It might seem that in this manner Nicole drains the meaning of our love of truth, but he does not do so entirely. It becomes apparent that "men would not be men, did they not run after some true, or false light".[83]

If men always have to justify to themselves that they are looking for something that is good and true, it is equally natural that they think that ultimately they are in search of harmony. The "life of a true Christian", Nicole writes, would be "a life of peace", but the life of a man driven by his concupiscence is a constant motion searching for peace that he cannot find. God's will is "im-

---

78 Ibid., III, 31/ III, 35.

79 Ibid., III, 30/ III, 35.

80 Ibid., III, 108/ III, 128.

81 Nicole, "A discourse of the necessity of not trusting the conduct of ones life to chance, and of not guiding it by the rules of fancy," in *Moral essays*, II, 122/ "Discours sur la necessité de se nepas conduire du hazard, et par des regles de fantaisie," in *Essais de morale*, II, 7.

82 Nicole, "Of the knowledge of one's self," in *Moral essays*, III, 30/ "De la connoissance de soimême," in *Essais de morale*, III, 35.

83 Nicole, "A discourse of the necessity of not trusting the conduct of ones life to chance, and of not guiding it by the rules of fancy," in *Moral essays*, II, 122/ "Discours sur la necessité de se nepas conduire du hazard, et par des regles de fantaisie," in *Essais de morale*, II, 7.

moveable" and "the bent and inclination of a virtuous man is towards silence as much as possible he can".[84] The inclination of the common sinner is "to fly from himself" believing that 'his happiness consists in being forgetful of himself, and running headlong into this forgetfulness'.[85]

As mistaken as they might be, men are genuinely and naturally aiming for the satisfaction that is not to be found Nicole underlines in his essay *Of the knowledge of one's self.* The scenario is further complicated by the fact that even when men are constantly turning their eyes away from themselves, they have a natural desire to think that they are doing the very opposite. A Nicolean man is truly a paradox. We have "two inclinations". "One", which "makes us to fly" from ourselves, and "the other", which makes us "to seek the knowledge of our selves". They are both "natural" and "spring" from "the same fountain".[86] Knowing and not knowing ourselves is difficult. A "vain" man, sooner or later, "will" always "see" his meaningless and worthless self.[87] "Truth always makes it self a little light through all those clouds wherewith men strive to obscure it". Once *amour-propre* is at the brink of acquiring satisfaction, there are "always some rays" that come and "incommode pride"and "trouble" the "false quiet which it endeavours to procure it self".[88] Naturally, a man "avoids seeing" his actual state, "because being vain he is not able to suffer the sight of his faults and miseries". "To accord these two contrary desires" a man has to be extremely astute to find "means" that are "worthy his vanity" and "satisfy" both of these inclinations "at the same time". It truly takes "craft or subtility" from the Nicolean man to be able to "cover all his faults" and "only to include' to "the image which he" forms "of himself" those "qualities which may raise him in his own thoughts".[89] It is interesting that Pierre Nicole puts so much effort to show that a man has to genuinely succeed in deceiving himself (not merely other people) and believe that he is as worthy as he would like to think. *Of the knowledge of one's self* is a timely intervention on the human condition.

Meanwhile, what happens is that these Nicolean men are constantly forced to "renew the *idea* of their *me*". It is "this *idea*" of self that causes "their pleasure

84 Nicole, "Of submissions to the will of God," in *Moral essays*, I, 76/ "De la soumission à la volonté de Dieu," in *Essais de morale*, I, 158.
85 Nicole, "Of the knowledge of one's self," in *Moral essays*, III, 4/ "De la connoissance de soi-même," in *Essais de morale*, III, 4.
86 Ibid., III, 5/ III, 6.
87 Ibid., III, 6/ III, 7.
88 Ibid., III, 25/ III, 29.
89 Ibid., III, 6/ III, 7.

during their fortune" and "their displeasure during their disgrace".[90] Once the former ground where men had placed the idea of their own excellence (or virtue) crumbles down – as it always does – they have to find some new ground where they can build it anew or at least support the old foundation. They are in constant motion and renewing the idea of self. There is "no other end" than "amour-propre" for their "actions", but ultimately what is directing these actions is the need to "joyn always to the *idea* that they have of themselves, new ornaments and new titles".[91] Nicole's explanation of the cause of human progress is admirable. The idea is that 'our vanity remains' only "half satisfied" – at best.[92] Thus, our whole personal identity becomes dependent upon movement. We are, at least in some sense, continuously refining and progressing, but only because there is no end to it. There is no goal and no true satisfaction that we can achieve in this world. If the motion ceases we simply cannot bear ourselves. The only way that our love for ourselves is supported is by "leaning to a number of petty supports" and we need an innumerable amount of these "little props and helps" to "keep it in repose".[93] But once we come to realise (as we sooner or later always do) that the old supports were not enough to fully satisfy our vanity, we have to start looking for some new ones and the circle continues. "It is" only "by continual changes the soul maintains it self in a condition it can away with, and that it hinders it self from being overwhelmed with grief and melancholy". Nicole's dramatic summary is that "the soul subsists only by art".[94] Thus, we manage to create a vicious circle that is not completely tinted off track, because we have to genuinely believe that what we are looking for is true and good and we are also fully dependent on the opinion and approval of others. Life is but a postponement of melancholy and sadness. Yet, men keep on searching and refining their petty little ways. Meanwhile, bridges are built, fashions change and hats come off. In short, at least all the necessities of life are supplied for and conversations are more or less agreeable.

Without the idea that the truth and God are implanted in us, Nicole's scheme would go astray. Even when we are constantly fooling ourselves and desperately renewing the image we have of ourselves, we need to be able to believe that the things we love are actually good and real – that we are true and good. A man would not be a man if he did not think that he is searching for the truth. But

90 Ibid., III, 9/ III, 10.
91 Ibid., III, 8/ III, 9.
92 Ibid., III, 17/ III, 19.
93 Nicole, "Of the weakness of man," in *Moral essays*, I, 28/ "De la faiblesse de l'homme," in *Essais de morale*, I, 59.
94 Ibid., 1, 29/ I, 61.

if you are not looking from the right place, Nicole in his normative doctrine lectures, you will never find it. Your vanity will always remain, at best, half-satisfied. However, the choice that Nicole has to offer does not look too appealing for the common sinner. In fact, a fallen man is not too willing to look for inner peace, because the price to pay is too high. It would take too much to accept his worthlessness. Even the idea of facing the fact that he is not as great or virtuous as he would like to be shuns him. Thus, more often than not, people keep trying to satisfy their self-liking, time and again, using their able imagination to think of different ways how to achieve the impossible.

Conclusion

Pierre Nicole has received attention from modern scholars because he is one of the first early-modern authors to outline the idea how a secular society can be rendered peaceful based on enlightened self-interest.[95] "One may say truly", Nicole writes, "that absolutely to reform the world, that's to say to banish all the vices", all you need to do is "to give every one an enlightened amour-propre" [*amour-propre éclairé*]. Such a "society" might be "corrupt" inside, but "there would be nothing better ordered, more civil, more just, more peaceable, more honest, more generous" and, significantly, more "admirable" than this. The reason why this society would be admirable, according to Nicole, is that even when nothing but *amour-propre* would move it, *amour-propre* "would not appear there" at all.[96]

This idea of "*amour-propre éclairé*" has usually been understood in the narrow Hobbist sense as "enlightened self-interest".[97] If anything, we have to take into consideration both sides of Nicole's conception of amour-propre and put

95 On this point see particularly Dale Van Kley, "Pierre Nicole, Jansenism, and the Morality of Enlightened Self-Interest," in *Anticipations of the Enlightenment in England, France and Germany*, ed. A. C. Kors and Paul Korshin (Philadelphia: University of Pennsylvania Press, 1987), 69–85.

96 Nicole, "Of charity and self-love," in *Moral essays*, III, 165/ "De la charité et de l'amour-propre," in *Essais de morale*, III, 197.

97 See, however, Van Kley, "Pierre Nicole, Jansenism, and the Morality of Enlightened Self-Interest," 69–85, which implicitly points out that Nicole is adding something to Hobbes's account, but which however does not bring out the clear and apparent theoretical framework that is Nicole's actual contribution to Enlightenment thought. The overall question is not whether enlightened self-interest is pointed out as morally good, as Van Kley seems to think. The question is what do we mean by *amour-propre éclairé* in the first place and how do we derive moral institutions from *amour-propre*.

a strong emphasis on the self-liking, instead of self-love, since this is Nicole's theoretical invention. Even when "true interests" are certainly involved in this society, curiously the self-liking side, which is the crux of Nicole's line of reasoning, has partly escaped modern scholars. To summarise my argument, it is both justice and politeness that have to be accounted for if we want to talk about Nicole's idea of enlightened *amour-propre.*[98] And for Nicole, it is the idea of the self-liking side of *amour-propre* that plays the foundational role in rendering a secular society tolerable.

The idea that two moral institutions, justice and politeness, (both derived from *amour-propre*) are needed to render a society enlightened follows consistently throughout Nicole's essays. As he clearly points out, "we owe some things to our neighbour by certain laws of justice; which are properly call'd laws". Analogously, we owe him some other things "by the bare laws of civility". Even when these laws of civility are not laws in the strict sense of the word, "the obligation" to follow them "springs from a consent amongst men" who have agreed "to blame such as shall be defective in them". Ultimately, it is "men" who "have established all these laws".[99] Based on "justice" and the "motion of interest" men can "expect" certain "duties from us". It is exactly "the same" that "happens in the duties of civility". Just like in our debts, if we "are wanting" in civility, "others are effectively offended".[100]

By and large, it is the rules of "civility" (not honesty, as the anonymous English translator repeatedly suggests) and "justice" that are needed in civil society.[101] As

---

98 In other words, Nicole anticipates what I have argued about Mandeville and Hume in Tolonen, *Mandeville and Hume: Anatomists of Civil Society* (Oxford: SVEC, 2013).

99 Nicole, "Of the means to conserve peace amongst men," in *Moral essays*, I, 141/ "Des moyens de conserver la paix avec les hommes," in *Essais de morale*, I, 282.

100 Ibid., I, 143/ I, 285–286.

101 Nicole, "Of the remedy against suspicion," in *Moral essays*, III, 315/ "De la guérison des soupçons," in *Essais de morale*, III, 315: 'lès regles de l' honnêté et de la justice'. Nicole is consistently using this parallel between civility and justice in his essays when he is discussing the principle moral institutions. Yet, the English translation repeatedly mistakes honesty for civility. Cf. Nicole, "Of reports," in *Moral essays*, III, 268 'those who are wanting in what may lawfully be expected from them, do undoubtedly wrong honesty [sic!] and justice, and 'tis enough to judge them guilty of infidelity' Nicole, "Des rapports," in *Essais de morale*, III, 322 'ceux qui manquent à ce qu' on peut attendre legitimement d' eux, blessent sans doute l' honnêteté et la justice, et il suffit pour les juger coupables d' infidelité'. And Nicole, "Of the remedy against suspicion," in *Moral essays*, III, p. 317 'they may observe in this point, in respect of others, what honesty [sic!], charity, and justice demands of us.' Nicole, "De la guérison des soupçons," in *Essais de morale*, III, 317 'garder sur ce point à l' égard des autres ce que l' honnêteté, la charité et la justice demandent de nous.' Keohane has pointed out that when talking about 'the idea of *l'Honnête*' in 'the last half of the seventeenth century in France' the word 'honesty is surely the wrong English word to use here' and in-

Nicole describes, "men are link'd together by an infinite number of wants". Thus, they are obliged "out of necessity to live in society" since "each particular" is not "able to subsist without others". Now, it is obvious that this implies different kinds of interests and commerce. However, what Nicole particularly wants to stress is that "for keeping up society amongst men", it is of "absolute necessity" that "they should respect and love one another". As always, Nicole wants to specifically point out that in this moral institution there are no interests or money involved. "There are a number", he writes, "of small matters" which are "highly necessary for life". People should realise that they "are bestowed *gratis*" and never "to be sold" because they "can only be had for love". It is precisely the fact that the "society" is "compos'd of men full of love and esteem for themselves" that special "care" has to be taken "reciprocally to please and humour one another". If not, "it would prove a loose company", "ill pleas'd and dissatisfied amongst themselves" and, in the end, not able to "continue united". Logically, "since this mutual love and esteem appears not outwardly, they have thought convenient to establish amongst themselves certain devoirs, which should be so many tokens of respect and affection". Thus, it is the institution of politeness that is of importance in the concept of "enlightened amour-propre".[102]

Only when we take into account that Nicole's broad definition of *amour-propre* has two different sides may we understand how he thinks that a secular civil society is able to function. My argument is that this forms the blueprint for Bernard Mandeville, David Hume and Adam Smith who follow Nicole's path in this overall distinction.[103] They all take their cue for their political philosophy from the idea that we may derive justice and politeness from human nature, namely from the two different sides of *amour-propre*. Of course, Mandeville, Hume and Smith seriously modify the description of civil society by paying close attention to natural and artificial moral qualities and the evolutionary nature of moral institutions in the conjectural history of civil society. However, it

---

stead 'the best terms' for 'capturing the meaning of *l'honnêté*' are 'civility, politeness' and 'propriety'. Keohane, *Philosophy and state in France*, 283–284. It is interesting that the translator of Nicole's essays was making this precise mistake and thus this mistake in English was deeply rooted already in the seventeenth century. According to Rogers' "In Praise of Vanity", the best study of the many on *honnêté* is Jean-Pierre Dens, *Honnête homme et la critique du goût: Esthétique et société au XVIIe siècle* (Lexington: French Forum, 1981).

102 Nicole, "Of the means to conserve peace amongst men," in *Moral essays*, I, 144–145/ "Des moyens de conserver la paix avec les hommes," in *Essais de morale*, I, 288.

103 I have advanced this reading of Adam Smith in the Mandevillean context, for example, in Mikko Tolonen, "Pride and moral fitness in the sceptical sentimentalism of Mandeville, Hume and Smith" (paper presented at *Inclusion and Exclusion in the History of Ideas* Conference of the Helsinki Centre for Intellectual History, Helsinki, December 14–15, 2017).

was Pierre Nicole who first outlined the overall blueprint for this project that still plays a mediated role in some of our conceptions of the relationship between human nature and civil society.

Aino Lahdenranta

11 Hutcheson's Ambivalence about the Passions: Must Virtue and Fittingness Come Apart?

Francis Hutcheson is famous for his sentimentalist account of moral qualities. The account builds on Hutcheson's claim that human beings are determined to be pleased as such with certain motivations – a determination he calls a "moral sense". Hutcheson further maintains that benevolence is the one motive that the moral sense approves of, rendering the motive virtuous.[1] It is then unsurprising that Hutcheson, never a moral sceptic, is equally renowned for his defense of genuine benevolence; for him, establishing the reality of virtue requires establishing the reality of benevolent desires. Against the "scheme" that reduces all desires to self-love, or the desire for pleasure, Hutcheson argues that there are benevolent desires in human nature besides selfish ones.[2]

Hutcheson's early work comprises four treatises that complement one another. The third treatise, *An Essay on the Nature and Conduct of the Passions and Affections*, contains his most detailed treatment of human motivation.[3] As the title

---

1 Hutcheson's exact position on moral ontology is under debate but there is wide agreement that he rejects robust realism about moral qualities. The notable exception is David F. Norton, *David Hume: Common-Sense Moralist, Sceptical Metaphysician* (Princeton, NJ: Princeton University Press, 1982). For critique, see Martin J. Stafford, "Hutcheson, Hume and the Ontology of Morals," *The Journal of Value Inquiry* 19 (1985): 133–151; Kenneth Winkler, "Hutcheson's Alleged Realism," *Journal of the History of Philosophy* 23 (1985): 179–194; Elizabeth S. Radcliffe, "Hutcheson's Perceptual and Moral Subjectivism," *History of Philosophy Quarterly* 3 (1986): 407–421; P. J. E. Kail, "Hutcheson's Moral Sense: Skepticism, Realism, and Secondary Qualities," *History of Philosophy Quarterly* 18 (2001): 57–77.

2 I will speak of motivational hedonism (or simply hedonism) to refer to the reductive view of human motivation that Hutcheson wishes to refute. Hutcheson mentions Epicurus as the originator and Hobbes as the reviver of the view, but it is the arguments by Mandeville and John Clarke of Hull he is particularly concerned with.

3 The first treatise contains Hutcheson's theory of aesthetics, which is explicitly analogous to his moral sense theory. The second treatise concerns the moral sense and the motives it approves of; the fourth argues against competing, rationalist accounts. The treatises appeared in sets of two. My references are to Francis Hutcheson, *An Inquiry into the Original of Our Ideas of Beauty and Virtue*, ed. Wolfgang Leidhold (Indianapolis, IN: Liberty Fund 2008, rev. ed.) [1st ed. 1725; **2nd ed. 1726;** 3rd ed. 1729; 4th ed. 1738]; *An Essay on the Nature and Conduct of the Passions and Affections, with Illustrations on the Moral Sense*, ed. Aaron Garrett (Indianapolis, IN: Liberty Fund 2002) [**1st ed. 1728;** 2nd ed. 1730; 3rd ed. 1742]. Hereafter cited as *Inquiry* and *Essay.*

https://doi.org/10.1515/9783110679861-013

suggests, one finds here a division pertaining to the conative part of human nature separating passions (what we would call emotions) from affections. Both are essentially desire-like states, but the passions are more complex than the affections and involve sensations. Due to the connotations of sentimentalism perhaps, one is struck by Hutcheson's strong preference for the desires that are *void of sensation.* Yet, despite his critical stance on the passions, Hutcheson is not willing to disregard them in his search for virtuous, benevolent motives. Rather, he remains ambivalent about the worth of the passions throughout the works.

The aim of this article is to make sense of Hutcheson's ambivalent attitude. For this purpose, I turn to Nicolas Malebranche, whom Hutcheson considers an important authority on the subject. I argue that Hutcheson follows Malebranche in holding that passions are caused by present sensations of pleasure and pain but that pleasure and pain may not be their intentional object. I suggest that this feature of the passions both enables Hutcheson to escape motivational hedonism and makes him prefer the affections over the passions. An uneasy position seems inevitable: On the one hand, Hutcheson cannot dispense with the passions since they alone can be disinterested and hence qualify as virtuous. On the other hand, he agrees with Malebranche who finds the passions lacking in terms of fittingness with respect to their object.[4]

I begin by introducing Malebranche's theory of the passions in *Recherche de la vérité*[5] and his idea that a compelling feel of fittingness accompanies all passions. In the second section, I present Hutcheson's psychological theory in the *Essay*, which relies heavily on Malebranche. I argue that Hutcheson's theory does not allow for benevolent affections that would be disinterested by his own lights. Namely, the benevolent affections *aim* at the pleasures of the public sense (basically, empathetic pleasures). In the third section, I turn to Hutcheson's *Inquiry* where he endorses Malebranche's idea about the judgment of fittingness while discussing the precise role of sensation in passion. It becomes clear that Hutcheson shares Malebranche's views about the intentionality of passions. Since pleasure and pain are the causes but not necessarily the objects of passion, passions can be disinterested in the sense that Hutcheson requires.

4 To be clear, I am not saying that the position is incoherent: the uneasiness I have in mind is normative. Namely, the position requires addressing a further normative question about the sort of desires one should cultivate and act upon. Should one aim for virtuousness, fittingness, or both?

5 My references are to the English translation: Nicolas Malebranche, *The Search after Truth*, ed. and trans. Thomas M. Lennon and Paul J. Olscamp (Cambridge: Cambridge University Press, 1997). Hereafter cited as *Search*.

In the final section, I suggest why Hutcheson is inclined to agree with Malebranche that the judgments of fittingness involved in passion are false. I argue that for Hutcheson a desire is fitting if and only if human nature determines us to desire its object. In the absence of false beliefs, affections are necessarily fitting. Passions, on the other hand, may yet be unfitting insofar as they stem from passing bodily states or habitual associations. The contingency of the passions is problematic in that it results in transient and contrary pursuits. Hutcheson can maintain that some passions, such as benevolence, are fitting but the worry is whether he is positing internal senses selectively to reach certain normative outcomes.

I

Malebranche uses the term passion in two senses. In a narrow sense, a passion is the mind's sensible impulse, or emotion, towards an object. The sensible impulses can be contrasted with the mind's inclinations. Both are movements of the will but whereas sensible impulses are caused by bodily motions, inclinations are caused by the perception of some good. If the human mind were a pure spirit, it would only have inclinations, but since mind and body are united, our inclination to any object is followed by a sensible impulse to it.[6] In a wide sense of the term, a passion is an episode of mental and bodily states that includes a sensible impulse of the will.[7]

A passion in the latter sense can consist of up to seven components. (Some lack the first three and do not start out as inclinations.) The first is a perception of some object as being either good or bad for us. Since we have a general inclination to good, this judgment determines our will towards or away from the object (2). The third component is an accompanying sensation, which varies depending on the object's perceived quality and nearness. The determination of the will corresponds to agitations in the brain that set the animal spirits in motion in order to dispose the body appropriately. This fourth component, the flow of the spirits, produces a new impulse of the will that is sensible and stronger than the original impulse (5) along with a sensation that is livelier (6). The

6 Malebranche, *Search*, 337–338.

7 I disagree here with Taylor, who argues that passions in the narrow sense are sensations. Jordan Taylor, "Emotional Sensations and the Moral Imagination in Malebranche," in *The Discourse of Sensibility: The Knowing Body in the Enlightenment*, ed. Henry Martyn Lloyd (Cham: Springer, 2013), 75–78.

main thing in each passion is the fifth component: the sensible emotion towards or away from the object.[8]

The final component of a passion is a sensation of joy "that fixes the soul in its passion and assures it that it is in the proper state with regard to the object it is considering".[9] The soul receives this joy if it does not try to arrest the flow of animal spirits and control the body by will. In experiencing a passion, Malebranche explains, the pleasure that is always involved in letting the body take its course is taken by the soul as assurance that its *own state* is appropriate with respect to the object. Malebranche maintains that this judgment is always false for passions attach and attract us to worldly objects while the soul's true good and hence the proper object of love is God.[10]

The pleasure of giving in to the passion and the pain of attempting to resist it make the deceiving feeling of appropriateness hard to overcome.[11] They provide an incentive to a form of self-deception where the passion's object is judged solely in the light that it presently appears. In Malebranche's words, all passions "seek their own justification; they unceasingly represent to the soul the object agitating it in the way most likely to maintain and increase its agitation".[12] For instance, we are apt to make favorable judgments about the person we love, and everything related to him, to sustain our love.[13]

Besides deceptive justifying judgments, Malebranche discusses other errors of the passions, which he compares to the errors of sense perception. These include attributing our inner state to the object that apparently causes it, as well as believing that the object causes equal states in other people.[14] Indeed, similar attribution or projecting takes place already within the seven components of a passion: The initial perception of the good that sets the will in motion is followed by a sensation. According to Malebranche, this makes the perception of the good

---

8 Malebranche, *Search*, 347–357, 394 – 395. Malebranche argues for the basic passions of desire, joy, and sadness, since the sensible impulse, or emotion, is very different in each. Every particular passion can be characterised as one of the basic passions or as their combination. The more specific names distinguish between passions further, in relation to the initial judgment, bodily effect, or accompanying sensation. Malebranche, *Search*, 394–396.

9 Malebranche, *Search*, 349.

10 Ibid., 355 – 356.

11 Ibid., 399.

12 Ibid., 397. Schmitter characterises the mechanism aptly as a feedback loop in the supplement on Malebranche in Amy M. Schmitter, "17th and 18th Century Theories of Emotions," in *The Stanford Encyclopedia of Philosophy* (Winter 2016), ed. Edward N. Zalta, https://plato.stanford.edu/archives/win2016/entries/emotions-17th18th/.

13 Malebranche, *Search*, 370–371, 400.

14 Ibid., 370.

"more sensible",[15] which strengthens the impulse towards the object, which in turn reinforces the sensation. The same mutual reinforcing takes place between the new impulse and its accompanying sensation, which are stronger to begin with due to the involvement of the body. All along the mind becomes more fixated to the passion's object: once the will is first determined, all the following sensations are attributed to the object so that the direction of the will's growing impulse remains the same.[16]

I suggest that Malebranche holds that a passion involves an experience of being moved by the object itself and a feeling of *fittingness* between the object and one's inner state. The seventh component of joy that results from not resisting the bodily effects affirms this initial judgment and provides a motive to sustain the passion in similar but more deliberate ways.[17] I shall argue that Hutcheson endorses Malebranche's idea that we project our emotions and sensations to the object of our passion and hence experience the passion as fitting.[18]

---

15 The mind's immediate way of using pleasure to determine what is good is not wholly without basis, for pleasure is both good in itself and a "sign" by which nature helps us distinguish what is good for our body. However, we are deeply confused about the causes of our sensations – the one true cause being God. Malebranche, *Search*, 310–311, 347–348, 359–360.

16 Malebranche, *Search*, 349–450, 355. See also p. 331, where Malebranche highlights that whereas sensation makes us feel connected to our body, passions make us feel connected to the things arounds us.

17 The idea of emotions seeming justified is quite familiar to contemporary philosophy of emotion. Peter Goldie argues that an emotion, say fear, involves perceiving an object as having the relevant "emotion-proper property", like being frightening, as well as an emotional feeling toward the object, which is experienced as reasonable or justified. Goldie, "Emotion, Feeling, and Knowledge of the World," in *Thinking About Feeling: Contemporary Philosophers on Emotions*, ed. Robert C. Solomon (Oxford & New York: Oxford University Press, 2004), 94–100.

18 Hutcheson did not remain the only sentimentalist to endorse Malebranche's idea and the thesis about self-justification of the passions. Smith does so explicitly (and indeed builds his theory of moral sentiments around the notion of "propriety" between a passion and its object). See Adam Smith, *The Theory of Moral Sentiments*, ed. D. D. Raphael and A. L. Macfie (Indianapolis, IN: Liberty Press, 1982), 157; "The Principles which lead and direct Philosophical Enquiries; illustrated by the History of Astronomy," ed. W. P. D Wightman, in *Essays on Philosophical Subjects*, ed. D. D. Raphael and A. S. Skinner (Oxford: Clarendon Press, 1980), 48. A convincing case has been made that Hume employs the thesis in the *Treatise* and in a letter to Hutcheson. Éléonore La Jallé, "Hume, Malebranche, and the Self-Justification of the Passions," *Hume Studies* 38 (2012): 201–220; D. D. Raphael, Review of Motivation and the Moral Sense in Francis Hutcheson, *Journal of the History of Philosophy* 12 (1974): 263–264. See David Hume, *A Treatise of Human Nature*, ed. L. A. Selby-Bigge, 2nd. ed., rev. P. H. Nidditch (Oxford: Oxford University Press, 1978), 351; *The Letters of David Hume, vol. 1*, ed. J. Y. T. Graig (Oxford: Clarendon Press, 1932), 47. Still, much more work is called for to clarify precisely how each sentimentalist interprets and applies Malebranche's idea.

First, however, let us turn to Hutcheson's *Essay* and its theory of the passions and affections.

II

Hutcheson characterises affections as modifications of mind that result from beliefs concerning pleasures and pains. All affections arise from an "*Opinion* of Good and Evil in their Objects";[19] and, for Hutcheson, good and evil refer simply to pleasure and pain.[20] Desire and aversion arise at the thought of such an object being attainable; joy and sorrow at the thought of it being present or certain. In a strict sense, Hutcheson claims, only desire and aversion are affections: a species of conative state.[21] Joy and sorrow, on the other hand, are agreeable and disagreeable sensations, though calm and distinct from those sensations that are raised by the object itself.[22] Hutcheson criticises Malebranche for failing to see that joy and sorrow are sensations rather than conative states but adopts eventually the division of the affections into desire, joy, and sorrow.[23]

Hutcheson invokes Malebranche likewise when distinguishing between passions and affections (where the latter correspond roughly to inclinations). Passions, or "passionate affections", are more complicated counterparts of affections. In addition to an affection, a passion involves a "confused" sensation of pleasure or pain, connected with violent bodily motions. Most often, a passion also involves some "propensity", an instinctive determination to an object or action. The passion of anger, for example, involves a propensity to cause misery to the offender. Hutcheson notes that alternatively the term "passion" could be reserved for mere propensities, attended with violent sensations. In this alternative meaning, a passion would not contain any "rational desire".[24]

Believing that an object is attainable and immediately productive of pleasure (or a means to some such object) necessarily raises desire. There are, however, numerous senses by which we receive pleasant and painful perceptions inde-

---

19 Hutcheson, *Essay*, 67.
20 Ibid., 15, 34–35.
21 The causal generation differentiates affections from appetites like hunger and lust, for example. Appetites too are conative states, or ones that excite action, but they do not presuppose beliefs about attainable pleasures or avoidable pains. Hutcheson, *Essay*, 67–68.
22 Hutcheson, *Essay*, 30.
23 Ibid., 49–51. Cf. Malebranche, *Search*, 390–396.
24 Hutcheson, *Essay*, 30–31, 51–53.

pendently of our will, resulting in the fundamental variety of human desire.[25] Accordingly, Hutcheson opens the *Essay* by classifying our desires based on the sense that the desired object is fitted to please. Besides the external senses and the sense of beauty, Hutcheson argues for a public sense, a moral sense, and a sense of honor: namely, that we are determined to feel pleasure upon perceiving that others are happy, upon perceiving benevolent affections, and upon perceiving that others approve of us.[26] I will refer to these determinations as "reflective senses" since their pleasures and pains are attached to complex ideas.[27]

The resulting taxonomy of desires contains five groups. The third group is based on the public sense. It consists of "Desires of the Pleasures arising from *Publick Happiness,* and Aversion to the Pains arising from the *Misery of others*".[28] All benevolent affections and their passionate counterparts, such as gratitude, compassion, natural affection, friendship, and universal benevolence, are included in this group. As we know, Hutcheson is at pains to establish a difference between benevolent and selfish desires because the moral sense approves of benevolence alone as virtuous (whereas self-love as such is morally neutral). The rationale of insisting on a public sense is to underline that happiness of others need not be advantageous to us – instead, it is desired as one of the immediate goods.[29]

However, as Luigi Turco points out, the public sense that Hutcheson introduces in the *Essay* threatens to turn benevolence into one type of interested desire: "After he revised his views Hutcheson considered the public sense and moral sense to be the causes of social affections, rather than their effects. [...] The blind and generous instinct of the first *Inquiry* is now less instinctive or less blind."[30] More straightforwardly, T. H. Green concludes that Hutcheson is unable to escape motivational hedonism. Hutcheson merely shows that the supposedly benevolent desires do not aim at the pleasure of satisfying the desire itself or at any pleasure *other than* the pleasant consciousness of other people's happiness.[31]

---

25 Ibid., 15, 17–19.

26 In the *Essay*'s last edition, Hutcheson takes great care to clarify that it is the thought of others being happy or unhappy, and not some visual perception, that affects the public sense (Hutcheson, *Essay,* textual notes, 207, 3rd ed. addition to p. 17).

27 Hutcheson, *Essay,* 16–19.

28 Ibid., 18–19.

29 Ibid., 24–27.

30 Luigi Turco, "Sympathy and Moral Sense: 1725–1740," *British Journal for the History of Philosophy* 7 (1999): 86.

31 Thomas Hill Green, "Introductions to Hume's *Treatise of Human Nature,*" in *Works of Thomas Hill Green, vol. 1,* ed. R. L. Nettleship (London: Longmans, Green, and Co., 1885), 325–328.

I find the above argument convincing. Hutcheson equates selfish or interested desire with desire for private pleasure and aversion to private pain.[32] The criteria for a desire counting as selfish is manifest in Hutcheson's subsequent denial that benevolent desires would aim at the pleasures of the public sense or removal of the corresponding pains.[33] In denying this to be the case, Hutcheson appears to contradict his causal account of the affections and the related, sense-based taxonomy.[34] How might Hutcheson defend the possibility of genuine benevolence while staying true to his psychological views and without limiting the explanatory scope of the public sense? I suggest that the passions, as opposed to the affections, make excellent candidates for disinterested desire. In order to see this, we must turn to the *Inquiry* and its discussion of Malebranche's observation that we approve of our present passions.

III

Hutcheson introduces the idea of self-justification of the passions while defending genuine benevolence against two different ways a proponent of hedonism might try to reduce it to self-love. This two-fold purpose is more pronounced in the *Inquiry*'s later editions (3rd and 4th) where Hutcheson inserts the relevant passage on Malebranche into a new section[35] that rearranges and supplements the material of the second edition.

Here is how Hutcheson characterises the phenomenon in the second edition:

32 Hutcheson, *Essay*, 22–23, 37.
33 Ibid., 27–28.
34 Most scholars do not see motivational hedonism (as I have defined it) lurking in Hutcheson's psychological theory. According to Bishop's interpretation of Hutcheson's early work, for instance, desires are caused by beliefs about future pleasures and pains – irrespective of who they belong to. Self-love might come out stronger, but desiring pleasure for others is just as basic. John D. Bishop, "Moral Motivation and the Development of Francis Hutcheson's Philosophy," *Journal of the History of Ideas* 57 (1996): 283–284. A different reading of the *Essay* is offered by Jensen who argues that benevolence is primarily one of the appetites. Henning Jensen, *Motivation and the Moral Sense in Francis Hutcheson's Ethical Theory* (The Hague: Martinus Nijhoff, 1971), 18–19, 24–25. I find both interpretations to be in contradiction with the *Essay*'s sense-based taxonomy of desires. For critical reviews of Hutcheson's attempt to refute motivational hedonism (that is, to prove it to be false), see Robert M. Stewart, "John Clarke and Francis Hutcheson on Self-Love and Moral Motivation," *Journal of the History of Philosophy* 20 (1982): 261–277; John J. Tilley, "Francis Hutcheson and John Clarke on Desire and Self-Interest," *The European Legacy* 21 (2019): 1–24.
35 Hutcheson, *Inquiry*, textual notes, 223–231.

> 'Tis true, all the Passions, and Affections justify themselves; or, we approve our being affected in a certain manner on certain Occasions, and condemn a Person who is otherwise affected. So the Sorrowful, the Angry, the Jealous, the Compassionate, think it reasonable they should be so upon the several Occasions which move these Passions; but we should not therefore say that Sorrow, Anger, Jealousy, or Pity are pleasant, and that we chuse to be in these Passions because of the concomitant Pleasure. The matter is plainly this. The Frame of our Nature, on such Occasions as move these Passions, determines us to be thus affected, and to approve our being so: Nay, we dislike any Person who is not thus affected upon such occasions, not-withstanding the uneasiness of these Passions.[36]

The passage is part of Hutcheson's attack on the hedonist's first argument, which is that people bring benevolent affections upon themselves because they find these affections pleasant or a means to some pleasure. Hutcheson's reply is that affections are involuntary: one cannot simply choose to experience a passion when its proper object is lacking or prevent another when its appropriate object is in sight. Malebranche would agree, but Hutcheson brings up his idea about approval as a potential threat to his own position. Hutcheson has just stated that desire in general is uneasy and that compassion in particular involves pain. But if all passions approve of themselves, does that make all passions pleasant? If so, Hutcheson's opponent could claim that people seek the company of suffering people in order to enjoy the pleasure that attends compassion.[37]

The paragraph's dialectic suggests that according to Hutcheson approving is pleasant given how he proceeds to the effects of pains and pleasures that may accompany affections. Also, given both Malebranche's view on the matter and Hutcheson's account of moral approval, it seems safe to assume that the approval involves pleasure. However, whereas Malebranche claims that all passions are pleasant if not resisted,[38] Hutcheson maintains that the pleasant element is not enough to make every passion pleasant as a whole. Most importantly, this is the case with compassion and hence the self-approving nature of passions could not endanger its disinterestedness.[39]

---

36 Hutcheson, *Inquiry*, 110–111. The later version of the passage is very similar but characterises the evaluations in slightly different terms and mentions Malebranche by name: "'Tis true, indeed, all the Passions and Affections justify themselves; while they continue, (as Malebranch expresses it) we generally approve our being thus affected on this Occasion, as an innocent Disposition, or a just one, and condemn a Person who would be otherwise affected on the like Occasion. [...]" (Hutcheson, *Inquiry*, textual notes, 224–225).

37 Hutcheson, *Inquiry*, textual notes, 223–225.

38 Malebranche, *Search*, 387.

39 The reading gains further support from an addition to the later versions of the *Inquiry's* fourth edition where Hutcheson insists that insofar as there is pleasure accompanying compassion it is manifestly inferior to the pain involved (Hutcheson, *Inquiry*, textual notes, 251: 99).

Hutcheson finds the second argument on behalf of hedonism more plausible. Applied to compassion, the suggestion is that we are moved to benevolent action with the intention of freeing ourselves from the pain of compassion. To tackle this argument, Hutcheson presents various observations to show that we are *not attending* to our own pain during compassion (while acknowledging that indeed all our desires are generally accompanied by an uneasy sensation)[40]. We typically seem unaware of the suggested intention when we attempt to relieve others' distress and we rather relieve others' distress than divert our thoughts from it. In a later section, Hutcheson reappeals to Malebranche's idea: given that we approve of our compassionate response and expect others to share it, we cannot immediately be thinking of how to rid ourselves from the pain involved.[41] Notice too that Hutcheson makes an equal claim about our typical intention in relation to the delight we take in others' happiness and doing "generous Offices".[42]

At this point, the opponent might ask if Hutcheson does really mean to argue that we are indifferent to the sensations of passion. Surely these pleasures and pains have some effect on us. Hutcheson answers at the end of the paragraph on Malebranche where he clarifies what role the accompanying sensations play. In the later editions, he writes:

> Uneasiness generally attends our Desires of any kind; and this Sensation tends to fix our Attention, and to continue the Desire. But the Desire does not terminate upon the Removal of the Pain accompanying the Desire, but upon some other Event: the concomitant Pain is what we seldom reflect upon, unless when it is very violent.[43]

Instead of drawing attention to itself, the uneasy sensation makes us more focused on the desired event. In the second edition, the passage contains a similar claim but this time it is not about desires in general but about the painful passions of sorrow, anger, jealousy, and pity. Here, uneasiness does something more

---

40 In the *Essay* too, Hutcheson leaves open the possibility that all *human* affections are passionate to some extent, meaning that perhaps our conative states are never completely void of sensation (Hutcheson, *Essay*, 31).

41 Hutcheson, *Inquiry*, 161.

42 Hutcheson, *Inquiry*, textual notes, 224–225, 227–228. A related view that Hutcheson criticises is that desire would consist of a felt uneasiness. His more general comment appears to be the following: if in desiring an object we are actually desiring to free ourselves from an uneasiness at the object's absence, nothing has been said about desire – on the other hand, if desire is taken presuppose an uneasiness at the object's absence, nothing has been said about the possible objects of desire. Hutcheson, *Inquiry*, textual notes, 228–229.

43 Hutcheson, *Inquiry*, textual notes, 225.

than strengthen a desire; namely, it "determines us to endeavor an Alteration in the state of the Object".[44] In these passions then, pain causes a desire for a certain event. Bringing to mind Hutcheson's terminology in the *Essay*, the resulting desire may be called a "propensity" since we are determined to the object without expectation of pleasure or advantage from it.[45] I take it that insofar as all human affections are somewhat passionate, even a desire that is raised by a belief about attainable pleasure or avoidable pain acquires some additional strength from present sensations at the thought of the object.

Hutcheson confronts the latter hedonist argument again in the *Essay* (stated here in terms of pleasures and pains of the public sense). The suggestion that we desire the happiness of others "*as the Means of obtaining the Pleasures of the public Sense, from the Contemplation of their Happiness*" is claimed by Hutcheson to constitute the "chief Difficulty" in defending disinterested benevolence.[46] Hutcheson replies along familiar lines: he notes that we often seem to desire the happiness of others without awareness of any such intention and reckons that few have even considered that they possess a public sense. In support of his position, Hutcheson argues that we can desire others' future happiness on what we know to be our last moment; and although our public sense may be perfectly acute "at our Exit", it can hardly supply an interested motive for desiring the happiness of our posterity.[47]

We are now able to complete Hutcheson's answer to the chief difficulty. Our disinterested, benevolent desires are passions that result from present sensations of the public sense at the thought of someone else's happiness or misery. This matches well with Hutcheson remark in the *Essay* that we experience passions towards objects that are immediately presented to some sense.[48] Moreover, since the public sense and other reflective senses can have possible states of affairs as their object, they seem particularly suited to generating propensity-like desires. Now, whereas "calm desires" are caused by beliefs about possible pleas-

44 Hutcheson, *Inquiry*, 111.
45 Hutcheson, *Essay*, 51.
46 Ibid., 27. Hutcheson attributes the argument to John Clarke of Hull, distinguishing him from others who deduce benevolence from self-love "in a less specious manner" (Hutcheson, *Essay*, 23). Indeed, in the *Essay*'s preface, Clarke's case for hedonism is characterised as "more ingenious" than any which Hutcheson has seen in print (*Essay*, 6–7). For a comprehensive analysis of the debate between Hutcheson and Clarke, see Stewart, "Self-Love." Stewart argues persuasively that both thinkers fail in their a priori arguments concerning motivational hedonism.
47 Hutcheson, *Essay*, 27–28. Hutcheson advances the "exit argument" (without invoking the public sense) also in the *Inquiry*'s later editions (Hutcheson, *Inquiry*, textual notes, 228; see also 234: 125).
48 Hutcheson, *Essay*, 31.

ures and pains, the passionate desires are caused by pleasures and pains upon perceiving a possibility. Private pleasure or pain, thereby, need not constitute a passion's intentional object. I conclude that the passions let Hutcheson escape motivational hedonism. Further, passionate benevolence provides an object for the approval of the moral sense, which renders it a virtuous motive.

Hutcheson never makes this point expressly. Far from privileging the passions over the affections, the *Essay* discusses persistently why the passions pose a serious threat to rational action. In the *Inquiry*'s preface, Hutcheson even speculates that with better reasoning capacities and without the passions, people would act in accordance with virtue without any guidance from a moral sense.[49] In the remaining section of my article, I suggest that the way in which disinterested desires are generated is the very reason Hutcheson remains suspicious of the passions.

IV

The fact that Hutcheson shares Malebranche's view about the role of sensations in passion and refers to the passions' self-approving nature lends support to the reading that he too takes these things to be connected. The *Inquiry* does not elaborate on the nature of the unavoidable approval in passion but it seems implausible that Hutcheson is invoking the moral sense in this context. (For instance, there is no mention of a momentary appearance of benevolence.) I believe that Hutcheson has in mind the same interplay between representation, desire, and sensation that we find in Malebranche. In other words, I argue that the approval he refers to is a spontaneous judgment about the fittingness of a motivational state and its object. In what follows, I wish to analyse the *Essay*'s treatment of the difference between affections and passions, or calm and passionate desires, with regard to the idea of fittingness.

Hutcheson holds that although every desire *feels* fitting with respect to its object, only calm desires are reliably fitting in this way. In characterising calm desires as "rational" desires,[50] Hutcheson is arguably leaning on the following reasoning about ends: First, we are determined to feel pleasures and pains upon perceiving certain objects of sense and reflection. Second, we are determined to desire whatever we think would provide such pleasures or diminish pains. For Hutcheson, this makes pleasure, or happiness, the natural and proper

49 Hutcheson, *Inquiry*, 9.
50 Hutcheson, *Essay*, 52

end of human action. Calm desires are always perfectly rational with respect to this end insofar as they are raised by true beliefs – meaning that their direction and strength is proportionate to the amount of pleasure and pain that the object can produce. Passionate desires, on the contrary, are highly unlikely to be proportionate to the object's actual qualities.

Hutcheson brings up two explanations for this disproportion. The first is due to the passion's confused sensation,

> which keeps the Mind much employed upon the present Affair, to the exclusion of every thing else, and prolongs or strengthens the Affection sometimes to such a degree, as to prevent all *deliberate Reasoning* about our Conduct.[51]

Another cause for the disproportion of passion is the association of ideas. For example, one might associate the pleasant idea of being esteemed by others with an external object that is indifferent in itself to all senses. The effect of associations is "that they raise the Passions into an extravagant Degree, beyond the proportion of real Good in the Object: And commonly beget some secret Opinions to justify the Passions".[52]

It is tempting to understand the irrationality of passionate desire in terms of false beliefs about the object's pleasant and painful effects. The suggestion would be that passionate desires are typically irrational because the other elements involved in passion are apt to maintain and produce false beliefs. However, Hutcheson continues his remark about opinions by contrasting them with associations:

> *Confutation* of these false Opinions is not sufficient to break the *Association*, so that the *Desire* or *Passion* shall continue, even when our Understanding has suggested to us, that the Object is not good, or not proportioned to the Strength of the Desire.[53]

I take it that insofar as association gives rise to false beliefs, the resulting desire could be perfectly calm. For instance, I might want to redecorate my kitchen because I mistakenly believe that this would be a means to social pleasures. I think

---

51 Ibid., 31.

52 Ibid., 69.

53 Ibid., 69. Hutcheson's example illustrates the point nicely: "The *Luxurious* are often convinced, when any Accident has revived a *natural Appetite*, of the superior Pleasures in a plain Dinner, with a sharp Stomach: but this does not reform them; they have got all the Ideas of *Dignity*, *Grandure*, *Excellence*, and *Enjoyment of Life* joined to their Table. Explain to a Miser the Folly of his Conduct, so that he can alledg nothing in his Defence; yet he will go on" (Hutcheson, *Essay*, 70).

that what Hutcheson rather has in mind is that I might be passionate about redecorating my kitchen without noticing that I am associating a fancier kitchen with the idea of good company. Only the latter idea is naturally attended with pleasure but somehow it makes the mere prospect of a new kitchen immediately attractive. What is problematic about my passion is that it is resistant to reasoning about the object's tendencies and still – although I would get momentary pleasure from satisfying my passion – I would probably find living with the new kitchen strangely disappointing.[54]

Jeffrey Barnouw has argued that for Hutcheson passions are "confused" primarily in the sense that they rely on association of ideas.[55] While I agree that associations are apt to make desires passionate (and suspect), I would qualify that this must happen via present pleasures and pains and that these can just as well stem from some bodily state. What makes a passion confused lies in the fact that these sensations are projected to the passion's object. As it turns out then, Hutcheson's account of the passions stays surprisingly faithful to the psychology of Cartesian confusion. It is because the inner feelings and sensations are perceived as belonging to the represented object that they move us in determinate ways, and that the resulting desires feel fitting with respect to their object.

This brings us to Hutcheson's justification for maintaining that the feeling of fittingness is usually misleading in the case of passions. According to my suggestion, Hutcheson does not begin with the normative claim that pleasure is the proper end of human action – rather, his normative or perhaps analytical claim is that whatever human nature is ultimately determined to desire is a proper end. Somehow Hutcheson must argue that we are not determined to desire things like revenge or wealth as such, for otherwise they would count as desirable in themselves. His idea appears to be that the sensations that cause or

---

54 Hutcheson, *Essay*, 85. Contrary to Gill, I would not say that association can corrupt the senses on Hutcheson's account. Michael Gill, "Fantastick Associations and Addictive General Rules: A Fundamental Difference between Hutcheson and Hume," *Hume Studies* 22 (1996): 24–27; cf. Hutcheson, *Inquiry*, 22. Rather, desires, joys, and sorrows can be corrupted because we may fail to distinguish which perceptions are responsible for our pleasures and pains. Hence, we are easily lead to objects that will eventually disappoint us. Hutcheson, *Essay*, 85–86, 92, 104–105.

55 Jeffrey Barnouw, "Passion as 'Confused' Perception or Thought in Descartes, Malebranche, and Hutcheson," *Journal of the History of Ideas* 53 (1992): esp. 420–421. In his excellent treatment of Hutcheson's relation to Malebranche on the passions, Barnouw asks what Cartesian confusion can mean for Hutcheson, who does not share the opposition of mind and body and equates good with pleasure. In reply, Barnouw argues that the confused nature of sense perception is replaced with confusion between the perception of an object and associated, additional ideas.

strengthen passionate desires are *accidental* in relation to the passion's object.[56] Hence, we may come to recognise that our desire for a particular object depended on a passing bodily state or associative habit and that the object raises no desire in itself. This realisation might lead us to take precautions against passions and their deceptive feel of fittingness.[57]

Conclusion

In the title of my article, I ask whether virtue and fittingness must come apart. Passionate forms of benevolence alone qualify as disinterested and hence virtuous, but it seems that all passions are likely to be more or less unfitting with respect to their object. Hutcheson has a way of avoiding this disturbing outcome. I have argued that passions are liable to be unfit with respect to their object given the contingency of their generation. However, when a present sensation of a reflective sense generates a passionate desire, the desire may be a necessary result of perceiving its object. It follows that a passion can be fitting even if its object fails to raise calm desire, for passions of the reflective senses render happiness of others, virtue, and honor proper ends.[58]

I have two worries about this solution. Firstly, in the *Essay* Hutcheson is averse to the idea that honor and virtue would have value as such – that is, independently of pleasure to oneself or others. He is critical of the propensity to after-death fame where "one has lost all notion of *Good*, either publick or private, which could be the Object of a distinct Desire".[59] Similarly, Hutcheson warns us that passionately pursuing the "lovely Form" of virtue can prevent one from enjoying the reflection of one's past benevolent conduct.[60] Maybe Hutcheson's deepest commitment is after all to the normative view that happiness of sensitive natures, understood in terms of pleasure, is the only thing of ultimate value. However, in his later work, *A System of Moral Philosophy*, Hutch-

56 Relatedly, I think that Hutcheson is not troubled by the immediate attribution or Cartesian confusion that takes place in sense perception because the former has an indisputable constancy that the passions lack.

57 Hutcheson, *Essay*, 47–48, 85–86, 110–111, 129–132.

58 By the same reasoning, one could perhaps argue that appetites render survival desirable irrespective of the possibility of pleasure.

59 Hutcheson, *Essay*, 51.

60 Ibid., 71.

eson presents "love of moral excellence" as a further virtuous motive.[61] Therefore, it is probable that he at least came to conceive of virtue as a proper end.

My second worry is the coherence and eventual plausibility of the proposed view. It appears that Hutcheson is stipulating which sensations manifest a natural sense in order to legitimise those passionate ends that are to his liking. Arguably, there is also a sense of revenge: a determination to feel pleasure upon the thought of making one's offender regret and feel pain in their turn. This should make revenge a proper end. I think Hutcheson might have done well to drop the idea of reflective senses altogether. In reply to motivational hedonism, he could simply have observed that many thoughts other than thoughts about attainable pleasures and pains raise our affections. Which desires count as virtuous, and what it is for something to have value in the first place, is another matter. Many are probably doubtful of Hutcheson's attempt to define value in terms of attitudes that are more natural than others.

61 Bishop, "Moral Motivation," esp. 288–291; Francis Hutcheson, *Collected Works of Francis Hutcheson, Volume V: A System of Moral Philosophy (1755)*, ed. Bernhard Fabian (Hildesheim: Georg Olms Verlag, 1990), 67–70.

Adriana Luna-Fabritius

12 Pufendorf's Sociability in (Italian) Translation

In 2005 the Italian historian Maurizio Bazzoli wrote about the rising interest in Pufendorf in recent decades in Italy. He affirmed that the increasing number of contemporary studies on the works of the German author enhanced Italian scholarship on Pufendorf's natural law and its diffusion across Europe.[1] Primarily, he noted that Pufendorf's studies contributed to the development of Italian legal culture since the eighteenth century. In his essay, Bazzoli recognised that the twentieth-century pioneer in the transformation of interest on Pufendorfian studies was Fiammetta Palladini[2] following the work of Norberto Bobbio, whose seminal works trained spotlights on the German author during the first half of the twentieth century.[3]

In a celebratory tone, Bazzoli indicated that in recent decades Italy has produced great scholars on Pufendorf's studies, such as Franco Todescan[4], Massimo

---

1 Maurizio Bazzoli, "Aspetti della Recezione di Pufendorf nel Settecento Italiano," in *Dal 'De jure naturae et gentium' di Samuel Pufendorf alla Codificazione Prussiana del 1794*, ed. Marta Ferronato Padua: Cedam, 2005), 43–60; Id., "Le concezione pufendorfiane della politica internazionale," in *Samuel Pufendorf filosofo del Diritto e della Politica*, ed. Vanda Fiorillo (Naples: Città del Sole, 1996), 29–72. Id., *Il Pensiero Politico dell'assolutismo illuminato* (Florence: La Nuova Italia, 1986); Id., "Giambattista Almici e la diffusione di Pufendorf nel Settecento Italiano," 16 *Critica Storica* (1979): 3–100.

2 Fiammetta Palladini, *Discussioni seicentesche su Samuel Pufendorf. Scritti Latini: 1663–1700* (Bologna: Il Mulino, 1978); Id., "Volontarismo e laicità del diritto naturale la critica di Pufendorf a Grozio," in *Reason in Law. Proceedings of the Conference Held in Bologna in 1984*, ed. Carla Faralli (Milan: Giuffrè, 1988), 397–420; Id., "Di una critica di Leibniz a Pufendorf," in *Percorsi della ricerca filosofica*, ed. Fiametta Palladini et. al. (Rome: Edizioni Nuova Cultura, 1990), 9–27; Id., *Samuel Pufendorf Discepolo di Hobbes. Per una reinterpretazione del giusnaturalismo moderno* (Bologna: Il Mulino, 1990); Id., "Appetitus Societatis in Grozio e Socialitas in Pufendorf" in *Filosofia Politica* 10 (1996): 61–70; Id., "Stato, Chiesa e Tolleranza nel pensiero di S. Pufendorf" *Rivista Storica Italiana* 109 (1997): 436–482.

3 Samuel Pufendorf, *Principi di diritto naturale*, ed. Norberto Bobbio. (Turin: G. B. Paravia & C., [1943] 1952); Norberto Bobbio, *Da Hobbes a Marx. Saggi di storia della filosofia* (Naples: Morano, 1965), especially the chapter "Leibniz e Pufendorf", 129–145. For a history of the philosophy of law in Italy, see Guido Fassò, *Storia della filosofia del diritto*, vol. II, L'età moderna (Bologna: Il Mulino, 1968), 173–185.

4 Franco Todescan, *Le radici teologiche del giusnaturalismo laico vol. III: Il Problema della secolarizzazione nel pensiero giuridico di Samuel Pufendorf* (Milan: Giuffrè, [1983] 2001); Id., "Dalla persona ficta alla persona moralis. Individualismo e matematismo nelle teorie della persona

https://doi.org/10.1515/9783110679861-014

Mori,[5] Oliviero Macini,[6] Vanda Fiorillo,[7] and Anna Lisa Schino, the editor of an anthology of Pufendorf's texts in Italian.[8] To this list, we should include Bazzoli himself, amongst other scholars. In Bazzoli's view, thanks to the accomplishments of twentieth-century Italian scholarship, studies on Pufendorf's natural law theory have expanded to encompass what have normally been considered his minor works.

According to Bazzoli, within Pufendorfian studies, one of the most important lines of research has undoubtedly been the historical reconstruction of its influence (sic) in the development of Italian civil culture in the eighteenth century. This line of research has primarily concentrated on the study of the translations of Pufendorf's texts into Italian, mainly, *De jure naturae et gentium* (1672) and *De officio hominis et civis* (1673).[9] Within these works, *Elementa Jurispudentiae universalis* (1660) was considered minor and did not circulate in Italy during the period in question.

Studies on the translations of Pufendorf's texts have been developed hand-in-hand with the following components: i) the elaboration of a periodisation that allowed Italians to establish the process of forming civil culture in the eighteenth

giuridica del secolo XVII," *Quaderni Fiorentini per una Storia del Pensiero Giuridico Moderno* I (1982–1983): 59–93.

5 Massimo Mori, "Giusnaturalismo e Crisi dell'Ordine Naturale," *Rivista di Filosofia* 77 (1986): 7–40.

6 Oliviero Mancini, "Diritto naturale e potere civile in Samuel Pufendorf" in *Il Contratto Sociale nella Filosofia Politica Moderna*, ed. Giuseppe Duso (Bologna: Il Mulino, 1987), 109–148.

7 Vanda Fiorillo, "La 'Socialitas' nell'antropologia giuridica pufendorfiana," *Materiali per una Storia della Cultura Giuridica* 20 (1990): 479–495; Id., *Tra Egoismo e Socialità. Il Giusnaturalismo di Samuel Pufendorf* (Naples: Jovene, 1992); Vanda Fiorillo (ed.), *Samuel Pufendorf filosofo del Diritto e della Politica* (Naples: Città del Sole, 1996); Hans Welzel, *La dottrina giusnaturalistica di Samuel Pufendorf. Un Contributo alla Storia delle Idee dei Secoli XVII e XVIII*, trans and ed. Vanda Fiorillo (Turin: Giappichelli, 1993).

8 Anna Luisa Schino, *Il Pensiero Politico di Pufendorf*, (Rome and Bari: Laterza, 1995); Id. (ed.), *De statu hominum naturali* (Lecce: Conte, 2009).

9 Diego Panizza, "La traduzione italiana del *De iure naturae* di Pufendorf: giusnaturalismo moderno e cultura cattolica nel Settecento," *Studi Veneziani* XI (1969): 483–528; Diego Quaglioni, "Pufendorf in Italia. Appunti e notizie sulla prima diffusione della traduzione italiana del *De jure naturae et gentium*," *Il Pensiero Politico* XXXII (1999): 235–250; Stefania Stoffella, "Assolutismo e diritto naturale in Italia nel Settecento," *Annali dell'Istituto Italo-Germanico in Trento* XXVI (2000): 137–175; Id., "Il diritto di resistenza nel Settecento Italiano. Documenti per la storia della traduzione del *De iure naturae et Gentium* di Pufendorf," *Laboratoire italien. Politique et société* 2 (2001): 173–199 and Id., "Il diritto naturale nella corrispondenza e negli scritti di Giovanni Battista Graser e di Clementi Baroni Cavalcabò," in *Aufklärung cattolica ed età delle riforme. Giovanni Battista Grasser nella cultura europea del Settencento*, ed. Serena Luzzi (-Rovereto: Accademia Roveretana degli Agiati, 2004): 191–205.

century; ii) the identification of certain themes within the process of forming Italian civil culture; iii) the development of methodologies *ad hoc* for a better understanding of the Italian process; and iv) an awareness and understanding of the interaction of different confessions involved in that process.

Regarding the periodisation of the circulation of Pufendorf's texts and its contribution to the development of Italian civil culture in the eighteenth century, Italian scholars have distinguished Pufendorf's studies as expanding their goals concerning Italian civil culture. Specifically, such studies changed the understanding of the relationship between Pufendorf and Grotius, between Pufendorf and Wolff, as well as the relationship between Pufendorf and other great exponents of European Enlightenment.[10]

Turning to methodology, perhaps one of the most interesting accomplishments of Pufendorfian studies in Italy lies in its affiliation to historical contextualisation. This contextualisation has thus stimulated the emergence of certain structures of thought and the *ad hoc* development of approaches to this particular case. More specifically, Italian scholars have acknowledged the relevance and worked on the concepts of *sociabilitas* and *perseitas* as crucial concepts for the development of Italian civil culture in the eighteenth century. Although, Bazzoli has shown how some authors managed to tackle the main concepts within Pufendorf's natural law theory, he pointed that not all of these authors have fully understood the meaning of some of early-modern fundamental concepts nor have they been able to identify the correct contexts to grasp their meaning. Fortunately, some examples of intellectual finesse exist. In relation to other European cases, Italian scholars have studied the concepts differently and reached varying conclusions. For instance, in 1764, J. F. Bonifacio Finetti (1707–1782) accused Pufendorf together with Hobbes and Spinoza of having linked the concept of *socialitas* to *utilitas* in such a manner that *socialitas* became more a political principle than a concept related to natural law. [11] Nowadays, we know that the diffusion of this binomial *socialitas–utilitas* should be attributed to Ferdinando Facchinei, who popularised it in his 1765 critique of Beccaria's *Dei delitti e*

---

10 Bazzoli cited Giuliana D'Amelio, *Illuminismo e scienza del diritto in Italia* (Milan: Giuffre, 1965). For a European study, see Ian Hunter, *Rival Enlightenments: Civil and Metaphysical Philosophy in Early Modern Germany* (Cambridge: Cambridge University Press, 2009).

11 Joannis Francisci Finetti, *De principiis iuris naturae et gentium adversus Hobbesium Puffendorfium, Thomassium, Wolfium et alios* (Venice: Thomam Bettinelli, 1764), I: 40; Ferdinando Facchinei, *Note e osservazioni sul libro intitolato Dei Delitti e Delle Pene* (Venice: Antonio Zatta, 1765). On Finetti, see Merio Scattola "Protestantismo e diritto natural cattolico nel XVIII secolo," in *Illuminismo e Protestantesimo*, ed. Giulia Cantarutti and Stefano Ferrari (Milan: Franco Angeli, 2010): 131–148.

delle pene. Moreover, nowadays we understand that in reality these authors popularised the arguments and terms used by the German Benedict friar Anselmo Design. Through those arguments and terms the *Juris naturae larva detracta* emphasised the lack of any religious dimension in Pufendorf's conception of society.[12] Thus previous evidence allows for the conclusion that in the early-modern Italian context the concept of sociability was associated with *utilitas* within Pufendorf's natural law. This association stems from the commentary from Design and from the understanding that a distinction existed between the principles of natural law and political thought.

In terms of methodology and themes, in his articles Bazzoli has certainly greatly stimulated discussions and interest on 'Pufendorfian themes' amongst scholars examining this period. Yet, Bazzoli has also noted that most of these themes have been developed through the historical and cultural filters of generations of scholars. Furthermore, he has insisted that these filters have likely guided studies on Pufendorf's natural law in order to tackle contemporary problems possibly beyond relevance to the understanding of Pufendorf's texts in early-modern time.[13] An example of this would lie in the insistence on the importance and way of approaching the confessionalisation divide that is a more a twentieth-century topic than an early-modern one.

Nevertheless, the importance regarding eighteenth-century Pufendorfian studies remains on understanding in which circles Pufendorf's texts were promoted. Specifically, we refer here to who the main promoters were and what their political agendas encompassed. This information is crucial to evaluating whether Pufendorf's natural law theory crucially impacted the specific contexts of the time or if in Italy it reached a more theoretical significance that assisted Italian thinkers to renew the foundations of early-modern political thought. Mainstream understanding has pointed out that Muratori and Genovesi can be counted amongst the primary promoters of Pufendorf's works in 1722 and 1755, respectively, although we continue to lack a full portrait of Muratori and Genovesi as Pufendorf's Italian publicists, and the same can be said for the rest of them.[14]

According to the results of this line of inquiry, circulation of Pufendorf was filtered through theological and moral philosophy problems already present in

---

12 Anselmo Desing, *Juris naturae larva detracta compluribus libris sub titulo juris naturae prodeuntibus, ut puffendorfianis, heineccianis, wolffianis & c.* (Munich: Joannis Urbani Gastl, 1753), 3 vols. Cfr. also Franco Venturi, *Utopia e riforma nell'illuminismo* (Turin: Einaudi, 1970), 128–129.
13 Bazzoli, "Aspetti della Recezione di Pufendorf," 43–45.
14 Ludovico Antonio Muratori, *Opere*, ed. Giorgio Falco and Fiorenzo Forti (Milan and Naples: Ricciardi, 1964).

the Catholic tradition across the Italian states.[15] This was particularly true in the north of Italy, where Pufendorf's theory was used in the theological and political controversies between Jansenists Rigorists and Jesuits amongst others. However, as pointed out above the theological and moral filters could also have reflected twentieth-century interests and approaches.

Be that as it may, in Bazzoli's view all of these above-mentioned elements serve as evidence that Pufendorf's natural law theory arrived in a fragmented Italy, which apart from Vico's theoretical and methodological proposal lacked original contributions. It was in that context of fragmented and lacking authority that the models coming from beyond the Alps found fertile soil in Italy. And, yet, for Bazzoli it is also crucial to remember that despite the endemic need for theoretical proposals these contributions were neither easily nor widely assimilated across different Italian states, nor were the proposals made by vernacular *novatori* that indeed found great reactions.

For this reason Pufendorf's contribution became even more significant, because important members of the Italian circles proposed it. Notwithstanding difficulties, Bazzoli affirmed, especially for the northern case, it was thanks to the circulation of Pufendorf's texts that natural law became a common language. Through this language, the culture of the ancient Italian states found new conceptual nets and practical implications amongst men of ethics, theology, morals, law, economy, and politics.[16] In the south of Italy, however, Grotius had the lead in this process.[17]

Still, much time has passed since Bazzoli's commentary from 2005 and his account of the undoubtedly significant contribution of Italian scholarship to Pufendorfian studies. Furthermore, room for improvements continue to exist in Italian scholarship. Amongst the most indispensable actions, there is an immense need for better coverage of the geographical territory, since Italian historiography has primarily concentrated on the north of Italy overlooking connections with the rest of the peninsula.[18] This study thus aims to unveil the forms of circulation

15 Bazzoli, "Aspetti della Recezione di Pufendorf," 43–45.

16 Maurizio Bazzoli, "Una controversia settecentesca sull'embriotomia," *Studi e Fonti di Storia Lombarda. Quaderni Milanesi* 8 (1988): 7–49.

17 Adriana Luna-Fabritius, "Providence and Uses of Grotian Strategies in Neapolitan Political Thought 1650–1750" in *Sacred Polities*, ed. Hans Blom (Leiden: Brill, forthcoming).

18 There is also a need for a better chronological coverage of Italian Pufendorfian studies that encompass the second half of the seventeenth and the first decades of the eighteenth centuries. For the kingdom of Naples, see Adriana Luna González, "*From Self-preservation to Self-liking in Paolo Mattia Doria: Civil Philosophy and Natural Jurisprudence in the Early Italian Enlightenment*" (PhD diss., Florence: European University Institute, 2009) and Luna-Fabritius, "Providence and Uses of Grotian Strategies".

of Pufendorf's works mainly, in their original language and their translations, as well as in book reviews and correspondence that circulated in the Italian Peninsula. The first part of this study reconstructs the general context where Pufendorf's translations appeared to draw some general lines, whilst the second focuses on a closer reading of the eighteenth-century Italian translations of Pufendorf's texts to disclose the main themes and concepts. The primary aim of this study is to enlarge the map of the dissemination of Pufendorf's ideas in Italy through discussions on human sociability, as this concept is common to the diverse Italian contexts.

Combining the study of eighteenth-century Italian translations of Pufendorf and the centrality of discussions on human sociability reveal the various aspects that Pufendorf's natural law theory acquired beyond its former context. Studying the impact of Pufendorf's natural law theory in the Italian context improves the evaluation of its relevance as a theoretical model for the foundations of early-modern political language in Italy and thus contributes the state of the art in Pufendorf's studies. Likewise, contributes to the history of readership since this allows us to better understand the obstacles related to the circulation and appropriation of Pufendorf's natural law as well as those of other forbidden authors in various Catholic contexts within the Italian Peninsula. In addition, this study aims to unveil the main centres of printing culture in eighteenth-century Italy. In this manner, this study aims to improve the history of the development of civil culture in Italy in the early-modern period.

The Italian context

External and internal confrontations marked the first half of the eighteenth century in the Italian states. From the international perspective, Italian states suffered before the redefinition of the European balance of power. Various Italian states faired that the major wars and the Pope's fights to reaffirm his political power in Europe under the framework of the Counterreformation era took place on the Italian Peninsula. The Pope threatened the exiting balance of power in different European states through constant interventions, most of the times, via the Inquisition through major attempts to stabilise his power in the Christendom. In such fights, the Pope counted on not only his Castilian ally, but also the various religious communities that fought for the Pope's preference in his enterprise.

The eighteenth century began with the War of the Spanish Succession from 1701 to 1714 (Utrecht 1713 and Rastatt and Baden 1714), continued with the War of the Polish Succession of 1733 to 1735 (the Treaty of Vienna 1738), and with the

War of the Austrian Succession of 1740 to 1748 (the Treaty of Aix-la-Chapelle 1748). As is well known, these events not only changed the balance of power in Europe, but most of all the configuration of the small Italian states where these wars had a massive impact. The first European conflict carried repercussions particularly in the Italian territory, where the leading families – specifically, the Habsburgs and the Bourbons – had to contend with their power in a fight mediated by the Pope and his policies within the Counterreformation programme. After signing the peace treatises of Utrecht in 1713 and Rastatt and Baden in 1714 marking the end of the War of the Spanish Succession, which did not satisfy the contesting parties, the Bourbons continued challenging the power of the Habsburgs in the following decades, particularly in Central Europe.[19]

By 1714, the Spanish monarchy officially lost the southern Netherlands (Belgium and Luxemburg) as well as two-thirds of Italy, that is, 'the garden of the Empire', which one of Charles V's chancellors used to denominate Spanish Italy. [20] The Duchy of Milan, Piombino in Tuscany, and the island of Sardinia passed to the emperor Charles VI (1685–1740) as well as the Kingdom of Naples, which remained within the sphere of the Holy Roman Empire until it was made an independent kingdom in 1734. The kingdom of Sicily, however, passed to the Duke of Savoy Victor Amadeus II (1666–1732), who in 1718 exchanged it with the emperor for the island of Sardinia. Yet, he retained its crown, which actually rendered him a king. There were also enormous changes regarding other Spanish territories both in Europe and in the Americas, but those lie beyond our interest here.

Despite all of these changes depicted by the great Giovanni Battista Tiepolo (Venice 1696–Madrid 1770), in the second half of the eighteenth century the Spanish monarchy was still considered the secular arm of the papacy, the sole guardian of political stability within Europe, and the champion of Christian cultural values. Spain is depicted as a female figure amongst lions representing the province of Leon. The old woman beside the castle represented Castile and Hercules symbolised the traditional protector of Spain with a column that symbolised Gibraltar. This was the strongest image publicising the strength of the Spanish monarchy after losing important territories in Europe.

From an internal perspective, within the Italian Peninsula the first half of the eighteenth century was a time of political and economic crisis for all of the Ital-

---

19 Joel Colton, Robert R. Palmer, and Alfred Knopf, *A History of the Modern World* (New York: Random House, 1984), 234.

20 See Anthony Pagden, *Spanish Imperialism and the Political Imagination* (New Haven and London: Yale University Press, 1990), 4.

ian states, exacerbated by the threat of the great powers taking the subsequent succession wars to Italian soil. This would bring destruction and ruin to the peninsula. Another important element that could threaten the fragile stability of the peninsula after the war of Spanish succession was the extensive European interests of Rome. Rome certainly reacted to these wars and changes in an attempt to consolidate its political power and slowly re-establish its prominent position in the new situation, until the European powers – more specifically Spain – reaffirmed what Tiepolo depicted in the 1760s. Rome critically needed to maintain its position in this new international situation.

The 1730s were marked by the beginning of the Polish Succession War (1733–1735). Charles Emmanuel III (1701–1773), the Duke of Savoy and King of Sardinia, entered the war. In contrast to his father's position, this time he did so by siding with the Bourbons with the sole objective of winning Lombardy to Piedmont. However, this time Austria and France reached an agreement relatively quickly. A preliminary peace agreement was signed in 1735, but the war formally ended with the Treaty of Vienna in 1738. Augustus III was confirmed as the king of Poland, and France awarded to his opponent the Duchy of Lorraine. The former Duke of Lorraine obtained as compensation for his loss the Grand Duchy of Tuscany and, in this manner, Austria could preserve most of the Lombard territory in addition to the Duchy of Parma. Charles of Parma took the crown of the Kingdom of Naples in 1734, declaring it independent. Yet, this act represented territorial gains for the Bourbons. Finally, Novara and Tortona passed to the Savoy family.

As far as the War of the Austrian Succession is concerned, it extended across most of the 1740s. Despite lasting eight years, it did not significantly modify the balance already created by Utrecht and Rastatt and Baden. The Holy Roman Empress Maria Theresa (1717–1780) retained the thrones of Austria, Bohemia, and Hungary, and in Italy the Duchies of Parma, Piacenza, and Guastalla were restored to the Spanish monarchy. Thus, whilst the first war of the eighteenth century brought considerable changes to the Italian Peninsula, the second and the third wars carried small modifications to that initial map.

In this context the ancient republics resisted maintaining their status. The Republic of Genoa was threatened but not attacked. Whilst the *Serenissima* Republic of Venice ratified its neutrality, Tuscany survived an awkward moment before the possible extinction of the Medici family, as well as Parma before the disappearance of the Farnese lineage. Most likely, the lack of heirs in Tuscany and Parma allowed them to be easily swept up in the massive modifications accompanying the eighteenth-century succession wars.

By the mid-eighteenth century, Italian thinkers from all of the Italian states awaited the collapse of ancient structures and prepared various political remedies. However, together they constituted a fascinating laboratory where old and new political solutions were ready to respond to whatever European eventuality emerged. Nonetheless, this situation was valid not only for the reality of the Italian Peninsula, but also for other European states. This period witnessed the rise of lofty discussions on rights, privileges, and pretentions to principalities and duchies, but also to monarchies and empires. Moreover, the fragile equilibriums between cities and their rulers were particularly shocked before major redefinitions and the emerging reform plans.[21]

The political and juridical experiments that sought a balance between principalities, kingdoms, and empires, between cities and their rulers were mediated by the popes, who used their resources to strengthen the Vatican's power by tipping the scales at the regional and international levels towards their families and their states. Pope Clement XII was Pope from 1730 until his death in 1740 and was the last pope to belong to one of the great Italian families. Following him, as pointed out by the historiography, the Vatican remained in the hands of smaller and more miserable families of provincial nobility.[22]

Finally, the religious communities contended amongst themselves for the preference of the Pope to assist him in his struggle to maintain the political power of the Vatican. Various religious communities contended the power of the Jesuits in Rome. In the north of Italy, Jansenists and Rigorists were active members of cultural milieus. This is relevant since the historiography has established that the circulation of Pufendorf's texts was linked to debates amongst Jesuits and Jansenists and because Italian Jansenists were supporters of Joseph II's reforms.[23] Although this connection explains why Pufendorf's texts circulated around Jansenists milieus in late eighteenth century, it is not valid for the earlier circulation, which obeyed to different European political contexts.

Pufendorf's natural law in Italian translation

It was in this late eighteenth-century political context marked by the European redefinition of the balance of power that modern natural law theorists – mainly Grotius, Hobbes, Pufendorf, and Heineccius amongst others – were discussed and translated. In what follows, this chapter focuses on the circulation and

---

21 Franco Venturi, *Il Settecento Riformatore* (Turin: Giulio Einaudi, 1969).
22 Venturi, *Il Settecento Riformatore*, 251–252.
23 Bazzoli, *Il Pensiero Politico dell'Assolutismo Illuminato*, see chapter 7.

forms of the appropriation of Pufendorf's texts in eighteenth-century Italian states.[24]

On 20 January 1757, the Lombard Jurist Giovanni Battista Chiaramonti wrote to jurist and celebrated member of the Republic of Letters the Florentine Giovanni Lami to announce the publication of the first volume of Pufendorf's *De jure naturae et gentium* by Giambattista Almici. In his letter, Chiaramonti communicated to Lami that the first volume of Pufendorf's *De jure* published in Venice, carefully corrected, enlarged, and illustrated by Almici, was receiving a favourable response and judgment amongst learned men.[25]

The translator of *De jure* Giambattista Almici was born in Brescia, one of the seven most powerful cities in Lombardy. Almici most likely had positioned himself amongst the learned men of the region through his brother, Pietro Camillo, who happened to be of one of the main pillars of Jansenism in northern Italy.[26] Research shows that Pufendorf's works circulated in northern Italy in circles in Italian historiography identified as 'Rigorist Catholic' groups. These groups were particularly strict followers of the Counterreformation programme during the second half of the eighteenth century.[27] That is, Pufendorf's translation of *De jure* circulated amongst groups that did not need to prove their loyalty to the Pope and the Christian faith in that moment.

However, recent research has shown that the publication of this book was not as welcome in Brescia as Chiaramonti affirmed to Lami in the letter referred to above. Indeed, its publication provoked a significant scandal amongst orthodox groups. Pufendorf's translation was, ultimately, the text of a protestant author included in *Index Librorum Prohibitorum,* a fact which did not pass as unnoticed as Chiaramonti wanted to persuade.[28] It is reasonable to think that Chiaramonti's intent was to convince Lami in Florence regarding the positive reception of the text in Brescia and Venice to encourage its circulation in Florence. The most important matter was that, although the men involved in the enterprise

---

24 For an account of studies on the cirulation of Grotius during this period, see Luna-Fabritius, "Providence and Uses of Grotian Strategies."

25 Giovanni Battista Chiaramonti, "Letter to Giovanni Lami, Brescia, January 20, 1757," (Florence: Biblioteca Riccardiana), ms 3719, c 169r and Id., "Letter to Giovanni Lami, Brescia, March 12, 1757," (Florence: Biblioteca Riccardiana), mS. 3719, c 171r. The information on the translator is enclosed in the correspondence of Giovanni Lami. On Almici, see also Bazzoli, "Giambattista Almici e la diffusione di Pufendorf", 3–100.

26 Quaglioni, "Pufendorf in Italia," 235–250; Bazzoli, "Giambattista Almici e la diffusione di Pufendorf," 3–100; Id., "Aspetti della recezione di Pufendorf", 41–60.

27 Bazzoli "Giambattista Almici e la diffusione di Pufendorf".

28 Patrizia Delpiano, *Il governo della lettura. Chiesa e libri nell'Italia del Settecento* (Bologna: Il Mulino, 2007), 90–91.

of translating and disseminating *De jure* were convinced that Almici's commentaries and amendments to Pufendorf's text rendered it ready for Catholic audiences, its circulation would not be unproblematic. Interestingly enough, despite the reaction produced by the publication of the first two volumes in 1757, the third came out in 1758 and the fourth in 1759.[29] Thus this evidence is another confirmation that despite the difficulties related to censored texts important levels of toleration also existed in the Catholic contexts.

Yet, the story of Pufendorf's texts did not end with the publication of Almici's translation. Between 1753 and 1758, a Latin edition of Pufendorf's *De officio hominis et civis secundum legem naturalem* was published in Venice by Giuseppe Bettinelli, but with the false indication of Frankfurt and Leipzig.[30] Likewise, in 1758, Girolamo Dorigoni, one of the principal Venetian editors, published Mascuvius's Latin edition of *De jure.*[31]

In addition to the previous Latin publications from 1753 and 1758 of *De officio* and *De jure* and from Almici's translations of *De jure* from 1757, 1758 and 1759, between 1761 and 1767 Michele Grandi (1718–1786)[32] published the first translation into Italian of *De officio hominis*, which was published in Venice from the French translation of Barbeyrac with corrections, additions, and illustrations.[33] Grandi was a priest born in Udine, another city in north-eastern Italy, where he had studied philosophy and theology. He obtained his doctorate in law, however, from the University of Padua. According to the historiography, the main difference between Grandi's and Almici's aims was quite evident. It has been noted

---

29 Panizza "La traduzione italiana del *De Iure naturae*," 483–528 and Bazzoli "Giambattista Almici e la diffusione di Pufendorf".

30 The edition indicates Samuel Pufendorf, *De jure naturae et gentium* (Francfurti: Lipsiae impensis Heinrici Broenneri, 1757).

31 Pufendorf, *De jure naturae et gentium*. Cfr. Mario Infelise, *L'editoria veneziana nel 700'* (Milan: Franco Angeli, 1989), 87–88, 94; Antonio Rotondò, "La censura ecclesiastica e la cultura," in *Storia d'Italia*, vol. V, ed. Ruggiero Romano and Corrado Vivanti (Turin: Einaudi, 1973), 1397–1492; Marino Berengo, *La società veneta alla fine del Settecento* (Florence: Sansoni, 1956), 134–161. Francesco Ruffini, *La Libertà religiosa: storia dell'idea* (Milan: Feltrinelli, 1967). On the circulation of Almici's translation in Tuscany and the confiscation of books in the house of Rigaci in Florence, see Niccolò Rodolico, *Stato e Chiesa in Toscana durante la reggenza lorenese (1737–1765)* (Florence: Le Monnier, 1910), 166–167, 327; Sandro Landi, *Il governo delle opinioni. Censura e formazione del consenso nella Toscana del Settecento* (Bologna: Il Mulino: 2000), n.31, 61, n.36, 63.

32 On Grandi see Carlo Morelli di Schönfeld, *Osservazioni ed Aggiunte di G.D. Della Bona. Istoria della Contea di Gorizia* (Gorizia: Tipografia Paternolli, 1856), 305–308.

33 As Samuele Pufendorf, *I doveri dell'uomo e del cittadino tali che a lui sono prescritti dalla legge natural, dalla versione francese di Giovanni Barbeyrac*, 3 vols., trans. and ed. Michele Grandi Accademico di Udine, (Venice: Pietteri, 1761–1767).

that despite Grandi's solid moralist and orthodox leaning, he was committed to the dissemination of enlightened ideas. Part of that project was the diffusion of Barbeyrac's interpretation of Pufendorf himself that he certainly considered an enlightened author. According to these objectives, Grandi was known in Italy for being a defender of Barbeyrac and in opposition to Almici. Evidence of this position primarily relies on the publication of an appendix to his translation of Pufendorf's *De officio*, Barbeyrac's *Discours sur la permission des Loix* (1715)[34] to the Academy of Lausanne, *Discours sur le Bénéfice des Loix* (1716),[35] and *Jugement d'un Anonyme sur l'original de cet Abrégé.*[36]

To close the section on Pufendorf's Italian translations and Latin editions, let us move to that completed by the Neapolitan lawyer Domenico Amato. He published his translation of *De officio hominis* in Naples in 1780,[37] with the second edition following in 1785. In the translator's preface, Amato affirmed that although he was familiar with Barbeyrac's translation of *De officio* he decided to use the Latin edition published in Lund in 1683 [1682]. However, in his notes, Amato commented on what he considered the main problem with Barbeyrac's translation, most notably, on the bond of men to laws and men's will – that is, the problem of human's sociability.[38] Be that as it may, it is remarkable that according to the historiography, Pufendorf's *De officio* and Grotius's *De Iure*

---

34 Jean Barbeyrac, *Discours sur la permission des Loix* (Geneva: Fabri & Barrillot, 1715). Italian translation,"Discorso sulla permissione delle leggi: nel quale si fa vedere che non è sempre giusto ed onesto quello ch'è dalle leggi permesso" in Pufendorf , *I doveri dell'uomo.*

35 Jean Barbeyrac, *Discours sur le Bénéfice des Loix* (Geneva: Fabri & Barrillot, 1716). Italian translation "Discorso sul benefizio delle leggi: nel quale si fa vedere che non può sempre un uomo onesto *prevalersi* dei diritti e dei privilegj che le leggi accordano," in Pufendorf, *I doveri dell'uomo.*

36 Jean Barbeyrac, "*Jugement d'un Anonyme sur l'original de cet Abrégé, avec des réflexions du Traducteur,*" in Samuel Pufendorf, *Le devoirs de l'homme et du citoyen*, trans. Jean Barbeyrac (Trévoux: L'impimerie de S. Altesse Serenissime, 1741). Italian translastion "Giudizio di un Anonimo sopra l'originale di questo ristretto, colle riflessioni di Mr. Barbeyrac, le quali serviranno ad illustrare alcuni principj dell'Autore", in Pufendorf, *I doveri dell'uomo.* See also Bazzoli "Giambattista Almici e al diffusione di Pufendorf," 46, and Elisabetta Fiocchi Malaspina, *L'eterno ritorno del Droit des gens di Emer de Vattel (sec XVIII-XIX). L'impatto sulla cultura giuridica in prospettiva globale* (Frankfurt am Main: Max Planck Institute, 2017), 57.

37 Samuel Pufendorf, *De' doveri dell'uomo e del cittadino secondo la Legge Naturale, libri due*, trans. Domenico Amato (Naples: Fratelli Raimondi, 1780) and the second edition *De' doveri dell'uomo e del cittadino secondo la Legge Naturale libri due*, trans. Domenico Amato (Naples: Petraroja, 1785).

38 Ibid., 24–25.

Belli ac Pacis (1777)[39] in Latin or in Italian translated from the French editions of Barbeyrac represented compulsory reading for an entire generation of Neapolitan political economists.[40]

On *socialitàs*

As discussed above, the historiography of Almici's translation of *De jure* identified human's sociability as a Pufendorfian theme. However, the reality is that no study has examined whether this theme stemmed from the original text in Latin or from Finetti and Facchinei's commentaries on the text of the German Benedictine Anselmo Desing and his *Juris naturae larva detracta.* [41] The intellectual connection has not been established nor the channels of dissemination between the northern Italian states and the Holy Roman Empire have been visualised. Yet, the understanding the political situation points to the strong intellectual connection and the possibility that this discussion could have also passed through strong cultural transfers with this milieu, most probably created before the European balance of power crisis.[42]

Despite the polemic created by Italian translations of Barbeyrac's French editions of Pufendorf's texts and that some editions being published in Latin in Italy during the period in question, it is noteworthy that Almici decided to publish Barbeyrac's translations with extensive notes and commentaries rather than reverting to the original versions. Particularly when it was his main intention to publicise Pufendorf and not Barbeyrac as it has been supposed for the case of Grandi.[43] It was only Amato in his Neapolitan edition of *De officio* who undertook this initiative of going back to Pufendorf's original text. Amato's decision could be read as a confirmation of the common place that circulated amongst Italian readers that Pufendorf's texts were included in the *Index Librorum* in

39 Hugo Grotius, *Il diritto della guerra e della pace di Ugone Grozio colle note dello stesso autore, e di Giovanni Barbeyrac*, trans. Antonio Porpora (Naples: Giuseppe de Dominicis, 1777).

40 See Salvo Mastellone, "Parole introduttive," in *La recezione di Grozio a Napoli nel Settecento*, ed. Vittorio Conti (Florence: Centro Editoriale Toscano, 2002), 7–12 and Luna-Fabritius, "Providence and Uses of Grotian Strategies".

41 See Desing, *Juris naturae larva* and Venturi's insights in *Utopia e riforma*, (Turin: Einaudi, 1970), 128–129.

42 Luna González, "*From Self-preservation to Self-liking*" and Luna-Fabritius, "Providence and Uses of Grotian Strategies".

43 Bazzoli, "Aspetti della Recezione di Pufendorf nel Settecento Italiano," 53–54 and Fiocchi Malaspina, *L'eterno ritorno del Droit des gens*, 57–58.

1711 due to Barbeyrac's additions.[44] So without Barbeyrac's modifications Pufendorf's texts could circulate in wider audiences. Likewise, Grandi's decision to use the French translation makes stronger the claim that Barbeyrac was associated with enlightened ideas and thus worth the effort of making the French author known and acceptable to Italian audiences.

Regarding the northern translators that used the French editions of Barbeyrac, it is notorious that although Almici expressly announced that he would attempt to render Pufendorf's writings, particularly *De jure* ready for wider Italian audiences through his intervention and emendations to the problematic areas, Grandi distinguished himself in this enterprise with his more complex translation of *De officio.*

In his translation of *De jure*, Almici introduced significant corrections to Barbeyrac's edition and notes.[45] In a letter to Giovambattista Lami from 26 May 1768, Almici explained his full plan of modifications. This letter is long. In a nutshell, Almici's main concern focused on correcting the accounts of human's sociability, natural law as a duty, and stressing God's binding force of laws and human beings to society. Almici then defined sociability as the human's capacity to understand natural law commands, as well its bonds to laws and their fellow men, which he insisted, all human beings have. For Almici the discussion of human sociability served as the foundation of human communality as well as the main principle Pufendorf's science. Defined in this manner, sociability was human beings' moral capacity to organise civil life, which every human being has. In Almici's words this passages reads:

> [i]t is not possible to conceive an operative and compulsory society without the intervention of conventions, and thus it is [crucial] to establish civil conventions to which the members of the society are obliged when they joined the society, and to defend each other under certain rules of government, from the diversity of which then come the various forms of civil societies and republics.... that is, monarchist, aristocratic, or democratic in which the will and forces of all the members of the society converge. While regarding the governing body, its power to command derives from the submission of the will and strengths of the members to his command. From which results in a correspondent obligation between the emperor and the members, that is, submission and obedience, the preservation and defence of them.[46]

44 For further details on the practices of the Inquisition in controlling readership in eighteenth century, see Delpiano *Il governo della lettura*, 82, for the date of the censorship of Pufendorf's *De Iure Natuarae*, 91.

45 Diego Panizza "La traduzione Italiana," 483–528; Berengo, *La società veneta alla fine del Settecento*, 152 and Venturi, *Il Settecento Riformatore*, 251–252.

46 Gio Battista Almici, "Lettera a Giovanni Lami, 26 Maggio 1768," *Novelle Letterarie pubblicate in Firenze* (Florence: Stamperia Granducale, 1768), 456–461 (author's translation).

According to Almici, this principle of the new science tackles the problem of human sociability posed by Pufendorf's natural law theory. It establishes civil conventions for the defence of all citizens under specific rules of government. Consequently, from this diversity derives the various forms of civil societies and republics. Therefore, by establishing and following these rules of governing body, rulers' powers to command and the obligation between the emperor and citizens naturally follow given that they are grounded in their self-preservation and their defence.[47]

Furthermore, Almici discussed the obligations and duties prescribed by natural law and the division of natural laws according to the 'improved' account of men's sociability. He stressed that this 'improved account' should be enough to *keep the religious bonds needed to ensure men's self-preservation* without offending any society that benefits from the protection of the rights shared by its members. [48] Moreover, in the political context of Brescia at that time this statement could also be read as an argument in favour of religious tolerance.

Thus far, it was Almici's plan to intervene in Pufendorf's *De jure* and to have it removed from the *Index Librorum Prohibitorum.* In Almici's opinion, after adjusting human's sociability in this manner, *De jure* was ready for discussion not only in the Academies and debating societies, but also at Italian universities. From Almici's reactions, it is clear that Barbeyrac's edition was notorious for the stress placed on human's unsocial sociability, which Almici thought was corrected in his translation. This appeared to be the most problematic element of Pufendorf's natural law theory in this northern-Italian context.

However, as is widely known, Almici did not achieve his objective to have *De jure* removed from the *Index* and this might have served as motivation to Michele Grandi, who published the first Italian translation of *De officio* in 1761 in three volumes in Venice. The case for a second attempt at popularising Pufendorf's natural law theory seemed to stem from the emerging gap created by the conflict and further the suppression of the Company of Jesus that concluded with the expulsion of the Jesuits in 1773. During that period, Grandi became a professor of moral philosophy, law, and history of the Church following the general reform from Vienna. It was at that precise moment that Grandi accomplished his enterprise. Grandi translated *De officio* using Barbeyrac's French edition,[49] and included sixty-five notes and corrections to the translation. As previously mentioned, Grandi's translation included three additional lectures in appendix,

47 Ibid.

48 Ibid. (author's emphasis).

49 Pufendorf, *Dei doveri dell'uomo.*

which Barbeyrac had delivered to the Academy of Lausanne, and which he included in his translation of *De officio* from 1717.[50]

Current historiography has interpreted this attitude as an attempt to engage in a broader discussion with Almici on the main Pufendorfian themes, most notably on *perseitas*.[51] According to it, for Michele Grandi, it was fundamentally necessary to discuss Pufendorf's understanding of good and bad in moral actions as an independent external imposition of God. In the view of the commentators, in his annotations Grandi analysed *perseitas* through a historical perspective. That is, he revised the views of the Dominicans, Franciscans' voluntarism, the Second Scholastic, and the most respectful theologians from Salamanca until seventeenth-century philosophical, juridical, and other theological debates thereof.[52] For some Italian commentators, Pufendorf's theory of natural indifference related to human actions is relevant since it was indeed the rational foundation of his theory of duty.[53]

According to Grandi in his annotations to *De officio*, Pufendorf approached the question of *perseitas* in such a different manner that it gave binding force to the laws. His conclusion was that natural laws are i) expressly communicated by the legislator or ii) transmitted somehow to men. In Grandi's view, in his attempt to detach from Hobbes's natural law, Pufendorf opted for the second option and affirmed that God wanted natural law to rule human actions. The direct transmission from God to men was indeed the essence of the law. According to Grandi, Barbeyrac had emphasised that the same occurred in the relationship between the sovereign and his subjects. However, in the absence of a command, duty could also be transmitted through rational judgments of the sovereign allowing him to guide his acts towards what he considers in accordance with the legislator's will.[54]

---

50 Barbeyrac, *Discours sur le bénéfice des loix; Jugement d'un Anonyme sur l'original de cet Abrégé* and *Discours sur le bénéfice des loix.*

51 For an Italian discussion of *perseitas* in Pufendorf see Todescan, *Le radici teologiche del giusnaturalismo laico*, 71 and Bazzoli, "Aspetti della Recezione di Pufendorf", 56.

52 On Pufendorf's discussions against his Lutherans critics, cfr. Fiammetta Palladini, *Discusioni seicentesche su Samuel Pufendorf*, 39 – 40; Id., "Pufendorf and Stoicism", *Grotiana:* 22 – 23 (2001 – 2002): 245 – 256.

53 Palladini, "Pufendorf and Stoicism".

54 Maurizio Bazzoli, "Aspetti della Recezione di Pufendorf," 56 – 60 and for an interpretation of Barbeyrac's commentary on this topic, see Petter Korkman, "Civil Sovereign and the King of Kings: Barbeyrac and the Creator's Right to Rule", in *Natural Law and Civil Sovereignty: Moral Right and State Authority in Early Modern Political Thought*, ed. Ian Hunter and David Saunders (London: Palgrave Macmillan, 2002), 109 – 122.

Grandi ensured that law is a command that stands in accordance with reason even without the explicit endorsement of God's will through the Bible. However, Grandi's struggle continued when he noted that good and bad moral actions could not be automatically deduced through the imposition of a divine or human legislator or through their intrinsic nature. That is, Grandi did not accept that God's will as a legislator could be understood as an undifferentiated and omni-comprehensive notion.[55]

Defined in this manner, *perseitas* required correction along with Almici's passive attitude towards this concept.[56] According to Grandi, understanding that God manifests His will not through one act but two was necessary: one act as a creator and the second as a legislator. The first distinguishes men from their fierce condition. This act is the act that commands human beings that God has created them to live according to religion, self-preservation, and sociability. In Grandi's view, human's rational condition allows them to understand that God has created them to live a life according to these principles. Thus, those principles should not be viewed only as ruling all of their moral actions, but also as the foundations of natural law. Accordingly, Grandi argued that the possibility to understand these ideas serves as sufficient proof that every single human being possesses the freedom to act.[57] In the pages that followed, Grandi proposed some examples. These included, for example, blasphemy as an act against religion and suicide as a bad act by nature because it goes against the principle of self-preservation. Homicide and robbery are bad actions in themselves because they go against the principle of sociability. Therefore, God's will as creator alongside human reason are sufficient to determine if actions are intrinsically good or bad. In addition, there is no need for the manifestation of God's divine will through the Bible to assert that, as Hobbes affirmed. Nor was the manifestation needed, as a previous divine act of legislative will as Pufendorf and Barbeyrac stated.

Grandi concluded his analysis stating that Pufendorf distanced himself from Hobbes by affirming that the moral acts deduced by reason result from natural law and obligatory law. Likewise, honest and dishonest acts should subsist by themselves before the legislative will of God. For Grandi, this position was not clear enough in Pufendorf's or Barbeyrac's texts. Thus, they seemed closer to Hobbes, creating the idea of a closeness across the three authors and that is why he felt compelled to comment on these matters.[58]

---

55 Maurizio Bazzoli, "Aspetti della Recezione di Pufendorf," 56–60.
56 Pufendorf, *I doveri dell'uomo*, cit, vol. 1:193.
57 Ibid.
58 Ibid., vol. 1: 196.

For some Italian scholars, Grandi's account of Pufendorf's theory of indifferent good and bad acts looked closer to Grotius's theory of obligation creating a vicious cycle[59] – despite Pufendorf's express critique thereof. For other Italian scholars, Grandi's position was in reality closer to Daniele Concina. In his *Revealed Religion* (Venice 1754)[60] Concina tied together Hobbes and Pufendorf.[61] However, a third position of Italian historiography has suggested that Grandi's discussion on *perseitas* and his position were also motivated by a contemporary practical discussion on usury. Be that as it may, along the lines of the rigorist thesis Grandi argued that usury transgresses the principles of natural law contradicting God's will as a creator – that is, of sociability.[62] In his conclusion to his commentary on this matter, Grandi affirmed that moral order could never be indifferent. However, according to Grandi, despite the strengths and weaknesses of the emergent discussion, Jesuits' casuistry was undoubtedly worse than Pufendorf's and Barbeyrac's position.

In line with Italian historiography, one could argue that the echoes of northern discussions on sociability resonated in Naples, thereby motivating Domenico Amato to complete his translation of *De officio*. However, it is possible that a contemporary practical discussion illuminated the matter, since it was the case of usury in Grandi's context. Nevertheless, the reality is that a gap exists within this line of research. Amato's translation was published in Naples in two editions in 1780 and 1785.[63] In the first edition, it was associated with cultural circles frequented by Antonio Genovesi and Ferdinando Galiani.[64]

Yet, new evidence regarding the circulation of Grotius texts in Naples during the last decades of the seventeenth century led us to confirm that Pufendorf's ideas circulated directly or indirectly in Naples earlier. Evidence exists that the circulation of modern natural law texts in Naples had begun a century earlier and that dissemination was long and continuous throughout this period.[65]

59 Bazzoli, "Aspetti della Recezione di Pufendorf," 59.

60 Cfr., Daniele Concina, *Della religione rivelata contra gli Ateisti, Deisti, Materialisti, Indifferentisti che negano la verità de' Misterj, libri ciqnue*, 2 vols (Venice, 1754).

61 See Alberto Vecchi, *Correnti religiose nel Sei-Settecento Veneto*, (Venice and Rome: Istituto per la collaborazione culturale, 1962). Alfonso Prandi, *Religiosità e cultura nel '700 italiano* (Bologna: Il Mulino, 1966); Mario Rosa, *Politica e Religione nel Settecento Europeo* (Florence: Sansoni, 1974), 37 and Bazzoli, "Aspetti della Recezione di Pufendorf," 58.

62 Pufendorf, *I doveri dell'uomo*, 2, 299.

63 Pufendorf, *De' doveri dell'uomo.*

64 Bazzoli, "Aspetti della Recezione di Pufendorf," 47.

65 Luna González, "*From Self-preservation to Self-liking*", and Luna-Fabritius, "Providence and Uses of Grotian Strategies".

This line of inquiry has shown that Genovesi was indeed associated with that Neapolitan milieu, whereas it appears that Galiani forged his own path.[66]

In the preface of his translation, Domenico Amato commented that although he knew about the publication of Barbeyrac's translation of *De officio* he had decided to use the Latin edition from Lund from 1682 instead. Amato began his commentary on what he considered the main problem of Barbeyrac's translation. Most notably, the bond of men to laws and human being's will – that is, again, the problem of human sociability as already defined by Almici.[67] The way this debate was settled by Amato leads us to believe that either he was aware of the on-going debate in northern Italy or that the problem of human sociability was rather common.

For Amato, the book that readers had in their hands was the most important instruction for their lives, since it informed them about their duties to society and provided them with knowledge about laws. Accordingly, the science of knowing one's duties towards God and our fellow men could not be perfect. Yet, that instruction could not be set aside, especially if one is involved in public or private affairs, since ignoring ones' duties represented an offence to the laws of honesty. Given the close connection between honesty and eternal happiness, men's duties should be understood in depth. According to Amato, the laws of nature form all others since they contained the justice and authority reinforcing its binding force. Amato affirmed that natural laws are not an invention to the human spirit nor an arbitrary creation of the people, but represent the expression of the eternal reason that rules the universe.

Therefore, for Amato natural law promotes the virtues and stops any vices in society against the fatherland, settling fortitude into the hearts of the people. Natural law is a law according to the nature of all human beings, which is constant, immutable, and eternal. Natural law is only able to conduct men to fulfil their duties and avoid evil. Amato's commentary, however, denotes a remaining need to solve the problem already raised by unsocial sociability discussed in Neapolitan academies a century earlier.[68] In Amato's straightforward opinion, for this reason, natural law does not allow removing, changing, or abolishing

---

66 Luna González, "*From Self-preservation to Self-liking*"; Adriana Luna-Fabritius, "Visions of Sociability in Early Modern Neapolitan Political Thought," in *Processes of Enlightenment – Essays in Honour of Hans Erich Bödeker*, ed. Jonas Gerlings, Ere Nokkala, and Martin van Gelderen (Liverpool: Liverpool University Press, forthcoming) and Id., "Providence and Uses of Grotian Strategies".

67 "Delle cose, alle quali uno è forzato and 25.8 Delle azioni di quelli, che non han l'uso della ragione". Cfr. Pufendorf, *De' doveri dell'uomo*, 24.7.

68 Luna-Fabritius, "Visions of Sociability".

anything from natural laws. Natural laws are clear in themselves and do not require any interpretation. Natural laws do not differ in Rome or in Athens and will be the same tomorrow in comparison to today. This situation is so because God is the author of them and He is the only sovereign of all human beings. That is, no prince nor Senate nor people are capable of abolishing or derogating them. Furthermore, whomever attempts to violate them would be renouncing his human nature, detaching himself from his nature. Based on the tone of these statements providing more than a summary of Pufendorf's natural law, it seems that Amato is instructing his audience regarding the proper interpretation. The normative tone is predominant.

In his preface as well, Amato stated that by publishing Pufendorf's work he aimed to demonstrate through the use of Christian and Pagan philosophy the utility and authority of natural law. Moreover, Amato wanted to clarify the divine origin and the need to learn its precepts to acquire the knowledge of the divine and human affairs. He also wanted to clarify the right way to address one's actions towards honesty. According to Amato, Pufendorf, together with Grotius – given their understanding of the chaos amongst ancient jurists, decided to create a new order in which men could live in a methodical system of moral discipline to instruct men on natural law. This served as the foundation of society, primarily the duties resulting from it.

All in all, Amato considered Pufendorf's work on natural law and on nations as excellent, an elegant collection of humans' and citizens' duties. This was his primary motivation in bringing this work to Naples in the vernacular. He confessed that Barbeyrac's edition with commentaries by Immanuel Weber (1659–1726),[69] Gershom Carmichael (1672–1729),[70] Sebastien Masson,[71] Gottlieb Gherard Titius (1661–1714),[72] and Everard Otto (1685–1756)[73] among others was un-

69 He is referring to Samuel Pufendorf, *De officio hominis et civis juxta legem naturalem libri duo, curante Immanuele Webero*, editio 6ta, (Francofurti et Lipsiae: sumptibu E. Bronkce, 1700).

70 Samuel Pufendorf, *De officio hominis et civis, juxta legem naturalem. Libri duo. supplementis et observatiionibus in Academicae Juventutis usum auxit et illustravit Gershomus Carmichael* (Glasgow: 1718), (Edinburgh 1724). See also James Moore and Michael Silverthorne, "Gershom Carmichael and the Natural Jurisprudence Tradition in Eighteenth-Century Scotland," *Man and Nature. L'Homme et la Nature* 1 (1982): 41–53.

71 Samuel Pufendorf, *De officiis hominis et civis, prout ipsi praescribuntur lege naturali libri duo: cum notis, viri Consultissimi ac Celebrerrimi Dn Io Barbeyracii ex Gallico in Latinum Sermonem versis a Seb. Masson, Giessae, Sumptibus Ioannis Philippi Krieger* (Giessen: Sumptibus Ioannis Philippi Krieger, 1728).

72 Samuelis Pufendorffii, *De officio hominis et civis juxta legem naturalem Libri duo. Obeservationibus antea separatim editis*, D. Gottlieb Gerhard Titio, Lipsiae: Sumptibus Haered, Lanckisii, 1709).

doubtedly relevant. Yet, he had made his own decision. He recommended to his readers that they experience the utility of this book that he was presenting to the public to silence the noise caused by passions that lead them to ignore their duties. Amato asserted that by reading his translation of *De officio* readers would hear the sweet invitation to fulfil their duties and feel the love of God that comes from piety, from loving one's self, from wisdom, from loving his fellow men and from all social virtues. That is, Amato was trying to reconcile what in that time was known as religious and secular forms of happiness.[74]

Christian virtues were crucial to developing human beings' sociability since they keep individuals bound to their duties. More importantly, Amato added, Christian virtues were paramount since they made human beings suitable for commerce in civil life. According to Amato, if someone who claims to profess Christian values cannot stop being turbid, seditious, and unsociable, we could frankly proclaim that Christian religion is only on their lips, but not in their heart.[75]

According to his plan, Amato presented the natural law in the following manner: Jesus Christ should be seen as the summary of all moral laws included in two rules, namely, i) the love of God and ii) the love of their fellow men. Accordingly, in Amato's account, in the state of nature in which human beings were in a fallen condition, only these two natural laws applied. The duty to love of our fellow men and sociability derive from the need to overthrow that fallen condition. In turn, we can only infer particular maxims derived from these principles, and only a slight or no difference should be recognised in the integrity between moral theology and natural rights. Similarly, the distinction between them, which was considerable after the fall from paradise, would vanish.[76]

---

73 Samueli Pufendorffii, *De officio hominis & civis, secundum Legem Naturalem, Libri Duo. Everardus Otto, Jctus. Repetita praelactione recensuit & Adnotationibus illustravit. In quibus Utilitas Juris Naturae in Studio Juris Civilis, & hujus in illo abusus ostenditur. Accedunt Dl. Titti ad eosdem libros Observationes. Trajecti ad Rhenum*, (Utrecht: Apud Joannem Broedelet, 1740 [1737]).

74 Adriana Luna-Fabritius, "The Secularisation of Happiness in Early Eighteenth-century Italian Political Thought: Revisiting the Foundations of Civil Society," in *Trust and Happiness in the History of European Political Thought*, ed. *László* Kontler and Mark Somos (Leiden: Brill, 2017), 169–195.

75 Pufendorf, *De' doveri dell'uomo*, 22.

76 Pufendorf, *De' doveri dell'uomo*, 9. For the consequences of the fallen condition in Pufendorf, cfr. Palladini, *Discussioni*; Kari Saastamoinen, *The Morality of the fallen man: Samuel Pufendorf on natural law* (Helsinki: Societas Historica Finlandiae, 1995) and Knud Haakonssen, *Natural Law and Moral Philosophy: from Grotius to the Scottish Enlightenment* (Cambridge: Cambridge University Press, 1996), 37–45.

For Amato, the rules set by natural law are necessary for the development of contracts, since they are the guarantee against a coin's false weights and amongst other crucial matters. However, if the debtor finds a problem, he should always have the right to return the money to the borrower within an agreed upon period. Natural laws were established, have been observed for a long time, and since then have defined not only civil government but also the duties of citizens. Currently, natural law commands assistance to the poor and that the miserable change their former mission.[77]

Conclusion

In the middle of one of the major political crises in European history, Italian authors established historical, theoretical, and juridical laboratories to rebuild the political foundations of their civil states and relationships amongst human beings through laws. For them, those natural laws were the solution to the problem of sociability characteristic of their time. For the authors and translators analysed here, Pufendorf's natural law theory proved quite useful to their enterprise. Evidence of that lies in the number of translations and editions that appeared in the second half of the eighteenth century in Lombardy and in Naples.

Following from the evidence presented here, we have little doubt of the contribution of Pufendorf's natural law to Italian civil culture. Yet, by studying the translations, it remains unclear whether the problem of human beings' unsociability arrived in Italy through the translations of Pufendorf's natural law theory or the debates generated by it via other channels from the Republic of Letters. The other channels may include the book reviews in the main journals and correspondence between its agents, but especially in the communicating circles created around Vienna's milieu. It is unquestionable that natural law provided the concepts upon which to build a common language through which the ancient Italian states developed conceptual nets, as Bazzoli has pointed out in one of his pioneering studies. Still, the evidence demonstrates that this phenomenon occurred one century earlier than the publication of Pufendorf's translations. The members of the *Accademia degli investiganti* identified the problem of sociability a century earlier. This problem was passed on to the eighteenth century to their heirs, primarily, Valletta, Doria, Vico, and Gravina, and became the core of

77 Ibid.

the development of Genovesi's political economy.[78] It is true that Grotius, Pufendorf, Hobbes, Spinoza, and Locke occupied a significant position in that earlier process too. In passing from the language of natural law to political economy, in turn, the social sciences as we now know them, arose. Likewise, the division between jurists, scientists, and men of politics coincided with this process and not the other way around as Bazzoli presumed. The indivisible connection between law, politics, and the economy endured until its division took place at universities during the first decades of the nineteenth century. However, regarding the Neapolitan case, the chief distinction between the earlier and later circulation of Pufendorf's natural law lied in the secularisation of the foundations of sociability. Whilst the former enterprise led to the secularisation of the theories of the state's foundations started by the *Investiganti*, their heirs, and continued by Genovesi and his school, the later started by Amato reverted to a previous state of the secularisation revitalising the urge of God's binding force to the laws and amongst human beings.

Regarding the perception of Barbeyrac, it is undoubted that for eighteenth-century Italian thinkers, Barbeyrac's new translations of Pufendorf's texts significantly modified the original. For Italian thinkers as well as among their European counterparts, Barbeyrac's work led to an extreme version of Pufendorf's natural law theory.[79] According to the Italians, Barbeyrac's translations affected the way in which people read these texts in different parts of Europe and they were very much aware of this. The French versions of these texts stimulated the reformulation of new lines of thought not only in Europe, but also in European kingdoms overseas. [80] For the Italian thinkers, this was the reason for the condemnation by the Roman Inquisition and the *Index Librorum Prohibitorum*. The result led Pufendorf to more closely align with Hobbes's natural law theory and thus, led to a desire to correct it. This was their primary motivation in returning to former Latin editions, as was the case with the translations of Pufendorf's *De officio* by Amato in 1780 in Naples.

---

78 See Luna-Fabritius, "Visions of sociability' and Id., 'Providence and Uses of Grotian Strategies."

79 For a study of Barbeyrac's reformulations, see Tim J. Hochstrasser, "Conscience and Reason: the Natural Law Theory of Jean Barbeyrac," *The Historical Journal* 36 (1993): 289–308; Id, *Natural Law Theories in the Early Enlightenment* (Cambridge: University Press, 2000); Korkman, "Civil Sovereigns," 109–122 and Id., "Voluntarism and moral obligation: Barbeyrac's defence of *Pufendorf* revisited," in *Early Modern Natural Law Theories: Contexts and Strategies in the Early Enlightenment*, ed. Tim J. Hochstrasser and Peter Schröder (Dordrecht: Kluwer Academic Publisher, 2003), 195–225; Giulia Maria Labriola, *Barbeyrac interprete di Pufendorf e Grozio* (Naples: Editoriale Scientifica, 2003).

80 Hochstrasser, "Conscience and Reason," 293.

Following from previous Italian discussions, Barbeyrac's conception of sociability stressed the opposition between what at that time was denoted as the law of self-love and the duties of sociability and what the Italian translators tried to solve through their corrections and notes. Yet, they did not succeed, since it corroborates the fact that the German author's texts remained in the *Index Librorum Prohibitorum* until the beginning of the nineteenth century. However, the controversies created by the circulation of these texts contributed enormously to the development of eighteenth-century Italian civil culture and the formation of a public sphere that made its way to the constitutional moments. These moments followed the Napoleonic invasions of the former kingdoms of the Spanish monarchy, particularly those that remained associated with the German Empire following the Spanish Succession War. The degree of refinement reached by the resulting Italian debate is evidenced by their significant knowledge and discussions on editions and translations of Pufendorf's texts. The peculiarities of the diverse Italian contexts presented here disclose different forms of appropriation completing the wider European map thereof. Finally, all of this serves as evidence that despite the censorship of the Counterreformation era Protestant texts circulated extensively across Catholic territories formerly associated with the Habsburg German Empire, evidencing the ineffectiveness of confessional borders during this period.

Ere Nokkala

13 Rethinking the Pursuit of Happiness – Johann Heinrich Gottlob von Justi's Critique of Paternal Rule

This chapter offers a re-interpretation of Johann Heinrich Gottlob von Justi's (1717–1771) account of paternal rule. Justi was one of the leading German political writers in the 1750s and 1760s,[1] and he has been variously interpreted as an advocate of enlightened absolutism,[2] of liberalism,[3] and of republicanism.[4] In this chapter, I study Justi's political thought by analyzing his essay "Considerations on Monarchies and Aristocracies" (1761).[5] This essay has been overlooked; however, it offers a key to understanding the nature of Justi's political thought. The reason not enough attention has not been paid to this essay is that it has been considered a translation and not an original piece by Justi. For instance, Ulrich Adam suggested in his seminal book on Justi that "Considerations on Monarchies and Aristocracies" was Justi's translation of a passage from Count Giovanni Cattaneo's (1691–1761) *The Source, the Strength, and the True Spirit of Laws*

---

1 Polish-British lawyer-historian C. H. Alexandrowicz considered Justi to be "one of the greatest German political writers of the eighteenth-century." See C. H. Alexandrowicz, *The Law of Nations in Global History*, eds. David Armitage and Jennifer Pitts (Oxford: Oxford University Press, 2017), 163; Ere Nokkala, *From Natural Law to Political Economy: J. H. G von Justi on State, Commerce and International Order* (Münster: Lit Verlag, 2019), 1.

2 Diethelm Klippel and Martin Fuhrmann, "Der Staat und die Staatstheorie des aufgeklärten Absolutismus," in *Der aufgeklärte Absolutismus im europäischen Vergleich*, ed. Helmut Reinalter and Harm Klueting (Wien: Böhlau, 2002), 223–43.

3 Uwe Wilhelm, "Das Staats- und Gesellschaftsverständnis von J. H. G. von Justi: Ein Beitrag zur Entwicklung des Frühliberalismus in Deutschland," *Der Staat* 30 (1991), 415–441; Uwe Wilhelm, *Der deutsche Frühliberalismus: von den Anfängen bis 1789* (Frankfurt am Main: Peter Lang, 1995); Marcus Obert, *Die naturrechtliche "politische Metaphysik" des Johann Heinrich Gottlob von Justi (1717–1771)* (Frankfurt am Main: Peter Lang, 1992).

4 Horst Dreitzel, *Absolutismus und ständische Verfassung in Deutschland: Ein Beitrag zu Kontinuität und Diskontinuität der politischen Theorie in der frühen Neuzeit* (Mainz: von Zabern, 1992), 100–120.

5 Johann Heinrich Gottlob von Justi, "Betrachtungen über die Monarchien und Aristocratien," in *Gesammelte Politische und Finanzschriften über wichtige Gegenstände der Staatskunst, der Kriegswissenschaften und des Cameral- und Finanzwesens*, 3 vols. (Copenhagen: Rothe, 1761–1764), 2: 176–190.

https://doi.org/10.1515/9783110679861-015

(1752).[6] Cattaneo was a Venetian author active in the court of Frederick II in Berlin. Cattaneo's book was a conservative, reactionary, commentary on Montesquieu's political philosophy – above all a critical discussion of Montesquieu's *Spirit of Laws* (1748) – and it is true that Justi polemically translated a passage on the origin of governments from it to be included to his collected political and financial writings.[7] However, "Considerations on Monarchies and Aristocracies" is Justi's lengthy introduction and critique of the arguments presented in the short translation. Therefore, it truly is an original text by Justi. The question Justi wanted to address with his introduction and translation was: Is the unlimited power of a monarch or an aristocratic assembly of natural origin? In other words, Justi asked whether unlimited monarchy or unlimited aristocracy was a natural – this is to say legitimate – form of government. Significant in answering this question was the figure of a patriarch (*Patriarche*, *Altvater*). As a result of trying to answer this most fundamental question, "Considerations on Monarchies and Aristocracies" is Justi's most elaborate critique of the arguments used in favour of paternal rule, in the context of eighteenth-century debates on unlimited power and political representation. Several competing reform concepts emerged in Germany in the second half of the eighteenth century: One emphasised the role of Estates balancing the power of the king; one had essentially anti-Estates politics combined with admiration of England's mixed government as mediated by Montesquieu; and one advocated the idea of "enlightened reform bureaucracy".[8] Building on these findings and in the footsteps of Barbara Stollberg-Rilinger, I interpret Justi as being among the anti-Estates admirers of mixed constitutions. However, departing from Stollberg-Rilinger, who unlike me inter-

---

6 Ulrich Adam, *The Political Economy of J. H. G. Justi* (Oxford: Peter Lang, 2006); Jean de Cattaneo, *La source, la force et le véritable esprit des loix: essais du J. de Cattaneo; on y joint aussi un essais sur l'origine naturelle des Gouvernemens politiques dans la Soc. humaine, par le même auteur* (Berlin: Voss, 1752), 181–185; Conte Giovanni Cattaneo, *The source, the strength, and the true spirit of laws: In three parts. In which the errors of M. de Montesquieu, and some other eminent writers, are occasionally considered. To which are added, Essays on the natural origin of political* (London: Lockyer Davis, 1753).

7 Justi translated pages 181–185 of the original French version of Cattaneo's *La source*. Justi's translation, "Gedanken von dem Ursprunge der Monarchien und Aristocratien," is published in Justi, *Gesammelte Politische und Finanzschriften über wichtige Gegenstände der Staatskunst, der Kriegswissenschaften und des Cameral- und Finanzwesens*, 3 vols. (Copenhagen: Rothe, 1761–1764), 2: 190–196.

8 Barbara Stollberg-Rilinger, *Vormünder* des *Volkes? Konzepte landständischer Repräsentation in der Spätphase des Alten Reiches* (Berlin: Duncker & Humblot, 1999), 189–233, 298–304. On Justi in the context of eighteenth-century German debate on representation, see especially pages 200–211.

prets Justi as a defender of pure unlimited monarchy,[9] special emphasis in this chapter will be given not to the anti-Estates views of Justi but to the virtue of not giving unlimited power to the monarch. Recovering the critique of paternal unlimited rule in Justi is an important aspect in reinterpreting Justi's political thought and in reinterpreting eighteenth century German political economy, known as cameral sciences (*Kameralwissenschaften*) in general, whose main advocate Justi was. As this chapter will argue, Justi contributed significantly to debate in his time on unlimited power instead of just recycling well-known arguments on paternal rule. Justi advocated the freedom of citizens to evaluate politics and to legislate. Thereby, he considerably contributed to the politicisation of the German Enlightenment – to making the phenomenon of paternal rule disputable and changeable.[10]

In recent literature, Justi has been regarded as an advocate of paternal rule and of the tutelary interventionist state. This is also linked with a more general interpretation of cameral sciences, whose main representative Justi was. Cameralists, the practitioners and theoreticians of cameral sciences, have been regarded to be in the service of the princely chamber and the interests of the ruler. Key in this respect is the concept of happiness (*Glückseligkeit*), a difficult concept to translate into English, but the connotations of happiness come very close to those of well-being and welfare.[11] In this line of interpretation cameralists are seen as puppets of the prince, and it is the task of the prince to guide his subjects to happiness. Very little attention is given to the pursuits of the individuals as actors.[12]

---

9 Stollberg-Rilinger, *Vormünder des Volkes*, 210.

10 On politicisation of the German Enlightenment, see Hans Erich Bödeker, "Aufklärung über Aufklärung? Reinhart Kosellecks Interpretation der Aufklärung," in *Zwischen Sprache und Geschichte: Zum Werk Reinhart Kosellecks*, ed. Carsten Dutt und Reinhard Laube (Göttingen: Wallstein Verlag, 2013), 128–174. On contingency and cameralism, see Marcus Sandl, "Development as possibility: Risk and chance in the Cameralist discourse," in *Economic Growth and the Origins of Modern Political Economy: Economic Reason of State, 1500–2000*, ed. Philipp Rössner (New York & Milton Park: Routledge, 2016), 139–155.

11 On happiness in early modern German economic thought, see Lars Magnusson, "On Happiness: Welfare in Cameralist Discourse in the Seventeenth and Eighteenth Centuries," in *Cameralism and the Enlightenment: Happiness, Governance and Reform in Transnational Perspective*, ed. Ere Nokkala and Nicholas B. Miller (London: Routledge, 2019), 23–46.

12 Douglas Moggach, "Freedom and Perfection: German Debates on the State in the Eighteenth Century," *Canadian Journal of Political Science* 42 (2009): 1003–1023; Andre Wakefield, *The Disordered Police State: German Cameralism as Science and Practice* (Chicago: University of Chicago Press, 2009); Andre Wakefield, "Cameralism: A German alternative to Mercantilism," in *Mercantilism Reimagined: Political Economy in Early modern Britain and its Empire*, ed. Philip J. Stern and Carl Wennerlind (Oxford: Oxford University Press, 2013), 134–150.

In this essay, I argue that the above-mentioned interpretation of Justi's thought – and simultaneously of the character of cameral sciences[13] – has been coloured by Immanuel Kant's negative assessment of happiness as the aim of the state and as a guideline for legislation. I begin this chapter with an overview of the historiography of happiness and the aim of state doctrine. From there, I move on to discuss Kant's critique of the doctrine and demonstrate to what extent the recent historiographical interpretations have been variations of backward-looking Kantian accounts. The last section of the chapter reveals that in contrast to the traditional reading among scholars, Justi placed the individual householder's freedom before the state. Contrary to common misconceptions, Justi did not see citizens as immature children who needed to be guided towards happiness. Indeed, he advocated the interests of a *Bürger*, conceptualised as a *Hausvater*, and was willing to grant a wide private sphere to this figure, who in many ways was a *homo economicus*. I will show that in Justi's account neither an unlimited monarchy nor an unlimited aristocracy founded originally by a patriarch was a natural form of government.

In relation to the Kantian account of happiness I highlight the significant differences between the political theories of Justi and Christian Wolff (1679 – 1754), the leading German political philosopher of the time. I will demonstrate that – contrary to numerous existing accounts – Justi certainly did not follow Wolff in his conception of the principles of civil legislation. Whereas Kantian criticism can still be successfully applied to Wolff, it does not do full justice to Justi's thought. This becomes clear when considering the central role played by freedom in Justi's political thought. It is particularly clear regarding the relationship between the ruler and the ruled. Here Justi embodies a major shift within the tradition of cameralism, which took place at a conceptual level: For Justi, the focus of interest is not the economy of the ruler, but the political economy (*Staatswirthschaft*) based on citizens' active pursuit of their own happiness. In line with this, unlike many of his predecessors, Justi granted citizens the right to evaluate the policies of a given government. In his view, if the ruler was not advancing the benefit of the political economy, and granting the citizens sufficient freedom, he or she was neglecting his or her duties.

---

13 For recent studies on cameral sciences written from a pan-European and transnational perspectives, see Philipp R. Rössner, ed., *Economic Growth and the Origins of Modern Political Economy: Economic Reason of State, 1500 – 2000* (New York & Milton Park: Routledge, 2016); Marten Seppel and Keith Tribe, eds., *Cameralism in Practice: State Administration and Economy in Early Modern Europe* (Woodbridge: Boydell & Brewer, 2017) and Ere Nokkala and Nicholas B. Miller (eds.), *Cameralism and the Enlightenment: Happiness, Governance and Reform in Transnational Perspective* (London: Routledge, 2019).

In sum, this chapter argues that if paternalism is understood in a Kantian sense, where fatherly government (*väterliche Regierung*) treats the people as immature children who do not know how best to pursue their own happiness,[14] then Justi was not a paternalist. These findings beg a rethinking of cameral sciences in general. It cannot be that cameral sciences were purely in service of the prince and represented some kind of escape from politics to management. Rather, I suggest that they contributed to the politicisation of the German Enlightenment.

Prehistory: The Aim of the State Doctrine

In the context of early-modern German political thought, the concept of happiness is inseparably linked with the doctrine of the aim of the state (*Staatszwecklehre*).[15] Discussing the aims of the political commonwealth was of course nothing new in early-modern Europe. Common aims had been a matter of discussion since antiquity and the Aristotelian notions of *bonum commune* and *beatitudo civilis* continued be of great interest to early-modern political thinkers. A significant shift in the doctrine of the aim of the state took place in the seventeenth century, when the aim of the state was for the first time reformulated in the context of the modern concept of the state as laid down by Thomas Hobbes and Samuel Pufendorf.[16] Another significant redefinition took place in the course of the eighteenth century.[17] For Pufendorf, maintenance of social peace was the main aim of the state. This is understandable in light of the contemporary situation

---

14 Immanuel Kant, "Über den Gemeinspruch: Das mag in der Theorie richtig sein, taugt aber nicht für die Praxis (1793)," in *Akademie Ausgabe von Immanuel Kants Gesammelten Werken, Bd. 8* (Abhandlungen nach 1781), 290–91, https://korpora.zim.uni-duisburg-essen.de/kant/aa08/290.html (web page visited 30 September 2019). "Eine Regierung, die auf dem Prinzip des Wohlwollens gegen das Volk als eines Vaters gegen seine Kinder errichtet wäre, d.i. eine väterliche Regierung (*imperium paternale*), wo also die Untertanen als unmündige Kinder, die nicht unterscheiden können, was ihnen wahrhaftig nützlich oder schädlich ist, sich bloß passiv zu verhalten genötight sind . . . ist der größte denkbare Despotismus."

15 On the development of the aim of the State doctrine, see Michael Stolleis, "Staatszweck," in *Historisches Wörterbuch der Philosophie*, vol. 10, ed. Joachim Ritter and Karlfried Gründer (Basel: Schwabe, 1998), 80–84.

16 Stolleis, "Staatszweck"; On Pufendorf's natural law, see Kari Saastamoinen, *The Morality of the Fallen Man: Samuel Pufendorf on Natural Law* (Helsinki: Societas Historica Finlandiae, 1995); Heikki Haara, *Pufendorf's Theory of Sociability: Passions, Habits and Social Order* (Cham: Springer, 2018).

17 Ulrich Engelhardt, "Zum Begriff der Glückseligkeit in der kameralistischen Staatslehre des 18. Jahrhunderts (J. H. G von Justi)," *Zeitschrift für Historische Forschung* 8 (1981): 41.

in which he was writing. In the aftermath of the Thirty Years' War, his thought was focused on peace and security. Over the course of the eighteenth century most German political and economic thinkers started to appoint the state a much broader spectrum of activities. This can be detected in the way the main aim of the state changed from security to happiness. By far the most famous and influential political theorist advocating happiness as the aim of the state was Christian Wolff. In Wolff's philosophy happiness was understood as unhindered progress towards higher levels of perfection. In short, according to Wolff, the state was necessary in order to secure the common good through the most effective pursuit of perfection and happiness. Wolff set about explaining how the state should direct the perfection of the goods of the mind, the goods of the body and external goods (*tranquilitas, securitas, vitae sufficientia*). Wolff's philosophical system resulted in an extraordinary welfare state, where the state's pursuit of the welfare of its citizens had no theoretical limits.[18] At times Wolff has been regarded as one of the first theoreticians of the welfare state. For instance, it has been claimed that he was the founder of the "cameralistic welfare state".[19] The changing concept of happiness showed how great was the belief that state could produce welfare and bring happiness to its citizens. Simultaneously, this aim was monopolised in the hands of the state.[20]

Kant's Critique of the Paternalism of the Previous Generation

The view of the concept of happiness as the aim of civil legislation was widespread in eighteenth-century Germany. Kant's influence provides a clue as to why it is often overlooked that for the vast majority of eighteenth-century German political theorists the aim of the state was happiness.[21] The German philos-

---

18 Knud Haakonssen, "German Natural Law," in *The Cambridge History of Eighteenth-Century Political Thought*, ed. Mark Goldie and Robert Wokler (Cambridge: Cambridge University Press, 2006), 273.
19 Alexander Kaufman, *Welfare in the Kantian State* (Oxford: Oxford University Press, 1999), 57–58.
20 Engelhardt, "Zum Begriff der Glückseligkeit," 43. Engelhardt untenably holds that practically all cameralists adopted Wolff's idea of a welfare state and that Wolff was the philosopher who influenced the majority of cameralists' views on human nature and indeed played the greatest role in shaping their general worldview.
21 On Kant's critique on the doctrine of happiness as the aim of state, see Frank Grunert, "Die Objektivität des Glücks: Aspekte der Eudämonismus Diskussion in der deutschen Aufklärung,"

opher Moses Mendelssohn (1729–1786) famously called Kant the all-destroyer (*der Alles zermalmende*).[22] Among that which Kant stood accused of "destroying" was the notion that happiness could be the guiding principle of civil legislation. Kant's devastating critique of the usefulness of the concept of happiness in ethics and civil philosophy long dominated the views of the historians. Only recently has there been growing interest in studying happiness – a key concept in eighteenth-century German political thought – in its contemporary context and on its own terms, as opposed to in the light in which Kant portrayed it.[23]

Kant was very familiar with Wolff's work and the categories, and to a great extent the concepts that Kant used in his own philosophy came from Wolff. However, this certainly did not stop Kant from criticising Wolff. Kant directed his critique of the *Glückseligkeitslehre* against conservative politicians of his own time and possibly even more so against the political theory of Wolff.[24] However, it needs to be emphasised that Kant does not express his critique of happiness as the aim of the state explicitly against Wolff. Rather, this critique was an implicit consequence of how Kant developed his own philosophy. In addition, it is necessary to mention that Kant did not so much question Wolff's or anyone else's intentions when they advocated happiness as the aim of the state, rather Kant asserted that happiness as a principle of civil legislation inevitably leads to despotism, be it intended or not. Kant argued that happiness functioned as a principle of a paternalistic state prepared for far-reaching moral interventions into the lives of individual citizens. According to this view, under a paternal government subjects are only obliged to behave passively and rely on the judgments of the head of the state as to how they ought to achieve happiness. Kant associated the doctrine of the aim of the state understood as happiness with unlimited absolutist regimes in which the ruler was seen as a father guiding his subjects to happiness. After all, in *Glückseligkeitslehre* it was ultimately the ruler who decided how subjects ought to be happy and indeed of what that happiness consisted. This was the exact opposite to Kant's understanding of the Enlightenment as an

---

in *Aufklärung als praktische Philosophie: Werner Schneiders zum 65. Geburtstag*, ed. Frank Grunert and Friedrich Vollhardt (Tübingen: De Gruyter, 1998), 351–368. See especially pages 351 and 368.

22 Moses Mendelssohn, *Morgenstunden oder Vorlesungen über das Daseyn Gottes* (Berlin: Voß, 1785), Preface, 2.

23 For a path-breaking study from this new viewpoint, see Clemens Schwaiger, *Das Problem des Glücks im Denken Christian Wolffs: Eine quellen-, begriffs- und entwicklungsgeschichtliche Studie zu Schlüsselbegriffen seiner Ethik* (Stuttgart: Frommann-Holzboog, 1995). For a new important treatment of happiness in European political thought, see László Kontler and Mark Somos, ed., *Trust and Happiness in the History of European Political Thought* (Leiden: Brill, 2018).

24 Kaufman, *Welfare*, 40.

escape "from the self-imposed immaturity" caused by a lack of courage and resolve and an inability to use reason without external guidance. According to Kant, in a paternalistic government (*väterliche Regierung, imperium paternale*) citizens were treated as immature children, which for Kant exemplified the greatest of possible despotisms (*der größte denkbare Despotismus*).[25]

Indeed, Kant's perceptions on happiness as the aim of the state were not without merit; the paternalistic character of the political thought of Christian Wolff is beyond question. Wolff wrote explicitly that ruling persons were to their subjects as fathers to their children. The task of the ruler was the same as a father's: to provide their children with means necessary for their advancement in perfecting their internal and external condition. The ruler or father should also guide their actions towards perfection and happiness.[26] According to Wolff, subjects were simply not able to direct themselves towards the highest perfection and happiness. It does not go too far to say that Wolff was writing political theory for a tutelary interventionist state.[27] As Frank Grunert has argued, Wolff's theory built on dual absolutisms. First, the philosopher was to provide proper insights into the truth of the common good. Second, true knowledge would be implemented as the right policy. In this way Wolff's theoretical absolutism became a political absolutism. Ultimately, practically everything, even natural law, could be subordinated to the aim of the state, which itself was defined by philosophers.[28] Ideally the ruler would be a philosopher as well. In Wolff's philosophy, the concept of happiness served to legitimise the paternalistic state, which executed far-reaching moral interventions into the lives of individual subjects. Subjects were expected to behave passively and rely on the superior judgements of the head of the state regarding the way in which they ought to pursue their happiness. Even more importantly, the ruler not only decided how subjects ought to become happy, he decided what happiness meant. The ruler was the one to decide on the common good, happiness, and welfare. In sum, Wolff was an advocate of a paternalistic government as he stated openly

---

25 Kant, "Über den Gemeinspruch," 290.

26 Christian Wolff, *Vernünfftige Gedancken von dem gesellschaftlichen Leben der Menschen und insonderheit dem Gemeinen Wesen* (Frankfurt: Renger, 1747 [1721]), § 264, 200–201. For a more extensive discussion, see Frank Grunert, "Absolutism(s): Necessary Ambivalences in the Political Theory of Christian Wolff," *Tijdschrift voor Rechtsgeschiedenis* 73 (2005): 141–52.

27 Moggach, "Freedom and Perfection," 1004–1009. Moggach argues that "Wolff's affinities with the theory and practice of cameralism are apparent" (page 1008).

28 Grunert, "Absolutism(s)"; Frank Grunert, "Vollkommenheit als (politische) Norm: Zur politischen Philosophie von Christian Wolff (1679–1754)," in *Politische Theorien des 17. und 18. Jahrhunderts: Staat und Politik in Deutschland*, ed. Bernd Heidenreich and Gerhard Goehler (Mainz: von Zabern, 2011), 164–184.

himself, and under this paternalistic government citizens were treated as immature children.[29]

Kant's evaluation of happiness as the main principle of civil legislation has long dominated the historiography of eighteenth-century German political and economic thought, and it is still often taken for granted in research. For instance, it is often argued that in the name of the happiness of the state and its citizens, any state action could be legitimised. Therefore, in this line of interpretation the old *Staatszwecklehre* – prior to the very end of the eighteenth century – is associated with a profoundly hostile attitude towards freedom.[30] According to this view, in the society organised by the state with happiness in mind there existed no noteworthy free sphere for the citizen that remained out of bounds for the rulers. Furthermore, it has been argued that by taking the discussion of the aim of the state on the level of individuals, of subjects, the notion of happiness justified an extension of state activity not only theoretically but also in terms of the practice of statecraft. This was even more so because the maintenance and support of freedom was excluded from the definition of happiness. Another aspect of the older German natural law was that it emphasised the duties of citizens over their rights. Moreover, in eighteenth-century German political theory the distinction between state (*Staat*) and state of nature (*Naturzustand*) was central, yet, unlike in the English tradition of natural law, the aim of the contract as the basis of the state was not to secure the rights of individuals in the state. In other words, in Germany the social contract served merely as a tool to undermine individual freedom. Neither the making of the contract nor its content was in the power of the people. Therefore, the social contract neither ensured the minimal rights of individuals nor set limits to the power of the sovereign.[31] Interestingly, Justi has been interpreted as a representative of an older natural law that was hostile towards freedom and emphasised duties over rights. According to this line of interpretation, the major change in the aims of the state took place no sooner than

29 Wolff, *Vernünfftige Gedancken*, § 264, 201. "Derowegen ist klar, daß Obrigkeiten oder regierende Personen eben das in Ansehung ihrer Unterthanen ablieget, was Vätern in Ansehung ihrer Kinder und sowohl Untherthanen, als Kinder zum Gehorsam bereit und willig seyn sollen. Und dannenhero werden auch regierende Personen mit Recht Landes-Väter und Väter des Vaterlands genennt."

30 Jan Rolin, *Der Ursprung des Staates: die naturrechtlich-rechtsphilosophische Legitimation von Staat und Staatsgewalt im Deutschland des 18. und 19. Jahrhunderts* (Tübingen: Mohr Siebeck, 2005), 52.

31 Diethelm Klippel, "Reasonable Aims of Civil Society: Concerns of the State in German Political Theory in the Eighteenth and Early Nineteenth Centuries," in *Rethinking Leviathan: The Eighteenth-Century State in Britain and Germany*, ed. John Brewer and Eckhart Hellmuth (Oxford: Oxford University Press, 1999), 78.

at the end of the eighteenth century when the role of the state was limited to providing security.[32] This coincided with the time when the first critiques of the older aim of the state doctrine were published.[33] Kant's critique belonged to this wave of criticism and due to his prominence, it was the most influential one. This line of interpretation overlooks that one of the most influential writers, Justi, does not fit into this framework at all, as I will show in the following section. The Wolffian part of the history of eighteenth-century German political thought has been adequately studied, whereas Justi's accounts are strongly at odds with the overall historiographical interpretations of the aim of state doctrine.

Justi's Critique of Paternal Rule

Scholars who argue that *Glückseligkeitslehre* underwrote absolutism have tended to interpret Wolff's position as representative of German political thought in the second half of the eighteenth century. According to this interpretation, happiness as the aim of the state served to justify almost any action of the state. In addition, the security and happiness of a state were tightly intertwined with that of the ruler. It has often been argued that the happiness of the state, ruler, and subject existed harmoniously, without any conflict of interests. Consequently, the role and freedom of an individual or citizen were subordinated to that of the state and prince.

Justi did set theoretical limits to the actions of the state as well as to the power of the sovereign. In addition, he was very decisive in his critique of equating the power of the state, or political power, with paternal rule. Furthermore, Justi represents an important departure from the rule that the maintenance and support of freedom was not included in the aims of the state prior to the end of the eighteenth century. In fact, the concept of freedom is the key to understanding Justi's doctrine about the aim of the state. Justi argued that civil freedom (*bürgerliche Freyheit*) is an indistinguishable part of the aim of the state. Maintenance and the support of civil freedom were high on his agenda. In his *Nature and Essence of the States* (1760), Justi stated that every government is obliged to interfere in the natural liberty of its subjects (*die natürliche Freyheit ihrer Unterthanen*) as little as possible. The best government was that which managed

---

32 Diethelm Klippel, "Der liberale Interventionsstaat: Staatszweck und Staatstätigkeit in der deutschen politischen Theorie des 18. und der ersten Hälfte des 19. Jahrhunderts," in *Recht und Rechtswissenschaft im mitteldeutschen Raum*, ed. Heiner Lück (Köln: Böhlau, 1998), 77–78.
33 Stolleis, "Staatszweck," 80–84.

to serve the republic's final aim without endangering natural freedom. For Justi, the latter consisted of the freedom enjoyed in the state of nature, within which the only laws men need obey are the laws they have given to themselves. Of course, this was not possible once the state had been established, yet, Justi's point was that the number of laws imposed by the state should be kept to a minimum. As far as possible everyone should lead himself to happiness. Men were to be active, above all in economic affairs. Justi went as far as to argue for a citizen's right to pursue his own happiness.[34]

Justi gave his clearest exposition of the question of the best art of government in his essay "Considerations on Monarchies and Aristocracies". Here Justi took a clear stand against any form of unlimited power. For Justi, unlimited power was a system in which legislative and executive power were held either by one person (*Person eines Einzigen*), or by a single senate, collegium or group of people.[35] In either system the people had no say in legislative matters. Justi called the first form of unlimited power a simple monarchy and the second a simple aristocracy. He approved of neither, arguing that the greatest and happiest states have always been those that have given legislative power to the people. As reasonable beings, humans were meant to govern themselves.[36] Justi's conviction was that every thinking being ought to govern himself, and following the definition of governing oneself, he stated that the people should always have at least a part in legislative power.[37] It was here that he concluded that it was never in the interest of any people to hand unlimited power to anyone.[38] As we see, Justi was definitely not a defender of pure and unlimited monarchy.

---

34 Justi, Johann, *Natur und Wesen der Staaten als die Quelle aller Regierungswissenschaften und Gesetze* (Mittau: Haude und Spener, [1760] 1771), 40.

35 Justi, "Betrachtungen über die Monarchien und Aristocratien," 176. "Durch die uneingeschränkte oder einfache Monarchie verstehe ich hier die Regierung eines einzigen, welcher in seiner Person alle Arten von Gewalt in Staate, nämlich sowohl die gesetzgebende, als vollziehende Macht, davon ich in der ersten Abhandlung dieses Bandes gehandelt habe, vereinigt. Unter der einfachen Aristocratie hingegen ist zu verstehen, wenn diese beyden höchsten Arten von Gewalt, bey einem Senat, Collegio, oder besondern Classe des Volkes allein beruhet, ohne daß das Volk an der gesetzgebenden Gewalt den geringsten Antheil hat."

36 Ibid., 177. "Ein jedes verständige Wesen soll sich selbst regieren."

37 Ibid., 182. "Sich selbst regieren, bestehet darinnen, daß man sich selbst Gesetze giebt; und wenn die Menschen in den bürgerlichen Verfassungen die Gesetzgebung sich selbst vorbehalten und blos zu Vollziehung der Gesetze eine Regierung über sich setzen; so thun sie dasjenige, was verständigen und freyen Wesen, die in bürgerlichen Gesellschaften mit einander leben wollen, gemäß ist."

38 Ibid.

In paternalist political theories, those with superior abilities and means to look out for the well-being of the less fortunate were to take the leading role.[39] As we saw, Christian Wolff's political theory was exemplary in this sense. Justi reflected on this question and asked whether it would not be better to let the more reasonable people guide the less reasonable ones towards their happiness. His answer was straightforwardly in the negative: Justi acknowledged that many people were uneducated and ignorant; however, this did not mean that they did not have any reason. According to Justi, the right to guide oneself to happiness should be respected, because even meagre reason was enough for people to enable them to pursue their own happiness and therefore they should not forcibly be directed by others.[40] Justi emphasised that citizens were always better in a position to legislate than even the wisest government ever could be. This was a consequence of the fact that no single individual or small group of individuals acting as a state knew the circumstances, needs, and powers of the people as well as they did. This was a critique of the simple forms of "enlightened reform bureaucracy" where the state was perceived to have superior knowledge of the circumstances of the people. In Justi's view, the simplicity of the people was not an obstacle to legislation. Moreover, Justi explained that if people living in the state were ignorant, the matters that needed to be solved by legislation could not be of a complicated nature either. As an immediate corollary, Justi concluded that every householder living in the nation of Iroquois was equally skilled to contribute to the legislation of his nation as the most prudent member of Parliament in England.[41]

Justi found historical examples in favour giving the legislative power to the people. He pointed out that in ancient times the successful Roman and German

---

39 Gaby Mahlberg, "Patriarchalism and the Monarchical Republics," in *Monarchism and Absolutism in Early Modern Europe*, ed. Cesare Cuttica and Glenn Burgess (London: Routledge, 2012), 54–55.

40 Justi, "Betrachtungen über die Monarchien und Aristocratien," 178. "Ein Mensch erkennet leicht, daß er ungelehrt und unwissend it. Allein dem ohngeachtet ist er weit davon entfernet, zu erkennen, *daß* er keinen Verstand besitze und deshalb nöthig habe, von einem andern regieret zu werden. Die Natur eines freyen und verständigen Wesens wirket allemal so viel, daß es sich zutrauet, sich selbst leiten zu können."

41 Ibid., 182–183. "Die Bürger eines Staats sind auch allemal zur Gesetzgebung besser geschickt, als die weiseste Regierung niemals seyn kann. Niemand kann ihren Zustand, ihre Bedürfnisse, ihre Noth, ihre Kräfte besser kennen, als sie selbst; und die Einfalt der Bürger ist in dieser Gesetzgebung niemals eine Hinderniß. Wenn sie sämtlich einfältig und unwissend sind; so werden auch gewiß allemal die Angelegenheiten des Staates von einem sehr geringen Umfange seyn. Ein jeder Hausvater bey der Nation der Iroquoisen ist eben so geschickt über die Gesetzgebung seines Volkes zu stimmen, als das Klügste Parlamentsglied in Engelland."

nations had granted legislative power to the people. Among contemporary states England represented the most powerful and happy nation, and it had indeed given the legislative power to the people.[42] Justi also observed that at no point in history had people voluntarily relinquished legislative power; to do so was simply not in the interest of any reasonable being. Basically, Justi was here supporting the mixed form of government as represented by England. In this context, it is important to remember that many of the works of Justi, including his "Considerations on Monarchies and Aristocracies" were written and published in the context of Seven Years' War. He participated in the conflict by writing Pro-Prussian and Pro-English pamphlets. However, this immediate occupation did not hinder him criticising the dynastic foreign policy practiced by European emperors. Justi identified the will to dominate and conquer, so widespread in the Europe of his lifetime, as the cause of non-freedom in Europe. This sad state of affairs explained why legislative power was so rarely found in the hands of the people in his own time. The imperial vices, Justi argued, had buried the freedom of the people.[43] This point was an implicit criticism of the foreign policy of his own patron, Frederick II.

Justi's essay "Considerations on Monarchies and Aristocracies" and his translation of the passage from Giovanni Cattaneo's *The Source, the Strength, and the True Spirit of Laws* aimed at questioning the legitimacy of paternal rule. According to Justi, simple monarchy was not a "natural form of government". He was not able to imagine a situation where a king would have been so impudent that he would have required the whole legislative power to be in his hands. Such a demand would have been equal to telling his future citizens that they should leave themselves to the arbitrary will of the king; the king would say: Just expect your happiness to follow from my will and passions.[44] Here Justi's position was that being dependent on the arbitrary will of anyone is a state of un-freedom. Justi noted that human beings want to be masters of

---

42 Ibid., 189. "Die größten und glücklichsten Staaten sind diejenigen gewesen, die nach der Natur verständiger Wesen die Gesetzgebung dem Volke überlaßen haben. Bey Römern hatte das Volk die gesetzgebende und der aristocratische Senat die vollziehende Macht. Die teutschen Völker, welche das römische Reich zu Grunde richteten, nachdem es sich in eine Monarchie verwandelt hatte, hatten alle die gesetzgebende und ihre Könige die vollziehende Macht und heutiges Tages giebt uns Großbritannien ein überzeugendes Beyspiel, wie reich, mächtig und glücklich ein solcher Staat werden kann."

43 Ibid., 189–190.

44 Ibid., 183. "Bey Errichtung eines neuen Staats wird auch niemals ein König so unverschämt seyn, daß er die gesetzgebende Gewalt verlangen sollte. Diese Forderung würde im Grunde eben das seyn, als wenn er zu seinen künftigen Bürgern sagte: Ueberlaßet euch gänzlich meiner Willkühr! Erwartet euer Glück lediglich von meinem Willen und Leidenschaften."

their own fate. He explained that we do need judges and commanders in war, but an unlimited legislator was not something that would be desired by anyone. According to Justi, this was because we – as reasonable beings – could best decide what was beneficial for our common good (*gemeinschaftlichen Besten*), and this was exactly because of the above-mentioned reason: No one knows our needs and shortcomings as well as we do.[45]

Justi elaborated on his point about distinguishing the political power from the paternal rule by returning to the analogy regarding the unlimited power of a father over his children. Justi acknowledged that a father had unlimited power over his children. However, this was only for the limited period of time during which the children did not possess enough reason and were immature. At the time the children became reasonable beings (*verständige Wesen*), the father had no power over his children, and the children had the right to guide themselves to their own happiness.[46] In short, Justi argued that human beings should have the right to pursue their own happiness, and in line with this the legislative power in the state should lie in the hands of people, who as reasonable beings – no matter how meagre that reason – were best prepared to decide what was best for them. It is worth emphasising that Justi spoke explicitly about citizens' right (*Recht*) to pursue for their happiness. This finding is in stark contrast with the earlier interpretations of Justi's political thought and with overall interpretations of the character of cameral sciences, as paternal in character or as mere propaganda of the princely chamber.

Conclusion

My aim in this chapter has been to re-interpret Justi's political thought with a focus on his essay on simple monarchies and simple aristocracies published in his collected political and financial writings. I have argued that if paternalism is understood in a Kantian sense, according to which fatherly government (*väter-*

---

45 Ibid., 184. "Allein wir wollen immer selbst Meister über unser Schicksal bleiben. Wir haben einen Richter und Anführer im Kriege nöthig, aber wir bedürfen keinen uneingeschränkten Gesetzgeber; weil wir als verständige Wesen selbst im Stande sind, zu beschließen, was zu unsern gemeinschaftlichen Besten zuträglich ist, und weil unsere Bedürfnisse und Mängel niemand so gut empfinden kann, als wir selbst."

46 Ibid., 185. "Die Natur giebt dem Vater allerdings eine uneingeschränkte Gewalt über seine Kinder; aber man muß hinzusetzen: so lange sie noch unverständig und unerwachsen sind. Sobald sie selbst verständige Wesen sind; so haben sie unstreitig das Recht ihre Glückseligkeit selbst zu leiten."

liche Regierung) is a government that treats the people as immature children who do not know how best to pursue their own happiness, then Justi's thought cannot be included in such a characterisation. According to Justi, paternal government, as it had been advocated, for instance, by Christian Wolff, was an unnatural form of government. The points made by Justi in his "Considerations on Monarchies and Aristocracies" bear resemblance to John Locke's views presented in his *Two Treatises of Government* (1690). In debate with Robert Filmer, Locke argued that political power was to be differentiated from paternal power.[47] Perhaps it is not completely out of place to state in Kari Saastamoinen's words that "Justi could almost be considered as some kind of poor man's Locke". However, it is best to contextualise Justi within contemporary German and European proposals for reform. The more immediate German context of Justi's proposal was to support a reform of government to appreciate the principles of a mixed constitution. Justi's advocacy for change and recognition of the open-endedness of future were part and parcel of the politicisation of the German Enlightenment.

Instead of focusing conventionally on the canon of great political philosophers only the focus on contemporary discussions helps us to avoid the major problem present in several of the previous interpretations of Justi's political thought and of cameral sciences in general. This problem is the so-called "dead hand of philosophy".[48] We first arrange arguments into "systems of thought" that are rationalised according to philosophic principles; then we plunder the archive for proofs of the validity of such "systems", treating individual "thinkers" as exemplars or critics or deviationists from the system that has been used to frame them. In this chapter, I have demonstrated that Justi has been "framed" by the Kant-inspired critique of Wolff, a critique that did highlight real differences, but which converted all intervening writing into one of two categories: post-Wolffian or pre-Kantian. However, as we have seen, this framework does not fit Justi and the cameral sciences as he advocated them.

---

47 John Locke, *Two treatises of government: in the former, the false principles and foundation of Sir Robert Filmer and his followers are detected and overthrown, the latter is an essay concerning the true original, extent, and end of civil government* (London: Awnsham Churchill, 1690); Cesare Cuttica, *Sir Robert Filmer (1588–1653) and the Patriotic Monarch: Patriarchalism in Seventeenth-Century Political Thought* (Manchester: Manchester University Press, 2013).

48 I want to thank Keith Tribe for discussions on this topic.

Laura Tarkka-Robinson

14 An Empire of Renewed Ambitions: Political Economy and National Character in the *Travels* (1782) of William Macintosh

Upon the appearance of William Macintosh's *Travels in Europe, Asia, and Africa* in 1782, British reviewers directed attention to the author's account of how the day was "commonly spent by an Englishman in Bengal". Since this caricature resonated vividly with rumors about British "nabobs" exploiting the territorial dominions of the English East India Company (EIC), both *The Monthly Review* and *The Critical Review* quoted the story in full.[1] As the account suggested, such Company servants were making "the most splendid fortunes" while leading a corrupt life of indolence and luxury.[2] Though based on the characters of the most prominent Englishmen in Bengal – Governor Robert Clive and Governor-General Warren Hastings – the account also constituted a general warning against the effect of a colonial career on young men intent on following their example.[3] As such, rather than providing any specific new facts, this section of the *Travels* made a political statement aiming to convince the public of the necessity to change how the British dominions in India were governed.

As demonstrated by this example, Macintosh's epistolary *Travels* was not a plainly descriptive travel narrative, but a carefully crafted contribution to the political debate concerning the past and the future of the EIC in relation to national interest and public opinion.[4] Accordingly, those eyewitness observations which it

1 Tillman W. Nechtman, *Nabobs: Empire and Identity in Eighteenth-Century Britain* (Cambridge: Cambridge University Press, 2010), 9–21; Robert Travers, *Ideology and Empire in Eighteenth-Century India: The British in Bengal* (Cambridge: Cambridge University Press, 2007), 5–7, 52.

2 William Macintosh, *Travels in Europe, Asia, and Africa: describing characters, customs, manners, laws, and productions of nature and art: containing various remarks on the political and commercial interests of Great Britain; and delineating in particular, a new system for the government and improvement of the British settlements in the East Indies: begun in the year 1777, and finished in 1781* (London, 1782), I: 214–219; *The Monthly Review* 67 (1782): 245–256; *The Critical Review* 53 (1782): 337–343, 424–432.

3 Macintosh, *Travels*, I: 243, 251–252; Nechtman, *Nabobs*, 81–85, 102–104, 198.

4 Innes M. Keighren, "Circulating Seditious Knowledge: The 'Daring Absurdities, Studied Misrepresentations, and Abominable Falsehoods' of William Macintosh," in *Mobilities of Knowledge*, ed. Heike Jöns et al. (Cham: Springer, 2017), 73–75.

https://doi.org/10.1515/9783110679861-016

did contain ought to be considered subservient to its political message: that improving the system of government in Bengal would be more advantageous for Britain than fighting over the rebellious colonies in America. Interestingly, to recommend his own approach to colonial policy, Macintosh embarked on a dialogue with the works of Adam Smith.[5] This was not an entirely unique strategy, because Company servants were likewise drawing support for their mercantile sovereignty in India from current theories of political economy and the Montesquieuan idea of adjusting government to local "genius".[6] Yet, Macintosh portrayed himself as a patriot rather than a Company man, and this gives his *Travels* a special relevance to the evolution of political language during a period of crisis.

Considering Macintosh's propositions in the context of the European commercial rivalry invoked by Smith in *The Wealth of Nations*, the following pages will hence interpret the *Travels* as an attempt to solve the moral issues associated with the English East India Company's transformation into a territorial power, collecting revenue under the auspices of the British Parliament. I aim to show that Macintosh sought to legitimate a system of imperial rule by redefining ambition with reference to national character. Accordingly, his *Travels* suggested that the ambition to strengthen the British Empire in Asia could and should be perceived as something more noble than a reprehensible desire for conquest. The argument was that in India, European "ardour of improvement" would be naturally complemented by the "gentle" character of the native population, and that it was therefore possible to build a morally sustainable system of imperial economy.

Thus, via a selective application of ideas put forward by Smith, Macintosh delineated a way of protecting "the glory of the British name" in the eyes of those members of the public who had been outraged and disillusioned by the behavior of British "nabobs".[7] Perceived in the context of the American War and the constitutional crisis defining the terms of political language when the *Travels* was published, Macintosh's suggestions were meant to instill confidence in the exploitation of Indian resources for the sake of beneficial commerce.[8] The conceptual challenges which the work faced in so doing are well illustrated by

---

5 Keighren, "Seditious Knowledge," 71.
6 Travers, *Ideology*, 54–55.
7 See Keighren, "Seditious Knowledge," 70.
8 Pasi Ihalainen, *Agents of the People: Democracy and Popular Sovereignty in British and Swedish Parliamentary and Public Debates, 1734–1800* (New York: Berghahn Books, 2010), 270.

John Bruce's later reference to British India as an accomplishment of "the character of a free, though conquering people".[9]

I

As might be expected, contemporary reviewers pointed out that the *Travels* contained some information on Indian customs and manners, but, as noted by *The Critical Review*, Macintosh had "studied" the world "rather to explore the foreign interests of Britain, than to gratify the public curiosity with reiterated description".[10] Indeed, the fact that several reviewers considered the descriptions too familiar to be worth quoting underlines the primacy of the political perspective.[11] Since it was not in the reviewers' interest to repeat what they perceived as truisms, such reactions indicate that the value of Macintosh's *Travels* as a publication was not based on first-hand observation.

Thus, while political intelligence did play a central role in the work, it should be read in light of Macintosh's concern about the bad reputation of Company servants, "whose measures are too public not to be known, and too unjustifiable to admit of defence".[12] Significantly, Macintosh also cursed the London-based *Courier de l'Europe* for circulating "the patriotic speeches" of Parliament "all over Europe" and encouraging "the enemies of Britain to join their aid to the American rebellion".[13] The tacit notions distinguishing the different national communities of readers to which he was referring surfaced in the processes of transfer and translation through which the *Travels* was introduced to new audiences.[14] For instance, *Le Journal encyclopédique* presented the work as evidence that the English were not being true to their acclaimed love of liberty, because they seemed to perceive it as an asset reserved solely for themselves.[15] This points to the moral dilemma of the public character of the British, which Macintosh had identified and attempted to resolve.

---

9 Travers, *Ideology*, 247; *Historical View of Plans, for the Government of British India, and the Regulation of Trade to the East Indies* (London 1793), 39. See also ibid., 51–53.

10 *The Critical Review* 53 (1782): 337.

11 *The Critical Review* 53 (1782): 426; *Le Journal encyclopédique* 54 (October 1782): 276; *Göttingische Anzeigen* (1783): 1233–1247.

12 Macintosh, *Travels*, I: 244.

13 Ibid., 31.

14 Keighren, "Seditious Knowledge," 68, 77–80.

15 *Le Journal encyclopédique* 54 (October 1782): 281.

However, Macintosh's appearance in the philosophical history of Johann Gottfried Herder exemplifies a different strand of contemporary reception. In this context, the *Travels* did not testify against the British character, but instead served to demonstrate that the characters of South Asian populations had remained fixed over a long period of time.[16] Indeed, with regard to the development of a historicised perspective on political philosophy, it is highly significant that scholars like Herder perused British publications on India in the hope of finding what might be called ethnographic descriptions. While two German reviews later complained about the dearth of such material in the *Travels*,Herder found it a useful source for his *Ideen zur Philosophie der Geschichte der Menschheit* and paraphrased some passages in German.[17] Making use of travel literature in this way was common practice, but the implications of Herder's references to Macintosh call for special attention, because the *Travels* was neither a modern narrative centered around "the experiencing self", nor a Baconian storehouse of experience-based observations.[18] However, rather than merely reading it as a reflection of the "epistemological disaster" of eighteenth-century Orientalism, it is worth emphasising that its aim was not to make different cultures "comprehensible", but to change the character of the British Empire.[19]

Indeed, according to its full title, the *Travels* provided "various remarks on the political and commercial interests of Great Britain". Since the notion of British "interests" related it to the early-modern notion of Europe as a system of competing commercial societies, an intelligent reader like Herder will hardly have missed its political message. Nevertheless, in *Ideen*, Macintosh figured simply as a modern traveler providing information on India.[20] As a consequence, it has been suggested that because Herder's notions of the Hindus derived "large-

---

16 See Keighren, "Seditious Knowledge," 78; Eva Piirimäe, "State-machines, Commerce and the Progress of *Humanität* in Europe: Herder's Response to Kant in *Ideas for the Philosophy of History of Mankind,*" in *Commerce and Peace in the Enlightenment* ed. Béla Kapossy, Isaac Nakhimovsky, and Richard Whatmore (Cambridge: Cambridge University Press, 2017), 171; Macintosh, *Travels*, I: 325–327.

17 *Allgemeine Literatur-Zeitung* (20 October 1785): 65–67; *Allgemeine deutsche Bibliothek* 70 (1786): 180; Sonia Sikka, *Herder on Humanity and Cultural Difference: Enlightened Relativism* (Cambridge: Cambridge University Press, 2011), 48.

18 See Kai Mikkonen, *Narrative Paths: African Travel in Modern Fiction and Nonfiction* (Columbus: The Ohio State University Press, 2015), 14–15, 18; Daniel Carey, "The Problem of Credibility in Early Modern Travel," *Renaissance Studies* 33 (2019): 528, 539–543.

19 See Jürgen Osterhammel, *Unfabling the East: The Enlightenment's Encounter with Asia* (Princeton, NJ: Princeton University Press, 2018), 11–12, 15, 31.

20 Johann Gottfried Herder, *Herders Sämmtliche Werke 13*, ed. Bernhard Suphan (Berlin, 1887), 150, 222, 261.

ly" from Macintosh, he shared the latter's "unbridled admiration" for "the gentlest of the races of men".[21] Looking at how one of Herder's references to Macintosh was translated back into English, the emphasis on the inherent gentleness and patience defining the "hindoos" as "happy lambs" certainly strikes the eye.[22] Yet, it should be noted that the corresponding passage of the original *Travels* did not describe the "Hindoos" in isolation, but in contrast to the French and the Dutch. The logic of these comparisons was hidden away in Herder's depiction of the Indian character, and what his *Ideen* likewise did not convey is that Macintosh had discussed the Indian character and "the influence of habit and custom on human sentiments" in conjunction with Smith's *Theory of Moral Sentiments.*[23] For this reason, it is crucial to consider Macintosh original account against the backdrop of the American war, and to ask how the works of Smith rendered support for the "new system for the government and improvement of the British settlements in the East Indies" that he laid out in the *Travels.*

II

Establishing how the *Travels* applied ideas put forward by Smith to solve the crisis of the British Empire helps us distinguish the multiple levels on which Smith's writing interacted with the political debates of his time.[24] This opens up a new perspective on the complex relationship between philosophical writing and interest-driven attempts to transform and translocate the British Empire. As the case of Macintosh's *Travels* demonstrates, how *The Theory of Moral Sentiments* and *The Wealth of Nations* contributed to the transformation of political language and to the creation of new policies was not necessarily in line with Smith's own intentions. Indeed, his works found a new and unexpected use in the hands of Macintosh – a former overseer of Caribbean plantations – and John Murray, his aspiring London-based publisher.[25]

---

21 A. Leslie Willson, "Herder and India: The Genesis of a Mythical Image," *PMLA* 70 (1955): 1051.

22 Johann Gottfried Herder, *Outlines of a Philosophy of the History of Man*, trans. T. Churchill (London, 1800), 253.

23 Macintosh, *Travels*, I: 321–322. On the dissonances between Smith's model and German Cameralism, see Fania Oz-Salzberger, "Adam Smith's Early German Readers: Reception, Misreception, and Critique," *The Adam Smith Review* 9 (2016): 201–209.

24 Compare with Jennifer Pitts, *A Turn to Empire: The Rise of Imperial Liberalism in Britain and France* (Princeton, NJ: Princeton University Press, 2005), 33–58; Marian Sawer, *Marxism and the Question of the Asiatic Mode of Production* (The Hague: Martinus Nijhoff, 1977), 25–36.

25 Keighren, "Seditious Knowledge," 69–70.

Macintosh and Murray presented the *Travels* as a contribution to the science of political economy, setting it up as a response to *The Wealth of Nations.*[26] Yet, Macintosh's proposal for the improvement of the colonial economy was not confined to strictly material considerations, for the moral psychology of national characters also played a central role in it. This was highlighted in the preface, which explained that

> The love of novelty and variety is a universal passion [...]. But in the present period of extended intercourse, when the rudest tribes of mankind may be brought to act in the general system [...] the real character, abilities, and circumstances of every people [...] form a necessary branch in the science of political economy.[27]

"National character" or "spirit" played a prominent role in the political language of the eighteenth century.[28] In contrast to what is sometimes assumed, however, it cannot be understood merely as a shorthand expression for later notions of ethnicity and race.[29] While such applications were certainly common, besides signifying human difference "national character" also had moral, political and even economic meanings, related to the idea of nations as public figures in an imaginary sphere of interaction. Accordingly, "national character" was not only a matter of customs, manners, and appearance, but also of honor, glory, and political virtue.

Taking the flexibility of the meaning of "national character" into account allows us to examine the dynamics of othering in eighteenth-century public debate from multiple angles. The case of Macintosh's *Travels* demonstrates that alertness to public opinion encouraged comparisons between the moral characters of national communities. Accordingly, in representations of commercial rivalry in the pursuit of material progress, this was conducive to demonstrations of the relative refinement of one's own nation. This, in turn, connected the moral and political dimensions of "national character" to the concept of emulation, or, the improvement of one's own condition and status through continuous efforts to exceed those of others. Indeed, as the *Travels* suggested, European national characters could be set apart from extra-European ones by virtue of their

---

26 Macintosh, *Travels*, I: iv, 206.
27 Ibid., iv.
28 Roberto Romani, *National Character and Public Spirit in Britain and France, 1750–1914* (Cambridge: Cambridge University Press, 2004), 1–4, 7–14; Joep Leerssen, *National Thought in Europe: A Cultural History* (Amsterdam: Amsterdam University Press, 2006), 17, 20–21, 39–70.
29 See Nechtman, *Nabobs*, 50–51.

sustained competitive interaction.[30] The advantage gained from the dynamics of emulation was therefore implicitly assumed in intra-European comparisons, while Macintosh's emphasis on the static nature of the Indian civilisation – embraced in Herder's *Ideen* – both reflected and justified the established colonial relationship between the British nation and the inhabitants of the Indian dominions of the EIC.

Before studying Macintosh's representation of national characters more closely, it is therefore important to consider the *Travels* as a publication aimed at an audience defined by an interest in colonial affairs. It consists of 72 letters, all of which had allegedly been sent to Europe during a voyage to India and back. Since many of them are devoted to the elaboration of what Macintosh considered sustainable imperial policy, the relatively few eyewitness observations ought to be read as supplementing this political message.[31] The second volume opens with an lengthy "enclosed letter", which had not been written by Macintosh himself, but instead by a "gentleman who has been for several years in the military service of the Company".[32] The richness of the detail on Indian customs and manners which this Company officer was able to provide is explained by his thorough immersion in his new habitat, as the letter states that "the operation of climate soon conformed me to the customs of this country".[33] In comparison with this section, other parts of the *Travels* retained a more distant perspective on India. Their authorial voice cannot, however, be fully equated with that of Macintosh, for although the *Travels* describe a voyage which he actually took, the shape of the published text derived from the pen of William Thomson, a professional writer who edited his manuscripts for the bookseller Murray.[34] This transpires from a footnote to a much later publication, in which Murray explained that

> A Gentleman from India, unpractised in literary composition, put sundry papers, which he wished to be published, into the hands of Mr. Thomson, who did his best to give them circulation by throwing them [...] into the form of letters to a friend in England, by mixing

30 Vera Keller, *Knowledge and the Public Interest, 1575–1725* (Cambridge: Cambridge University Press, 2015), 44–45, 153, 179; Istvan Hont, *Jealousy of Trade: International Competition and the Nation-State in Historical Perspective* (Cambridge, MA: Harvard University Press, 2005), 117–124. See also David Carrithers, introduction to *Charles-Louis de Secondat, Baron de Montesquieu*, ed. David Carrithers (London: Routledge, 2016), xxviii–xxix.

31 Macintosh, *Travels*, I: 259; Keighren, "Seditious Knowledge," 70–72.

32 Macintosh, *Travels*, II: 1.

33 Ibid., 5. See also: Nechtman, *Nabobs*, 90.

34 Keighren, "Seditious Knowledge," 72–75.

> them with various entertainment, furnished, for the most part, though not entirely, by his employer, and clothing them in tolerable language.[35]

Accordingly, while it is hard to distinguish the experience, observations, and opinions of Macintosh from Thomson's revisions and additions, the *Travels* was evidently not just a collection of "sundry papers" or "various entertainment" but a contribution to the political debate incited by EIC's territorial acquisitions. This is plainly demonstrated by the prominence of the theme of the American war in the first part of the work, which discusses the national characters of Britain's European rivals alongside their perspectives on American independence.[36] After this, the letters narrate Macintosh's voyage to India via the Cape of Good Hope, and by the 27th letter – of 15 September 1779 – he has finally reached Calcutta, his prime destination.[37] The following letter commences a sequence addressed to "J– M–, Esq" – the publisher John Murray, perhaps – and focuses on how India could be governed with the help of knowledge about the "Hindoo" character.[38] While Smith's ideas appear to have been "foremost in Macintosh's mind" when he composed this part of the manuscript, he did not, however, fain to implement *The Wealth of Nations* without amendment.[39]

Significantly, although the American War is mentioned as the context which had motivated the publication of the *Travels*, and although the work thus made a statement relating to British colonial politics, it argued against the public dissemination of British political speeches. Indeed, according to Macintosh, "the great advantage that an absolute has over a free government, lies in the secrecy and expedition of all its operations".[40] As this remark suggests, the aim of the *Travels* was to promote British interest in a way that did not necessarily depend on the transparency of policy-making. Thus, while the sixth letter of the *Travels* was, in practice, an open letter to the Prime Minister Lord North, this could be read as a plea for the future deliberation of colonial policy without public exposure.[41]

---

35 *The Defence of Innes Munro, Esq.* (London 1790), 17.
36 Macintosh, *Travels*, I: 12, 17, 26–27.
37 Ibid., 242.
38 Ibid., 250–482.
39 Keighren, "Seditious Knowledge," 71.
40 Macintosh, *Travels*, I: 30–31.
41 See Paul Seaward and Pasi Ihalainen, "Key Concepts for Parliament in Britain (1640–1800)," in *Parliament and Parliamentarism: A Comparative History of a European Concept*, ed. Pasi Ihalainen, Cornelia Ilie, and Kari Palonen (New York: Berghahn Books, 2016), 42–43.

In the letter to North, Macintosh underlined the need to pacify the British dependencies in India and "to counterbalance the influence of ambitious rivals, who will, no doubt, be industrious to alienate the affections of the natives from the English". As he suggested, "the natives being now instructed in the use of arms", the most stable "system of politics" would be "mild and wise", and either resemble "the original institutions of India" or be constructed upon "virtue and justice". In this way, Macintosh prefigured that a reformed system of government could give rise to "a spirit of commercial liberty", which would "gradually banish all ideas of despotism from European breasts, and dispel of course that melancholy distrust and apprehension, which unfortunately have so long hung over the minds of the gentle natives of the East". By way of explanation, he affirmed that there was no "people *naturally* more virtuous, more tractable and docile, or capable of arriving at greater perfection in those arts which give elasticity to the springs of commerce, than those over whom the English East India Company have extended their dominion in Asia".[42]

Significantly, the "spirit of commercial liberty" which the *Travels* invoked had very little to do with political liberty, and seems to have denoted something more like a spirit of industrial activity. A further explanation of how the new "mild" system would work was provided in the letters to "J– M–, Esq." In view of the argument about "commercial liberty", it is significant that the *Travels* included an appendix commenting on *The Wealth of Nations*, "the last and greatest work that hath appeared on the public stage, from the inimitable *pen* of Dr. Adam Smith".[43] In addition, Macintosh recounted how he had got hold of Smith's new book at the Cape of Good Hope, with five months to examine it before his arrival in India.[44] However, as already noted, the *Travels* was also informed by ideas that Smith had presented in his earlier *Theory of Moral Sentiments*. Thus, Smith's discussion of the influence of custom on moral sentiments provided Macintosh with a way of explaining how knowledge of the character of the Hindus would help in supporting the spirit of commerce and make London the "grand emporium of the world".[45]

The impact of the opinion of an "enlightened" public on the *Travels* is perceptible from the fact that, besides Smith, Macintosh also claimed to have read some Voltaire, Rousseau, and Raynal's *History of the Two Indies* on his way to the Cape.[46] Moreover, the *Travels* was furnished with explicit references to Montes-

---

42 Macintosh, *Travels*, I: 63–73.
43 Ibid., 206.
44 Ibid., 205.
45 Ibid., 262.
46 Ibid., 84.

quieu, and a seven-page footnote on James Dunbar's *Essays on the History of Mankind in Rude and Cultivated Ages* (1780), which had been published while Macintosh was on his way back to Britain.[47] While these references display an awareness of arguments against colonial aggression, the works of Smith were used to suggest that an economy based on the difference of national characters could secure the British Empire in the East while it was falling apart in the West.

In view of the language used in contemporaneous parliamentary debates, Smith's moral psychology and political economy offered an alternative both to the rhetoric revolving around an understanding of the British constitution as a tradition "refined by the wisdom of ages" and to the authoritative work of Montesquieu, which divided the world up according to climates.[48] The advantage of relying on the "spirit of commercial liberty" was that British policy in India would not have to be based on a pre-existing Mughal constitution, nor would there be a need to assume that members of the British Parliament represented the voice of the Indian population. This was important since, in the late 1770s, the sovereignty of "the people", and "public opinion" beyond Parliament, had become significant themes in British political debate.[49] In the aftermath of the American War, references to "the people" became even more common.[50] In this context, parliamentary involvement in the government of the EIC's dominions suggested the power of one "people" over another. Accusations of despotism could, however, be averted via the notion of British liberty as a product of commercial society and modern property relations, which provided a political narrative of British national interest as beneficial for the Empire at large.[51]

III

As Macintosh explained to the public, Hindostan had been a well-cultivated country, "inhabited by numerous and learned people, highly accomplished". Drawing a comparison to the British colonies in America, he stressed that a "country peopled with such inhabitants" was "an acquisition infinitely greater" and that in order to benefit from the Indian dominions, it was "only necessary to make the people happy, by a mild system of government adapted to their man-

47 Macintosh, *Travels*, I: 304–310; II: 53, 179, 458. See also Pitts, *Turn*, 26–27.
48 Travers, *Ideology*, 7–9; Ihalainen, *Agents*, 119.
49 Ihalainen, *Agents*, 256–260.
50 Ibid., 319.
51 See Travers, *Ideology*, 47–48; 217–218.

ners, customs, and educations".[52] Adopting the language of political economy, Macintosh added that "no other country in the world can afford to sell their labour so cheap as the Hindoos, the most temperate, persevering, and ingenious of all the sons of men".[53] By emphasising the impact of custom on national character in this way while in some passages also invoking the universal rationality of self-interest, the *Travels* bypassed the problems previously ascribed to the corrupting influence of local circumstances.[54] Most importantly, however, the *Travels* suggested that Indian happiness was compatible with British greatness.[55] This was because the Hindu character was neither savage like that of the natives of America, nor graced with the ambition for improvement which Macintosh associated with the competitive culture shared by the Europeans.

Indeed, while Macintosh claimed that the American colonies could perhaps have been appeased by the introduction of internal jealousies and luxury, his counsel with regard to India was different.[56] For although he suggested the application of the maxim of *divide et impera* by letting "the crown of Great Britain be invested with an independent sovereignty over certain provinces" while the king of Delhi would continue enjoying an "undisturbed dominion over the rest", the new system he recommended was to be founded on the use of "generous" sentiments:[57]

> By a captivating display of all the virtues, acquire the confidence of the native powers of India. There is not in the world, a race of men more grateful for favours than the Hindoos, or who have quicker feelings of right and wrong. Operate on the generous sensibility of their nature. It will not be difficult, by the exercise of humanity and justice, to make them more ambitious of the friendship of Britain, than jealous of its power.[58]

As indicated by this passage, the language of national character was instrumental to Macintosh's method of justifying the build-up of an imperial system of political economy, because it enabled him to articulate it in enlightened terms of progress and civilisation.[59] Since Macintosh was clearly preoccupied with the honor as well as the wealth of his nation, his stated aim was to offer "certain

---

52 Macintosh, *Travels*, I: 280–81.
53 Ibid., 283.
54 Nechtman, *Nabobs*, 30–58.
55 Compare with Adam Smith, *The Theory of Moral Sentiments* (London, 1759), 352.
56 Macintosh, *Travels*, I: 26–27.
57 Ibid., 385.
58 Ibid., 402.
59 See László Kontler, "William Robertson and His German Audience on European and Non-European Civilizations," *The Scottish Historical Review* 80 (2001): 68–69.

hints" to "men in power in Britain", to encourage "enquiries that may be productive of the greatest public benefits".[60] By such enquiries, he meant a closer study of the character, sentiments and circumstances of the people to be governed. Significantly, however, the system that he proposed was not only recommended by commercial gain but also by the promise of stability and mutual satisfaction.

What Macintosh suggested was that building a new system in India would serve the national interest better than the fight against American independence, because the latter had turned into a hopeless display of valor, represented as an antiquated type of ambition. As he stated, "while I glory in the spirit of my countrymen, I regret the cause in which it is now exerted, and see more matter of grief than of triumph in all their victories".[61] By defining military success as a "matter of grief", Macintosh referred to the notoriously destructive powers of avarice and the ambition for military conquest, thus distinguishing the policies he proposed from the failure of the British government to keep the American colonies under control. From this perspective, his representation of European nations as the most savage of all can be read as a rhetorical move encouraging his British audience to display the virtues expected of a civilized nation:[62]

> I have seen or had exact information of the principles and manners of many nations in Asia, and the Asiatic and African islands; and have not a doubt in my mind, that the nations of Europe are more savage than any of all these; if by term savage, I may be allowed to understand oppression, cruelty, and injustice. That people, in my mind, have the best title to the praise of civilization and refinement, who are the most humane, courteous, and just in the intercourses of social life.[63]

As suggested by this passage, the Europeans had let themselves down by practicing "oppression, cruelty, and injustice", but the British nation could still aspire to "the best title" of civilisation by demonstrating humanity, courteousness, and justice. Thus, even as Macintosh directed attention to the dangers of ambition, he suggested ways in which certain culture-specific ambitions could be turned to account in a system of political economy.[64] However, it is important to note that only the jealous ambition represented as characteristic of Europeans went along with the "love of novelty" and "ardour of improvement" driving societal progress. In contrast, he defined "the genius of the Hindoos" as "rather imitative than inventive", which allowed for the claim that in India, "the object

60 Macintosh, *Travels*, I: 264–265.
61 Ibid., 265.
62 Ibid., 303–307.
63 Ibid., 303.
64 Ibid., 154.

of emulation" was "not to invent anything new" but instead to preserve "the usages and doctrines of the most remote antiquity". This, in turn, was linked to perseverance and dexterity in "works of imitation".[65] Accordingly, Macintosh affirmed that the "imitative" habits of the Indian people had rendered

> Hindostan, of all countries in the earth, the fittest for that singular species of commerce, which will allow the lord-paramount to export its copious redundancy without violating justice, offending industry, or impoverishing the people; provided that government take care, that a necessary proportion of money, or other authentic currency, be constantly kept in circulation, to prevent a stagnation in the commerce of the inhabitants with merchants, manufactures, and each other.[66]

The justice of international relations in this imperial version of political economy was thus a matter of organising commercial relations in accordance with the allegedly inherent inclinations of the nations included in the system. In order for such an economy to work, however, national characters had to be consistent among those defined as a nation, and the ambitions driving their behavior had to be stable.[67]

To be sure, all of this was not explicitly laid out in the *Travels*, as it only offered some "hints". However, Macintosh's way of appealing to his readers by redefining current notions of ambition makes the *Travels* a significant example of the interaction of philosophical writing with private interest. It would also be wrong to presume that the meaning of ambition had been stable in early-modern discourse. For, according to Samuel Pufendorf, ambition counted among the evil imperfections of the fallen man, whereas Francis Bacon observed that some individuals had ambitious temperaments, which should be used well by the head of the state.[68] What is clear from the political discourse of the second half of the eighteenth century, however, is that a general mistrust of the notorious ambition and greed manifested by Company servants motivated the attempts to change how the EIC operated and, as such, this mistrust was also Macintosh's key concern.[69]

65 Ibid., 301–302, 332–333, 352.

66 Ibid., 255.

67 See Smith, *Theory* (1759), 397–398.

68 Heikki Haara, *Pufendorf's Theory of Sociability: Passions, Habits and Social Order* (Cham: Springer, 2018), 109–111; Jared Poley, *The Devil's Riches: A Modern History of Greed* (New York: Berghahn Books 2016), 90–91; Keller, *Knowledge*, 136.

69 See for example: Travers, *Ideology*, 224; A letter from Calcutta signed by John Day, Advocate General, 17 October 1779, *House of Commons Sessional Papers of the Eighteenth Century (1715–*

IV

In view of the public nature of national character, it is significant that the section "Of the origin of ambition, and of the distinction of ranks" in Smith's *Theory of Moral Sentiments* suggested that the purpose of "avarice and ambition" was vanity, or "the belief of our being the object of attention and approbation".[70] Moreover, Smith added that ambition was always admired when it kept "within the bounds of prudence and justice", but sometimes even "when it passes the limits of both these virtues, and is not only unjust but extravagant".[71] While Macintosh did not borrow these ideas to the letter, his writing displays an interest in using the idea of ambition as an object of public admiration, and this, I suggest, had an impact on his representation of the British national character.[72]

His approach was original, because even though Smith – along with Hume and others – suggested that individual self-interest could in the long run have beneficial consequences for the society at large, ambition had a decidedly negative ring due to its close association with military conquest.[73] To quote William Robertson's *History of the Reign of the Emperor Charles V* as an example, the opening of this seminal work presented Charles V's "ambition to be distinguished as a conqueror" as a contrast to young George III's ability to control his thirst for "military glory".[74] Interestingly, in Robertson's later *History of America*, the role played by ambition in the historical narrative began to change. At first, Robertson stated that "the intercourse among nations" had extended in "proportion as the knowledge of the advantages derived from navigation and commerce" had spread. As a result of this, the "ambition of conquest, or the necessity of procur-

1800): Reports on Justice in Bengal 1781 and 1782, 334; A speech by Charles James Fox on 1 December 1783, *Parliamentary Register (1780–1796)*, 289.

70 Smith, *Theory* (1759), 108–109.

71 Ibid., 304.

72 Ibid., 405–409.

73 Karen O'Brien, "Empire, History and Emigration: from Enlightenment to Liberalism," in *Race, Nation and Empire: Making Histories, 1750 to the Present*, ed. Catherine Hall and Keith McClelland (Manchester: Manchester University Press, 2010), 16–17; *A Short History of English Transactions in the East-Indies* (Cambridge 1776), xiv–xv, 46–47, 166–175.

74 Kontler, "William Robertson," 69, 73–80, 86; J. G. A. Pocock, *Barbarism and Religion: Vol. 2: Narratives of Civil Government* (Cambridge: Cambridge University Press, 1999), 276; Richard B. Sher, "*Charles V* and the Book Trade: An Episode in Enlightenment Print Culture," in *William Robertson and the Expansion of Empire*, ed. Stewart J. Brown (Cambridge: Cambridge University Press, 1997), 175.

ing new settlements, were no longer the sole motives of visiting distant lands", but were complemented by the "desire of gain".[75]

Hence, while ambition was still linked with conquest, this passion was partly replaced by economic interest. Further on, Robertson noted that due to "a spirit of curiosity and emulation", the ambition of Columbus "aimed at something more", which created distance between the common pair of ambition and avarice.[76] At times, Robertson also made this conventional connection, but in a note on the "characteristics of the Californians", he distinguished the ambitions of Europeans and native Americans in a manner resembling Macintosh's discussion of national characters. For, according to Robertson, the "objects of ambition with us, honour, fame, reputation, titles, posts, and distinctions of superiority, are unknown among them; so that this powerful spring of action, the cause of so much seeming good and real evil in the world", had "no power" over the minds of the people of California.[77]

In his *Travels*, Macintosh granted that "European avarice, and ambition", had taught some people in India "the necessity of securing to themselves some degree of happiness, by satiating the rapacity of strangers".[78] This, however, only served to prove that India could be governed in accordance with the "spirit of commerce". As the *Travels* suggested, the beneficial consequences of the modern commercial ambition did not really need to be unintended, since, when linked with the notion of progress, British ambition for empire-building became justified as a force driving societal progress and no longer signified the sheer will to conquer and to rule.[79]

This redefined relationship of ambition and national character was crucial to the relevance of the policies which the *Travels* proposed. Indeed, for someone like Macintosh, with practical experience from colonial government, it was clear that the British empire was a space of displacement where a contractual framework of reciprocal rights and duties did not work. Furthermore, while investment in the EIC put pressure on policymakers to ensure that the Company's territorial dependencies would become profitable, critical voices demanded reason and justice from those with power over the Company's affairs. As Smith suggested, "the contempt of mankind" was to be avoided, and in this situation, the notion of national difference provided a basis for an imperial system satisfying what the second edition of *The Theory of Moral Sentiments* called "the love of

75 William Robertson, *History of America* (London, 1777), I: 4.
76 Ibid., 62.
77 Ibid., 467–468.
78 Macintosh, *Travels*, I: 253.
79 Ibid., 274. See also: Pocock, *Barbarism*, 169–171.

what is honourable and noble, of the grandeur, and dignity, and superiority of our own characters".[80] Thus, the *Travels* implied that a system of political economy could ensure mutual satisfaction regardless of inequality.[81]

For this reason, the idea of consistent national characters was of key importance to Macintosh. This is not to say that he believed in the existence of such characters, or that he was blind to the malleable and multi-faceted relationship between individuals and their social surroundings.[82] Indeed, although the *Travels* sometimes resorted to typologies building on stereotypical reference even when describing Europeans, it is striking that in an isolated company sailing between continents, the antagonism between Britain and France could be lost in polite conversation. Thus, while onboard the French ship *Brisson*, Macintosh enjoyed the hospitality of captain Cheseaux, who willingly shared his "small but well chosen library". Another example of the things Macintosh found "comfortable in our little society" was that the French officers were "polite, easy, and happily united with one another in great intimacy and friendship".[83] Yet another letter describing his sea voyage shows that national character could be broken down into an array of different types, since Macintosh found himself "placed in a society not unlike that of the stage-coach in Tom Jones; a jumble of figures, constitutions, complexions, dispositions, professions, and sexes".[84]

However, in view of the relationship of the *Travels* with its aspired audience, and the aim of establishing an acceptable system of imperial economy, Macintosh's reaction to being detained onboard *Brisson* is most revealing. Concluding that the amiable French captain had let him down, Macintosh declared himself "almost" converted "to that system of moral philosophy which derives every thing that men do, or say, or feel, from the principle of self-love".[85] As this remark indicates, the *Travels* was informed not only by theories of political economy but also by the moralist tradition cautioning against self-interest. Thus, in presenting himself in the "important office" of an "arbiter between England and her colonies" and attempting to save the public character of the British, the textual figure of Macintosh performed a careful act of balancing between private interest and enlightened public opinion.[86]

---

80 Smith, *Theory* (1759), 140; Adam Smith, *The Theory of Moral Sentiments* (London, 1761), 214.
81 See also Travers, *Ideology*, 231.
82 See Macintosh, *Travels*, I: 377.
83 Ibid., 84.
84 Ibid., 150 – 157.
85 Ibid., 89, 153.
86 Ibid., I: 20.

Jussi Kurunmäki & Jani Marjanen

15 How Ideology Became Isms: A History of a Conceptual Coupling

Recent scholarly discussions about populism and neoliberalism as ideologies exemplify how changing political struggles are conceptualised through "isms" as navigating concepts.[1] These isms are further connected with the notion of ideology as a crucial category in politics. We argue that such couplings also constitute a redefinition of the concept even if it is often assumed that it has always been associated with political reasoning. In fact, there have been such redefinitions as long as ideology has been regarded as a key concept in the field of political conduct, both as an analytical category and as a rhetorical device. Our aim in this article is to trace the way in which "ideology" gained prominence in political vocabulary, and show that this happened largely through its coupling with "isms" in a period between the late nineteenth century and World War II.

Despite current questioning of what counts as an ideology, the common view seems to be that ideologies are omnipresent and trans-historical. According to the *The Oxford Handbook of Political Ideologies*, for instance, "ideologies are, have been and will be very much with us".[2] Studies that regard certain ages as more ideological also seem to assign them a trans-historical quality: it is stated in *The Cambridge History of Twentieth-Century Political Thought* that "the

---

1 Catherine Fieschi and Paul Heywood, "Trust, Cynicism and Populist Anti-politics," *Journal of Political Ideologies* 9 (2004): 289–309; Ben Stanley, "The Thin Ideology of Populism," *Journal of Political Ideologies* 13 (2008): 95–110; Cas Mudde and Cristóbal Rovira Kaltwasser, "Populism," in *The Oxford Handbook of Political Ideologies*, eds. Michael Freeden, Lyman Tower Sargent, and Marc Stears (Oxford: Oxford University Press, 2013), 493–512; Michael Freeden, "After the Brexit Referendum: Revisiting Populism as an Ideology," *Journal of Political Ideologies* 22 (2017): 1–11; Marco Tarchi, "Populism: Ideology, Political Style, Mentality?" *Politologický Časopis – Czech Journal of Political Science* 23 (2016): 95–109; Rajesh Venugopal, "Neoliberalism as Concept," *Economy and Society* 44 (2015): 165–187; Jamie Peck, "Explaining (with) Neoliberalism," *Territory, Politics, Governance* 1 (2013): 132–157.

2 Michael Freeden, Lyman Tower Sargent, and Marc Stears, "Preface," In *The Oxford Handbook of Political Ideologies*, eds. Michael Freeden, Lyman Tower Sargent, and Marc Stears (Oxford: Oxford University Press, 2013). v–vi, v; see also Michael Freeden, *Ideologies and Political Theory: A Conceptual Approach* (Oxford: Clarendon Press, 1996); Michael Freeden, "The resurgence of ideology studies: Twenty years of the JPI," *Journal of Political Ideologies* 2 (2016): 1–8; Andrew Vincent, "Political Ideology and Political Theory: Reflections on an Awkward Partnership," in *Liberalism as Ideology: Essays in Honour of Michael Freeden*, ed. Ben Jackson and Marc Stears (Oxford: Oxford University Press, 2012), 159.

https://doi.org/10.1515/9783110679861-017

twentieth century was pre-eminently an age of ideologies",[3] but there is no apparent interest in how the concept developed.

Most scholars in the field of ideology are aware of its several different layers of historical meaning as one of the most "elusive concepts one can find in the social sciences",[4] being "thoroughly muddied by diverse uses".[5] Nevertheless, there have been few attempts to understand the historical processes in which the concept assumed this complex character. From the perspective of conceptual history, we aim to show how its meaning and field of application have changed since the coining of the term in the late 1790s. We build on earlier studies that trace the historical manifestation of the concept,[6] but focus particularly on the historical connection between "ideology" and "isms", which we argue explains the transformation of the notion of ideology. Although such a link has been noted in strands of research on ideology focusing on language and symbols,[7] it has not thus far been analyzed as a historical process. Our examination of the historical coupling of ideology and isms clearly shows how the tendency to concentrate on a set of thinkers from Destutt de Tracy, Napoleon, Marx, Engels, Mannheim, Arendt, and Geertz to contemporary scholars in the fields of political theory and political sociology has underplayed the major semantic ruptures in the understanding of ideology in the early twentieth century. This shift, we argue, can only be grasped if one also pays attention to the more mundane language of ideology. As Michael Freeden points out, ideology as a concept has been "subjected to vernacular and professional meanings that are out of step

3 Terence Ball and Richard Bellamy, "Editors' introduction," in *The Cambridge History of Twentieth-Century Political Thought*, ed. Terence Ball and Richard Bellamy (Cambridge: Cambridge University Press, 2012), 2.
4 Jorge Larrain, *The Concept of Ideology* (London: Hutchinson, 1979), 13.
5 Kathleen Knight, "Transformations of the Concept of Ideology in the Twentieth Century," *American Political Science Review* 100 (2006): 619–626.
6 Ulrich Dierse, "Ideologie," in *Geschichtliche Grundbegriffe: Historisches Lexikon zur politisch-sozialen Sprache in Deutschland, Bd. 3 H–Me*, ed. Otto Brunner, Werner Conze and Reinhart Koselleck (Stuttgart: Klett-Cotta, 1982), 132–135; Bo Stråth, "Ideology and Conceptual History," in *The Oxford Handbook of Political Ideologies*, eds. Michael Freeden, Lyman Tower Sargent, and Marc Stears (Oxford: Oxford University Press, 2013), 3–4.
7 See Michael Freeden, *Ideology: A Very Short Introduction* (Oxford: Oxford University Press, 2003), 1; Freeden, *Ideologies and Political Theory*; Jussi Kurunmäki and Jani Marjanen, "A Rhetorical View of Isms: An Introduction," *Journal of Political Ideologies* 23 (2018): 241–255; Jussi Kurunmäki and Jani Marjanen, "Isms, Ideologies and Setting the Agenda for Public Debate," *Journal of Political Ideologies* 23 (2018): 256–282. A kindred interpretation is to be found in Duncan Bell, "What Is Liberalism?" *Political Theory* 42 (2014): 682–715.

with each other".[8] It is our claim that the dynamics between vernacular and professional meaning were strengthened in the period from the 1910s until the aftermath of World War II.

We bring in the vernacular uses of the term ideology to give a better picture of how the concept has been understood in somewhat contradicting ways. To this end, we use parliamentary records from Britain and Sweden, newspaper reports from Austria, Sweden, Britain, and the Netherlands, and journal articles from JSTOR, thereby allowing access to textual examples and simple quantitative information about the changing frequency of the use of ideology and its coupling with different isms. Although the data sets may come across as disparate, they provide different entry points to the more general developments in the understanding of ideology that also affected professional, more sophisticated discourses.

In tracing the transformation of ideology from the post-French-Revolution era to the Cold War we chose three analytical distinctions for scrutiny: politicisation, democratisation, and historicisation. Although these processes are loosely chronological, they also overlap such that the politicisation of ideology continued when the concept became democratised and historicised, for instance. We argue that the concept of ideology was almost immediately politicised after its introduction, and it was used as invective throughout the nineteenth century. Nevertheless, it was only when it started to be used more frequently that it acquired more abstract meanings and became more commonly used as a hypernym for several individual types of ideology. Whereas individual isms were sometimes rhetorically described as empty playing with words and ideas, in other words ideology in its old sense, in this new setting the notion of ideology as a meta-category for individual isms took over. At this point, ideologies also became the subject of history writing. Perhaps paradoxically, their historicisation meant that the historical constitution of the links between isms and ideology was forgotten. Our aim is to bring such links to light.

The Politicisation of Ideology

The concept of ideology coined by Antoine Destutt de Tracy in 1796 (published in 1801) did not refer to grand sets of ideas that people (wittingly or unwittingly)

---

8 Michael Freeden, "Ideology and Conceptual History: The Interrelationship between Method and Meaning," in *Political Concepts and Time: New Approaches to Conceptual History*, ed. Javier Fernández Sebastián (Santander: Cantabria University Press, 2011), 73.

needed when they acted politically, but rather concerned an Enlightenment program for a science of ideas, understood in the sensationalist tradition of Condillac. "Ideology" purported to deal with perception and theory of mind, and thereby to develop the means for categorising and teaching ideas.[9] Destutt de Tracy's conceptions became commonly recognised, and this positivist notion soon became prevalent around Europe and in the United States. It was described as a "theory of ideology" that had "modified all modern languages in correspondence to that theory".[10] It also made its way to university curricula as a separate topic alongside grammar, ethics, rhetoric and *belle lettres*, and the fine arts.[11]

Destutt de Tracy maintained that the meaning of "ideology", unlike that of terms such as "metaphysics" and "psychology", was clear to everyone, being the Greek word for the science of ideas.[12] However, the word soon came to be associated with metaphysics when Napoleon turned his back on his former protégés around 1800, and labelled them "ideologues". According to Napoleon, they were meddling in political praxis with a philosophical theory, and aimed to devise a political system based on metaphysical and fanatical speculation.[13] As he argued in 1812, the troubles France had experienced were due to "ideology, that shadowy metaphysics which subtly searches for first causes on which to base the legislation of peoples, rather than making use of laws known to the human heart and of the lessons of history".[14] Such pejorative use by Napoleon and in subsequent debates politicised the notion, which was soon taken as an expression of republicanism and atheism, and was associated with well-known republicans and critics of Napoleon such as Georges Cabanis, Stendahl, Emmanuel-Joseph Sieyès, and Benjamin Constant.[15]

The Napoleonic conception of ideology spread quickly. As early as in 1804, a German account of the circumstances in Napoleonic France rhetorically associated it with politically laden terms such as "democrat", "Jacobins", and "terrorists".[16] F. H. Jacobi even used the ism form (*Ideologisme*) in a private letter in

9 See Emmet Kennedy, "'Ideology' from Destutt de Tracy to Marx," *Journal of the History of Ideas* 40 (1979), 353–354; Dierse, "Ideologie"; Freeden, *Ideology*, 4–5; Stråth, "Ideology and Conceptual History," 3–4.
10 P. A., "On the Word Picturesque," *The Belfast Monthly Magazine* 6, February 28, 1811, 118.
11 "Proceedings and Report of the Commissioners for the University of Virginia, Presented 8th of December 1818," *The North-American Review and Miscellaneous Journal* 10, January 1820, 119.
12 Kennedy, "'Ideology' from de Tracy to Marx," 355.
13 Dierse, "Ideologie," 136–138.
14 Quoted in Kennedy, "'Ideology' from de Tracy to Marx," 360.
15 Ibid., 358.
16 Dierse, "Ideologie," 141.

1805.[17] The coining and early evolvement of "ideology" goes well together with Reinhart Koselleck's interpretation of the formation of modern political language during and after the French Revolution.[18] For instance, the ways in which "ideology" was used in post-Napoleonic Europe show important strong similarities with the ways in which "liberalism" was treated in conservative and reactionary rhetoric, being associated with the French Revolution, liberalisation, the sovereignty of the people, freedom of the press, and constitutional principles.[19] A later example of this sentiment expressed in German came to light in the early 1840s when the Prussian political culture was contrasted with "French liberalism, the idea of emancipation and constitutionalism", and "papery ideology".[20] The Napoleonic conception is reflected in some conservative Swedish newspapers in descriptions of ideology as "political opportunism",[21] or "the encyclopedic Lockean materialism" and "fanaticism".[22] A curious outlier in the use of ideology occurred in 1845 when the prominent intellectual E. G. Geijer was described in a positive tone as endorsing a "democratic ideology".[23] This instance, although very interesting, is not representative of the established use of the terms ideology or democracy at the time.

Despite the widespread use of ideology as a pejorative label of political ideas and conduct throughout the nineteenth century, most accounts of nineteenth-century ideology have focused on Marx and Engels. This is understandable in many ways, but it is also somewhat problematic given our attempt to understand the historical trajectory. The main source for Marx and Engels' view of ideology, *Die Deutsche Ideologie*, although written in 1845 to 1846, remained basically unknown until most of it was published as late as in 1903 to 1904, and all of it in

17 Ibid.

18 Reinhart Koselleck, "Einleitung", in *Geschichtliche Grundbegriffe. Historisches Lexikon zur politisch-sozialen Sprache in Deutschland. Band 1*, ed. Otto Brunner, Werner Conze and Reinhart Koselleck (Stuttgart: Klett-Cotta, 1972), xiii–xxvii; Reinhart Koselleck, "Introduction and Prefaces to the *Geschichtliche Grundbegriffe*," *Contributions to the History of Concepts* 6 (2011): 1–37; Kurunmäki and Marjanen, "Isms, Ideologies and Setting the Agenda for Public Debate."

19 Dierse, "Ideologie," 141–142. In Britain, Lady Morgan's *France in 1829–30* (1830) stated that the "theory of constitutional freedom had been stigmatized as ideology" in France. Quoted in the review, "Lady Morgan's 'France'," *The National Magazine* 1 November 1830, 510–511.

20 Quoted in Dierse, "Ideologie," 143. For other examples, see G. Croom Robertson, "Les Idéologues by F. Picavet," *Mind* (1892): 119–120; Lucien Arréat, "Literary Correspondence," *The Monist* 2 (1892): 390.

21 *Post- och Inrikes Tidningar*, 26 November 1835.

22 *Svenska Biet*, 5 March 1841.

23 *Östgöta Patrioten*, 13 December 1845.

1932.[24] Although the view endorsed by Marx and Engels came to be known via their other works, especially the introduction to *Zur Kritik der Politischen Ökonomie* (1859) and Engels's elaboration of the concept in "Ludwig Feuerbach und der Ausgang der klassischen deutschen Philosophie" (1886), in fact they wrote little about ideology and, as David Leopold points out, what they did write were inchoate and opaque observations rather than a sustained discussion.[25]

The impact of Marx and Engels' view of ideology emerged at a later date than indicated in a commonly held narrative starting from Destutt de Tracy and continuing to Marx and Engels and finally Mannheim and other twentieth century theoreticians. It is nevertheless worth pointing out the emergence of the notion as an expression of class-based false consciousness. Marx and Engels followed the pattern set by Napoleon and conservative rhetoric in their critical view of ideology, but they also put it in a theoretical framework. For them, ideologies such as romanticism, idealism, religion, and philosophy were disconnected from the material conditions of the people, and thus served the interests of the ruling classes.[26] The question that followed was whether the class-based ideological nature of ideas also dealt with the proletariat, or whether it was immune to ideology. According to Dierse, Marx and Engels did not have any positive conception of a socialist ideology, although they admitted that the working class had to be conscious of the ideological nature of the means of production in a bourgeois society.[27] However, it has also been maintained that Marx was shifting "back and forth between reductionism and the affirmation of his belief in the constructive role of ideas."[28] Referring to the positive role given to "bourgeois ideologists" who would go over to the side of the proletariat, as argued in the *Manifesto of the Communist Party*, Reinhard Bendix held that Marx and Engels were trying to circumvent the need to state that even the proletariat would act ideologically.[29]

Nevertheless, it is worth noting that it was not common in the time of Marx and Engels to regard socialism and communism as ideologies. Whereas socialism was understood as a future-oriented doctrine, the notion of ideology was not yet

24 Dierse, "Ideologie," 146.
25 David Leopold, "Marxism and Ideology: From Marx to Althusser," in *The Oxford Handbook of Political Ideologies*, ed. Michael Freeden, Lyman Tower Sargent, and Marc Stears (Oxford: Oxford University Press, 2013), 20.
26 See, e.g., Freeden, "Ideology and Conceptual History," 83.
27 Dierse, "Ideologie," 154.
28 Reinhard Bendix, "The Age of Ideology: Persistent and Changing," in *Ideology and Discontent*, ed. David E. Apter (London: The Free Press of Glencoe, Collier-Macmillan, 1964), 309.
29 Ibid., 309.

properly coupled with it. The ways in which two Swedish Social Democratic newspapers touched upon the question of ideology in 1889 and 1890 provide an illustrative example of the confusion caused by the "ideological dilemma." The paper that is usually regarded as hardline Marxist projected a socialist line by making a distinction between "the decadent ideology of the bourgeoisie" and "the modern ideology of our revolutionary proletariat",[30] whereas the organ of the party denounced (without mentioning its sister paper) the idea that the proletariat had an ideology, which was restricted to the ruling classes.[31]

The question of the ideological status and the role of the working class was raised in connection with debates on historical materialism in the 1890s when some leading Marxist socialists developed the conception of an ideology that not only belonged to the working class but was also neutral or even positive in tone. Ideology was used both as an analytical concept and a potential asset for the working class. Eduard Bernstein, to take a prominent example, maintained that proletarian ideas were more than just reflections of their material conditions: they were, in fact, forward-looking and value-based, in other words ideological. He also made an explicit connection between "ideology" and "socialism" in his article "Das realistische und das ideologische Moment im Sozialismus" (1898).[32]

At the same time, the meaning and sphere of the term ideology diversified further as it was becoming an analytical concept of the social sciences.[33] Drawing on the earlier positivist ambitions of the ideologues, the new social sciences took the term to the sphere of social phenomena. Although there were intellectual and political links to socialist political thinking, sociologist and political scientists even introduced the notion of ideology into the non-socialist analysis of society and politics.[34] This ultimately opened up a way of linking ideology with several different isms.

---

30 *Arbetet*, 2 March 1889.

31 *Social-Demokraten*, 8 November 1890.

32 Dierse, "Ideologie," 158–159; see also Eduard Bernstein, *The Preconditions of Socialism*, ed. by Henry Tudor (Cambridge: Cambridge University Press, [1899] 1993), 17–20. A conservative Swedish newspaper published a positive review of Bernstein's Kantian view of socialism, maintaining that, for Bernstein, materialism was "a deceptive ideology." *Svenska Dagbladet*, April 7, 1901.

33 See, e.g., Erville Bartlett Woods, "Progress as a Sociological Concept," *American Journal of Sociology* 12 (1907): 804; James Melville Coleman, Review of "Essays on the Materialistic Conception of History, by Antonio Labriola," *The American Journal of Psychology* 16 (1905): 137.

34 See also Stråth, "Ideology and Conceptual History," 9.

The Democratisation of Ideology

By the 1910s it was no longer uncommon, even in scholarly accounts, to write about "the working class" or "the proletariat" as having their own ideology that was not presented in a pejorative manner,[35] although it was still open to discussion. George D. H. Cole, for instance, opened the chapter "Proletarianism" in *Labour in the Commonwealth* (1919) by maintaining that "it is a question that has been posed again and again in the history of Labour and Socialist agitation how far the working class, or proletariat, ought to have a culture and an 'ideology' of its own".[36] Cole's answer to this question was in the affirmative: in his book on the history of the British working-class movement, published a year later, he held that socialism was becoming Labour's "official ideology".[37] The coupling of ideology with socialism and the Labour Party made it something that belonged to modern party politics.

Although the question of socialism dominated the articles that mentioned political ideology in the journals investigated here, the 1920s was also the age of bolshevism and fascism. For instance, according to an article on the class-based theory of morals, the main principle of bolshevism was the assertion of the "supremacy of the 'ideology' of the working class".[38] Peter Struve, a former Russian Marxist who became a White and then emigrated to Paris, wrote that a "hybrid ideology" existed in Russia, "the so-called Eurasianism and the so-called national Bolshevism".[39] Fascism, in turn, was often labelled as an ideology, although Mussolini claimed that it was, in fact, "action" not ideology: for him, ideologies such as liberalism meant "programs and a superstitious reverence for the formal democracy of the ballot box".[40]

---

35 E.g., A. A. Goldenweiser, "Russia and the Socialists: A Protest and a Reply," *The North American Review* 206 (1917): 808–809.

36 George D. H. Cole, *Labour in the Commonwealth: A Book for the Younger Generation* (London: Pelican Press, 1919), 166; see also Laura A. Thompson, "Worker's Education: A List of References (in English)," *Monthly Labor Review* 14 (1922): 181.

37 S. Perlman, Review of "A Short History of the British Working Class Movement by G. D. H. Cole," *The American Economic Review* 18 (1928): 318; see also Emil Frankel, "Present-Day Tendencies in the German Socialist Movement," *Journal of Political Economy* 33 (1925): 71–72.

38 M.W. Robieson, "The Theory of Morals on a Class Basis," *International Journal of Ethics* 29 (1919): 294–295.

39 Peter Struve, "Russia," *The Slavonic Review* 1 (1922): 27.

40 William Yandell Elliot, "Mussolini, Prophet of the Pragmatic Era in Politics," *Political Science Quarterly* 41 (1926): 167; Carl Joachim Friedrich, "Review of Sozialismus und Faschismus in Italien by Robert Michels," *The American Political Science Review* 22 (1928): 198.

A major consequence of the broadened use of "ideology" was that it was, at times, discussed in connection with many isms. For instance, a volume dealing with the progress of Latin America published in 1913 included a chapter entitled "Political Ideology", in which topics such as "liberalism, radicalism, Jacobinism" are discussed.[41] It also made sense to write about "progressivism" in a positive tone and to maintain that the author's way of proceeding was "ideological and historical rather than scientific and economic".[42] However, such early couplings of ideology and certain isms were rare and by no means imply that the two were commonly understood as self-evidently belonging together, let alone being synonymous. For instance, none of the renowned British authors included the word ideology in their accounts of socialism, liberalism and conservatism in books published around 1910.[43]

To obtain some idea of when ideology and different isms were coupled we turned to newspaper collections from Sweden and Austria, which provide easily searchable data sets. They indicate that writing about a particular ism and ideology in conjunction with one another became common only later (see Table 1 for Sweden and Table 2 for Austria).

Table 1: Occurrences of the word ideology together with selected ism words in Swedish newspapers. The years reflect the first occurrences within a window of 50 and 10 words before and after the word ideology, as well as adverbial use. The results were extracted from *https://tidningar.kb.se*.

	window of 50	window of 10	adverbial use
socialism	1916	1920	1929 (socialist ideology[44])
Marxism	1916	1935	1929 (Marxist ideology[45])
liberalism	1928	1938	1917 (liberal ideology[46])
conservatism	1921	1931	1944 (conservative ideology[47])
fascism	1933	1933	1925 (fascist ideology[48])

41 Roscoe R. Hill, "Review of Latin America: Its Rise and Progress, by F. Garcia Calderon," *Political Science Quarterly* 28 (1913): 701.

42 William English Walling, "Review of Progressive Democracy, by Herbert Croly," *American Economic Review* 5 (1915): 380–381.

43 See J. Ramsay MacDonald, *Socialism and Society* (London: Independent Labour Party, 1908); L. T. Hobhouse, *Liberalism* (London: Oxford University Press, 1911); H. Cecil, *Conservatism* (London: Oxford University Press, 1912).

44 *Signalen*, 15 August 1829, 3.

45 *Dagens Nyheter*, 29 October 1829, 15.

Two words appearing within a certain window in historical texts obviously do not give a precise measure of individual speech acts, but they may serve as a proxy for how ideology and particular isms were gradually associated. Turning to the Austrian collection of newspapers,[49] we see that the timing is different, but only slightly. The period of coupling isms and ideology in the Swedish press seemed to be from the 1910s to the 1930s, whereas the process seems to have started in the 1890s in the Austrian press (as the first co-occurrence with liberalism is an outlier).

Table 2: Occurrences of the word ideology together with selected ism words in the collection of Austrian newspapers (not only from present-day Austria). The years reflect the first occurrences within a window of 50 and 10 words before and after the word ideology, as well as adverbial use. The results were extracted from http://anno.onb.ac.at/anno-suche.

	window of 50	**window of 10**	**adverbial use**
socialism	1894	1926	1913 (socialist ideology), 1926 (ideology of socialism)[50]
Marxism	1898	1899	1916 (Marxist ideology), 1924 (ideology of Marxism)[51]
liberalism	1873 (outlier)	1873 (outlier)	1921 (liberal ideology), 1908 (ideology of liberalism)[52]
fascism	1922	1922	1927 (fascist ideology), 1925 (ideology of fascism)[53]

Several interlinked factors affected the ways in which ideology and isms were understood in the 1930s. These include Hitler's rise to power in Germany and the deterioration of international order that was built on the League of Nations; the great depression and its repercussions; and the widely held opinion that parliamentary democracy was in crisis even in countries that were not subjected to

---

46 *Göteborgs Aftonblad*, 12 November 1917, 6. Next uses: *Dagens Nyheter*, May 11, 1924, 10; *Svenska Dagbladet*, 3 February 1930, 11.
47 *Svenska dagbladet*, 14 February 1944, 10.
48 *Norrskensflamman*, 22 June 1925, 4.
49 http://anno.onb.ac.at/anno-suche.
50 *Arbeiterwille*, 23 August 1913, 7; *Der Hausbesitzer/Hausherren Zeitung*, 15 October 1926, 1.
51 *Freiheit!*, March 4, 1916, 3; *Neue Freie Presse*, 13 April 1924, 4.
52 *Die Rote Fahne*, 29 May 1921, 6; *Arbeiter Zeitung*, 27 February 1908, 2. This included the qualifier (older liberalism). The first occurrence without qualifiers such as "economic" or "progressive" is from 1929.
53 *Arbeiter Zeitung*, July 10,1927, 3; *Arbeiter Zeitung*, 21 June 1925, 4.

dictatorship or autocratic rule. We make two general observations about the consequences of that development with regard to how ideology and isms were understood in the parts of Europe that did not become totalitarian.

First, fascism, National Socialism, and Bolshevism/communism were sometimes portrayed in English-language texts as basically one and the same ideology.[54] Not only was ideology regarded as something false and negative, it was also seen as a political force that was utterly dangerous and against which free and democratic countries should defend themselves. As German born American novelist Ludwig Lewisohn wrote in 1934, for instance, "the patterns of the Russian, the Italian Fascist and the German Nazi revolutions are one hundred per cent identical", and the ideology these revolutions displayed was "identified with absolute truth and with the power of the state".[55] His conclusion was that it was "possible today to disregard completely the merits of any case or any ideology", and that this type of revolution "must be resisted if we are not all to become quite literally filthy savages in the howling wilderness of a desolate earth".[56]

Lewisohn's powerful style may not be representative of the ways in which ideology was discussed in academic journals, but it spelled out a common sentiment that reflects an increasing trend to see danger in isms in general. It was held, for instance, that there was an "epidemic of 'isms'", as US sociologist Howard Odum put it,[57] and a governmental report in the US used the expression "those fearsome European isms" in 1936.[58] It is worth pointing out that during and after World War II, isms in general were associated with one in particular, totalitarianism, which had a strong impact on the ways in which ideology was understood.[59] Carlton J. H. Hayes, who became famous as one of the pioneers of the study of nationalism, was among the first to identify the link between ideology, communism, fascism, and totalitarianism. In his article "The Challenge of Totalitarianism", published in 1938, he denies the alleged difference between communism and fascism as ideologies:

---

54 See, e.g., Ludwig Lewisohn, "The New Meaning of Revolution," *The North American Review* 238 (1934): 211; Ernest Barker, "The Conflict of Ideologies," *International Affairs* 16 (1937): 348.

55 Lewisohn, "New Meaning of Revolution," 211.

56 Ibid.

57 Howard W. Odum, "Orderly Transitional Democracy," *American Academy of Political and Social Science* 180 (1935): 38.

58 Quoted in M. Hilson, "Consumer Co-operation and Economic Crisis: The 1936 Roosevelt Inquiry on Co-operative Enterprise and the Emergence of the Nordic 'Middle Way,'" *Contemporary European History* 22 (2013): 182.

59 Kurunmäki and Marjanen, "Isms, Ideologies and Setting the Agenda for Public Debate," 267–268.

> When we turn from the actual political functioning of the totalitarian state to the philosophy of totalitarianism – to its ideology, as we nowadays like to describe it – many of us are apt to be confused by apparent differences between Communism and Fascism and to imagine that there is no similarity of thought or ultimate goal among the variously designated brand of totalitarianism. [. . .] Nevertheless, if we will but look behind all the phrases and catch-words and discount the propaganda of Fascists against Communists and the counter-propaganda of Communists against Fascists, we shall perceive that their seemingly diverse ideologies have actually much in common, that there is in reality an intellectual pattern for all totalitarianism.[60]

Hayes positioned totalitarianism against democracy and, not unlike Karl Loewenstein[61] for instance, maintained that totalitarianism flourished in countries that had never, or only very briefly, been democratic.[62] This brings us to our second observation: "ideology" was also something that even democratic and liberal countries could have. Defenses of democracy against totalitarian doctrines tended to idealise one's own political system and culture as more democratic and as belonging to national tradition more than warranted by social practices, constitutional law, and political institutions.[63] "Democratic ideology" belonged to this kind of rhetorical defense of democracy in the same manner as "American ideology".[64]

The viewing of democracy as an ideology is one indication that the word was becoming so commonly used that it was difficult to avoid, let alone ignore. Following the analytical terminology of Reinhart Koselleck, we understand the increase in its use as a process of democratisation. This obviously has nothing to do with the question of whether or not ideology as a word had more democratic undertones than before.[65] It is difficult to pinpoint when this democratisation happened. If anything, the process was gradual, but it can be traced through three historical indicators: 1) historical actors started reflecting upon the popu-

60 Carlton J. H. Hayes, "The Challenge of Totalitarianism," *The Public Opinion Quarterly* 2 (1938): 21–22.

61 Karl Loewenstein, "Militant Democracy and Fundamental Rights, I," *The American Political Science Review* 31 (1937): 417–432.

62 Hayes, "The Challenge of Totalitarianism," 26.

63 See Jussi Kurunmäki, "Democracy both Young and Old: Finland, Sweden and the Interwar Crisis of Democracy," *Journal of Modern European History* 17 (2019): 1–14; Francis Dupuis-Déri, "History of the Word 'Democracy' in Canada and Québec: A Political Analysis of Rhetorical Strategies," *World Political Science Review* 6 (2010): 1–23.

64 Howard W. Odum, "Orderly Transitional Democracy," 32; Walter James Shepard, "Democracy," *The Annals of the American Academy of Political and Social Science* 180 (1935): 96.

65 For a discussion on democratization of concepts, see Koselleck, "Einleitung," XIII–XXVII; Koselleck, "Introduction and Prefaces," 10–11.

larity and ambiguity of the concept of ideology; 2) the semantic shifts stemming from the coupling of ideology, and different isms were recorded in lexicons and dictionaries of general language use; 3) ideology experienced a growth in relative frequency that can be measured in different digital corpora.

The association of ideology with democracy serves as our first example of an awareness among historical actors of the increasingly common and ambiguous nature of the concept. Ernest Barker, a renowned advocate of British parliamentarism, clearly sensed that he was taking steps in a new direction when he spoke about democracy as an ideology at Chatham House in 1937. Acknowledging the controversial nature of associating ideology and democracy, Barker asked whether it was right to speak of an ideology of liberal-democratic states. His answer was that if the definition of ideology was related "both to aim and to method, both to the purpose and to the process of community-action", then it was right to claim that liberal-democratic states with their "doctrine of discussion" did have an ideology that stood against the doctrine of fascist and communist states. It is worth pointing out, however, that Barker began his speech by acknowledging the ambiguous, polysemic, and contextually shifting nature of ideology, which he maintained was "a barbarous term" that had been popularised by the British Foreign Minister and had "undergone a new change in the twentieth century". Having been adopted by Marxists, as he put it, it had "flowed from the peculiar vocabulary of Marxism into the peculiar vocabulary of statesmen and publicists. Distorted from its original meaning of a science of ideas, or a thinking of ideas, it has come to mean ideas themselves".[66]

Barker's argument was that not only fascism and communism were ideologies, but also liberal democracy and the Catholic Church could be seen as such. This was exceptional but not unique. Illinois professor Francis G. Wilson referred to "the war of ideologies" in which democracy needed "some clear principles of 'internal evidence' that may be applied in its own defence".[67] As he saw it, democracy was "the technique of popular participation and control" and was focused, "like other ideologies", on the future.[68]

Barker and Wilson represented something new. The more common take on ideology as a false opinion was put forward in an unsigned response to Barker: "I always thought ideologies referred to other people's erroneous opinions [. . .] I agree that Communism and Fascism are both ideologies, but I am quite certain that Liberal-Democracy is not an ideology, and I am also quite certain, although

66 Barker, "The Conflict of Ideologies," 341.
67 Francis G. Wilson, "The Structure of Modern Ideology," *The Review of Politics* 1 (1939): 387.
68 Wilson, "The Structure of Modern Ideology," 388.

I happen to disagree with it, there is not an ideology of the Roman Catholic Church".[69]

The association of ideology with democracy signaled a semantic shift that rendered the term ideology more ambiguous and open to further theoretical inquiry. A clear landmark in this sense was Karl Mannheim's *Ideologie und Utopie* (1929) and its extended English version (1936). Mannheim famously argued that, as the Marxists had maintained, ideology was something that was dependent on social position, but he also claimed that this referred to all social positions including the working class. His theory was not a class theory as such but a sociological theory of the dependence of ideas on social position. Many contemporary readers of Mannheim's work accepted the notion that ideology did not escape any political or class position, but his claim that intellectuals could move beyond their ideological positions and study ideology in an objective manner was largely repudiated. Although the political context of the late 1930s clearly affected the ways in which the theory was discussed, the tone tended to be sociological and analytical rather than directly connected to ideologies that were topical at the time.[70] In line with Barker, although on a more theoretical level, Mannheim also captured a semantic ambiguity that we relate to the democratisation of ideology, pointing out that "we have to disentangle all the different shades of meaning which are blended here into a pseudo-unity".[71]

With this in mind, Mannheim made an analytical distinction between the particular and total meanings of ideology. According to him, the particular conception of ideology is implied "when the term denotes that we are skeptical of the ideas and representations advanced by our opponent", whereas the total conception is at play when "we refer to the ideology of an age or of a concrete historico-social group, e. g. of a class".[72] Taking an analytical rather than a proper historical perspective on these two conceptions of ideology, Mannheim interpreted the discursive landscape of his time such that the "particular conception of ideology now merges with the total". He claimed that this had changed the

69 Barker, "The Conflict of Ideologies," 354.
70 See, e. g., Hans Speier, "Ideology and Utopia, by Karl Mannheim," *American Journal of Sociology* 43 (1937): 155–166; T. V. Smith, "Ideology and Utopia by Karl Mannheim, by Karl Mannheim, Louis Wirth, Edward A. Shils." *International Journal of Ethics* 48 (1937): 120–128; Robert K. Merton, "The Sociology of Knowledge," *Isis* 27 (1937): 493–503; Wilson, "The Structure of Modern Ideology." For the German reception of the 1929 volume, see Lyman Tower Sargent, "Ideology and Utopia: Karl Mannheim and Paul Ricoeur," *Journal of Political Ideologies* 13 (2008): 264.
71 Mannheim, *Ideology and Utopia*, 49.
72 Ibid.

communicative abilities of different groups: "previously, one's adversary, as the representative of a certain political-social position, was accused of conscious or unconscious falsification. Now, however, the critique is more thoroughgoing in that, having discredited the total structure of his consciousness, we consider him no longer capable of thinking correctly".[73]

Both Barker and Mannheim were astute observers who captured the topicality of ideology in their time, and both ended up making propositions that would play a major role in the study of the phenomenon. Their insights related to semantic ambiguity of ideology were also reflected in the ways in which dictionaries presented ideology, which is our second theme. Dictionaries tend to be somewhat conservative, only including new words and meanings that are considered well established in the language. When this happens, and the inclusion coincides with a rise in frequency in other sources, one can assume a link between the semantic shift and the democratisation of the term. *A new English dictionary on historical principles; founded mainly on the materials collected by the Philological society* (1901), an earlier version of the *Oxford English Dictionary* (OED), gives three senses of the word ideology: the first pertaining to "the science of ideas" and the "study of the way in which ideas are expressed in language"; the second being "ideal or abstract speculation"; and the third simply labeled "idealism", i. e., understood as philosophical idealism and shown to be a counter concept to materialism.[74] The first meaning dates back to Destutt de Tracy, the second is closer to Napoleon's (and even Marx's) use of the term as invective, whereas the third expands on the first and comes closer to scholarly discussions on the role of sociology. All these uses were still prevalent in 1901.

The current edition of the OED provides four different senses of the word ideology, three of which roughly correspond to those in the 1901 edition whereas the fourth is a new concise definition reflecting the currently predominant meaning related to political ideologies: "ideology" is a "systematic scheme of ideas, usually relating to politics, economics, or society and forming the basis of action or policy; a set of beliefs governing conduct".[75] In our view, the emergence of uses that correspond to the fourth sense of the term came about through a process of contestation and negotiation that began in the late nineteenth century and led to the growth in the frequency of its use in the first four decades of the twen-

73 Ibid., 61–62.

74 James H. Murray, ed., *A new English dictionary on historical principles; founded mainly on the materials collected by the Philological society, Vol. 5: H to K* (Oxford: Clarendon Press, 1901).

75 "ideology, n.," in *Oxford English Dictionary*. Oxford: Oxford University Press, https://oed.-com/view/Entry/91016?redirectedFrom=ideology, accessed 8 October 2019.

tieth century, helping to make the notion of ideology an irreplaceable part of political discourse.

This semantic drift was not limited to English. As in the OED, we find additional meanings of ideology in different editions of the *Dictionnaire de L'Académie Française*. The eighth edition from 1932 to 1935 gives only one meaning, *idéologie* described as a science of ideas. The edition also notes the predominantly pejorative use of the word. The current ninth edition provides two new senses: one denoting a collection of ideas that are typical for a society, an epoch or an intellectual movement (e.g., the ideology of the Enlightenment), and the other referring to ideology as a political doctrine.[76] In the case of German, we have to resort to dictionaries without historical examples. The 1911 edition of the *Brockhaus Kleines Konversations-Lexikon* contains an entry for *Ideolog*, which is simply defined as dreamer ("Schwärmer, Träumer"), but nothing for *Ideologie*.[77] The *Sprach-Brockhaus* from 1935 defines *Ideologie* as a doctrine that is alien to the world ("Weltfremde Lehre"), echoing the pejorative definition of ideologue, but also suggests a specific system of visions and values ("Bestimmte Vorstellungs- und Wertungswelt").[78] The 1958 edition repeats the two above definitions, whereas the 1972 edition loses the first, much more pejorative reference to an alien doctrine, but maintains the definition of ideology as a worldview and value system.[79] For Swedish, we turn to *Svenska Akademiens Ordbok* (SAOB), which like the OED provides historical examples of word use. The entry *ideologi* was written in 1933, and has not been updated since. It provides two familiar senses: the science of ideas and the negatively laden idealist theory of the world. The 1933 edition of the SAOB did not give a clear meaning of ideology as a system of thought.[80]

Dictionaries are seldom useful in pinpointing the birth of new meanings, but it is noteworthy that it is difficult to find dictionary definitions of ideology as a political doctrine in editions published before the 1930s. There is textual evidence of a shift in meaning in the first three or four decades of the twentieth cen-

---

76 We consulted the online version here: *Dictionnaire de L'Académie Française*. https://www.dictionnaire-academie.fr/article/A9I0063.

77 *Brockhaus Kleines Konversations-Lexikon, fünfte Auflage, Bd. 1* (Leipzig, 1911), 847, http://www.zeno.org/nid/2000120677X.

78 *Der Sprach-Brockhaus: Deutsches Bilderwörterbuch für jedermann* (Leipzig: Brockhaus, 1935).

79 *Der Sprach-Brockhaus: Deutsches Bilderwörterbuch für jedermann* (Wiesbaden: Brockhaus, 1958); *Der Sprach-Brockhaus: Deutsches Bilderwörterbuch* (Wiesbaden: Brockhaus, 1972).

80 "ideologi," in *Svenska Akademiens Ordbok* https://www.saob.se/artikel/?seek=ideologi&pz=1#U_I1_89220 ("Liberalismen var (för Marx) inbegreppet av all världens ideologi och illusioner").

tury, and we claim that the breakthrough is traceable through simple word frequencies. The emergence of this new sense was a gradual process in which the different meanings were not as neatly separated as the definitions in dictionaries might lead us to believe. The senses were rather linked in language use, and the term ideology carried several older layers of meaning.[81] It was now more commonly invoked in the sense of competing political doctrines, but old meanings referring to the science of ideas and irrational reasoning were, and still are, retained for particular purposes.

Our third source, the examination of digital corpora, reveals that not only was the word ideology changing in terms of meaning and context, it was also much more common. All the diachronic corpora we consulted indicate a similar trend: the word ideology gradually became more popular in the early twentieth century, and the 1930s was a decade of particular intensification. The Google Books data set,[82] although justifiably criticised for its biased selection of books,[83] provides the largest corpus available for studying frequencies. Its datasets in English, German and French all indicate a rise in the relative frequency of the word ideology in the first three or four decades of the twentieth century.[84]

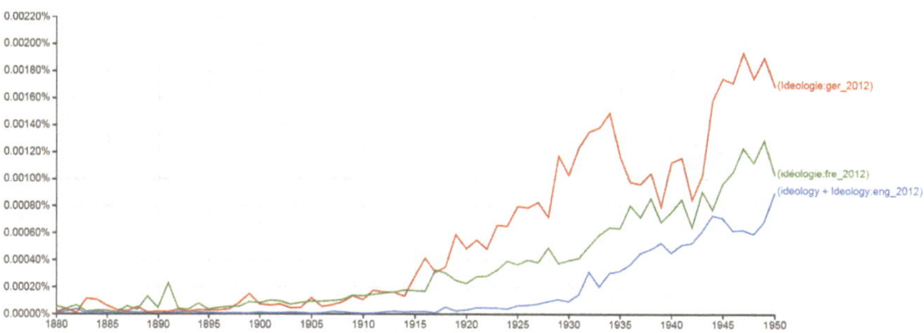

Figure 1: Relative frequencies of ideology, Ideologie and idéologie in the English, German and French data sets of Google Books, respectively. The plot was produced here: *http://books.google.com/ngrams*

81 Reinhart Koselleck, *Zeitschichten: Studien zur Historik* (Frankfurt: Suhrkamp, 2003).

82 Jean-Baptiste Michel et al., "Quantitative Analysis of Culture Using Millions of Digitized Books," *Science* 331 (2011): 176–182.

83 Eitan Adam Pechenick, Christopher M. Danforth, and Peter Sheridan Dodds, "Characterizing the Google Books Corpus: Strong Limits to Inferences of Socio-Cultural and Linguistic Evolution," *PLOS ONE* 10 (2015): e0137041.

84 Google. http://books.google.com/ngrams.

Although the trends are similar, there are clear differences between the countries. Usage of the term increased earlier in German-speaking Europe and occurred more frequently overall in German than in English or French. A perusal of digitised German-language newspapers in the ANNO collection of the Austrian National Library also indicates its earlier usage in connection with political movements or parties, and individual isms. Because ANNO does not provide relative frequencies, we had to look at absolute frequencies of the term in individual Austrian newspapers published during the first, second, and third decades of the twentieth century: occurrences of the term ideology became more frequent in the 1910s and 1920s, as evidenced in the newspapers *Arbeiter Zeitung* (59 for the 1900s, 184 for the 1910s, 351 for the 1920s), *Reichspost* (15 for the 1900s, 31 for the 1910s, 99 for the 1920s), and *Salzburger Wacht* (10 for the 1900s, 50 for the 1910s, 182 for the 1920s).[85]

Other European countries followed a similar trend. Delpher, a collection of Dutch newspapers, provides absolute frequencies, which also point to the sporadic use of '*ideologie*' until the first decade of the twentieth century, followed by a sharp increase up to the 1930s.[86] The Times Digital Archive, containing all issues of *The Times* between 1785 and 2012, is a significantly smaller data set, but provides parallel trajectories. The first uses of ideology in it are from 1827,[87] 1846,[88] and 1862.[89] There were very few occurrences of the word during the last decades of the nineteenth century (between zero and seven per decade), but from 1910 onwards it clearly became part of everyday language, with 11 occurrences for the 1910s, 30 for the 1920s, 284 for the 1930s, and 349 for the 1940s. Absolute word frequencies are not normalised per decade according to the size of the data set, but bearing in mind that the Times Digital Archive covers only one newspaper, the absolute figures do give an indication of the trend. The stories in *The Times* also indicate that ideology tended to be increasingly used in explicitly political settings once it become more frequent. Usage relating to language or as the opposite of facts were replaced with a more general take in which ideologies were seen as something that competed for space, supporters or influence.[90]

85 *Arbeiter Zeitung*. Searches were done in http://anno.onb.ac.at/anno-suche.
86 Delpher. https://www.delpher.nl/.
87 "Portugal," *Times*, 15 September 1827, 2. *The Times Digital Archive*, http://tinyurl.gale.com/tinyurl/CCJH53, accessed 11 November 2019.
88 "The debate in the Chamber of Deputies which," *Times*, 7 September 1846, 4. *The Times Digital Archive*, http://tinyurl.gale.com/tinyurl/CCJZ99, accessed 11 November 2019.
89 "Arches' Court, Feb. 25," *Times*, 26 February 1862, 11. *The Times Digital Archive*, http://tinyurl.gale.com/tinyurl/CCJdP6, accessed 11 November 2019.
90 For an example, see "The Soviet Structure," *Times*, 2 September 1948, 5.

Turning to the Hansard corpus comprising British parliamentary debates between 1803 and 2005 reveals the change in use of the word ideology more clearly: there is not a single occurrence of "ideology" or "ideological" before the 1920s, and even then both words appear only once. The breakthrough was in the 1930s: ideologies are often "political", "rival", "offensive" or used in conjunction with particular isms, most often socialism, communism or fascism.[91] The British Parliament was not in the least concerned with issues of ideology as the science of ideas, but once it assumed its new meaning it entered the sphere of Parliament. The Swedish Riksdag serves as a further example of parliamentary talk about ideology. The first use of the term in the Riksdag was in 1874 in a statement advising against rushing into the metric system. Swedish parliamentary debates not only include the word ideology earlier than the British debates, they also show much more awareness of its history and Napoleonic uses of it. Whereas nineteenth-century uses are close to Napoleonic uses, the Swedish Parliament referred to ideologies as something political and competitive as early as in the 1910s and the 1920s.[92] Nevertheless, the trend is similar in that usage of the term rocketed in the discourse of the Swedish Riksdag during the 1930s.

As ideology was entering new language domains, we also observed a shift in semantic context related to the popularity of the term. It was not only the word ideology, but also and in particular the phrase "political ideology", that were increasingly used in English in the 1930s (the first uses were obviously earlier). As part of this semantic change, we also note the rise of the plural form: the proportion of "ideologies" in all forms of the word rose from around 10 percent in the 1910s to around 20 percent in the period after 1930 in the Google Books data set, meaning that it was more common to have a comparative outlook on competing ideologies.[93] Had ideology only meant the science of ideas or wishful and irrelevant thinking, the plural form would have been less relevant.

Having been part of the theoretical discussion in philosophy, sociology, and other academic disciplines, ideology as a term became much more common in newspapers and parliamentary debates. The rise in frequency and the semantic changes described above are related, and probably reciprocally constitutive.

---

91 Results were obtained through a search on "ideolog*" in https://www.english-corpora.org/hansard/.

92 Occurrences of ideology in the Swedish Riksdag were extracted by downloading all Riksdag documents from before 1970 and searching them as text files. The data is to be found here: https://data.kb.se/datasets/2017/09/riksdagstryck/.

93 Both claims are based on http://books.google.com/ngrams, so further corpus linguistic verification would be welcome.

When the term became more common, more people thought in terms of ideology and perhaps consciously used the word in new ways. In these new contexts, it was also more likely to be associated with different ism words. It is clear that different periods of time produced new ideologies (such as the notion of totalitarianism in the 1930s, 1940s, and 1950s),[94] but we should also point out that the coupling of different isms with it also helped to transform the notion of ideology as a meta-category.

The Historicisation of Ideology

We have focused in the previous sections on when and how the word ideology acquired a new meaning and how isms have come to be understood as competing ideologies. As noted, ideology was occasionally coupled with different isms even in early nineteenth-century pejorative rhetoric against ideologues and ideology, but this was rather uncommon and based on an old sense of ideology. A more modern use was when an ism was described as one ideology among others. Although it is sometimes difficult to separate the two senses, our contention is that the latter became more common in the 1920s and 1930s, as indicated above in our discussion about Swedish and Austrian newspapers and supported by parliamentary material from Britain and Sweden. At this time, ideology was coupled with socialism, communism, Marxism, fascism, anarchism, totalitarianism, and liberalism, although not necessarily simultaneously. According to Michael Freeden, ideology became a focal concept of political analysis and gained prominence in political vocabulary with the rise of totalitarian ideologies.[95] Our interpretation resembles Freeden's, but we highlight the gradual coupling of different isms, as a result of which ideology came to be perceived as omnipresent on the political spectrum. No longer did only political adversaries have ideologies (although this sentiment still occasionally recurs), but ideologies were perceived as being held also by one's own political movement and the academics analyzing them.

The experience of ideology as omnipresent provoked historical accounts of the phenomenon. The original Ideologues gained their place in the history of

94 Kurunmäki and Marjanen, "Isms, ideologies and setting the agenda," 267; Juan Francisco Fuentes, "Totalitarian Language: Creating Symbols to Destroy Words," *Contributions to the History of Concepts* 8 (2013): 45–66; Id., "How Words Reshape the Past: The 'Old, Old Story' of Totalitarianism," *Politics, Religion & Ideology* 16 (2015): 282–297.

95 Freeden, "Ideology and Conceptual History," 73.

ideology.[96] Although there were already books about liberalism, conservatism, and socialism in the early twentieth century,[97] they were not presented as historical studies of ideology, nor were the historical accounts of the ideologues tied to isms. A relative frequency search shows that terms such as "history of ideology", "study of ideology", and "age of ideology" appear in Google Books data set from the 1920s, but became more common in the postwar period.[98] Moreover, ideology was commonly associated with isms during and after World War II and, vice versa, isms were understood as ideologies, which called for an account of their history. For instance, the *Handbook of Political 'Isms'*, published in 1941, was presented as "a dictionary of ideologies",[99] and the chapters in a volume on European ideologies was organised according to different isms.[100] The age of ideology as a notion stemmed from the need to provide historical explanations for the experience of totalitarianism.[101] Although this meant that the history of particular isms was written as the history of ideology, the historical coupling of the two was lost. The link was readily postulated as far back in time as one could write the history of a particular ism.

Works that describe the age of ideology, or that claim the end of it, tend to have a dual temporality. On the one hand, they clearly arose from the experience of World War II and the Cold War as an age of ideology, but on the other hand they provide an extensive historical account, most often depicting the nineteenth century as the age of ideologies.[102] However, these interpretations had different starting points. It is possible to find influential accounts of ideology that go back to Francis Bacon and religious conflicts,[103] to the birth of modern politics around

---

96 See, e.g., François Picavet, *Les ideologues: Essai sur l'histoire des idées et des théories scientifiques, philosophiques, religieuses, etc. en France depuis 1789* (Paris, 1891).

97 See, e.g., Hobhouse, *Liberalism*; Guido de Ruggiero, *The History of European Liberalism* (London: Oxford University Press, [1925] 1927); Cecil, *Conservatism*; J. Ramsay MacDonald, *Socialism and Society* (London: Independent Labour Party, 1908). On liberalism as an ideology and Ruggiero, see also Bell, "What Is Liberalism?".

98 http://books.google.com/ngrams.

99 Louis Wasserman, *Handbook of Political 'Isms'* (New York: Association Press, 1941), 5.

100 Feliks Gross and Robert M. Maciver (ed.), *European Ideologies; A Survey of 20th Century Political Ideas* (New York: Philosophical Library, 1948).

101 See, e.g., Karl Dietrich Bracher, *The Age of Ideologies: A History of Political Thought in the Twentieth Century* (London: Methuen & Co, 1985), ix. For a critical view on understanding ideology merely through totalitarianism, see Freeden, "Ideology and Conceptual History," 87–89.

102 Henry D. Aiken, *The Age of Ideology* (Boston: Houghton & Mifflin, 1957); L. Wasserman, *Handbook of Political 'Isms'*, 5.

103 Bendix, "Age of Ideology: Persistent and Changing," 294–295.

the Enlightenment in the late eighteenth century,[104] to the period after the 1848 revolutions,[105] or to the age of mass society and totalitarianism.[106] Most accounts also acknowledge Destutt de Tracy's coinage of the term ideology after the French Revolution, but none of them seem to consider the introduction of the word the starting point of an age of ideology.[107] Interestingly, Quentin Skinner, an ardent critic of conceptual anachronism in the study of political thought, readily placed ideology as a category in the medieval and early-modern periods in his magnum opus on political thought, *The Foundation of Modern Political Thought* (1978).[108] James Tully has without any reservations described Skinner's book as "a map of the great political ideologies of early-modern Europe."[109]

The notion of a currently experienced age of ideology is particularly plain in some of the early volumes on the history of ideologies. As the above-mentioned 1948 volume *European Ideologies* states: "In our day it has surely become clear to every thinking person that mankind is now, whatever it was before, governed by ideas, activated by ideologies, and ridden by myths".[110] Thinking about ideologies was as topical as it could get, but their roots were most often placed in the nineteenth century. Similarly, Hans Kohn provided historical accounts of ideologies starting from the revolutions of 1848, but the prefaces of his book clearly show how his work grew out of an uneasiness with ideology in the present. This perspective also changed over the years: whereas the first edition from 1949 still reveled in the experience of an international conflict between ideologies, the third edition from 1967 echoed the end of the ideology thesis, as Kohn recognised a different present: "But winds of change are blowing which in 1914 or even 1945 few would have expected. The ideologies of the first part of the century are undergoing a subtle transformation without giving up their distinct charac-

104 Clifford Geertz, "Ideology as a Cultural System," in *Ideology and Discontent*, ed. David E. Apter (London: The Free Press of Glencoe, Collier-Macmillan, 1964), 64.

105 Hans Kohn, *Political Ideologies of the Twentieth Century* (New York, Harper Torchbooks, 1967), xi.

106 Hannah Arendt, *The Origins of Totalitarianism*. New edition with added prefaces (San Diego: A Harvest Book, Harcourt Brace & Company, 1973), 45.

107 The conceptual histories of ideology by Dierse, Stråth, and Freeden are exceptions, but they do not make claims about a particular age of ideology.

108 See e.g., Quentin Skinner, *The Foundations of Modern Political Thought, Vol. 1* (Cambridge, Cambridge University Press, 1978), xii.

109 On this point, see Vincent, "Political Ideology and Political Theory," 165.

110 Robert M. MacIver, "Introduction," in *European Ideologies: A Survey of 20th Century Political Ideas*, ed. Felix Gross (New York: Philosophical Library, 1948), xiii.

ter" and "ideologies count less than twenty years ago and national and imperial interests count more".[111]

Some Western intellectuals, such as Edward Shils, Daniel Bell, Seymor Martin Lipset, Albert Camus, and Raymond Aron, had been advancing the theory of the end of ideology in Western democracies since the late 1940s. Claiming the end of ideology in developed countries was intended to limit the influence of communism and left-wing radicalism in the West.[112] Such theories tended to build on the belief that ideologies such as socialism, communism, and liberalism emanated from Enlightenment thought, but degenerated in the era of the mass society into xenophobic nationalism, doctrinaire socialism, communism, and fascism – in other words, totalitarianism. This interpretation placed ideology outside the liberal democratic sphere. If the Marxist understanding of ideology presented it as something negative and as something that the bourgeoisie held, the end of ideology thesis turned this on its head. The liberal or social-democratic position was now non-ideological, whereas communism and fascism were deemed the opposite and as belonging to the past.

Many historical treatises on ideology became foundational works in the field. Two scholars are particularly noteworthy in the way they historicise the concept: Hannah Arendt and Clifford Geertz. Arendt gives a brief history in *The Origins of Totalitarianism* (1951), in which she identifies ideology with totalitarianism, but she also builds her argument on the long-term development of totalitarianism, describing antisemitism and imperialism as ideologies.[113] She maintains that only a few nineteenth-century ideas became "full-fledged ideologies", which she describes as "systems based upon a single opinion that proved strong enough to attract and persuade a majority of people and broad enough to lead them through the various experiences and situations of an average modern life". According to her, "an ideology differs from a simple opinion in that it claims to possess either the key to history, or the solution for all the 'riddles of the universe'".[114] For her, the two full-fledged ideologies had defeated all oth-

---

111 Kohn, *Political Ideologies of the Twentieth Century*, xi.

112 See Edward Shils, "The End of Ideology?" *Encounter* 5 (1955): 52–58; Raymond Aron, *The Opium of the Intellectuals* (New York: Norton 1962 [1955]); Daniel Bell, *The End of Ideology: On the Exhaustion of Political Ideas in the Fifties. With a New Afterword* (Cambridge, MA: Harvard University Press, 1988 [1960]); Seymour Martin Lipset, *Political Man: The Social Bases of Politics* (New York: Doubleday & Co., 1960). For an analysis, see Howard Brick, "The End of Ideology Thesis," in *The Oxford Handbook of Political Ideologies*, ed. Michael Freeden, Lyman Tower Sargent, and Marc Stears (Oxford: Oxford University Press, 2013), 90–112.

113 Arendt, *Origins of Totalitarianism*, 45; see also Fuentes, "How Words Reshape the Past," 287.

114 Arendt, *Origins of Totalitarianism*, 159.

ers: "the ideology which interprets history as an economic struggle of classes, and the other that interprets history as a natural fight of races".[115] They were not universal, but every "full-fledged ideology has been created, continued and improved as a political weapon and not as a theoretical doctrine".[116] Arendt explicitly equates ideologies with isms in her article "Ideology and Terror" (1953), which was added to the second edition of the book on totalitarianism: "ideologies – isms which to the satisfaction of their adherents can explain everything and every occurrence by deducing it from a single premise – are a very recent phenomenon and, for many decades, this played a negligible role in political life". She further explains that the political potential of ideology was not realised before the time of Hitler and Stalin.[117]

Arendt's understanding of these two full-fledged and totalising ideologies was widely acknowledged during the following years. Drawing on her analysis, in the early 1960s Bernard Crick presented a powerful denunciation of ideology by contrasting it to what he called "politics", arguing that totalitarian rule "marks the sharpest contrast imaginable with political rule, and ideological thinking is an explicit and direct challenge to political thinking".[118] Like Arendt, he viewed totalitarian regimes as the product of a democratic age and ideology as the womb from which both totalitarianism and modern sociology had evolved.[119]

Geertz, on the other hand, produced a longer history of ideologies that ended up being an interpretation of the birth of modern political culture, reminiscent of the way in which historians Reinhart Koselleck and R. R. Palmer saw the emergence of liberalism, socialism, and conservatism in the aftermath of the French Revolution.[120] In his seminal article on ideology as a cultural system, Geertz maintains that the function of ideology "is to make an autonomous politics possible by providing the authoritative concepts that render it meaningful, the suasive images by means of which it can be sensibly grasped".[121] Referring to Burke and de Maistre, he considered the emergence of ideology as part of the modern era:

---

115 Ibid.

116 Ibid.

117 Hannah Arendt, "Ideology and Terror: A Novel Form of Government," *The Review of Politics* 15 (1953): 315.

118 Bernard Crick, *In Defence of Politics* (Harmondsworth: Penguin Books, [1962]) 1966), 34.

119 Ibid., 35, 38.

120 See Kurunmäki and Marjanen, "Isms, ideologies and setting the agenda," 257.

121 Geertz, "Ideology as a Cultural System," 63.

> It is, in fact, precisely at the point at which a political system begins to free itself from the immediate governance of received tradition, from the direct and detailed guidance of religious or philosophical canons on the one hand and from the unreflective precepts of conventional moralism on the other, that formal ideologies tend first to emerge and take hold.[122]

He described the French Revolution as "the greatest incubator of extremist ideologies, 'progressive' and 'reactionary' alike", because "the central organizing principle of political life, the divine right of kings, was destroyed".[123] Geertz's take on ideology was very different from that of Arendt, and opened up a perspective from which the end of the ideology thesis no longer made sense: ideologies were everywhere, and they were needed to "render otherwise incomprehensible social situations meaningful". He described them as "maps of problematic social reality and matrices for the creation of collective conscience".[124] Geertz's account of ideology as a symbolic phenomenon has inspired many contemporary analysts who view it as an elementary aspect of politics and not degeneration or deviation from it, and who have a constructive and rhetorical view of the role of language in history, politics, and, consequently, ideology. Michael Freeden's morphological analysis of ideologies is perhaps the best and most influential example of this line of thinking.

According to Geertz, a variety of things could reasonably be called ideologies, and consequently he imagined a large range of isms and their hybrids as cultural systems. He further argued that the search for symbolic frameworks in reaction to political problems "whether in the form of nationalism, Marxism, liberalism, populism, racism, Caesarism, ecclesiasticism, or some variety of reconstructed traditionalism (or, most commonly, a confused mélange of several of these) is therefore tremendously intense".[125] Any new political situation could constitute a setting in which new ideological systems could emerge, which also meant that whereas ideology was a phenomenon of the post-French revolution setting, individual ideologies have their distinct histories. In making this move Geertz opened up a very flexible framework in which to discuss individual ideologies, but again, the historicisation of ideology and its historical coupling with individual isms was, in a sense, lost. In such an interpretation, ideologies could not be invective, as in Napoleon, or forms of false consciousness as in Marx, but rather had their own intellectual trajectories. In tracing those trajec-

---

122 Ibid., 63–64.
123 Ibid., 64.
124 Ibid.
125 Ibid., 65.

tories the historical linking of the notion of ideology and individual isms did not make sense. Ideology was purely a meta-category.

This more open notion of ideology also made it easier to label political movements as ideologies. The fact that Ceasarism, populism, agrarianism, and trade unionism could at least be discussed as ideologies is indicative not only of the link between ideology and particular isms, but also of the increasingly strong link between ideology and almost any ism. One chapter in a 1969 volume on populism was devoted to populism as an ideology, but it is characteristic of the volume that all the authors except American historian Richard Hofstadter, who had published a book that was mainly about the impact of nineteenth-century populism on the political culture in the US, were clearly very uncertain about what populism was at that time.[126] Nevertheless, ideology was included in the book through the ism. Something similar is happening in the current discussion about populism and neoliberalism as ideologies, although the meanings of ideology are also being renegotiated. Whereas the discussion on populism tends to build on the notion of ideology as a cultural system, the discussion on neoliberalism seems to build on something that is closer to Arendt's thinking – neoliberalism as a distorted form of nineteenth-century liberalism – or even to Marx's – neoliberalism as false consciousness that is prevalent in new public management.

Conclusion

The transformation of ideology as a concept can be traced through the slightly overlapping processes of politicisation, democratisation, and historicisation. Politicisation took place almost immediately after the coinage of the term as it was immediately contested and used as invective. This feature is still present in the use of the word ideology. Democratisation, the process in which ideology was much more commonly used, took place in the early twentieth century, in particular the 1920s and 1930s. The term also entered various different language domains, and assumed an ambiguous meaning in vernacular use. Historicisation is the process in which ideology was understood as a meta-category that covered a potentially endless selection of individual ideologies (usually called isms of

126 Ghita Ionescu and Ernest Gellner, *Populism: Its Meanings and National Characteristics* (London: Weidenfeld and Nicolson, 1969); Richard Hofstadter, *The Age of Reform: From Bryan to F. D. R.* (New York: Vintage Books, 1955); see also Anton Jäger, "The Semantic Drift: Images of Populism in Post-War American Historiography and Their Relevance for (European) Political Science," *Constellations* 24 (2017): 310–323.

some sort), and thus prompted the writing up of these individual ideologies as a feature of the history of political thought.

It was common in the early coupling of ideology and particular isms to take an outside position by presenting one or several isms as ideologies but not identifying one's own position as an ideology. Marx is a typical example of this, whereas Bernstein was an early exception. The tradition was a direct continuation of Napoleon's use of ideology as invective (which was also a dominant feature of isms). It is also evident in quite late characterisations like in many analyses of totalitarianism and in the end of ideology thesis in the 1950s and 1960s, and still occurs today in less reflected uses.

It is difficult to pinpoint which isms were first associated with ideology, because it depends on the political culture and the types of source consulted. Nevertheless, it seems that Bernsteinian revisionsim and discussions on the position of ideology in sociology made socialism and communism the first isms to be regularly associated with it. The rise of fascism and National Socialism gave it a new focus in the 1920s and 1930s. At this time, too, it was surprisingly common in British and American discourse to regard fascism, National Socialism, and Communism as one and the same ideology. Although we found examples of liberalism being called an ideology in the 1870s, it still seems that the notion of liberalism as an ideology became more common only around World War II, if even then.

What characterised the discourse of ideologies in the period before World War II was that they were considered to be few in number. This changed in the postwar period as it became more common to regard ideologies as indispensable such that everyone had them. At the time it made more sense to provide long lists of ideologies to describe the essentials of the ideological spectrum. Many of them had in individual cases been called ideologies already earlier (this applies even to isms such as feminism and anarchism), but then it became more common to consider them all as ideologies at the same time (although probably giving them different prominence). It also meant that even academic analysts of ideologies reflected upon their own positions as persons with ideologically founded opinions. This was evident in the case of democracy being an ideology, for instance, but it is also a feature of current literature on ideologies.[127] Once ideology was regarded as being everywhere, and as it had gained a higher level of abstraction it could not really be seen as a science of ideas that could be juxtaposed with other takes on creating knowledge (even the Mannheimian take on ideology as a sociology of knowledge was marginalised). Instead, it

127 See e.g., Ball and Bellamy, "Editors' introduction," 1–4.

became a meta-category that could not have a clear counter-concept. Instead it was the different ideologies that could be juxtaposed, opposed, and historicised. However, older meanings did not disappear altogether, and are visible in the current use of the adjective "ideological" as invective in political debate, for instance. In this meaning, ideological is often presented as a counter-concept to pragmatism or the pragmatic, but when the talk is of ideology as a meta-category, the only feasible antonym is anti-ideological or non-ideology.

Contributors

Tatiana Artemyeva is a Professor at the Herzen State Pedagogical University of Russia at the Department of Theory and History of Culture and Director of research programmes in St Petersburg Centre for History of Ideas, and both co-founder and co-editor of the almanac 'Philosophical Age'. She has been a Fellow of Helsinki Collegium for Advanced Studies, Aleksanteri Institute, Herzog August Bibliothek, Kennan Institute and the NYU Jordan Center. Her research has been supported by DAAD and Fulbright programmes. She is an author of 16 books and 298 papers devoted to the history of philosophy and intellectual culture of the Enlightenment in Russia. Among them: *Intellectual Culture of the Enlightenment in Russia* (together with M. Mikeshin) (2020); *From the Glorious Past to the Bright Future. Philosophy of History and Utopia in Russia in the Epoch of Enlightenment* (2005); *Philosophy at Petersburg Academy of Sciences in the 18th Century* (1999) and *The History of Metaphysics in 18th-century Russia* (1996).

Justin Begley is a Postdoctoral Researcher in the Humanities Division at the University of Helsinki, who focuses on early-modern literature and intellectual history, with special interests in substance theories, classical reception, comparative anatomy, and plant studies. Having published in journals such as *Intellectual History Review, The Review of English Studies*, and *The Seventeenth Century*, he is currently completing a monograph entitled *Margaret Cavendish: The Last Natural Philosopher*; in addition, he is working on an edition of the Cavendishes' medical manuscript. Along with Cavendish, Justin has also published on major figures including Nehemiah Grew, Pierre Gassendi, Thomas Tryon, and Kenelm Digby.

Çağlar Çömez is a doctoral student in a cotutelle programme at Boğaziçi University and Martin-Luther-Universität in Halle-Wittenberg. His research is currently funded by the Deutscher Akademischer Austauschdienst (DAAD). His PhD thesis concerns the relation between morality and law, in general, and an assessment of how Immanuel Kant characterised this relation within the context of contemporary legal philosophy, in particular. His research interests include moral philosophy, legal philosophy and German philosophy. He wrote his master's thesis on Martin Heidegger's *Being and Time.*

Ben Dew is a Senior Lecturer in the School of Area Studies, History, Politics and Literature at the University of Portsmouth, UK. His research is principally concerned with the history of historical writing in the seventeenth, eighteenth and nineteenth centuries. He has published in a range of journals including *Modern Intellectual History, Intellectual History Review*, and the *Journal for Eighteenth-Century Studies.* He is the editor of two books: *Tea and Politics* (Pickering and Chatto, 2010) and *British Historical Writing, 1688–1830* (Palgrave, 2014); and the author of *Commerce, Finance and Politics: Histories of England, 1600–1780* (Manchester University Press, 2018).

Heikki Haara is a Senior Lecturer of Political History in the Faculty of Social Sciences at the University of Helsinki. He has been a visiting researcher at the universities of California, Berkeley and Oxford. His research interests have principally been early-modern moral and political thought. He has published articles in academic journals such as *Journal of the History of Ideas, Political Theory* and *Journal of Scottish Philosophy.* He is the author of *Pufendorf's*

Theory of Sociability: Passions, Habits and Social Order (Springer, 2018) and the co-editor of *Rights at the Margins: Historical, Philosophical and Legal Perspectives* (Brill, 2020).

Mikko Immanen is an Academy of Finland Postdoctoral Researcher at the Department of Social Sciences and Philosophy at the University of Jyväskylä, Finland. His research interests focus on Critical Theory, modern European intellectual history, and German history. His publications include *Toward a Concrete Philosophy: Heidegger and the Emergence of the Frankfurt School* (Cornell University Press, 2020). During 2018–2019, he was Fulbright visiting scholar at the CUNY Graduate Center in New York.

László Kontler is Professor of History at Central European University (Budapest/Vienna). His research and publications focus on intellectual history, the history of political thought, translation and reception, and the production and circulation of scientific knowledge in early-modern Europe, mainly the Enlightenment. His books include *Translations, Histories, Enlightenments: William Robertson in Germany, 1760–1795* (Palgrave, 2014) and (with Per Pippin Aspaas) *Maximilian Hell (1720–1792) and the Ends of Jesuit Science in Enlightenment Europe* (Brill, 2020).

Jussi Kurunmäki is an Associate Professor at Tampere University, Finland, where he is a specialist in nineteenth- and twentieth-century conceptual history of parliamentary democratisation and political ideologies in Finland and in Sweden. He is one of the editors of the volumes *Rhetorics of Nordic Democracy* (2010) and *Democracy in Modern Europe: A Conceptual History* (2018), as well as the special issue "The Political Rhetoric of Isms" in *Journal of Political Ideologies* (2018). In recent years, he has also published in *Journal of Modern European History*. Kurunmäki is the chairperson of the international network Concepta – International Research Seminars in Conceptual History and Political Thought.

Aino Lahdenranta is a doctoral student of philosophy at the University of Jyväskylä. Aino's research interests comprise early-modern moral philosophy and contemporary metaethics. In her dissertation research on eighteenth-century sentimentalism, she examines the relationship between emotions and moral judgment.

Adriana Luna-Fabritius is a University Researcher at the University of Helsinki. She works on the languages of republicanism, natural law and political economy in the Spanish monarchy, especially Naples and Piedmont. Luna-Fabritius is the current President of the European Society for the History of Political Thought and Associate Editor of its book series on the History of European Political and Constitutional Thought (Brill). She is affiliated with the research groups: "Cameralism as a European Political Science: A Reassessment"; "International Research Network: Natural Law 1625–1850"; and the Helsinki Centre for Intellectual History.

Jani Marjanen is a Postdoctoral Researcher at the University of Helsinki, where he also earned his PhD in 2014. During 2014–2015, he was Visiting Scholar at the Max Planck Institute for Human Development, Berlin. He specializes in late eighteenth-century and early nineteenth-century language of economic patriotism in Scandinavia, the theory and method of conceptual history, and the history of ideology. He co-edited *The Rise of Economic Societies in the Eighteenth Century* (2012) and the special issue "The Political Rhetoric of Isms" in *Jour-*

nal of Political Ideologies (2018). He is one of the editors of *Contributions to the History of Concepts.*

Fabio Mengali completed his PhD in Political Philosophy at the University of Trento (Italy). His doctoral and research interests concern the history of the intertwining concepts of labour and citizenship in early-modern England, with particular focus on Locke's political theory and the intellectual milieu of the fifteenth and sixteenth centuries. His publications in Italian and international journals span the debates on labour and citizenship in Western intellectual history, Italian workerism and its legacy, the impairment and contradictions of European citizenship, as well as authoritarian populism. He wrote a book aimed at a wider public on Donald Trump's electoral victory in relation to the global populist upsurge. He is currently interested in the history of the concept of labour within the Scottish Enlightenment and American Liberalism.

Ere Nokkala is a University Researcher at the University of Helsinki. He is a member of the Helsinki Centre for Intellectual History with a focus on eighteenth-century Germany, Scandinavia and Finland. His publications include *From Natural Law to Political Economy: JHG von Justi on State, Commerce and International Order* (LIT Verlag, 2019) and the co-edited volume *Cameralism and the Enlightenment: Happiness, Governance and Reform in Transnational Perspective* (Routledge, 2020). He has published widely on aspects of cameralism and early-modern republicanism, including in *History of European Ideas*, *European Review of History*, and *Contributions to the History of Concepts*. Nokkala earned his PhD in 2010 from the European University Institute, Florence, and has held fellowships at the Swedish Collegium for Advanced Study, Lichtenberg-Kolleg – The Göttingen Institute for Advanced Study, and the Herzog August Bibliothek.

Markku Peltonen is Professor of History at the University of Helsinki. His publications include *Classical Humanism and Republicanism in English Political Thought, 1570–1640* (1995), *The Duel in Early Modern England: Civility, Politeness and Honour* (2003) and *Rhetoric, Politics and Popularity in Pre-Revolutionary England* (2013), all published by Cambridge University Press. He has also edited *The Cambridge Companion to Bacon* (1996) for Cambridge University Press. He is completing a book on the political thought of the English free state.

Eva Piirimäe is Associate Professor of Political Theory at the Johan Skytte Institute of Political Studies, University of Tartu, Estonia. She earned her PhD in 2007 from the University of Cambridge. Piirimäe's research interests include early-modern moral and political philosophy, historical and contemporary theories of patriotism, cosmopolitanism and nationalism, as well as the intellectual history of human rights and the self-determination of peoples. She has recently published "State-Machines, Commerce and the Progress of *Humanität* in Europe", in *Commerce and Peace in the Enlightenment*, edited by Béla Kapossy et al. (CUP, 2017) as well as co-edited (with Liina Lukas and Johannes Schmidt) *Herder on Empathy and Sympathy/ Einfühlung und Sympathie im Denken Herders* (Brill, 2020).

Koen Stapelbroek is an Associate Professor at Erasmus University Rotterdam and Director of the Helsinki Centre for Intellectual History. He published *Love, Self-Deceit and Money: Commerce and Morality in the Early Neapolitan Enlightenment* (University of Toronto Press, 2008) and a range of articles and edited volumes on European eighteenth-century political thought and the history of commercial institutions. He is currently completing two monographs on European perceptions of the rise and fall of the Dutch trade republic and on the history of free trade and its regulatory institutions and frameworks.

Tim Stuart-Buttle is Lecturer in Politics at the University of York. His research interests centre on early-modern theories of sociability and politics, with a particular focus on the pervasive interest in mankind's desire for esteem and recognition. He has published articles in journals, including *History of Political Thought* and *Political Theory*, and his first monograph, *From Moral Theology to Moral Philosophy: Cicero and Visions of Humanity from Locke to Hume*, was published by Oxford University Press in 2019. He is co-editor, with Subha Muhkerji, of *Literature, Belief and Knowledge in Early Modern England: Knowing Faith* (Palgrave Macmillan, 2018).

Laura Tarkka-Robinson is a Postdoctoral Researcher at the School of Languages and Translation Studies at the University of Turku, Finland. She defended her thesis *"Rudolf Erich Raspe and the Anglo-Hanoverian Enlightenment"* at the University of Helsinki in January 2017 and has since specialised on the meaning of 'national character' in the multilingual public sphere of the Enlightenment period. In 2018, she held a Visiting Research Fellowship at the Sussex Centre for Intellectual History. Her research interests now revolve around cultural transfer and translation, the construction of national cultures, and the uses of travel literature in the long eighteenth century.

Mikko Tolonen is a tenure-track Professor at the Faculty of Arts in the University of Helsinki. His background is in intellectual history and he is the leader of the Helsinki Computational History Group. His current research is focused on an integrated study of public discourse and knowledge production that combines metadata from library catalogues as well as full-text libraries of books, newspapers and periodicals in early-modern Europe. He has published widely on Mandeville, Hume and the Scottish Enlightenment, including a monograph: *Mandeville and Hume: Anatomists of Civil Society* (2013).

Richard Whatmore is Professor of Modern History and Co-Director of the Institute of Intellectual History at the University of St Andrews. He is the author of *Republicanism and the French Revolution* (Oxford, 2000), *Against War and Empire* (Yale, 2012), *What is Intellectual History?* (Polity, 2015) and *Terrorists, Anarchists and Republicans* (Princeton, 2019).

Bibliography

Abizadeh, Arish. "Hobbes on the Causes of War: A Disagreement Theory." *American Political Science Review* 105 (2011): 298–315.

Abulafia, David. *The Discovery of Mankind: Atlantic Encounters in the Age of Columbus.* New Haven and London: Yale University Press, 2008.

Acosta, Joseph de [sic]. *The Natural and Moral History of the Indies.* London: The Hakluyt Society, 1880.

Adam, Ulrich. *The Political Economy of J. H. G. Justi.* Oxford: Peter Lang, 2006.

Aiken, Henry D. *The Age of Ideology.* Boston: Houghton & Mifflin, 1957.

Alexandrowicz, C. H. *The Law of Nations in Global History.* Edited by David Armitage and Jennifer Pitts. Oxford: Oxford University Press, 2017.

Allen, Don Cameron. "The Rehabilitation of Epicurus and His Theory of Pleasure in the Renaissance." *Studies in Philology* 41 (1944): 1–15.

Almici, Gio Batista. "Lettera scrittami dall'illustre Sig. Gio. Batista Alimici to Giovanni Lami, 26

Maggio 1768." *Novelle Letterarie pubblicate in Firenze*, 456–461. Florence: Stamperia Granducale, 1768.

Anderson, Adam. *An Historical and Chronological Deduction of the Origin of Commerce, from the earliest accounts to the present time.* 2 vols. London, 1764.

Anderson-Gold, Sharon. *Cosmopolitanism and Human Rights.* Cardiff: University of Wales Press, 2001.

—. "Kant and Herder." In *A Companion to the Philosophy of History and Historiography*, edited by Aviezer Tucker, 457–467. Oxford: Wiley, 2008.

—. *Unnecessary Evil: History and Moral Progress in the Philosophy of Immanuel Kant.* Albany: State University of New York Press, 2001.

Anichkov, Dmitry Sergeevich. *Slovo o raznyh sposobah, tesneishii soyuz dushi s telom iz'yasnyayushih.* Moscow: V Universitetskoi tipografii u N. Novikova, 1783.

—. *Slovo o svoistvah poznaniya chelovecheskago i o sredstvah predohranyayushih um smertnago ot raznyh zabluzhdenii.* Moscow: Pechatano pri Imperatorskom Moskovskom universitete, 1770.

Appleby, Joyce. *Liberalism and Republicanism in the Historical Imagination.* Cambridge, MA: Harvard University Press, 1992.

—. "Recovering America's Historic Diversity: Beyond Exceptionalism." *Journal of American History* 79 (1992): 419–431.

—. "Republicanism and Ideology." *American Quarterly* 37 (1985): 461–473.

—. "Republicanism in Old and New Contexts." *William and Mary Quarterly* 43 (1986): 20–34.

Arendt, Hannah. *The Human Condition.* Chicago: University of Chicago Press, 1968.

—. "Ideology and Terror: A Novel Form of Government." *The Review of Politics* 15 (1953): 303–327.

—. *The Origins of Totalitarianism.* New edition with added prefaces. San Diego: A Harvest Book, Harcourt Brace & Company, 1973.

Aristotle. *Parts of Animals. Movement of Animals. Progression of Animals.* Translated and edited by E. S. Forster and A. L. Peck. Cambridge, MA: Harvard University Press, 2014.

https://doi.org/10.1515/9783110679861-019

—. *Physics*. Translated and edited by F. M. Cornford and P. H. Wicksteed. Cambridge, MA: Harvard University Press, 2014.
Arkhimandrit, Gavriil. *Istoriia filosofii v 6 chchastiakh*. Ch. III. Kazan': V Universitetskoi tipografii, 1839.
Armitage, David. "Globalizing Jeremy Bentham." *History of Political Thought* 32 (2011): 63–82.
—. "What's the Big Idea? Intellectual History and the Longue Durée." *History of European Ideas* 38 (2012): 493–507.
Aron, Raymond. *The Opium of the Intellectuals*. New York: Norton [1955] 1962.
Arréat, Lucien. "France." *The Monist* 2 (1892): 266–272.
Artemyeva, Tatiana. "Kak prepodavat' filosofiyu? Mnenie universitetskogo chinovnika." *Filosofskii vek, al'manakh* 30 (2005): 67–80.
—. "Nauki o cheloveke v pervyh izdaniyah Britanskoi enciklopedii." *Chelovek* 6 (2003): 670–685.
Ashcraft, Richard. *Locke's Two Treatises of Government*. London: Unwin Hyman Ltd, 1987.
—. "Revolutionary Politics and Locke's *Two Treatises of Government:* Radicalism and Lockean Political Thought." *Political Theory* 8 (1980): 429–486.
Augustine of Hippo. *The City of God against the Pagans*. Translated by Robert W. Dyson. Cambridge: Cambridge University Press, 1988.
Avramescu, Cătălin. *An Intellectual History of Cannibalism*. Princeton, NJ: Princeton University Press, 2009.
Bejan, Teresa M. "Teaching the Leviathan: Thomas Hobbes on Education." *Oxford Review of Education* 36 (2010): 607–626.
Ball, Terence and Richard Bellamy. "Editors' introduction." In *The Cambridge History of Twentieth-Century Political Thought*, edited by Terence Ball and Richard Bellamy, 1–5. Cambridge: Cambridge University Press, 2012.
Barbeyrac, Jean. "Discorso sul benefizio delle leggi: nel quale si fa vedere che non può sempre un uomo onesto *prevalersi* dei diritti e dei privilegj che le leggi accordano. Lausanne: 1716." In Samuel Pufendorf, *I doveri dell'uomo e del cittadino tali che a lui sono prescritti dalla legge natural, dalla versione francese di Giovanni Barbeyrac*. 3 Vols. Translated and edited by Michele Grandi. Venice: Pietteri, 1761–1767.
—. "Discorso sulla permissione delle leggi: nel quale si fa vedere che non è sempre giusto ed onesto quello ch'è dalle leggi permesso. Laussane: 1715." In Samuel Pufendorf, *I doveri dell'uomo e del cittadino tali che a lui sono prescritti dalla legge natural, dalla versione francese di Giovanni Barbeyrac*. 3 Vols. Translated and edited by Michele Grandi. Venice: Pietteri, 1761–1767.
—. "Giudizio di un Anonimo sopra l'originale di questo ristretto, colle riflessioni di Mr. Barbeyrac, le quali serviranno ad illustrare alcuni principj dell'Autore, 1717." In Samuel Pufendorf, *I doveri dell'uomo e del cittadino tali che a lui sono prescritti dalla legge natural, dalla versione francese di Giovanni Barbeyrac*. 3 Vols. Translated and edited by Michele Grandi. Venice: Pietteri, 1761–1767.
Barker, Ernest. "The Conflict of Ideologies." *International Affairs* 16 (1937): 341–360.
Baumeister, Friedrich Christian. *Khristiana Baumeistera Metafizika / Perevod s latinskago [Aleksandra Pavlova] vnov' vysmotren i na mnogikh mestakh ispravlen professorom Dmitriem Sin'kovskim*. Moscow: Universitetskaya tipografiya u Novikova, 1789.

Bazzoli, Maurizio. "Aspetti della Recezione di Pufendorf nel Settecento Italiano." In *Dal 'De jure naturae et gentium' di Samuel Pufendorf alla Codificiazione Prussiana del 1794*, edited by Marta Ferronato, 43–60. Padua: Cedam, 2005.

—. "Giambattista Almici e la diffusione di Pufendorf nel Settecento Italiano." *Critica Storica* 16 (1979): 3–100.

—. *Il Pensiero Politico dell'assolutismo illuminato.* Florence: La Nuova Italia, 1986.

—. "Le concezione pufendorfiane della politica internazionale." In *Samuel Pufendorf filosofo del Diritto e della Politica*, edited by Vanda Fiorillo, 29–72. Naples: Città del Sole, 1996.

—. "Una controversia settecentesca sull'embriotomia." *Studi e Fonti di Storia Lombarda. Quaderni Milanesi* 8 (1988): 7–49.

Beattie, James. *An Essay on the Origin and Immutability of Truth, in Opposition to Sophistry and Scepticism.* Philadelphia: Wieatt, 1809.

Becker, Ron. "The Ideological Commitment of John Locke: Freemen and Servants in the *Two Treatises of Government.*" *History of Political Thought* 4 (1992): 631–656.

Bell, Daniel. *The End of Ideology: On the Exhaustion of Political Ideas in the Fifties.* With a New Afterword. Cambridge, MA: Harvard University Press, [1960] 1988.

Bell, Duncan. "What Is Liberalism?" *Political Theory* 42 (2014): 682–715.

Bendix, Reinhard "The Age of Ideology: Persistent and Changing." In *Ideology and Discontent*, edited by David E. Apter, 294–327. London: The Free Press of Glencoe, Collier-Macmillan, 1964.

Berengo, Marino. *La società veneta alla fine del Settecento.* Florence: Sansoni, 1956.

Bernstein, Eduard. *The Preconditions of Socialism.* Edited by Henry Tudor. Cambridge: Cambridge University Press, [1899] 1993.

Bevir, Mark. "The Contextual Approach." In *The Oxford Handbook of the History of Political Philosophy*, edited by George Klosko, 11–23. Oxford: Oxford University Press, 2011.

—. *The Logic of the History of Ideas.* Cambridge: Cambridge University Press, 1999.

Blanckaert, Claude. *Monogénisme et polygénisme.* In *Dictionnaire du darwinisme et de l'évolution*, edited by Pierre Tort. Paris: PUF, 1996.

Blom, Hans. "Sociability and Hugo Grotius." *History of European Ideas* 41 (Sociability in Enlightenment Thought, ed. Eva Piirimäe et al.) (2015): 589–604.

Bobbio, Norberto. *Principi di diritto natural.* Turin: G. B. Paravia & C [1943] 1952.

—. *Saggi di storia della filosofia*, Naples: 1971.

Boonin-Vail, David. "The Vegetarian Savage: Rousseau's Critique of Meat Eating." *Environmental Ethics* 15 (1993): 75–84.

Bowers, Rick. "Roger Crab: Opposition Hunger Artist in 1650s England." *The Seventeenth Century* 18 (2003): 93–112.

Bracher, Karl Dietrich. *The Age of Ideologies: A History of Political Thought in the Twentieth Century.* London: Methuen & Co, 1985.

Brady, Michelle E. "Locke's *Thoughts* on Reputation." *The Review of Politics* 75 (2013): 335–356.

Braude, Benjamin. "The Myth of the Sephardi Economic Superman." In *Trading Cultures: The Worlds of Western Merchants: Essays on Authority, Objectivity and Evidence*, edited by Jeremy Adelman and Stephen Aron, 163–191. Turnhout: Brepols, 2001.

Brett, Annabel. *Changes of State: Nature and the Limits of the City in Early Modern Natural Law.* Princeton, NJ: Princeton University Press, 2011.

Brick, Howard. "The End of Ideology Thesis." In *The Oxford Handbook of Political Ideologies*, edited by Michael Freeden, Lyman Tower Sargent and Marc Stears, 90–112. Oxford: Oxford University Press, 2013.

Broberg, Gunnar. "Homo sapiens: Linnaeus's Classification of Man." In *Linnaeus: The Man and His Work*, edited by Tore Frängsmyr, 156–194. Berkeley and Los Angeles: University of California Press, 1983.

Brockhaus Kleines Konversations-Lexikon, fünfte Auflage, Bd. 1. Leipzig, 1911.

Brooke, Christopher. "A Response to James Tully." In *Self-Evident Truths? Human Rights and the Enlightenment*, edited by Kate Tunstall, 35–42. New York: Bloomsbury, 2012.

Brooke, John L., and Carl Spencer Larsen. "The Nurture of Nature: Genetics, Epigenetics, and Environment in Human Biohistory." *American Historical Review* 119 (2014): 1500–1513.

[Bruce, John]. *Historical View of Plans, for the Government of British India, and the Regulation of Trade to the East Indies.* London, 1793.

Brundell, Barry. *Pierre Gassendi: From Aristotelianism to a New Natural Philosophy.* Dordrecht: Reidel, 1987.

Burnett, James, Lord Monboddo, *Of the Origin and Progress of Language.* 2nd. ed. Edinburgh: Balfour, London: Caddell, 1774.

Burrow, John W. "Intellectual History in English Academic Life: Reflections on a Revolution." In *Advances in Intellectual History*, edited by Richard Whatmore and Brian Young, 8–24. London: Palgrave Macmillan, 2006.

Bödeker, Hans Erich. "Aufklärung über Aufklärung? Reinhart Kosellecks Interpretation der Aufklärung." In *Zwischen Sprache und Geschichte: Zum Werk Reinhart Kosellecks*, edited by Carsten Dutt und Reinhard Laube, 128–174. Göttingen: Wallstein Verlag, 2013.

Carey, Daniel. "The Problem of Credibility in Early Modern Travel." *Renaissance Studies* 33 (2019): 524–547.

Carey, David. *Locke, Shaftesbury, and Hutcheson: Contesting Diversity in the Enlightenment and Beyond.* Cambridge: Cambridge University Press, 2006.

Carrithers, David. Introduction to *Charles-Louis de Secondat, Baron de Montesquieu*, edited by David Carrithers, xiii–xli. London: Routledge, 2016.

Cattaneo, Giovanni Conte. *The source, the strength, and the true spirit of laws: In three parts. In which the errors of M. de Montesquieu, and some other eminent writers, are occasionally considered. To which are added, Essays on the natural origin of political.* London: Lockyer Davis, 1753.

Cattaneo, Jean de. *La source, la force et le véritable esprit des loix: essais du J. de Cataneo; on y joint aussi un essais sur l'origine naturelle des Gouvernemens politiques dans la Soc. humaine, par le même auteur.* Berlin: Voss, 1752.

Cavallar, Georg. *Kant's Embedded Cosmopolitanism: History, Philosophy, and Education for World Citizens.* Berlin/Boston: De Gruyter, 2015.

Cecil, H. *Conservatism.* London: Oxford University Press, 1912.

Chambers, Ephraim. *Cyclopædia.* London: Printed for D. Midwinter, W. Innys, 1741.

Chaplin, Joyce E. "Ogres and Omnivores: Early American Historians and Climate History." *The William and Mary Quarterly* 72 (2015): 25–32.

Chiaramonti, Giovanni Battista. "Letter to Giovanni Lami, Brescia, January 20, 1757." Florence: Biblioteca Riccardiana.

—. "Letter to Giovanni Lami, Brescia, March 12, 1757." Florence: Biblioteca Riccardiana.

Chuchmarev, Vladimir Ivanovich. *Leibnits i russkaia kul'tura: Iz istorii mezhdunarodnykh nauchnykh i kul'turnykh sviazei.* Moscow: Vysshaya shkola, 1968.

Cicero, Quintus Tullius. *De finibus bonorum et malorum.* Cambridge, MA: Harvard University Press, 2014.

Clark, Gillian. "Fattening the Soul: Christian Asceticism and Porphyry on Abstinence." In *Ascetica, Gnostica, Liturgica, Orientalia: Studia Patristica*, vol. 2, edited by M.F. Wiles and E.J. Yarnold, 41–51. Leuven: Peeters, 2001.

Clement of Alexandria. *Stromateis. Book 1–3.* Edited by John Ferguson. Washington, D.C.: Catholic University of America Press, 1991.

Clericuzio, Antonio. "Chemical and Mechanical Theories of Digestion in Early Modern Medicine." *Studies in History and Philosophy of Biological and Biomedical Sciences* 43, (2012): 329–337.

Cohon, Rachel. "The Common Point of View in Hume's Ethics." *Philosophy and Phenomenological Research* 57 (2007): 827–850.

Coke, Edward. *The Second Part of the Institutes of the Lawes of England.* London, 1642.

Cole, George D. H. *Labour in the Commonwealth: A Book for the Younger Generation.* London: Pelican Press, 1919.

Coleman, James Melville. "Review of Essays on the Materialistic Conception of History, by Antonio Labriola." *The American Journal of Psychology* 16 (1905): 137.

Colton, Joel, Robert R. Palmer, and Alfred Knopf. *A History of the Modern World.* New York: Random House, 1984.

Concina, Daniele. *Della religione rivelata contra gli Ateisti, Deisti, Materialisti, Indifferentisti che negano la verità de' Misterj, libri ciqnue.* 2 vols. Venice, 1754.

Condren, Conal. *The Status and Appraisal of Classic Texts.* Princeton, NJ: Princeton University Press, 1985.

Cooper, Julia E. "Vainglory, Modesty, and Political Agency in the Political Theory of Thomas Hobbes." *The Review of Politics* 72 (2010): 241–269.

Crick, Bernard. *In Defence of Politics.* Harmondsworth: Penguin Books, [1962] 1966.

Crome, Andrew. "English National Identity and the Readmission of the Jews, 1650–1656." *Journal of Ecclesiastical History* 66 (2015): 280–301.

Culpeper, Nicholas. *Galen's Art of Physick.* London, 1652.

Cuttica, Cesare. "Il primato della politica: Algernon Sidney commonwealthman." In *Ideali repubblicani in età moderna*, edited by Fiorella De Michelis Pintacuda and Gianni Francioni, 145–160. Pisa: ETS, 2002.

—. *Sir Robert Filmer (1588–1653) and the Patriotic Monarch: Patriarchalism in Seventeenth-Century Political Thought.* Manchester: Manchester University Press, 2013.

D'Amelio, Giuliana. *Illuminismo e scienza del diritto in Italia.* Milan: Giuffre, 1965.

Daniel, Samuel. *The Collection of the Historie of England.* London, 1618.

Darwin, Charles. *The Descent of Man and Selection in Relation to Sex.* London: Murray, 1871.

Dawson, Hannah. "The Normativity of Nature in Pufendorf and Locke." *Historical Journal*, Online First (2019).

The Defence of Innes Munro, Esq. London, 1790.

Delpiano, Patrizia. *Il governo della lettura. Chiesa e libri nell'Italia del Settecento.* Bologna: Il Mulino, 2007.

Dens, J. P. *Honnête homme et la critique du goût: Esthétique et société au XVIIe siècle.* Lexington: French Forum, 1981.

Dent, Nicholas. J. H. *A Rousseau Dictionary.* Oxford: Blackwell, 1992.
—. "Rousseau on amour-propre." *Supplement to the Transactions of the Aristotelian Society* 72 (1998): 57–73.
Der Sprach-Brockhaus: Deutsches Bilderwörterbuch für jedermann. Leipzig: Brockhaus, 1935.
Der Sprach-Brockhaus: Deutsches Bilderwörterbuch für jedermann. Wiesbaden: Brockhaus, 1958.
Der Sprach-Brockhaus: Deutsches Bilderwörterbuch. Wiesbaden: Brockhaus, 1972.
Desing, Anselmo. *Juris naurae larva detracta compluribus libris sub titulo juris naturae prodeuntibus, ut puffendorfianis, heineccianis, wolffianis & c.* 3 vols. Munich: 1753.
Desmond, Adrian, and James Moore, *Darwin's Sacred Cause: Race, Slavery, and the Quest for Human Origins.* Chicago: University of Chicago Press, 2011.
DeSouza, Nigel. "Herder's Theory of Organic Forces and its Kantian Origins." In *Kant and His Contemporaries*, edited by Corey Dyck and Daniel O. Dahlstrom, 109–130. Cambridge: Cambridge University Press, 2018.
Dew, Ben. *Commerce, Finance and Statecraft: Histories of England, 1600–1780.* Manchester: Manchester University Press, 2018.
Dierse, Ulrich. "Ideologie." In *Geschichtliche Grundbegriffe: Historisches Lexikon zur politisch-sozialen Sprache in Deutschland, Bd. 3 H*–Me, edited by Otto Brunner, Werner Conze, and Reinhart Koselleck, 131–169. Stuttgart: Klett-Cotta, 1982.
Dictionnaire de L'Académie Française. https://www.dictionnaire-academie.fr/article/A9I0063.
Dictionnaire géographique des Gaules et de la France. 6 vols. Paris: Desaint et Saillant 1762–1770.
Di Sciullo, Franco M. *Gestire l'indigenza. I poveri nel pensiero politico inglese da Locke a Malthus.* Roma: Aracne, 2013.
Domènech, Antoni. *El eclipse de la fraternidad. Una visión publica de la tradición socialista.* Barcelona: Critica, 2003.
Dreitzel, Horst. *Absolutismus und ständische Verfassung in Deutschland: Ein Beitrag zu Kontinuität und Diskontinuität der politischen Theorie in der frühen Neuzeit.* Mainz: von Zabern, 1992.
Dubichinskii, Vladimir. *Leksikografiya russkogo yazyka.* Moscow: Nauka, Flinta, 2008.
Duhovnaya ceremoniya proizvodivshayasya vo vremya vsevozhdelenneishago prisudstviya eya imperatorskago velichestva velikiya gosudaryni premudreishiya monarhini i popechitel'neishiya materi Ekateriny Vtoryya v Kazane. St. Petersburg: Pri Imperatorskoi Akademii nauk, 1769.
Dunn, John. "Individuality and Clientage in the Formation of Locke's Social Imagination." In John Dunn, *Rethinking Modern Political Theory: Essays 1979–83*, 13–33. Cambridge: Cambridge University Press, 1985.
—. "Justice and the Interpretation of Locke's Political Thought." *Political Studies* 16 (1968): 68–87.
—. *The Political Thought of John Locke.* Cambridge: Cambridge University Press, 1982.
Dupuis-Déri, Francis. "History of the Word 'Democracy' in Canada and Québec: A Political Analysis of Rhetorical Strategies." *World Political Science Review* 6 (2010): 1–23.
Edwards, G. Fay. "Reincarnation, Rationality, and Temperance: Platonists on not Eating Animals." In *Animals: A History*, edited by Peter Adamson and G. Fay Edwards, 27–55. Oxford: Oxford University Press, 2018.

Elliot, William Yandell. "Mussolini, Prophet of the Pragmatic Era in Politics." *Political Science Quarterly* 41 (1926): 161–192.
Encyclopédie, ou Dictionnaire raisonne des sciences, des arts et des métiers vols. 1–35. Paris, 1751–80.
Endelman, Todd M. *The Jews of Georgian England, 1714–1830: Tradition and Change in a Liberal Society.* Ann Arbor: University of Michigan Press, 1999.
Engelhardt, Ulrich. "Zum Begriff der Glückseligkeit in der kameralistischen Staatslehre des 18. Jahrhunderts (J. H. G von Justi)." *Zeitschrift für Historische Forschung* 8 (1981): 37–79.
Engin, Isin. *Being Political: Genealogies of Citizenship.* Minnesota: University of Minnesota Press, 2002.
Evrigenis, Ioannis D. *Images of Anarchy: The Rhetoric and Science in Hobbes's State of Nature.* Cambridge: Cambridge University Press, 2014.
Facchinei, Ferdinando. *Note e osservazioni sul libro intitolato Dei Delitti e Delle Pene.* Venice: Antonio Zatta, 1765.
Fainshtein, Mikhail Smilievich. *"I slavu Francii v Rossii prevzoiti": Rossiiskaya. akademiya* (1783–1841) i razvitie kul'tury i gumanitarnykh nauk. St. Petersburg: Dmitrii Bulanin, 2002.
Fassò, Guido. *Storia della filosofia del diritto.* vol. II. Bologna: Il Mulino, 1968.
Fieschi, Catherine and Paul Heywood. "Trust, Cynicism and Populist Anti-politics." *Journal of Political Ideologies* 9 (2004): 289–309.
Fiocchi Malaspina, Elisabetta. *L'eterno ritorno del Droit des gens di Emer de Vattel (sec XVIII-XIX). L'impatto sulla cultura giuridica in prospettiva globale.* Frankfurt am Main: Max Planck Institute, 2017.
Filmer, Robert. *Patriarcha or of The Natural Power of Kings.* London: Richard Chiswell, 1680.
Finetti, Joannis Francisci. *De principiis iuris naturae et gentium adversus Hobbesium Puffendorfium, Thomassium, Wolfium et alios.* 2 vols. Venice: Thomam Bettinelli, 1764.
Fiorillo, Vanda. "La 'Socialitas' nell'antropologia giuridica pufendorfiana." *Materiali per una Storia della Cultura Giuridica* 20 (1990): 479–495.
—. ed. *Samuel Pufendorf filosofo del Diritto e della Politica.* Naples: Città del Sole, 1996.
—. *Tra Egoismo e Socialità. Il Giusnaturalismo di Samuel Pufendorf.* Naples: Jovene, 1992.
Flourens, Marie-Jean-Pierre. "On the Natural History of Man." In *Race: The Origins of an Idea 1760–1850*, edited by Hannah Franziska Augstein, 181–187. Bristol: Thoemmes Press, 1996.
Force, Pierre, *Self-Interest before Adam Smith: A Genealogy of Economic Science.* Cambridge: Cambridge University Press, 2003.
—. "Self-Love, Identification, and the Origin of Political Economy." *Yale French Studies* 92 (1997): 46–64.
Forster, Georg. *A Voyage Round the World in His Britannic Majesty's Sloop, the Resolution, commanded by Capt. James Cook, during the Year 1772. 3, 4, and 5.* London: White, Robson, Elmsly and Robinson, 1777.
Forster, Johann Reinhold. *Observations Made during a Voyage round the World.* Edited by Nicholas Thomas, Harriet Guest and Michael Dettelbach. Honolulu: University of Hawaii Press, 1996.

Forster, Michael N. "Herder and Human Rights." In *Herder: Philosophy and Anthropology*, edited by Anik Waldow and Nigel DeSouza, 224–239. Oxford: Oxford University Press, 2017.

Foucault, Michel. *The Birth of Biopolitcs. Lectures at the Collège de France 1978–1979*. Translated by Graham Burchell. London: Palgrave Macmillan, 2008.

—. *Discipline and Punishment: The Birth of Prison*. Translated by Alan Sheridan. London: Allen Lane, Penguin, 1977.

—. *The Foucault Effect: Studies in Governmentality*. Edited by Graham Burchill, Colin Gordon, and Peter Miller. Chicago: University of Chicago Press, 1991.

—. *The History of Sexuality, Vol. I: An Introduction*. Translated by Robert Hurley. New York: Pantheon Books, 1978.

—. *Security, Territory, Population. Lectures at the Collège de France 1977–1978*. Translated by Graham Burchell and edited by Michael Senellart. London: Palgrave Macmillan, 2007.

—. *Society Must Be Defended. Lectures at the Collège de France 1975–1976*. Translated by David Macey. New York: Picador, 2003.

Foxe, John. *Actes and Monuments of Matters Most Speciall and Memorable, Happenyng in the Church*. London, 1583.

Foxley, Rachel. "From Native Rights to Natural Equality: The Agreement of the People (1647)." In *Revolutionary Moments: Reading Revolutionary Texts*, edited by Rachel Hammersley, 1–20. London: Bloomsbury Academic, 2015.

—. "John Lilburne and the Citizenship of 'Free-born Englishmen'." *The Historical Journal* 47 (2004): 849–874.

Frankel, Emil. "Present-Day Tendencies in the German Socialist Movement." *Journal of Political Economy* 33 (1925): 60–80.

Freeden, Michael. "After the Brexit Referendum: Revisiting Populism as an Ideology." *Journal of Political Ideologies* 22 (2017): 1–11.

—. *Ideologies and Political Theory: A Conceptual Approach*. Oxford: Clarendon Press, 1996).

—. "Ideology and Conceptual History: The Interrelationship between Method and Meaning." In *Political Concepts and Time: New Approaches to Conceptual History*, edited by Javier Fernández Sebastián, 73–100. Santander: Cantabria University Press, 2011.

—. *Ideology: A Very Short Introduction*. Oxford: Oxford University Press, 2003.

—. "The Resurgence of Ideology Studies: Twenty Years of the JPI." *Journal of Political Ideologies* 2 (2016): 1–8.

Freeden, Michael, Lyman Tower Sargent, and Marc Stears, eds. *The Oxford Handbook of Political Ideologies*. Oxford: Oxford University Press, 2013.

—. Preface to *The Oxford Handbook of Political Ideologies*, edited by Michael Freeden, Lyman Tower Sargent, and Marc Stears, v–vi. Oxford: Oxford University Press, 2013.

Friedrich, Carl Joachim. "Review of Sozialismus und Faschismus in Italien by Robert Michels." *The American Political Science Review* 22 (1928): 197–199.

Fudge, Erica. *Brutal Reasoning: Animals, Rationality, and Humanity in Early Modern England*. Ithaca: Cornell University Press, 2019.

Fuentes, Juan Francisco. "How Words Reshape the Past: The 'Old, Old Story' of Totalitarianism." *Politics, Religion & Ideology* 16 (2015): 282–297.

—. "Totalitarian Language: Creating Symbols to Destroy Words." *Contributions to the History of Concepts* 8 (2013): 45–66.

Gassendi, Pierre. *Opera Omnia*. Lyon, 1658.

Gauchet, Marcel. "De l'avènement de l'individu à la découverte de la société." *Annales E.S.C.* 34 (1979): 451–463.

Geertz, Clifford. "Ideology as a Cultural System." In *Ideology and Discontent*, edited by David E. Apter, 47–76. London: The Free Press of Glencoe, Collier-Macmillan, 1964.

Giglioni, Guido. "Life and Its Animal Boundaries: Ethical Implications in Early Modern Theories of Universal Animation." In *Ethical Perspectives on Animals in the Renaissance and Early Modern Period*, edited by Cecilia Muratori and Burkhard Dohm, 111–137. Florence: SISMEL edizioni del Galluzzo, 2013.

Gill, Michael B. "Moral Rationalism vs. Moral Sentimentalism: Is Morality More Like Math or Beauty?" *Philosophy Compass* 2 (2007): 16–30.

Glaser, Eliane. *Judaism without Jews: Philosemitism and Christian Polemic in Early-Modern England.* Basingstoke: Palgrave, 2007.

Gobetti, Daniela. "Sfera domestica e sfera politica nella riflessione del pensiero politico britannico del Settecento." *Annali della Fondazione Luigi Einaudi* 17 (1983): 291–332.

Goldenweiser, A. A. "Russia and the Socialists: A Protest and a Reply." *The North American Review* 206 (1917): 808–809.

Goldie, Peter. "Emotion, Feeling, and Knowledge of the World." In *Thinking About Feeling: Contemporary Philosophers on Emotions*, edited by Robert C. Solomon, 91–106. Oxford & New York: Oxford University Press, 2004.

Gooding, Nicholas, and Kinch Hoekstra. "Hobbes and Aristotle on the Foundation of Political Science." In *Hobbes's On the Citizen: A Critical Guide*, edited by Robin Douglass and Johan Olsthoorn, 31–50. Cambridge: Cambridge University Press, 2019.

Gramsci, Antonio. *Quaderni del Carcere. Vol. 1: Il Materialismo Storico e la Filosofia di Benedetto Croce.* Turin: Giulio Einaudi, 1966.

Grant, Ruth. "John Locke on Custom's Power and Reason's Authority." *Review of Politics* 74 (2012): 607–629.

Green, Thomas Hill. "Introductions to Hume's *Treatise of Human Nature.*" In *Works of Thomas Hill Green. Vol. 1*, edited by R. L. Nettleship, 1–371. London: Longmans, Green, and Co., 1885. Originally published in David Hume, *The Philosophical Works of David Hume. Vol. 1*, ed. T. H. Green & T. H. Grose (London: Longmans, Green, and Co., 1874).

Gross, Felix and Robert M. Maciver, eds. *European Ideologies: A Survey of 20th Century Political Ideas.* New York: Philosophical Library, 1948.

Grotius, Hugo. *Il diritto della guerra e della pace di Ugone Grozio colle note dello stesso autore, e di Giovanni Barbeyrac.* Translated by Antonio Porpora. Naples: Giuseppe de Dominicis: 1777.

—. *The Rights of War and Peace*, edited and with an Introduction by Richard Tuck, from the Edition by Jean Barbeyrac. Indianapolis: Liberty Fund, 2005.

Grunert, Frank. "Absolutism(s): Necessary Ambivalences in the Political Theory of Christian Wolff". *Tijdschrift voor Rechtsgeschiedenis* 73 (2005): 141–152.

—. "Die Objektivität des Glücks: Aspekte der Eudämonismus Diskussion in der deutschen Aufklärung". In *Aufklärung als praktische Philosophie: Werner Schneiders zum 65. Geburtstag*, edited by Frank Grunert and Friedrich Vollhardt, 351–368. Tübingen: De Gruyter, 1998.

—. "Vollkommenheit als (politische) Norm: Zur politischen Philosophie von Christian Wolff (1679–1754)". In *Politische Theorien des 17. und 18. Jahrhunderts: Staat und Politik in*

Deutschland, edited by Bernd Heidenreich and Gerhard Goehler, 164–184. Mainz: von Zabern, 2011.

Guerrini, Anita. "A Diet for a Sensitive Soul: Vegetarianism in Eighteenth-Century Britain." *Eighteenth-Century Life* 23 (1999): 34–42.

Guion, Béatrice. "The Fable of the bees: proles sine matre?" In *Bernard de Mandeville's Tropology of Paradoxes. Morals, Politics, Economics, and Therapy*, edited by Edmundo Balsemão Pires and Joaquim Braga, 91–104. Cham: Springer, 2015.

—. "Du traité des passions à l'art de se connaître soi-même: l'écrit moral au XVIIe siècle." In *L'Homme et ses Passions, Actes du XVIIe Congrès international de l'Association Guillaume Budé*, edited by Isabelle Boehm, Jean-Louis Ferrary et Sylvie Franchet d'Espèrey, 643–654. Paris: Les Belles Lettres, 2016.

—. *Pierre Nicole, moraliste.* Paris: Honoré Champion, 2002.

Gunnell, John G. "Interpretation and the History of Political Theory: Apology and Epistemology." *American Political Science Review* 76 (1982): 317–327.

Guthrie, William. *A Generaal History of England.* 3 vols. London, 1744–1751.

Guyer, Paul. "The Crooked Timber of Mankind." In *Kant's* Idea for a Universal History with a Cosmopolitan Aim: *A Critical Guide*, edited by Amélie Oksenberg Rorty and James Schmidt, 129–149. Cambridge: Cambridge University Press, 2009.

—. *Kant on Freedom, Law, and Happiness.* Cambridge: Cambridge University Press, 2000.

Gventsadze, Veronica. "Aristotelian Influences in Gassendi's Moral Philosophy." *Journal of the History of Philosophy* 45 (2007): 223–242.

Haakonssen, Knud. "German Natural Law." In *The Cambridge History of Eighteenth-Century Political Thought*, edited by Mark Goldie and Robert Wokler, 251–290. Cambridge: Cambridge University Press, 2006.

—. *Natural Law and Moral Philosophy: from Grotius to the Scottish Enlightenment.* Cambridge: Cambridge University Press, 1996.

Haara, Heikki. *Pufendorf's Theory of Sociability: Passions, Habits and Social Order.* Cham: Springer, 2018.

Haara, Heikki, and Aino Lahdenranta. "Smithian Sentimentalism Anticipated: Pufendorf on the Desire for Esteem and Moral Conduct." *Journal of Scottish Philosophy* 16 (2018): 19–37.

Haara, Heikki, and Tim Stuart-Buttle. "Beyond Justice: Pufendorf and Locke on the Desire for Esteem." *Political Theory* 47 (2019): 699–723.

Hartley, L. P. *The Go-Between.* Edited by Douglas Brooks-Davies. London: Penguin, 2004.

Hayes, Carlton J. H. "The Challenge of Totalitarianism." *The Public Opinion Quarterly* 2 (1938): 21–26.

Hedesan, Georgiana. *An Alchemical Quest for Universal Knowledge: The "Christian Philosophy" of Jan Baptist van Helmont (1579–1644).* London: Routledge, 2016.

Heilbron, Johan. "French Moralists and the Anthropology of the Modern Era." In *The Rise of the Social Sciences and the Formation of Modernity: Conceptual Change in Context, 1750–1850*, edited by Johan Heilbron, Lars Magnusson and Björn Wittrock, 77–106. Dordrecht: Springer, 1998.

Heinz, Marion. "Sympathie. Zur Palingenesie stoischen Denkens in Herders *Kalligone.*" In *Herder on Empathy and Sympathy/ Einfühlung und Sympathie im Denken Herders*, edited by Eva Piirimäe, Liina Lukas, and Johannes Schmidt. Leiden: Brill, forthcoming.

van Helmont, Jan Baptista. *Van Helmont's Works: Containing His Most Excellent Philosophy, Physick, Chirurgery, Anatomy.* Translated by J. Chandler. London, 1664.

Henry, Robert. *The History of Great Britain.* 6 vols. London, 1771–1793.

Herder, Johann Gottfried. *Briefe. Gesamtausgabe.* Edited by Wilhelm Dobbek and Günter Arnold. 8 vols. Weimar: Hermann Böhlaus Nachfolger, 1977–2016.

—. *J. G. Herder on Social and Political Culture.* Translated and edited by F. M. Barnard. Cambridge: Cambridge University Press, 1969.

—. *Herders Sämmtliche Werke* 13. Edited by Bernhard Suphan. Berlin, 1887.

—. *Outlines of a Philosophy of History of Man.* Translated by T. Churchill. London, 1800.

—. *Werke in zehn Bänden.* Edited by Jürgen Brummack and Martin Bollacher. 10 vols. Frankfurt am Main: Deutscher Klassiker Verlag, 1985–2000.

—. *Werke.* Vol. 3/1. Edited by Wolfgang Proß. Munich, Vienna: Carl Hanser Verlag, 2002.

Herman, Barbara. "The Practice of Moral Judgment." *The Journal of Philosophy* 82 (1985): 414–436.

Hill, Christopher. *The Century of Revolution 1603–1714.* New York: Norton & Company, 1961.

—. *Change and Continuity in Seventeenth-Century England.* London: Weidenfeld and Nicolson, 1974.

Hill, Roscoe R. "Review of Latin America: Its Rise and Progress, by F. Garcia Calderon." *Political Science Quarterly* 28 (1913): 700–703.

Hilson, M. "Consumer Co-operation and Economic Crisis: The 1936 Roosevelt Inquiry on Co-operative Enterprise and the Emergence of the Nordic 'Middle Way.'" *Contemporary European History* 22 (2013): 181–198.

Hirschman, Albert O. *The Passions and the Interests.* Princeton, NJ: Princeton University Press, 1977.

Hobbes, Thomas. *Leviathan.* Edited by Noel Malcolm. 3 vols. Oxford: Oxford University Press, 2012.

—. *Leviathan.* Harmondsworth: Penguin, 1981.

—. *On the Citizen.* Edited by Richard Tuck and translated by Michael Silverthorne. Cambridge: Cambridge University Press, 1998.

Hobhouse, L. T. *Liberalism.* London: Oxford University Press, 1911.

Hochstrasser, Tim J. "Conscience and Reason: the Natural Law Theory of Jean Barbeyrac." *The Historical Journal* 36 (1993): 289–308.

—. *Natural Law Theories In The Early Enlightenment.* Cambridge: Cambridge University Press, 2000.

Hoekstra, Kinch. "Hobbesian Equality." In *Hobbes Today: Insights for the 21st Century,* edited by S. A. Lloyd, 76–112. Cambridge: Cambridge University Press, 2012.

Hofstadter, Richard. *The Age of Reform: From Bryan to F. D. R.* New York: Vintage Books, 1955.

Holinshed, Raphael. *The First and Second Volumes of the Chronicles.* 3 vols. London, 1587.

—. *The First Volume of the Chronicles of England, Scotlande, and Irelande.* 2 vols. London, 1577.

Home, Henry, Lord Kames. *Sketches on the History of Man.* Edited by James A. Harris. Indianapolis: Liberty Fund, 2007.

Honneth, Axel. *Anerkennung: Eine europäische Ideensgeschichte.* Berlin: Suhrkamp, 2018.

—. *The Struggle for Recognition: The Moral Grammar of Social Conflicts.* Translated by Joel Anderson. Cambridge: Polity Press, 1995.

Hont, István. *Jealousy of Trade: International Competition and the Nation-State in Historical Perspective.* Cambridge, MA: Harvard University Press, 2005.
—. *Istvan Hont Papers, Special Collections.* University of St Andrews, St Andrews.
—. *Politics in Commercial Society: Jean Jacques Rousseau and Adam Smith*, edited by Béla Kapossy and Michael Sonenscher. Cambridge, MA: Harvard University Press, 2015.
Hume, David. *An Enquiry Concerning the Principle of Morals.* Edited by Jerome B. Schneewind. Indianapolis, NJ: Hackett, 1983.
—. *Essays, Moral, Political and Literary.* Edited by Eugene F. Miller. Indianapolis, IN: Liberty Fund, 1985.
—. *The History of England.* 6 vols. Indianapolis, IN: Liberty Fund, 1985.
—. *The Letters of David Hume.* Vol. 1. Edited by J. Y. T. Graig. Oxford: Clarendon Press, 1932.
—. *A Treatise of Human Nature.* Edited by David F. Norton and Mary J. Norton. Oxford: Clarendon Press, 2007.
—. *A Treatise of Human Nature.* Edited by L. A. Selby-Bigge. 2nd. ed., revised by P. H. Nidditch. Oxford: Oxford University Press, 1978.
Hunter, Ian. *Rival Enlightenments: Civil and Metaphysical Philosophy in Early Modern Germany.* Cambridge: Cambridge University Press, 2009.
Huscroft, Richard. *Expulsion: England's Jewish Solution: Edward I and the Jews.* Stroud: Tempus, 2006.
Hutcheson, Francis. *Collected Works of Francis Hutcheson, Volume 5: A System of Moral Philosophy (1755)*, facsimile edition prepared by Bernhard Fabian. Hildesheim: Georg Olms Verlag, 1990.
—. *An Essay on the Nature and Conduct of the Passions and Affections, with Illustrations on the Moral Sense.* Edited by Aaron Garrett. Indianapolis, IN: Liberty Fund 2002.
—. *An Inquiry into the Original of Our Ideas of Beauty and Virtue.* Edited by Wolfgang Leidhold. Indianapolis, IN: Liberty Fund 2008.
"ideologi." In *Svenska Akademiens Ordbok* https://www.saob.se/artikel/?seek=ideologi&pz=1#U_I1_89220.
"ideology, n.." In *Oxford English Dictionary.* Oxford: Oxford University Press, https://oed.com/view/Entry/91016?redirectedFrom=ideology.
Ihalainen, Pasi. *Agents of the People: Democracy and Popular Sovereignty in British and Swedish Parliamentary and Public Debates, 1734–1800.* New York: Berghahn Books, 2010.
Infelise, Mario. *L'editoria veneziana nel 700'.* Milan: Franco Angeli, 1989.
Ionescu, Ghita, and Ernest Gellner. *Populism: Its Meanings and National Characteristics.* London: Weidenfeld and Nicolson, 1969.
Israel, Jonathan. *European Jewry in the Age of Mercantilism, 1550–1750.* Oxford: Clarendon Press, 1985.
Jack, Malcolm. *Corruption and Progress: The Eighteenth-Century Debate.* New York: AMS Press, 1989.
James, E. D. *Pierre Nicole, Jansenist and Humanist: A Study of his Thought.* The Hague: Martinus Nijhoff, 1981.
Jardine, Lisa, and Anthony Grafton. "'Studied for Action': How Gabriel Harvey Read His Livy." *Past & Present* 129 (1990): 30–78.
Jensen, Henning. "Hume on Moral Agreement." *Mind* 86 (1977): 497–513.

—. *Motivation and the Moral Sense in Francis Hutcheson's Ethical Theory.* The Hague: Martinus Nijhoff, 1971.

Jones, Campbell. "The Meanings of Work in John Locke." In *History of Economic Rationalities: Economic Reasoning as Knowledge and Practice Authority*, edited by Jakob Bek-Thomsen et al., 51–62. Cham: Springer, 2017.

Jones, Peter. "Another Look at Hume's Views of Aesthetic and Moral Judgments." *Philosophical Quarterly* 20 (1970): 53–59.

Joy, Lynn. *Gassendi, the Atomist: Advocate of History in the Age of Science.* Cambridge: Cambridge University Press, 1987.

Jungkuntz, Richard. "Fathers, Heretics and Epicureans." *The Journal of Ecclesiastical History* 17 (1966): 3–10.

von Justi, Johann Heinrich Gottlob. "Betrachtungen über die Monarchien und Aristocratien." In *Gesammelte Politische und Finanzschriften über wichtige Gegenstände der Staatskunst, der Kriegswissenschaften und des Cameral- und Finanzwesens*, 3. vols., Vol. 2: 176–190. Copenhagen: Rothe, 1761–1764.

—. "Gedanken von dem Ursprunge der Monarchien und Aristocratien". In *Gesammelte Politische und Finanzschriften über wichtige Gegenstände der Staatskunst, der Kriegswissenschaften und des Cameral- und Finanzwesens*, 3. vols., Vol. 2: 190–196. Copenhagen: Rothe, 1761–1764.

—. *Natur und Wesen der Staaten als die Quelle aller Regierungswissenschaften und Gesetze.* Mittau: Haude und Spener, [1760] 1771.

Jäger, Anton. "The Semantic Drift: Images of Populism in Post-War American Historiography and Their Relevance for (European) Political Science." *Constellations* 24 (2017): 310–323.

Kail, P. J. E. "Hutcheson's Moral Sense: Skepticism, Realism, and Secondary Qualities." *History of Philosophy Quarterly* 18 (2001): 57–77.

Kant, Immanuel. *History, and Education.* Edited by Günter Zöller and Robert B. Louden. Cambridge: Cambridge University Press, 2007.

—. *Political Writings.* Edited by H. P. Reiss. Cambridge: Cambridge University Press, 1996.

—. *Practical Philosophy.* Translated and edited by Mary J. Gregor. Cambridge: Cambridge University Press, 1999.

—. "Über den Gemeinspruch: Das mag in der Theorie richtig sein, taugt aber nicht für die Praxis (1793)." In *Akademie Ausgabe von Immanuel Kants Gesammelten Werken, Bd. 8* (Abhandlungen nach 1781). https://korpora.zim.uni-duisburg-essen.de/kant/aa08/290.html.

Kapust, Daniel J. *That Glib and Oily Art: Flattery and the History of Political Thought.* Cambridge: Cambridge University Press, 2018.

Karp, Jonathan. *The Politics of Jewish Commerce: Economic Thought and Emancipation in Europe, 1638–1848.* Cambridge: Cambridge University Press, 2008.

Katz, David M. *The Jews in the History of England, 1485–1850.* Oxford: Clarendon Press, 1994.

Kaufman, Alexander. *Welfare in the Kantian State.* Oxford: Oxford University Press, 1999.

Keane, John. "On the 'New' History: Quentin Skinner's Proposal for a New History of Political Ideology." *Telos* 47 (1981): 174–183.

Keighren, Innes M. "Circulating Seditious Knowledge: The 'Daring Absurdities, Studied Misrepresentations, and Abominable Falsehoods' of William Macintosh." In *Mobilities of*

Knowledge, edited by Heike Jöns, Peter Meusburger, and Michael Heffernan, 67–84. Cham: Springer, 2017.

Keller, Vera. *Knowledge and the Public Interest, 1575–1725*. Cambridge: Cambridge University Press, 2015.

Kendall, Willmore. *Locke and the Doctrine of Majority-Rule*. Champaign: University of Illinois Press, 1960.

Kennedy, Emmet. "'Ideology' from Destutt de Tracy to Marx." *Journal of the History of Ideas* 40 (1979): 353–368.

Kidd, Colin. "Europe, what Europe?" *London Review of Books* 30 (2008): 16–17.

Kirilov, Ivan Kirillovich. *Atlas Vserossiiskoi imperii*. St. Petersburg, 1731.

Kleingeld, Pauline. *Kant and Cosmopolitanism: The Philosophical Ideal of the World Citizenship*. Cambridge: Cambridge University Press, 2013.

Klippel, Diethelm. "Der liberale Interventionsstaat: Staatszweck und Staatstätigkeit in der deutschen politischen Theorie des 18. und der ersten Hälfte des 19. Jahrhunderts." In *Recht und Rechtswissenschaft im mitteldeutschen Raum*, edited by Heiner Lück, 77–103. Köln: Böhlau, 1998.

—. "Reasonable Aims of Civil Society: Concerns of the State in German Political Theory in the Eighteenth and Early Nineteenth Centuries." In *Rethinking Leviathan: The Eighteenth-Century State in Britain and Germany*, edited by John Brewer and Eckhart Hellmuth, 71–98. Oxford: Oxford University Press, 1999.

Klippel, Diethelm, and Martin Fuhrmann. "Der Staat und die Staatstheorie des aufgeklärten Absolutismus." In *Der aufgeklärte Absolutismus im europäischen Vergleich*, edited by Helmut Reinalter and Harm Klueting, 223–243. Wien: Böhlau, 2002.

Knight, Kathleen. "Transformations of the Concept of Ideology in the Twentieth Century." *American Political Science Review* 100 (2006): 619–626.

Kohn, Hans. *Political Ideologies of the Twentieth Century*. New York, Harper Torchbooks, 1967.

Koikkalainen, Petri, and Sami Syrjämäki. "Quentin Skinner On Encountering the Past." *Finnish Yearbook of Political Thought* 6 (2002): 34–63.

Kontler, László. "William Robertson and His German Audience on European and Non-European Civilizations." *The Scottish Historical Review* 80 (2001): 63–89.

Kontler, László, and Mark Somos, Ed. *Trust and Happiness in the History of European Political Thought*. Leiden: Brill, 2018.

Kopievskij, Ilya Fedodrovich. *Latina grammatica in usum scholarum celeberrimae gentis Sclavonico-Rosseanae adornata*. Amsterdam, 1700.

—. *Latinorossiiskaya i nemeckaya slovesnaya kniga*. St. Petersburg, 1732.

—. *Vokabuly ili rechi na slavenskom, nemeckom i latinskom yazykah*. St. Petersburg, 1718.

Korkman, Petter. "Civil Sovereign and the King of Kings: Barbeyrac and the Creator's Right to Rule." In *Natural Law and Civil Sovereignty: Moral Right and State Authority in Early Modern Political Thought*, edited by Ian Hunter and David Saunders, 109–122. London: Palgrave Macmillan, 2002.

—. "Voluntarism and Moral Obligation: Barbeyrac's Defence of *Pufendorf* Revisited." In *Early Modern Natural Law Theories: Contexts and Strategies in the Early Enlightenment*, edited by Tim J. Hochstrasser and Peter Schröder, 195–225. Dordrecht: Kluwer Academic Publisher, 2003.

Koselleck, Reinhardt. "Einleitung." In *Geschichtliche Grundbegriffe. Historisches Lexikon zur politisch-sozialen Sprache in Deutschland. Band 1*, edited by Otto Brunner, Werner Conze and Reinhart Koselleck, xiii–xxvii; Stuttgart: Klett-Cotta, 1972.

—. "Introduction and Prefaces to the *Geschichtliche Grundbegriffe.*" *Contributions to the History of Concepts* 6 (2011): 1–37.

—. *Zeitschichten: Studien zur Historik.* Frankfurt: Suhrkamp, 2003.

Kurganov, Nikolaii Gavrilovich. "Slovar raznoyazychnyi, ili tolkovanie evreiskih, grecheskih, latinskih, francuzskih, nemeckih i prochih inozemskih upotreblyaemyh v russkom yazyke i nekotoryh slavyanskih yazykah slov (Russkii slovotolk)". In *Rossiiskaya universal'naya grammatika, ili vseobshee pis'moslovie.* St. Petersburg: Morskoi kadetskii korpus, 1769.

Kurunmäki, Jussi. "Democracy both Young and Old: Finland, Sweden and the Interwar Crisis of Democracy." *Journal of Modern European History* 17 (2019): 1–14.

Kurunmäki, Jussi, and Jani Marjanen. "Isms, Ideologies and Setting the Agenda for Public Debate." *Journal of Political Ideologies* 23 (2018): 256–282.

—. "A Rhetorical View of Isms: An Introduction." *Journal of Political Ideologies* 23 (2018): 241–255.

Kuznetsova, Irina. "Ob istochnike Nomenklatora na russkom, latinskom i nemeckom yazyke Il'i Kopievskogo". In *Materialy chtenii, posvyashennyh pamyati professora Iosifa Moiseevicha Tronskogo.* St. Petersburg: Nauka. 2009.

Labriola, Giulia Maria. *Barbeyrac interprete di Pufendorf e Grozio.* Naples: Editoriale Scientifica, 2003.

Las Casas, Bartolomé de. *A Brief Account of the Destruction of the Indies*, Project Gutenberg EBook edition (2007), http://www-personal.umich.edu/~twod/latam-s2010/read/las_casasb2032120321-8.pdf.

La Jallé, Éléonore. "Hume, Malebranche, and the Self-Justification of the Passions." *Hume Studies* 38 (2012): 201–220.

Landi, Sandro. *Il governo delle opinioni. Censura e formazione del consenso nella Toscana del Settecento.* Bologna: Il Mulino, 2000.

Larrain, Jorge. *The Concept of Ideology.* London: Hutchinson, 1979.

Laslett, Peter. *Preliminary Study to the Two Treatises.* Cambridge: Cambridge University Press, 1988.

Leclerc, Georges-Louis, Comte de Buffon. "From *A Natural History, General and Particular.*" In *Race and the Enlightenment: A Reader*, edited by Emmanuel Chukwudi Eze, 15–29. Oxford: Blackwell, 1997.

Leerssen, Joep. *National Thought in Europe: A Cultural History.* Amsterdam: Amsterdam University Press, 2006.

Leopold, David. "Marxism and Ideology: From Marx to Althusser." In *The Oxford Handbook of Political Ideologies*, edited by Michael Freeden, Lyman Tower Sargent, and Marc Stears, 493–512. Oxford: Oxford University Press, 2013.

Leslie, Margaret. "In Defence of Anachronism." *Political Studies*, 18 (1970): 433–470.

Levitin, Dmitri. *Ancient Wisdom in the Age of the New Science: Histories of Philosophy in England, c. 1640–1700.* Cambridge: Cambridge University Press, 2015.

Lewisohn, Ludwig. "The New Meaning of Revolution." *The North American Review* 238 (1934): 210–218.

Liebersohn, Harry. *The Traveler's World: Europe to the Pacific.* Cambridge, MA: Harvard University Press, 2006.

Linguarum totius orbis vocabularia comparativa: augustissimae cura collecta. Sectionis primae, linguas Europae et Asiae. Petropoli, 1786–1789.

von Linné, Carl. "*Homo* in *The System of Nature.*" In *Race and the Enlightenment: A Reader*, edited by Emmanuel Chukwudi Eze, 10–13. Oxford: Blackwell, 1997.

Lipset, Seymour Martin. *Political Man: The Social Bases of Politics*. New York: Doubleday & Co., 1960.

Lloyd, S. A. "Coercion, Ideology, and Education in Hobbes's *Leviathan.*" In *Reclaiming the History of Ethics: Essays for John Rawls*, edited by Andrews Reath, Barbara Herman, and Christine M. Korsgaard, 32–65. Cambridge: Cambridge University Press, 1997.

Locke, John. *The Correspondence of John Locke*. Edited by E. S. de Beer. 8 vols. Oxford: Clarendon Press, 1976–1989.

—. *An Essay Concerning Human Understanding*. Edited by Peter H. Nidditch. Oxford: Oxford University Press, 1975.

—. *John Locke: Political Writings*. Edited by David Wootton. Indianapolis, IN: Hackett Publishing Company, 2003.

—. *La ragionevolezza del cristianesimo*. Edited by Alfredo Sabetti. Florence: La Nuova Italia, 1976.

—. *A Letter concerning Toleration*. Edited by Mark Goldie. Indianapolis, IN: Liberty Fund, 2010.

—. *MS Locke*. Bodleian Library, Oxford.

—. *Saggio sull'intelletto umano*. Translated and edited M. G. D'Amico and V. Cicero. Milan: Bompiani, 2007.

—. *Second Treatise of Government*. Edited by C. B. Macpherson. Indianapolis, IN: Hackett Publishing Company, 1980.

—. *Some Thoughts concerning Education*. Edited by John W. Yolton and Jean S. Yolton. Oxford: Clarendon Press, 1989.

—. *Two Treatises of Government and a Letter on Toleration*. Edited by Ian Shapiro. New Haven and London: Yale University Press, 2003.

—. *Two Treatises of Government*. Edited by Peter Laslett. Cambridge: Cambridge University Press, 1988.

—. *Two treatises of government: in the former, the false principles and foundation of Sir Robert Filmer and his followers are detected and overthrown, the latter is an essay concerning the true original, extent, and end of civil government*. London: Awnsham Churchill, 1690.

—. *The Works of John Locke in Nine Volumes*. Aalen: Scientia Verlag, 1963.

Loewenstein, Karl. "Militant Democracy and Fundamental Rights, I." *The American Political Science Review* 31 (1937): 417–432.

Lolordo, Antonia. *Pierre Gassendi and the Birth of Early Modern Philosophy*. Cambridge: Cambridge University Press, 2007.

Louden, Robert B. "Cosmopolitan Unity: The Final Destiny of the Human Species." In *Kant's Lectures on Anthropology: A Critical Guide*, edited by Alix Cohen, 211–229. Cambridge: Cambridge University Press, 2014.

—. *Kant's Human Being: Essays on his Theory of Human Nature*. Oxford: Oxford University Press, 2011.

Lovejoy, Arthur. *Reflections on Human Nature*. Baltimore, MD: The Johns Hopkins University Press, 1961.

Lucretius, *De rerum natura*. Translated and edited by W. H. D Rouse and Martin F. Smith. Cambridge, MA: Harvard University Press, 1982.

Luna-Fabritius, Adriana. "Providence and Uses of Grotian Strategies in Neapolitan Political Thought 1650–1750." In *Sacred Polities*, edited by Hans Blom. Leiden: Brill, forthcoming.

—. "The Secularisation of Happiness in Early Eighteenth-century Italian Political Thought: Revisiting the Foundations of Civil Society.' In *Trust and Happiness in the History of European Political Thought*, edited by László Kontler and Mark Somos, 169–195. Leiden: Brill, 2017.

—. "Visions of Sociability in Early Modern Neapolitan Political Thought." In *Processes of Enlightenment – Essays in Honour of Hans Erich Bödeker*, edited by Jonas Gerlings, Ere Nokkala, and Martin van Gelderen. Liverpool: Liverpool University Press, forthcoming.

Luna González, Adriana. "*From Self-preservation to Self-liking in Paolo Mattia Doria: Civil Philosophy and Natural Jurisprudence in the Early Italian Enlightenment.*" PhD diss., European University Institute, 2009.

MacDonald, J. Ramsay. *Socialism and Society.* London: Independent Labour Party, 1908.

Macintosh, William. *Travels in Europe, Asia, and Africa: describing characters, customs, manners, laws, and productions of nature and art: containing various remarks on the political and commercial interests of Great Britain; and delineating in particular, a new system for the government and improvement of the British settlements in the East Indies: begun in the year 1777, and finished in 1781.* London, 1782.

MacIver, Robert M. "Introduction." In *European Ideologies: A Survey of 20th Century Political Ideas*, edited by Felix Gross, xiii–xv. New York: Philosophical Library, 1948.

Macpherson, Crawford Brough. *The Political Theory of Possessive Individualism: Hobbes to Locke.* Oxford: Oxford University Press, 1962.

Madox, Thomas. *The History and Antiquities of the Exchequer of the Kings of England, in two periods.* London, 1711.

Mahlberg, Gaby. "Patriarchalism and the Monarchical Republics." In *Monarchism and Absolutism in Early Modern Europe*, edited by Cesare Cuttica and Glenn Burgess, 47–60. London: Routledge, 2012.

Maksimovich, Lev Maksimovich. *Novyi i polnyi geograficheskii slovar' Rossiiskago gosudarstva.* St. Petersburg 1788–1789.

Malebranche, Nicolas. *The Search after Truth.* Edited and translated by Thomas M. Lennon and Paul J. Olscamp. Cambridge: Cambridge University Press, 1997.

Maliks, Reidar. *Kant's Politics in Context.* Oxford: Oxford University Press, 2014.

Mancini, Oliviero. "Diritto naturale e potere civile in Samuel Pufendorf." In *Il Contratto Sociale nella Filosofía Politica Moderna*, edited by Giuseppe Duso, 109–148. Bologna: Il Mulino 1987.

Mandrik, M. V. "Lavrenti Lavrentyevich Blyumentrost." In *Aktual'noe proshloe: vzaimodejstvie i balans interesov Akademii nauk i Rossijskogo gosudarstva v XVIII – nachale XX v.*, Part 1., edited by I. V. Tunkina. St. Petersburg: Renome, 2018.

Mann, Nicholas. "The Origins of Humanism." In *Cambridge Companion to Renaissance Humanism*, edited by Jill Kraye, 1–19. Cambridge: Cambridge University Press, 1996.

Manning, Brian. *The English People and the English Revolution. 1640–1649.* London: Heineman Educational Books, 1976.

Mantena, Karuna, "On Gandhi's Critique of the State: Sources, Contexts, Conjunctures." *Modern Intellectual History* 9 (2012): 535–63.
Marshall, John. *John Locke: Resistance, Religion and Responsibility.* Cambridge: Cambridge University Press, 1994.
Marshall, Thomas Humphrey. *Citizenship and Social Class.* Cambridge: Cambridge University Press, 1950.
Mastellone, Salvo. "Parole introduttive." In *La recezione di Grozio a Napoli nel Settecento*, edited by Vittorio Conti, 7–12. Florence: Centro Editoriale Toscano, 2002.
Matthew of Paris, *Chronicles of Matthew Paris: Monastic Life in the Thirteenth Century.* Edited and translated by Richard Vaughan. Gloucester: Alan Sutton, 1984.
—. *English History: from the Year 1235 to 1273.* 3 vols. Translated by J. A. Giles. London: Henry G. Bohn, 1847.
McColley, Diane Kelsey. *Poetry and Ecology in the Age of Milton and Marvell.* Aldershot: Ashgate, 2007.
McMahon, Darrin M., and Samuel Moyn. "Introduction: Interim Intellectual History." In *Rethinking Modern European Intellectual History*, edited by Darrin M. McMahon and Samuel Moyn, 3–12. Oxford: Oxford University Press, 2014.
Mehta, Uday Singh. *The Anxiety of Freedom: Imagination and Individuality in Locke's Political Thought.* Ithaca, NY: Cornell University Press, 1992.
Meiksins-Wood, Ellen. *Liberty and Property. A Social History of Western Political Thought from Renaissance to Enlightenment.* New York: Verso, 2012.
Menache, Sophia. "Faith, Myth, and Politics: The Stereotype of the Jews and Their Expulsion from England and France." *The Jewish Quarterly Review* 75 (1985): 351–374.
—. "Matthew Paris's Attitudes toward Anglo-Jewry." *Journal of Medieval History* 23 (1997): 139–162.
Mendelssohn, Moses. *Morgenstunden oder Vorlesungen über das Daseyn Gottes.* Berlin: Voß, 1785.
Mennell, Nicole. "'The Dignity of Mankind': Edward Tyson's *Anatomy of a Pygmie* and the Ape-Man Boundary." In *Seeing Animals after Derrida*, edited by Sarah Bezan and James Tink, 87–106. New York: Lexington Books, 2018.
Merton, Robert K. "The Sociology of Knowledge." *Isis* 27 (1937): 493–503.
Michel, Jean-Baptiste et al. "Quantitative Analysis of Culture Using Millions of Digitized Books." *Science* 331 (2011): 176–182.
Mikkeli, Heikki. *Hygiene in the Early Modern Medical Tradition.* Helsinki: Academia Scientiarum Fennica, 1999.
Mikkonen, Kai. *Narrative Paths: African Travel in Modern Fiction and Nonfiction.* Columbus: The Ohio State University Press, 2015.
Minogue, Kenneth. "Method in Intellectual History: Quentin Skinner's *Foundations*." In *Meaning and Context: Quentin Skinner and his Critics*, edited by James Tully, 176–193, Princeton, NJ: Princeton University Press, 1988.
Miqueu, Christophe. *Spinoza, Locke et l'idée de citoyenneté, une génération républicaine à l'aube des Lumières.* Parigi: Classique Garnier, 2012.
della Mirandola, Giovanni Pico. *On the Dignity of Man: On Being and the One: Heptaplus.* Translated by Charles Glenn Wallis, Paul J. W. Miller, and Douglas Carmichael. Indianapolis, IN: Hackett, 1998.

Mitchell, Joshua. "Hobbes and the Equality of the All under the One." *Political Theory* 21 (1993): 78–100.

Modèle du vocabulaire qui doit servir à la comparaison de toutes les langues. St. Petersburg, 1785.

Moggach, Douglas. "Freedom and Perfection: German Debates on the State in the Eighteenth Century." *Canadian Journal of Political Science* 42 (2009): 1003–1023.

Montaigne, Michel de. *The Complete Essays.* Translated by Donald M. Frame. Stanford: Stanford University Press, 1958.

Moore, James and Michael Silverthorne. "Gershom Carmichael and the Natural Jurisprudence Tradition in Eighteenth-Century Scotland." *Man and Nature. L'Homme et la Nature* 1 (1982): 41–53.

Morgan, Edmund S. *Inventing the People: The Rise of Popular Sovereignty in England and America.* New York: Norton and Company, 1988.

Morelli di Schönfeld, Carlo. *Istoria della Contea di Gorizia.* Gorizia: Tipografia Paternolli, 1856.

Mori, Massimo. "Giusnaturalismo e Crisi dell'Ordine Naturale." *Rivista di Filosofia 77* (1986): 7–40.

Moriarty, Michael. *Fallen Nature, Fallen Selves. Early Modern French Thought II.* Oxford: Oxford University Press, 2006.

Moyn, Samuel. "Afterword. The Self-Evidence of Human Rights." In *Self-Evident Truths? Human Rights and the Enlightenment*, edited by Kate Tunstall, 249–262. New York: Bloomsbury, 2012.

—. "Imperialism, Self-Determination, and the Rise of Human Rights." In *The Human Rights Revolution: An International History*, edited by Akira Iriye, Petra Goedde, and William I. Hitchcock, 159–178. Oxford: Oxford University Press, 2012.

—. *The Last Utopia: Human Rights in History.* Cambridge, MA: Belknap Press of Harvard University Press, 2010.

Mudde, Cas, and Cristóbal Rovira Kaltwasser. "Populism." In *The Oxford Handbook of Political Ideologies*, edited by Michael Freeden, Lyman Tower Sargent, and Marc. Stears, 493–512. Oxford: Oxford University Press, 2013.

Mundill, Robin R. *The King's Jews: Money, Massacre and Exodus in Medieval England.* London: Continuum, 2010.

Muratori, Cecilia. "Animals in the Renaissance." In *Animals: A History*, edited by Peter Adamson and G. Fay Edwards, 163–186. Oxford: Oxford University Press, 2018.

Muratori, Ludovico Antonio. *Opere.* Edited by Giorgio Falco and Fiorenzo Forti. Milan and Naples: Ricciardi, 1964.

Murray, James H., ed. *A new English dictionary on historical principles; founded mainly on the materials collected by the Philological society, Vol. 5: H to K.* Oxford: Clarendon Press, 1901.

Muthu, Sankar. "Conquest, Commerce, and Cosmopolitanism in Enlightenment Political Thought." In *Empire and Modern Political Thought*, edited by Sankar Muthu, 199–231. Cambridge: Cambridge University Press, 2012.

Nechtman, Tillman W. *Nabobs: Empire and Identity in Eighteenth-Century Britain.* Cambridge: Cambridge University Press, 2010.

Neuhouser, Frederick. "Rousseau on the Relation between Reason and Self-Love (amour-propre)." *Internationales Jahrbuch des Deutschen Idealismus* 1 (2003): 221–239.

—. *Rousseau's Theodicy of Self-Love: Evil, Rationality, and the Drive for Recognition.* Oxford: Oxford University Press, 2008.

Nevskaia, Nina., ed. *Letopis' Rossijskoi Akademii nauk.* St. Petersburg: Nauka, 2000.

Nicole, Pierre. *Essais de morale [Document électronique]: contenus en divers traittez sur plusieurs devoirs importans.* Reprod. de l'éd. de, Paris: G. Desprez, 1701, 1997.

—. *Moral essays, contain'd in several treatises on many important duties.* Vol. 3. London, 1680.

—. *Moral essays, contain'd in several treatises on many important duties.* Vol. 2. London, 1684.

—. *Moral essays, contain'd in several treatises on many important duties.* 3rd. ed. Vol. 1. London, 1696.

Noble, Louise. *Medicinal Cannibalism in Early Modern English Literature and Culture.* New York: Palgrave Macmillan, 2011.

Nokkala, Ere. *From Natural Law to Political Economy: J. H. G von Justi on State, Commerce and International Order.* Münster: Lit Verlag, 2019.

Nokkala, Ere, and Nicholas B. Miller, eds. *Cameralism and the Enlightenment: Happiness, Governance and Reform in Transnational Perspective.* London: Routledge, 2019.

Norton, David F. *David Hume: Common-Sense Moralist, Sceptical Metaphysician.* Princeton, NJ: Princeton University Press, 1982.

Novyi i polnyi geograficheskii slovar' Rossiiskogo gosudarstva Part III. Moscow: N. I. Novikov, 1788.

Obert, Marcus. *Die naturrechtliche "politische Metaphysik" des Johann Heinrich Gottlob von Justi (1717–1771).* Frankfurt am Main: Peter Lang, 1992.

O'Brien, Karen. "Empire, History and Emigration: from Enlightenment to Liberalism." In *Race, Nation and Empire: Making Histories, 1750 to the Present*, edited by Catherine Hall and Keith McClelland, 15–35. Manchester: Manchester University Press, 2010.

O'Dowde, Thomas. *The Poor Man's Physician, or The True Art of Medicine.* London, 1665.

Odum, Howard W. "Orderly Transitional Democracy." *American Academy of Political and Social Science* 180 (1935): 31–38.

Odzuck, Eva. "War by Other Means? Incentives for Power Seekers in Thomas Hobbes's Political Philosophy." *Review of Politics* 81 (2019): 21–46.

O'Hagan, Timothy. "Rousseau on amour-propre: on Six Facets of amour-propre." *Proceedings of the Aristotelian Society* 99 (1999): 91–107.

O'Neill, Onora. *Constructions of Reason.* Cambridge: Cambridge University Press, 1989.

—. "Kant and the Social Contract Tradition." In *Kant's Political Theory: Interpretations and Applications*, edited by Elisabeth Ellis, 25–41. University Park: Pennsylvania State University Press, 2012.

Osler, Margaret. "Baptizing Epicurean Atomism: Pierre Gassendi on the Immortality of the Soul." In *Religion, Science, and Worldview: Essays in Honor of Richard S. Westfall*, edited by Margaret Osler and Paul Farber, 163–183. Cambridge: Cambridge University Press, 1985.

—. *Divine Will and the Mechanical Philosophy: Gassendi and Descartes on Contingency and Necessity in the Created World.* Cambridge: Cambridge University Press, 1994.

—. "From Immanent Natures to Nature as Artifice: The Reinterpretation of Final Causes in Seventeenth-Century Natural Philosophy." *Monist* 79 (1996): 388–407.

Osterhammel, Jürgen. *Unfabling the East: The Enlightenment's Encounter with Asia*. Princeton, NJ: Princeton University Press, 2018.

Oz-Salzberger, Fania. "Adam Smith's Early German Readers: Reception, Misreception, and Critique." *The Adam Smith Review* 9 (2016): 201–217.

Pagden, Anthony. *The Fall of Natural Man: The American Indian and the Origins of Comparative Ethnology*. Cambridge: Cambridge University Press, 1982.

—. *Spanish Imperialism and the Political Imagination*. New Haven and London: Yale University Press, 1990.

Pagel, Walter. *Joan Baptista van Helmont: Reformer of Science and Medicine*. Cambridge: Cambridge University Press, 1982.

Palladini, Fiammetta. "Appetitus Societatis in Grozio e Socialitas in Pufendorf." *Filosofia Politica* 10 (1996): 61–70.

—. *Discussioni seicentesche su Samuel Pufendorf. Scritti Latini: 1663–1700*. Bologna: Il Mulino, 1978.

—. "Di una critica di Leibniz a Pufendorf." In *Percorsi della ricerca filosofica*, edited by Fiametta Palladini et. al, 9–27. Rome: Edizioni Nuova Cultura, 1990.

—. "Pufendorf and Stoicism." *Grotiana* 22–23 (2001–2002): 245–256.

—. *Samuel Pufendorf Discepolo di Hobbes. Per una reinterpretazione del giusnaturalismo moderno*. Bologna: Il Mulino, 1990.

—. "Stato, Chiesa e Tolleranza nel pensiero di S. Pufendorf." *Rivista Storica Italiana* 109 (1997): 436–482.

—. "Volontarismo e laicità del diritto naturale la critica di Pufendorf a Grozio." In *Reason in Law. Proceedings of the Conference Held in Bologna in 1984*, edited by Carla Faralli, 397–420. Milan: Giuffrè, 1988.

Palonen, Kari. "An Application of Conceptual History to Itself: From Method to Theory in Reinhart Koselleck's 'Begriffsgeschichte.'" *Finnish Yearbook of Political Thought* 1 (1997): 39–69.

Palter, Robert. "Hume and Prejudice." *Hume Studies* 21 (1995): 3–23.

Panizza, Diego. "La traduzione Italiana del De Iure naturae di Pufendorf: giusnaturalismo modern e cultura cattolica nel Settecento." *Studi Veneziani,* XI (1969): 483–528.

Parekh, Bhikhu, and R. N. Berki. "The History of Political Ideas: A Critique of Q. Skinner's Methodology." *Journal of the History of Ideas* 34 (1973): 163–184.

Pateman, Carol. *The Sexual Contract*. Stanford: Stanford University Press, 1988.

Pechenick, Eitan Adam, Christopher M. Danforth, and Peter Sheridan Dodds. "Characterizing the Google Books Corpus: Strong Limits to Inferences of Socio-Cultural and Linguistic Evolution." *PLOS ONE* 10 (2015): e0137041.

Peck, Jamie. "Explaining (with) Neoliberalism." *Territory, Politics, Governance* 1 (2013): 132–157.

Perlman, S. Review of "A Short History of the British Working Class Movement by G. D. H. Cole." *The American Economic Review* 18 (1928): 317–319.

Pesante, Maria Luisa. *Come servi. Figure del lavoro salariato dal diritto naturale all'economia politica*. Milan: FrancoAngeli, 2013.

Phillips, Mark Salber. *Society and Sentiment: Genres of Historical Writing*. Princeton, NJ: Princeton University Press.

Picavet, François. *Les ideologues: Essai sur l'histoire des idées et des théories scientifiques, philosophiques, religieuses, etc. en France depuis 1789*. Paris, 1891.

Piirimäe, Eva. "Herder and Cosmopolitanism." In *Critique of Cosmopolitan Reason: Timing and Spacing the Concept of World Citizenship*, edited by Rebecka Lettevall and Kristian Petrov, 181–212. Bern: Peter Lang, 2013.

—. "Sociability, Nationalism and Cosmopolitanism in Herder's Early Philosophy of History." *History of Political Thought* 36 (2015): 521–559.

—. "State-Machines, Commerce and the Progress of Humanität in Europe: Herder's Response to Kant in *Ideas for the Philosophy of History of Mankind.*" In *Commerce and Peace in the Enlightenment*, edited by Béla Kapossy, Isaac Nakhimovsky, and Richard Whatmore, 155–181. Cambridge: Cambridge University Press, 2017.

—. "Introduction. Herder on Empathy and Sympathy: Historicism, Stoicism and Contemporary Perspectives." In *Herder on Empathy and Sympathy/ Einfühlung und Sympathie im Denken Herders*, edited by Eva Piirimäe, Liina Lukas, and Johannes Schmidt. Leiden: Brill, forthcoming.

Piirimäe, Eva, and Alexander Schmidt. "Introduction: Between Morality and Anthropology – Sociability in Enlightenment Thought." *History of European Ideas* 41 (2015): 571–588.

Pitts, Jennifer. *A Turn to Empire: The Rise of Imperial Liberalism in Britain and France.* Princeton, NJ: Princeton University Press, 2005.

Plutarch. *Moralia*, Vol. 12. Translated by H. Cherniss and W. Helmbold. Cambridge, MA: Harvard University Press, 1957.

—. *Moralia*, Vol. 14. Translated by B. Einarson and P. de Lacy. Cambridge, MA: Harvard University Press, 1967.

Pocock, J. G. A. *The Ancient Constitution and the Feudal Law: A Study of English Historical Thought in the Seventeenth Century, A Reissue with a Retrospect.* Cambridge: Cambridge University Press, [1959] 1987.

—. *Barbarism and Religion, Vol. 2: Narratives of Civil Government.* Cambridge: Cambridge University Press, 2001.

—. *Barbarism and Religion., Vol. 3: The First Decline and Fall.* Cambridge: Cambridge University Press, 2005.

—. *Barbarism and Religion, Vol. 4: Barbarians, Savages and Empires.* Cambridge: Cambridge University Press, 2008.

—. "The Concept of a Language and the Métier d'Historien: Some Considerations on Practice." In *The Languages of Political Theory in Early-Modern Europe*, edited by Anthony Pagden, 19–38. Cambridge: Cambridge University Press, 1987.

—. *The Discovery of Islands: Essays in British History.* Cambridge: Cambridge University Press, 2005.

—. "Gaberlunzie's Return." *New Left Review* 5 (2000): 41–52.

—. "On the Unglobality of Contexts: Cambridge Methods and the History of Political Thought." *Global Intellectual History* 4 (2019): 99–109.

—. *Political Thought and History: Essays on Theory and Method.* Cambridge: Cambridge University Press, 2009.

—. *Politics, Language & Time: Essays on Political Thought and History.* Chicago: University of Chicago Press, 1989.

—. *The Machiavellian Moment.* Princeton, NJ: Princeton University Press, 1975.

—. *The Machiavellian Moment: Florentine Political Thought and the Atlantic Republican Tradition*, 2nd. ed. Princeton, NJ and Oxford: Princeton University Press, 2003.

—. *Virtue, Commerce, and History: Essays on Political Thought and History, Chiefly in the Eighteenth Century.* Cambridge: Cambridge University Press, 1985.
Pocock, J. G. A. et al. "Deconstructing Europe." *London Review of Books* 19 (1991): 6–10.
Pocock, J. G. A. et al. "Where are we now?" *London Review of Books* 38 (2016): 8–15.
Poley, Jared. *The Devil's Riches: A Modern History of Greed.* New York: Berghahn Books, 2016.
Polikarpov-Orlov, Fedor. *Leksikon treyazychnyi, sirech' rechenii slavenskih, ellinogrecheskih i latinskih sokrovishe.* Moscow, 1704.
Polnoe Sobranie Zakonov Rossiiskoi Imperii. T. XIV. St. Petersburg, 1830.
Polunin, Fedor Afanasievich. *Geograficheskii leksikon Rossiiskago gosudarstva.* Moscow: Napechatano pri Imperatorskom Moskovskom universitete, 1773.
Popkin, Richard H. "Medicine, Racism, Anti-Semitism: A Dimension of Enlightenment Culture." In *The Languages of Psyche: Mind and Body in Enlightenment Thought: Clark Library Lectures, 1985–1986*, edited by G. S. Rousseau, 405–444. Berkeley and Oxford: University of California Press, 1990.
Porphyry. *On Abstinence from Killing Animals.* Translated by Gillian Clark. London: Duckworth, 2000.
Prandi, Alfonso. *Religiosità e cultura nel '700 italiano.* Bologna: Il Mulino, 1966.
Preuss, Peter. *Epicurean Ethics: Katastematic Hedonism.* Lampeter, Wales: Mellen, 1994.
Proß, Wolfgang. "Anmerkungen." In Johann Gottfried Herder. *Werke,* Vol. 3/2, edited by Wolfgang Proß. Munich, Vienna: Carl Hanser Verlag, 1989.
—. "Die Begründung der Geschichte aus der Natur – Herders Konzept von 'Gesetzen' in der Geschichte." In *Wissenschaft als kulturelle Praxis*, edited by Hans Erich Bödeker, Peter H. Reill, and Jürgen Schlumbohm, 187–225. Göttingen: Vandenhoeck und Ruprecht, 1999.
—. "Geschichtliches Handeln und seine Nemesis: Visionäre der Geschichte im Zeitalter der Französischen Revolution." In *Die Gestaltbarkeit der Geschichte*, edited by Kurt Bayertz and Matthias Hoesch, 81–116. Hamburg: Meiner, 2019.
—. "*Ideen zur Philosophie der Geschichte der Menschheit.*" In *Herder Handbuch*, edited by Stefan Greif, Marion Heinz, and Heinrich Clairmont, 171–215. Paderborn: Wilhelm Fink, 2016.
—. "Kolonialismuskritik aus dem Geist der Geschichtsphilosophie: Raynal, Herder, Dobrizhoffer und der Fall Paraguay." In *Raynal – Herder – Merkel: Transformationen der Antikolonialismusdebatte in der europäischen* Aufklärung, edited by Mix York-Gothard and Hinrich Arend, 17–73. Heidelberg: Winter Verlag, 2017.
Prynne, William. *A Short Demurrer to the Jewes*, 2nd. ed. London, 1656.
Pufendorf, Samuel. *De jure naturae et gentium.* Edited by Frank Böhling. Berlin: Akademie Verlag, 2008.
—. *De jure naturae et gentium.* Francfurti: Lipsiae impensis Heinrici Broenneri, 1757.
—. *De officio hominis et civis juxta legem naturalem libri duo, curante Immanuele Webero.* Francofurti et Lipsiae: sumptibu E. Bronkce, 1700.
—. *De officio hominis et civis juxta legem naturalem Libri duo. Obeservationibus antea separatim editis*, D. Gottlieb Gerhard Titio, Lipsiae, Sumptibus Haered, Lanckisii, 1709.
—. *De officio hominis et civis, juxta legem naturalem. Libri duo. supplementis et observatiionibus in Academicae Juventutis usum auxit et illustravit Gershomus Carmichael.* Glasgow, 1718.

—. *De officiis hominis et civis, prout ipsi praescribuntur lege naturali libri duo: cum notis, viri Consultissimi ac Celebrerrimi Dn Io Barbeyracii ex Gallico in Latinum Sermonem versis a Seb. Masson.* Giessae, Sumptibus Ioannis Philippi Krieger, 1728.
—. *De officio hominis & civis, secundum Legem Naturalem,Libri Duo. Everardus Otto, Jctus. Repetita praelactione recensuit & Adnotationibus illustravit. In quibus Utilitas Juris Naturae in Studio Juris Civilis, & hujus in illo abusus ostenditur. Accedunt Dl. Titti ad eosdem libros Observationes. Trajecti ad Rhenum.* Apud Joannem Broedelet, Utrecht [1737] 1740.
—. *De' doveri dell'uomo e del cittadino secondo la Legge Naturale, libri due.* Translated by Domenico Amato. Naples: Vincenzo Orsino, 1780.
—. *De' doveri dell'uomo e del cittadino secondo la Legge Naturale libri due.* Translated by Domenico Amato. Second edition. Naples: Petraroja, 1785.
—. *I doveri dell'uomo e del cittadino tali che a lui sono prescritti dalla legge natural, dalla versione francese di Giovanni Barbeyrac.* Translated and edited by Michele Grandi. 3 vols. Venice: Pietteri, 1761–1767.
—. *Il diritto della natura e delle genti o sia Sistema generale de' principia li piu importanti di morale, giurisprudenza e politica di Samuele barone di Puffendorf.* Translated, rectified, and illustrated by Giovambatista Almici. 4 vols. Venice: Pietro Valvasense, 1757–1759.
—. *Of the Law of Nature and Nations.* Translated by Charles H. Oldfather and William A. Oldfather. Oxford: Clarendon Press, 1934.
—. *On the Duty of Man and Citizen.* Edited by James Tully and translated by Michael Silverthorne. Cambridge: Cambridge University Press, 1991.
—. *Principi di diritto natural.* Edited by Norberto Bobbio. Turin: G. B. Paravia & C., [1943] 1952.
—. *The Divine Feudal Law: Or Covenants with Mankind, Represented.* Edited by Simone Zurbuchen. Indianapolis, IN: Liberty Fund, 2002.
—. *The Political Writings of Samuel Pufendorf.* Translated by Michael J. Seidler and edited by Craig L. Carr. New York: Oxford University Press, 1994.
Quaglioni, Diego. "Pufendorf in Italia. Appunti e notizie sulla prima diffusione della traduzione italiana del *De jure naturae et gentium.*" *Il Pensiero Politico* XXXII (1999): 235–250.
Radcliffe, Elizabeth S. "Hutcheson's Perceptual and Moral Subjectivism." *History of Philosophy Quarterly* 3 (1986): 407–421.
Raphael, D. D. "Review of Motivation and the Moral Sense in Francis Hutcheson." *Journal of the History of Philosophy* 12 (1974): 263–264.
Raymond, Marcel. "Du jansénisme à la morale de l'intrétêt." *Mercure de France* 1126 (1957): 238–255.
Reddaway, William Fiddian, trans. *Documents of Catherine the Great: The Correspondence with Voltaire and the Instruction of 1767 in the English.* Cambridge: Cambridge University Press, 1931.
Richards, Judith, Lotte Mulligan, and John Graham. "Property and People: Political Usages of Locke and Some Contemporaries." *Journal of the History of Ideas* 42 (1981): 29–51.
Ripstein, Arthur. *Force and Freedom: Kant's Legal and Political Philosophy.* Cambridge, MA: Harvard University Press, 2009.
Robertson, G. Croom. "Les Idéologues by F. Picavet." *Mind* 1 (1892): 118–126.

Robertson, John. “Sacred History and Political Thought: Neopolitan Responses to the Problem of Sociability.” *Historical Journal* 56 (2013): 1–29.

Robertson, William. *The History of America.* London: Routledge/Thoemmes Press, [1777] 1996.

—. *History of America.* London, 1777.

Robieson, M.W. “The Theory of Morals on a Class Basis.” *International Journal of Ethics* 29 (1919): 294–317.

Rodolico, Niccolò. *Stato e Chiesa in Toscana durante la reggenza lorenese (1737–1765).* Florence: Le Monnier, 1910.

Roger, Jacques. *Buffon: A Life in Natural History.* Ithaca, NY: Cornell University Press, 1998.

Roger of Hoveden. *The Annals of Roger of Hoveden, Volume 2, part 1.* Translated by Henry T. Riley. Felinfach: Llanerch, 1997.

Roger of Wendover. *Roger of Wendover's Flowers of History.* 2 vols. Translated by J.A. Giles. London: Henry G. Bohn, 1849.

Rogers, Ben. “In Praise of Vanity: the Augustinian Analysis of the Benefits of Vice from Port-Royal to Mandeville.” PhD diss., University of Oxford, 1994.

Rolin, Jan. *Der Ursprung des Staates: die naturrechtlich-rechtsphilosophische Legitimation von Staat und Staatsgewalt im Deutschland des 18. und 19. Jahrhunderts.* Tübingen: Mohr Siebeck, 2005.

Rollin, Bernard. “Animal Pain: What It Is and Why It Matters.” *Journal of Ethics* 15 (2011): 425–437.

Romani, Roberto. *National Character and Public Spirit in Britain and France, 1750–1914.* Cambridge: Cambridge University Press, 2004.

Rosa, Mario. *Politica e Religione nel Settecento Europeo.* Florence: Sansoni, 1974.

Ross, David. *The Right and the Good.* Edited by Philip Stratton Lake. Oxford: Clarendon Press, 2007.

Rotondò, Antonio. “La censura ecclesiastica e la cultura.” In *Storia d'Italia.* vol. V, edited by

Ruffini, Francesco. *La Libertà religiosa: storia dell'idea.* Milan: Feltrinelli, 1967.

Ruggiero, Romano and Corrado Vivanti, 1397–1492. Turin: Einaudi, 1973

Rousseau, Jean-Jacques *The Basic Political Writings.* Translated and edited by Donald A. Cress. Indianapolis, In: Hackett, 1987.

Rubiés, Joan-Pau. *Travellers and Cosmographers: Studies in the History of Early Modern Travel and Ethnology.* London: Routledge, 2007.

Ruggiero, Guido de. *The History of European Liberalism.* London: Oxford University Press, [1925] 1927.

Runciman, David. *Political Hypocrisy: The Mask of Power, from Hobbes to Orwell and Beyond.* Princeton, NJ: Princeton University Press, 2008.

Russell, Edmund. “Coevolutionary History.” *American Historical Review* 119 (2014): 1514–1528.

Saarinen, Risto. *Recognition and Religion: A Historical and Systematic Study.* Oxford: Oxford University Press, 2016.

Saastamoinen, Kari. *The Morality of the Fallen Man: Samuel Pufendorf on Natural Law.* Helsinki: Societas Historica Finlandiae, 1995.

—. “Pufendorf on Natural Equality, Human Dignity, and Self-Esteem.” *Journal of the History of Ideas* 71 (2010): 39–62.

Sagar, Paul. *The Opinion of Mankind: Sociability and the Theory of the State from Hobbes to Smith.* Princeton, NJ: Princeton University Press, 2018.

Saltman, Avrom. *The Jewish Question in 1655: Studies in Prynne's Demurrer.* Jerusalem: Bar Ilan University Press, 1995.

Sarasohn, Lisa. *Gassendi's Ethics: Freedom in a Mechanistic Universe.* London: Cornell University Press, 1996.

Sargent, Lyman Tower. "Ideology and Utopia: Karl Mannheim and Paul Ricoeur." *Journal of Political Ideologies* 13 (2008): 263–273.

Sarti, Raffaella. "Servo o padrone, o della (in)dipendenza. Un percorso da Aristotele ai giorni nostri. I: Teorie e dibattiti." *Scienza & Politica* 2 (2015): 2–249.

Sawer, Marian. *Marxism and the Question of the Asiatic Mode of Production.* The Hague: Martinus Nijhoff, 1977.

Scattola, Merio. "Protestantismo e diritto natural cattolico nel XVIII secolo." In *Illuminismo e Protestantesimo*, edited by Giulia Cantarutti and Stefano Ferrari, 131–148. Milan: Franco Angeli, 2010.

Schiebinger, Londa. *Nature's Body: Gender in the Making of Modern Science.* New Brunswick, NJ: Rutgers University Press, 1993.

Schmidt, Johannes. "Herder's Political Ideas and the Organic Development of Religions and Governments." In *Herder on Empathy and Sympathy*, edited by Eva Piirimäe, Liina Lukas, and Johannes Schmidt. Leiden: Brill, forthcoming.

Schmitter, Amy M. "17th and 18th Century Theories of Emotions." In *The Stanford Encyclopedia of Philosophy* (Winter 2016 Edition), edited by Edward N. Zalta. https://plato.stanford.edu/archives/win2016/entries/emotions-17th18th/.

Schneewind, Jerome B. "Good Out of Evil: Kant and the Idea of Unsocial Sociability." In *Kant's Idea for a Universal History with a Cosmopolitan Aim: A Critical Guide*, edited by Amélie Oksenberg Rorty and James Schmidt, 94–111. Cambridge: Cambridge University Press, 2009.

Schino, Anna Luisa. ed. *De statu hominum naturali.* Lecce: Conte, 2009.

—. *Il Pensiero Politico di Pufendorf.* Rome and Bari: Laterza, 1995.

Schwaiger, Clemens. *Das Problem des Glücks im Denken Christian Wolffs: Eine quellen-, begriffs- und entwicklungsgeschichtliche Studie zu Schlüsselbegriffen seiner Ethik.* Stuttgart: Frommann-Holzboog, 1995.

Seaward, Paul, and Pasi Ihalainen. "Key Concepts for Parliament in Britain (1640–1800)." In *Parliament and Parliamentarism: A Comparative History of a European Concept*, edited by Pasi Ihalainen, Cornelia Ilie, and Kari Palonen, 32–48. New York: Berghahn Books, 2016.

Sebastiani, Silvia. "L'orang-outang, l'esclave et l'humain: une querelle des corps en régime colonial." *L'Atelier du Centre de recherché historiques* 11 (2013), 32, http://journals.openedition.org/acrh/5265.

—. *The Scottish Enlightenment: Race, Gender, and the Limits of Progress.* Houndmills: Palgrave Macmillan, 2013.

Seppel, Marten, and Keith Tribe, eds. *Cameralism in Practice: State Administration and Economy in Early Modern Europe.* Woodbridge: Boydell & Brewer, 2017.

Serres, Marcel de. "On the Unity of the Human Species." In *Race: The Origins of an Idea 1760–1850*, edited by Hannah Franziska Augstein, 195–202. Bristol: Thoemmes Press, 1996.

Seth, Suman. “Materialism, Slavery and the History of Jamaica.” *Isis* 105 (2014): 764–772.
Shapiro, James. *Shakespeare and the Jews.* New York: Columbia University Press, 1996.
Shepard, Walter James. “Democracy.” *The Annals of the American Academy of Political and Social Science* 180 (1935): 94–101.
Sher, Richard B. “*Charles V* and the Book Trade: An Episode in Enlightenment Print Culture.” In *William Robertson and the Expansion of Empire*, edited by Stewart J. Brown, 164–195. Cambridge: Cambridge University Press, 1997.
Shils, Edward. “The End of Ideology?” *Encounter* 5 (1955): 52–58.
A Short History of English Transactions in the East-Indies. Cambridge, 1776.
Sidney, Algernon. *Discourses Concerning Government.* Edited by Thomas G. West. Indianapolis, IN: Liberty Fund, 1996.
Sikka, Sonia. *Herder on Humanity and Cultural Difference: Enlightened Relativism.* Cambridge: Cambridge University Press, 2011.
Sinclair, John. *The History of the Public Revenue of the British Empire.* 2nd. ed. London, 1790.
Skinner, Quentin. *The Foundations of Modern Political Thought, Vol. 1.* Cambridge: Cambridge University Press, 1978
—. “Hobbes and the Purely Artificial Person of the State.” *Journal of Political Philosophy* 7 (1999): 1–29.
Slezkine, Yuri. *The Jewish Century.* Princeton, NJ and Oxford: Princeton University Press, 2004.
Slomp, Gabriella. “Hobbes on Glory and Civil Strife.” In *The Cambridge Companion to Hobbes's Leviathan*, edited by Patricia Springborg, 181–198. Cambridge: Cambridge University Press, 2007.
—. *Thomas Hobbes and the Political Philosophy of Glory.* Basingstoke: Palgrave Macmillan, 2000.
Slovar' Akademii Rossiiskoi. St. Petersburg: Imperatorskaya akademiya nauk, 1789–1794.
Slovar' mineralogicheskii. St. Petersburg: Imperatorskaya akademiya nauk, 1790.
Smith, Adam. *An Inquiry into the Nature and Causes of the Wealth of Nations*, edited by R. H. Campbell, A. S Skinner, and W.B. Todd. Indianapolis, IN: Liberty Fund, 1981.
—. “A Letter to the Authors of the Edinburgh Review.” In *Essays on Philosophical Subjects*, edited by W. P. D. Wightman and J. C. Bryce, 251–254. Indianapolis, IN: Liberty Fund, 1982.
—. “The Principles which lead and direct Philosophical Enquiries; illustrated by the History of Astronomy,” edited by W. P. D Wightman. In *Essays on Philosophical Subjects*, edited by D. D. Raphael & A. S. Skinner, 33–105. Oxford: Clarendon Press, 1980.
—. *The Theory of Moral Sentiments*, edited by D. D. Raphael and A. L. Macfie. Indianapolis, IN: Liberty Press, 1982.
—. *The Theory of Moral Sentiments.* London, 1759.
—. *The Theory of Moral Sentiments.* London, 1761.
Smith, Justin. “Diet, Embodiment, and Virtue in the Mechanical Philosophy.” *Studies in History and Philosophy of Biological and Biomedical Sciences* 43 (2012): 338–348.
Smith, T. V. “Ideology and Utopia by Karl Mannheim, Louis Wirth, Edward A. Shils.” *International Journal of Ethics* 48 (1937): 120–128.
Sombart, Werner. *The Jews and Modern Capitalism.* Translated by M. Epstein. New Brunswick and London: Transaction Books, 1982.

Sonenscher, Michael. *Sans-Culottes: An Eighteenth-Century Emblem in the French Revolution.* Princeton: Princeton University Press, 2008.

Speed, John. *The History of Great Britaine under the Conquests of ye Romans, Saxons, Danes and Normans.* London, 1611.

Speier, Hans. "Ideology and Utopia, by Karl Mannheim." *American Journal of Sociology* 43 (1937): 155–166.

Spencer, Colin. *The Heretic's Feast: A History of Vegetarianism.* London: University Press of New England, 1995.

Stafford, Martin J. "Hutcheson, Hume and the Ontology of Morals." *The Journal of Value Inquiry* 19 (1985): 133–151.

Stanley, Ben. "The Thin Ideology of Populism." *Journal of Political Ideologies* 13 (2008): 95–110.

Steinfeld, Robert J. *The Invention of Free Labour: The Employment Relation in English and American Law and Culture, 1350–1870.* Chapel Hill: University of North Carolina Press, 1991.

Stewart, Robert M. "John Clarke and Francis Hutcheson on Self-Love and Moral Motivation." *Journal of the History of Philosophy* 20 (1982): 261–277.

Stoffella, Stefania. "Assolutismo e diritto naturale in Italia nel Settecento." *Annali dell'Istituto Italo-Germanico in Trento* XXVI (2000): 137–175.

—. "Il diritto di resistenza nel Settecento Italiano. Documenti per la storia della traduzione del *De iure naturae et Gentium* di Pufendorf." *Laboratoire italien. Politique et société* 2 (2001): 173–199.

—. "Il diritto naturale nella corrispondenza e negli scritti di Giovanni Battista Graser e di Clementi Baroni Cavalcabò." In *Aufklärung cattolica ed età delle riforme. Giovanni Battista Grasser nella cultura europea del Settencento*, edited by Serena Luzzi, 191–205. Rovereto: Accademia Roveretana degli Agiati, 2004.

Stolleis, Michael. "Staatszweck". In *Historisches Wörterbuch der Philosophie*, Vol. 10, edited by Joachim Ritter et. al., 80–84. Basel: Schwabe, 1998.

Stow, John. *A Summarie of the Chronicles of England.* London, 1575.

—. *A Survey of London.* London, 1598.

Stow, John, and Edmund Howes, *Annales, or a Generall Chronicle of England.* London, 1631.

Struve, Peter. "Russia." *The Slavonic Review* 1 (1922): 24–39.

Stråth, Bo. "Ideology and Conceptual History." In *The Oxford Handbook of Political Ideologies*, edited by Michael Freeden, Lyman Tower Sargent, and Marc Stears, 3–19. Oxford: Oxford University Press, 2013.

Stuart, Tristram. *Bloodless Revolution: Radical Vegetarians and the Discovery of India.* London: HarperPress, 2006.

Stuart-Buttle, Tim. "'A Burthen Too Heavy for Humane Sufferance': Locke on Reputation." *History of Political Thought* 38 (2017): 644–680.

—. *From Moral Theology to Moral Philosophy: Cicero and Visions of Humanity from Locke to Hume.* Oxford: Oxford University Press, 2019.

Sutcliffe, Adam. "Anxieties of Distinctiveness: Walter Sombart's *The Jews and Modern Capitalism* and the Politics of Jewish Economic History." In *Purchasing Power: The Economics of Modern Jewish History*, edited by Rebecca Kobrin and Adam Teller, 238–258. Philadelphia: University of Pennsylvania Press, 2015.

—. *Judaism and Enlightenment.* Cambridge: Cambridge University Press, 2003.

—. "The Philosemitic Moment? Judaism and Republicanism in Seventeenth-Century European Thought." In *Philosemitism in History*, edited by Jonathan Karp and Adam Sutcliffe, 67–89. Cambridge: Cambridge University Press, 2011.

Tarchi, Marco. "Populism: Ideology, Political Style, Mentality?" *Politologický Časopis – Czech Journal of Political Science* 23 (2016): 95–109.

Tarlton, Charles D. "Historicity, Meaning, and Revisionism in the Study of Political Thought." *History and Theory* 12 (1973): 307–328.

Tatishev, Vasilii Nikitich. *Leksikon rossiiskoi istoricheskoi, geograficheskoi, politicheskoi i grazhdanskoi.* St. Petersburg: Tipografiya Gornogo uchilisha, 1793.

Taylor, Gabriele. "Hume's Views of Moral Judgments." *Philosophical Quarterly* 21 (1971): 64–68.

Taylor, Jordan. "Emotional Sensations and the Moral Imagination in Malebranche." In *The Discourse of Sensibility: The Knowing Body in the Enlightenment*, edited by Henry Martyn Lloyd, 63–83. Cham: Springer, 2013.

Teplov, Grigorii Nikolaevich. "Znaniia, kasaiushchiesia voobshche do filosofii, dlia pol'zy tekh, kotorye o sei materii chuzhestrannykh knig chitat' ne mogut, sobrany i iz'iasneny Grigoriem Teplovym". *Filosofskii vek, Al'manakh* 3 (1998): 207–289.

Thiele, Rüdiger. *Leonard Euler.* Kiev: Vishha shkola, 1983.

Thomas, Keith. *Man and the Natural World: Changing Attitudes in England, 1500–1800.* London: Allen Lane, 1983.

Thompson, Laura A. "Worker's Education: A List of References (in English)." *Monthly Labor Review* 14 (1922): 181–205.

Thompson, E. P. *Customs in Common: Studies in Traditional Popular Culture.* London: Merlin Press, 1991.

Tilley, John J. "Francis Hutcheson and John Clarke on Desire and Self-Interest." *The European Legacy* 21 (2019): 1–24.

Timofeev, Alexander. "Khr.Vol'f i sozdanie rossiiskoi Akademii nauk". In *Peterburgskaia Akademiia nauk v istorii akademij mira. Materialy Mezhdunarodnoi konferentsii.* T. IV. St. Petersburg: Nauka, 1999.

Todescan, Franco. "Dalla persona ficta alla persona moralis. Individualismo e matematismo nelle teorie della persona giuridica del secolo XVII," in *Quaderni Fiorentini per una Storia del Pensiero Giuridico Moderno* I (1982–1983): 59–93.

—. *Le radici teologiche del giusnaturalismo laico vol. III: Il Problema della secolarizzazione nel pensiero giuridico di Samuel Pufendorf.* Milan: Giuffrè, [1983] 2001.

Tolonen, Mikko. *Mandeville and Hume: Anatomists of Civil Society.* Oxford: SVEC, 2013.

—. "Pride and moral fitness in the sceptical sentimentalism of Mandeville, Hume and Smith." Paper presented at *Inclusion and Exclusion in the History of Ideas* Conference of the Helsinki Centre for Intellectual History, Helsinki, December 14–15, 2017.

Tovey, D'Blossiers. *Anglia Judaica: or the history and antiquities of the Jews in England.* London, 1738.

Travers, Robert. *Ideology and Empire in Eighteenth-Century India: The British in Bengal.* Cambridge: Cambridge University Press, 2007.

Trivellato, Francesca. "Credit, Honour, and the Early Modern French Legend of the Jewish Invention of Bills of Exchange." *The Journal of Modern History* 84 (2012): 289–334.

—. "Images and Self-Images of Sephardic Merchants in Early Modern Europe and the Mediterranean." In *The Self-Perception of Early Modern Capitalists*, edited by Margaret C. Jacob and Catherine Secretan, 49–74. Basingstoke: Palgrave Macmillan, 2008.

Tuck, Richard. *Philosophy and Government 1572–1651.* Cambridge: Cambridge University Press, 1993.

Tucker, Josiah. *A Second Letter to a Friend Concerning Naturalizations.* London, 1753.

Tully, James. *An Approach to Political Philosophy: Locke in Contexts.* Cambridge: Cambridge University Press, 1993.

—. *A Discourse on Property: John Locke and His Adversaries.* Cambridge: Cambridge University Press, 2006.

—. "Governing Conduct." In *Conscience and Casuistry in Early Modern Europe*, edited by Edmund Leites, 12–71. Cambridge: Cambridge University Press, 1988.

—. *Public Philosophy in a New Key.* 2 vols. Cambridge: Cambridge University Press, 2008.

—. "Rethinking Human Rights and Enlightenment: A View From the Twenty-First Century." In *Self-Evident Truths? Human Rights and the Enlightenment*, edited by Kate Tunstall, 3–35. New York: Bloomsbury, 2012.

Turco, Luigi. "Sympathy and Moral Sense: 1725–1740." *British Journal for the History of Philosophy* 7 (1999): 79–101.

Van Kley, Dale. "Pierre Nicole, Jansenism, and the Morality of Enlightened Self-Interest." In *Anticipations of the Enlightenment in England, France and Germany*, edited by A. C. Kors and Paul Korshin, 69–85. Philadelphia: University of Pennsylvania Press, 1987.

Vecchi, Alberto. *Correnti religiose nel Sei-Settecento Veneto.* Venice and Rome: Istituto per la collaborazione culturale, 1962.

Venturi, Franco. *Il Settecento Riformatore.* Turin: Giulio Einaudi, 1969.

Venugopal, Rajesh. "Neoliberalism as Concept." *Economy and Society* 44 (2015): 165–187.

Vergil, Polydore. *Anglica Historia.* Edited by Dana F. Sutton. Philological.bham.ac.uk., http://Philological.bham.ac.uk/polverg/.

Vincent, Andrew. "Political Ideology and Political Theory: Reflections on an Awkward Partnership." In *Liberalism as Ideology: Essays in Honour of Michael Freeden*, edited by Ben Jackson and Marc Stears, 159–177. Oxford: Oxford University Press, 2012.

Wakefield, Andre. "Cameralism: A German Alternative to Mercantilism." In *Mercantilism Reimagined: Political Economy in Early Modern Britain and Its Empire*, edited by Philip J. Stern and Carl Wennerlind, 134–150. Oxford: Oxford University Press, 2014.

—. *The Disordered Police State: German Cameralism as Science and Practice.* Chicago: University of Chicago Press, 2009.

Walling, William English. Review of "Progressive Democracy, by Herbert Croly." *American Economic Review* 5 (1915): 380–381.

Wasserman, Louis. *Handbook of Political 'Isms'.* New York: Association Press, 1941.

Watson, Robert N. "Protestant Animals: Puritan Sects and English Animal-Protection Sentiment, 1550–1650," *English Literary History* 81 (2014): 1111–1148.

Wear, Andrew. *Knowledge and Practice in English Medicine, 1550–1680.* Cambridge: Cambridge University Press, 2000.

Weber, Dominique. "Le 'commerce d'amour-propre' selon Pierre Nicole." *Astérion – Philosophie, histoire des idées, pensée politique* 5 (2007): 169–196.

Weber, Max. *L'etica protestante e lo spirit del capitalismo.* Edited by Giorgio Galli and translated by Anna Maria Marietti. Padua: Bur, 1991.

Welzel, Hans. *La dottrina giusnaturalistica di Samuel Pufendorf. Un Contributo alla Storia delle Idee dei Secoli XVII e XVIII*. Translated and edited by Vanda Fiorillo. Turin: Giappichelli, 1993.

Westphal, Kenneth R. *How Hume & Kant Reconstruct Natural Law: Justifying Strict Objectivity without Debating Moral Realism*. Oxford: Clarendon Press, 2016.

Whatmore, Richard. "The State of Intellectual History: Local and Global," in *Passions, Politics and the Limits of Society*, edited by Heikki Haara, Mikko Immanen, and Koen Stapelbroek, 5–15. Berlin: de Gruyter, 2020.

—. *What is Intellectual History?* Cambridge: Polity Press, 2015.

Wheeler, Roxann. *The Complexion of Race: Categories of Difference in Eighteenth-Century British Culture*. Philadelphia: University of Pennsylvania Press, 2000.

Wilhelm, Uwe. "Das Staats- und Gesellschaftsverständnis von J. H. G. von Justi: Ein Beitrag zur Entwicklung des Frühliberalismus in Deutschland." *Der Staat* 30 (1991): 415–441.

—. *Der deutsche Frühliberalismus: von den Anfängen bis 1789*. Frankfurt am Main: Peter Lang, 1995.

Willson, A. Leslie. "Herder and India: The Genesis of a Mythical Image." *PMLA* 70 (1955): 1049–1058.

Wilson, Francis G. "The Structure of Modern Ideology." *The Review of Politics* 1 (1939): 382–399.

Winkler, Kenneth. "Hutcheson's Alleged Realism." *Journal of the History of Philosophy* 23 (1985): 179–194.

Wokler, Robert. "The Gaze of Natural History." In *Inventing Human Science*, edited by Christopher Fox, Roy Porter, and Robert Wokler, 112–151. Berkeley and Los Angeles: University of California Press, 1995.

—. "The Professoriate of Political Thought in England since 1914: A Tale of Three Chairs." In *The History of Political Thought in National Context*, edited by Dario Castiglione and Ian Hampsher-Monk, 134–158, Cambridge: Cambridge University Press, 2001.

Wolff, Christian. *Razumnye mysli o silah chelovecheskago razuma*. St. Petesrburg, 1765.

—. *Vernünfftige Gedancken von dem gesellschaftlichen Leben der Menschen und insonderheit dem Gemeinen Wesen*. Frankfurt: Renger, 1736 [1721].

Wolfsdorf, David. *Pleasure in Ancient Greek Philosophy*. Cambridge: Cambridge University Press, 2012.

Woodhouse, Arthur Sutherland Pigott, ed. *Puritanism and Liberty, being the Army Debates (1647–49), from the Clarke Manuscripts with Supplementary Documents. Part I: The Putney Debates*. Chicago: University of Chicago Press, 1951.

Woods, Erville Bartlett. "Progress as a Sociological Concept." *American Journal of Sociology* 12 (1907): 779–821.

Yakimovich, Yulia. *Deyateli russkoi kul'tury i slovarnoe delo*. Moscow: Nauka, 1985.

Yanovskii, Nikolai Maksimovich. *Novyi slovotolkovatel', raspolozhennyi po alfavitu*. St. Petersburg: Imperatorskaja akademija nauk, 1803–1806.

Zammito, John Z. *The Genesis of Kant's* Critique of Judgement. Chicago: University of Chicago Press, 1992.

—. *Kant, Herder, and the Birth of Anthropology*. Chicago: University of Chicago Press, 2002.

Zhuchkov, Vladimir. "Metafizika Vol'fa i ee mesto v istorii filosofii Novogo vremeni". In *Khristian Vol'f i filosofiia v Rossii*. St. Petersburg: Russkaya hristianskaya gumanitarnaya akademiya, 2001.

Znamenskii, Petr Vasilievich. *Dukhovnye shkoly v Rossii do reformy 1808 goda*. St. Petersburg: Letnii Sad. 2001.

Index

FSC
www.fsc.org
MIX
Papier | Fördert gute Waldnutzung
FSC® C083411

Kolibri 360 GmbH
Ferdinand-Jühlke-Straße 7
99095 Erfurt, Deutschland
produktsicherheit@kolibri360.de